MAO ZEDONG ON DIPLOMACY

Compiled by
The Ministry of Foreign Affairs of
the People's Republic of China and
the Party Literature Research Center
under the Central Committee of
the Communist Party of China

FOREIGN LANGUAGES PRESS
BEIJING

First Edition   1998

The present book is a translation of the first Chinese edition of the *Mao Zedong on Diplomacy*, first published in December 1994 jointly by the Central Party Literature Publishing House and World Affairs Press. As the original transcripts of Mao Zedong's talks with foreign guests were not available, the official Chinese-language versions of those talks have been followed in the translation.

ISBN 7-119-01141-3

© Foreign Languages Press, Beijing, China

Published by Foreign Languages Press
24 Baiwanzhuang Road, Beijing 100037, China

Distributed by China International Book Trading Corporation
35 Chegongzhuang Xilu, Beijing 100044, China
P.O. Box 399, Beijing, China

Printed in the People's Republic of China

EDITORIAL NOTE

In order to make known Mao Zedong's contributions to China's foreign affairs, and enable people to study and inherit his ideas on diplomacy, the present book, *Mao Zedong on Diplomacy*, has been compiled, with the approval of the Central Committee of the Communist Party of China (CPC), by the Ministry of Foreign Affairs and the CPC Central Committee's Party Literature Research Center.

This book is a collection of 160 of Mao Zedong's writings, speeches, talks, comments and telegrams concerning diplomacy from July 1937 to May 1974. Most are published here for the first time.

Mao Zedong was a great diplomatic strategist of modern times. As the chief leader of the Communist Party and People's Republic of China, he laid out principles of external affairs and diplomatic strategies, tactics and policies during the War of Resistance Against Japan (1937-1945) and the War of Liberation (1946-1949). For 27 years after the founding of the People's Republic he made significant contributions to forming the country's strategic guidelines on international affairs, laying down diplomatic policies, planning important diplomatic activities and opening up a new prospect in China's foreign affairs. This book records Mao Zedong's fundamental views on international situations and diplomatic strategies as well as his stratagic and tactical concepts in and theoretical contributions to foreign affairs.

In compiling this book, the editors have remained loyal to the original editions or manuscripts of the articles included in this book. A few changes in language were made in the original manuscripts or articles published before. Transcripts of speeches and talks were edited, with errors of fact corrected and titles added. Notes on the sources are provided at the end of all the articles. Explanatory and editorial notes are also provided. The former can be found at the bottom of the first page of each article, and the latter are numbered and can be found in the appendix.

The Ministry of Foreign Affairs
of the People's Republic of China
Party Literature Research Center
of the Central Committee of
the Communist Party of China
June 1994

CONTENTS

ADOPT AN ANTI-JAPANESE FOREIGN POLICY (*July 1937-May 1941*) 1
SPEECH AT THE YAN'AN ANTI-AGGRESSION MEETING (*February 11, 1938*) 5
FIGHTING FOR PERPETUAL PEACE (*May 1938*) 7
THE PRINCIPAL TASKS OF THE WORLD'S YOUTH IN ASSISTING CHINA'S WAR OF RESISTANCE AGAINST JAPAN (*July 2, 1938*) 10
PRIMARILY RELYING ON OUR OWN EFFORTS, WHILE NOT SLACKENING IN SEEKING FOREIGN HELP (*October 1938*) 11
THE RELATIONSHIP BETWEEN THE WAR OF RESISTANCE AND FOREIGN AID—PREFACE TO THE ENGLISH TRANSLATION OF *ON PROTRACTED WAR* (*January 20, 1939*) 14
INTERVIEW WITH A *NEW CHINA DAILY* CORRESPONDENT ON THE NEW INTERNATIONAL SITUATION (*September 1, 1939*) 16
THE QUESTION OF WAR AND REVOLUTION (*July 13, 1940*) 21
ON THE INTERNATIONAL UNITED FRONT AGAINST FASCISM (*June 23, 1941*) 24
WELCOME, COMRADES-IN-ARMS OF THE U.S. MILITARY OBSERVATION GROUP (*August 15, 1944*) 25
A LETTER TO U.S. PRESIDENT ROOSEVELT (*November 10, 1944*) 29
THE PRESENT INTERNATIONAL SITUATION AND THE FUNDAMENTAL PRINCIPLE OF THE FOREIGN POLICY OF THE COMMUNIST PARTY OF CHINA (*April 24, 1945*) 31
THE REACTIONARY COUNTERCURRENT WILL BE SWEPT AWAY (*June 11, 1945*) 35
ON THE DANGER OF THE HURLEY POLICY (*July 12, 1945*) 36
WE MUST NOT STOP CRITICIZING THE U. S. POLICY OF SUPPORTING CHIANG KAI-SHEK AGAINST THE COMMUNISTS (*July 30, 1945*) 38
WE MUST NOT BELIEVE THE "NICE WORDS" OF THE IMPERIALISTS, NOR BE INTIMIDATED BY THEIR BLUSTER (*August 13, 1945*) 39
WHILE THE PROSPECTS OF THE WORLD ARE BRIGHT, THE ROAD HAS TWISTS AND TURNS (*October 17, 1945*) 41
SOME POINTS IN APPRAISAL OF THE PRESENT INTERNATIONAL SITUATION (*April 1946*) 43
TALK WITH THE AMERICAN CORRESPONDENT ANNA LOUISE STRONG

(*August 6, 1946*)	45
REPUDIATE THE TRAITOROUS FOREIGN POLICY (*October 10, 1947*)	49
THE STRENGTH OF THE WORLD ANTI-IMPERIALIST CAMP HAS SURPASSED THAT OF THE IMPERIALIST CAMP (*December 25, 1947*)	50
THE DANGER OF A WORLD WAR MUST AND CERTAINLY CAN BE OVERCOME (*September 8, 1948*)	53
REVOLUTIONARY FORCES OF THE WORLD UNITE, FIGHT AGAINST IMPERIALIST AGGRESSION! (*November 1948*)	55
WE SHOULD INCLUDE A DIRECT U.S. MILITARY INTERVENTION IN OUR BATTLE PLAN (*January 8, 1949*)	59
NO INTERFERENCE IN CHINA'S INTERNAL AFFAIRS IS PERMISSIBLE BY ANY FOREIGN COUNTRY OR THE UNITED NATIONS (*January 19, 1949*)	60
SYSTEMATICALLY AND COMPLETELY DESTROY IMPERIALIST DOMINATION IN CHINA (*March 5, 1949*)	62
PROTECT THE LIVES AND PROPERTY OF FOREIGN NATIONALS (*April 25, 1949*)	64
WE MAY CONSIDER ESTABLISHING DIPLOMATIC RELATIONS WITH THE UNITED STATES AND BRITAIN IF THEY SEVER TIES WITH THE KUOMINTANG (*April 28, 1949*)	65
ON THE OUTRAGES BY BRITISH WARSHIPS—STATEMENT BY THE SPOKESMAN OF THE GENERAL HEADQUARTERS OF THE CHINESE PEOPLE'S LIBERATION ARMY (*April 30, 1949*)	66
POINTS OF ATTENTION FOR HUANG HUA IN HIS TALK WITH JOHN LEIGHTON STUART (*May 10, 1949*)	68
THE CHINESE PEOPLE WISH TO HAVE FRIENDLY COOPERATION WITH THE PEOPLE OF ALL COUNTRIES (*June 15, 1949*)	70
UNITE WITH THOSE NATIONS OF THE WORLD WHICH TREAT US AS EQUALS AND WITH THE PEOPLES OF ALL COUNTRIES (*June 30, 1949*)	72
CAST AWAY ILLUSIONS, PREPARE FOR STRUGGLE (*August 14, 1949*)	75
FAREWELL, LEIGHTON STUART! (*August 18, 1949*)	81
THE CHINESE PEOPLE HAVE STOOD UP! (*September 21, 1949*)	87
THE CHINESE GOVERNMENT'S PRINCIPLE FOR ESTABLISHMENT OF DIPLOMATIC RELATIONS WITH FOREIGN COUNTRIES (*October 1, 1949*)	89
CAPITALIST COUNTRIES MUST NEGOTIATE WITH US TO ESTABLISH DIPLOMATIC RELATIONS WITH CHINA (*December 19, 1949*)	90
ANSWERS TO QUESTIONS OF A TASS CORRESPONDENT (*January 2, 1950*)	91
ZHOU ENLAI TO GO TO THE SOVIET UNION FOR PARTICIPATION IN NEGOTIATIONS AND SIGNING OF TREATY (*January 1950*)	92
APPROVAL OF A STATEMENT REPUDIATING THE LEGAL STATUS OF THE FORMER KUOMINTANG GOVERNMENT'S REPRESENTATIVE AT THE U.N. SECURITY COUNCIL (*January 7, 1950*)	95

ON CHINA'S SENDING REPRESENTATIVES TO THE UNITED NATIONS AND SOME OTHER MATTERS *(January 13, 1950)*   97

IN REFUTATION OF DEAN ACHESON'S SHAMELESS FABRICATIONS *(January 19, 1950)*   98

PREREQUISITES TO THE ESTABLISHMENT OF DIPLOMATIC RELATIONS BETWEEN CHINA AND BRITAIN *(February 8, 1950)*   101

THE GREAT SIGNIFICANCE OF THE CONCLUSION OF THE SINO-SOVIET TREATY AND AGREEMENTS *(April 11, 1950)*   102

REPLY ON RECEIVING THE CREDENTIALS PRESENTED BY INDIAN AMBASSADOR TO CHINA KAVALAM M. PANIKKAR *(May 20, 1950)*   104

A NEW WORLD WAR CAN BE AVERTED *(June 6, 1950)*   105

DEFEAT ANY PROVOCATION OF U.S. IMPERIALISM *(June 28, 1950)*   106

ON THE DECISION TO SEND VOLUNTEERS TO FIGHT IN KOREA *(October 2, 1950)*   107

ORDER TO ORGANIZE THE CHINESE PEOPLE'S VOLUNTEERS *(October 8, 1950)*   109

OUR TROOPS SHOULD AND MUST ENTER KOREA TO JOIN THE FIGHTING *(October 13, 1950)*   111

NO ROOM FOR SAY BY ANY FOREIGN COUNTRY IN THE MATTER OF CHINESE TROOPS ENTERING TIBET *(October 28, 1950)*   112

THE CHINESE PEOPLE'S VOLUNTEERS SHOULD CHERISH EVERY HILL, EVERY RIVER, EVERY TREE AND EVERY BLADE OF GRASS IN KOREA *(January 19, 1951)*   113

CONGRATULATORY SPEECH AT INDIA'S NATIONAL DAY PARTY HOSTED BY THE INDIAN AMBASSADOR TO CHINA *(January 26, 1951)*   114

THE WORLD FROM NOW ON MUST BE A WORLD THAT BELONGS TO THE PEOPLE *(October 23, 1951)*   115

SUCCESS OF THE KOREAN ARMISTICE NEGOTIATIONS HINGES ON WHETHER THE U.S. GOVERNMENT IS SINCERE *(February 14, 1952)*   118

TELEGRAM TO J.V. STALIN IN CELEBRATION OF THE SEVENTH ANNIVERSARY OF VICTORY IN THE WAR OF RESISTANCE AGAINST JAPAN *(September 2, 1952)*   119

FIGHT ON UNTIL U.S. IMPERIALISM IS WILLING TO GIVE UP *(February 7, 1953)*   120

TELEGRAM TO THE CONGRESS OF INDIANS IN SOUTH AFRICA *(May 28, 1954)*   121

ON THE INTERMEDIATE ZONE, PEACEFUL COEXISTENCE, SINO-BRITISH AND SINO-US RELATIONS *(August 24, 1954)*   122

APPLICATION OF THE FIVE PRINCIPLES OF PEACEFUL COEXISTENCE SHOULD BE EXTENDED TO STATE RELATIONS AMONG ALL COUNTRIES *(October 1954)*   126

All Countries in the East Have Been Bullied by Western Imperialist Powers *(October 19, 1954)* 126

Cooperation Between Countries Must Be Mutually Beneficial *(October 21, 1954)* ... 129

We Should Work Together to Prevent War and Win a Lasting Peace *(October 23, 1954)* 129

All Issues Between Countries That Can Cause Suspicion or Hamper Cooperation Should Be Resolved *(October 26, 1954)* 134

THE FIVE PRINCIPLES OF PEACEFUL COEXISTENCE ARE A LONG-TERM POLICY *(December 1954)* 136

We Should Promote Understanding in the Course of Cooperation *(December 1, 1954)* 136

Countries Should Be Equal, Irrespective of Size *(December 11, 1954)* 143

GREETING THE FIFTH ANNIVERSARY OF THE SIGNING OF THE SINO-SOVIET TREATY OF FRIENDSHIP, ALLIANCE AND MUTUAL ASSISTANCE *(February 12, 1955)* 151

ORDER ON TERMINATION OF THE STATE OF WAR BETWEEN THE PEOPLE'S REPUBLIC OF CHINA AND GERMANY *(April 7, 1955)* 154

CHINA AND PAKISTAN SHOULD BECOME GOOD FRIENDS *(April 27, 1955)* 156

THE UNITED STATES, THOUGH FRIGHTFUL, IS NOT SO FRIGHTFUL *(April 29, 1955)* 158

PEACE IS THE BEST *(May 26, 1955)* 160

HISTORY AND CURRENT REALITY DEMAND THAT WE UNITE AND COOPERATE *(June 30, 1955)* 165

REESTABLISHMENT OF DIPLOMATIC RELATIONS BETWEEN CHINA AND ITALY IS BENEFICIAL TO BOTH SIDES *(October 3, 1955)* 167

ON SINO-JAPANESE RELATIONS AND THE QUESTION OF A WORLD WAR *(October 15, 1955)* 169

OUR WISH IS TO PROMOTE FRIENDSHIP BETWEEN CHINA AND THAILAND *(December 1955 and February 1956)* 175

WE WISH TO LEARN FROM ALL COUNTRIES OF THE WORLD *(April 10, 1956)* 179

THE RELATIONSHIP BETWEEN CHINA AND OTHER COUNTRIES *(April 25, 1956)* 181

DO NOT BLINDLY BELIEVE THAT EVERYTHING IS GOOD IN A SOCIALIST COUNTRY *(June 28, 1956)* 185

ASIAN-AFRICAN COUNTRIES SHOULD UNITE TO SAFEGUARD PEACE AND INDEPENDENCE *(August 21, 1956)* 187

UNITING WITH FRATERNAL COUNTRIES AND ESTABLISHING FRIENDLY RELATIONS WITH ALL COUNTRIES *(August 29, 1956)* 189

THE CHINESE PEOPLE SUPPORT EGYPT'S RECOVERY OF THE SUEZ CANAL *(September 17, 1956)* 191

OVERSEAS CHINESE SHOULD OBSERVE THE LAWS OF THE COUNTRY IN WHICH THEY RESIDE (*September 18, 1956*)	194
DRAW HISTORICAL LESSONS AND OPPOSE BIG-NATION CHAUVINISM (*September 1956*)	195
ON RESTORATION TO CHINA HER LEGITIMATE SEAT IN THE UNITED NATIONS (*September 30, 1956*)	204
SPEECH AT THE BANQUET IN HONOR OF PRESIDENT SUKARNO OF INDONESIA (*October 2, 1956*)	213
IS IT RIGHT TO "LEAN TO ONE SIDE"? (*December 8, 1956*)	215
ON SINO-AMERICAN AND SINO-SOVIET RELATIONS (*January 27, 1957*)	217
ON A THIRD WORLD WAR AND INTERNATIONAL SOLIDARITY (*February 27, 1957*)	221
ON SOME POLICY ISSUES IN CHINA'S FOREIGN RELATIONS (*March, September 1957*)	222
SPEECH AT THE BANQUET IN HONOR OF VICE-PRESIDENT SARVEPALLI RADHAKRISHNAN OF INDIA (*September 19, 1957*)	224
A NEW TURNING POINT IN THE INTERNATIONAL SITUATION (*November 18, 1957*)	226
CHINA WILL NOT EXPAND OUTWARD (*December 14, 1957*)	233
TELEGRAM TO KIM IL SUNG ON THE WITHDRAWAL OF THE CHINESE PEOPLE'S VOLUNTEERS FROM KOREA (*January 24, 1958*)	237
FROM THE SOVIET UNION'S EXPERIENCE WE SHOULD CHOOSE ONLY THE GOOD THINGS (*March 1958*)	240
LEARN ADVANCED EXPERIENCE FROM ALL COUNTRIES IN THE WORLD (*April 2, 1958*)	242
WITHIN THE FOUR SEAS ALL MEN ARE BROTHERS (*May 16, 1958*)	244
ON THE SOVIET REQUEST TO ESTABLISH A SPECIAL LONG-WAVE RADIO STATION IN CHINA (*June 7, 1958*)	245
SELF-RELIANCE IS PRINCIPAL AND STRIVING FOR FOREIGN AID IS AUXILIARY (*June 17, 1958*)	247
DO AWAY WITH SUPERSTITION ABOUT IMPERIALIST "CIVILIZATION" (*July 12, 1958*)	248
TALK TO YUDIN, AMBASSADOR OF THE SOVIET UNION TO CHINA (*July 22, 1958*)	250
BIG NATIONS AND SMALL NATIONS SHOULD TREAT ONE ANOTHER AS EQUALS (*August 16, 1958*)	259
FIGHT FOR NATIONAL INDEPENDENCE AND DO AWAY WITH BLIND WORSHIP OF THE WEST (*September 2, 1958*)	260
SPEECH ON THE INTERNATIONAL SITUATION AT THE 15TH SESSION OF THE SUPREME STATE CONFERENCE (*September 1958*)	264
Views on the International Situation (*September 5, 1958*)	264

The U.S. Imperialists Are Caught in Their Own Noose (*September 8, 1958*)   269

THE NECESSITY IN DIPLOMATIC STRUGGLE TO OPERATE FROM A STRATEGICALLY ADVANTAGEOUS POSITION WITH IRRESISTIBLE FORCE (*September 19, 1958*)   273

JOHN F. DULLES IS THE BEST TEACHER BY NEGATIVE EXAMPLE IN THE WORLD (*October 2, 1958*)   274

CHINA AND THE U.S. HAVE NO WAR, SO THEY CAN HAVE NO CEASE-FIRE (*October 1958*)   277

THE WESTERN WORLD WILL INEVITABLY SPLIT UP (*November 25, 1958*)   280

ON THE ISSUE OF WHETHER IMPERIALISTS AND ALL REACTIONARIES ARE REAL TIGERS (*December 1, 1958*)   281

A LETTER IN REPLY TO CHAIRMAN FOSTER OF THE U.S. COMMUNIST PARTY (*January 17, 1959*)   284

GUARD AGAINST ARROGANCE IN FOREIGN RELATIONS (*February 13, 1959*)   285

AFRICA'S TASK IS TO STRUGGLE AGAINST IMPERIALISM (*February 21, 1959*)   286

WESTERN PACIFIC AFFAIRS SHOULD BE RUN BY WESTERN PACIFIC COUNTRIES (*March 18, 1959*)   288

SOME PEOPLE IN THE WORLD ARE AFRAID OF GHOSTS AND SOME ARE NOT (*May 6, 1959*)   290

INDIA IS NOT CHINA'S ENEMY, BUT CHINA'S FRIEND (*May 13, 1959*)   291

ON THE QUESTION OF TAIWAN (*May and October 1959*)   293

   The United States Must Withdraw Its Troops from Taiwan (*May 10, 1959*)   293

   The Relations Between China's Mainland and Taiwan Are Different from Those Between the Two Germanys, Two Koreas and Two Vietnams (*October 2, 1959*)   295

   The International Issue of the Taiwan Question Should Not Be Confused with the Domestic Issue (*October 5, 1959*)   296

IT IS POSSIBLE TO WIN A FAIRLY LONG PERIOD OF PEACE (*October 18, 1959*)   298

DÉTENTE IS BENEFICIAL TO THE PEOPLE OF BOTH THE SOCIALIST COUNTRIES AND THE CAPITALIST COUNTRIES (*October 26, 1959*)   301

THE SINO-NEPALESE BORDER SHOULD BE PEACEFUL AND FRIENDLY FOREVER (*March 18, 1960*)   302

WE ARE IN AN ERA WHEN IMPERIALISTS FEAR US (*May 3, 1960*)   308

IMPERIALISM IS NOTHING TO FEAR (*May 7, 1960*)   311

FIRMLY SUPPORT THE JAPANESE PEOPLE IN THEIR STRUGGLE AGAINST THE JAPANESE-U.S. MILITARY ALLIANCE (*May 14, 1960*)   319

OPPRESSED PEOPLE OUGHT NOT TO YIELD (*May 17, 1960*)   321

TALK WITH MARSHAL MONTGOMERY ON THE CURRENT INTERNATIONAL SITUATION (*May 27, 1960*)   325

U.S. IMPERIALISM IS THE COMMON ENEMY OF THE CHINESE AND JAPANESE PEOPLES *(June 21, 1960)*	335
SO LONG AS THE TWO SIDES KEEP FRIENDLY RELATIONS, THE BOUNDARY ISSUE IS EASY TO SOLVE *(September 29, 1960)*	341
TALK WITH EDGAR SNOW ON TAIWAN AND OTHER QUESTIONS *(October 22, 1960)*	344
THE IMPACT OF THE STRUGGLE OF THE JAPANESE PEOPLE IS FAR-REACHING *(January 24, 1961)*	349
AFRICA IS THE FOREFRONT OF STRUGGLE *(April 27, 1961)*	355
CHINA CAN HAVE ONLY ONE REPRESENTATIVE IN THE UNITED NATIONS *(June 13, 1961)*	359
ON THE TWO POSSIBILITIES OF A WORLD WAR *(August 19, 1961)*	361
TALKS WITH MARSHAL MONTGOMERY ON THE THREE PRINCIPLES AND THE QUESTION OF NUCLEAR WEAPONS *(September 1961)*	362
The Three Principles Are Well Put *(September 23, 1961)*	362
Nuclear Weapons Are to Scare People, Not to Use *(September 24, 1961)*	364
TALK WITH NEPAL'S KING MAHENDRA AND THE QUEEN *(October 5, 1961)*	366
THE JAPANESE PEOPLE HAVE A BRIGHT FUTURE *(October 7, 1961)*	368
THE COUNTRIES IN THE INTERMEDIATE ZONE VARY IN NATURE *(January 3, 1962)*	371
OUR RELATIONS WITH ALL AFRICAN PEOPLE ARE GOOD *(May 3, 1963)*	375
STATEMENT IN SUPPORT OF THE STRUGGLE OF THE AMERICAN BLACK PEOPLE AGAINST RACIAL DISCRIMINATION *(August 8, 1963)*	377
THE OPPRESSED WILL FINALLY RISE UP *(August 9, 1963)*	380
STATEMENT AGAINST U.S.-NGO DINH DIEM CLIQUE'S AGGRESSION IN SOUTH VIETNAM AND MASSACRE OF SOUTH VIETNAMESE PEOPLE *(August 29, 1963)*	385
THERE ARE TWO INTERMEDIATE ZONES *(September 1963; January and July 1964)*	387
THE CHINESE PEOPLE RESOLUTELY SUPPORT THE PEOPLE OF PANAMA IN THEIR PATRIOTIC AND JUST STRUGGLE *(January 12, 1964)*	390
KHRUSHCHEV IS HAVING A HARD TIME *(January 17, 1964)*	392
THE CHINESE PEOPLE SUPPORT THE GREAT PATRIOTIC STRUGGLE OF THE JAPANESE PEOPLE *(January 27, 1964)*	396
CHINA AND FRANCE SHARE COMMON GROUND *(January 30, 1964)*	398
OPPOSING EXTERNAL INTERVENTION, CARRYING OUT THE EIGHT PRINCIPLES *(June 14, 1964)*	402
WE SUPPORT THE OPPRESSED PEOPLE IN THEIR WARS AGAINST IMPERIALISM *(June 23, 1964)*	404
LOOKING AT THE PROSPECT OF THE PEOPLE'S STRUGGLE IN ASIA, AFRICA AND LATIN AMERICA FROM A HISTORICAL PERSPECTIVE	

(*July 9, 1964*) 408
PEOPLE OF THE WORLD ARE AGAINST KILLING BY ATOMBOMBS (*August 22, 1964*) 413
WE GREATLY APPRECIATE FRANCE'S INDEPENDENT POLICY (*September 10, 1964*) 415
TALK WITH EDGAR SNOW ON INTERNATIONAL ISSUES (*January 9, 1965*) 416
WE HOPE THE ARAB COUNTRIES WILL UNITE (*March 23, 1965*) 429
STATEMENT IN SUPPORT OF THE DOMINICAN PEOPLE'S OPPOSITION TO U.S. ARMED AGGRESSION (*May 12, 1965*) 432
FAITH IN VICTORY IS DERIVED FROM STRUGGLE (*October 20, 1965*) 434
A CLEAR DISTINCTION MUST BE MADE BETWEEN THE U.S. IMPERIALIST ELEMENTS AND THE AMERICAN PEOPLE (*November 25, 1965*) 437
STATEMENT IN SUPPORT OF THE AMERICAN BLACK PEOPLE'S STRUGGLE AGAINST VIOLENT REPRESSION (*April 16, 1968*) 439
WE AGREE WITH VIETNAM'S POLICY TO BOTH FIGHT AND NEGOTIATE (*November 17, 1968*) 441
THE PEOPLE OF THE WHOLE WORLD UNITE, DEFEAT THE U.S AGGRESSORS AND ALL THEIR LACKEYS (*May 20, 1970*) 444
IMPERIALISM IS AFRAID OF THE THIRD WORLD (*July 11, 1970*) 446
INTERNATIONAL ISSUES SHOULD BE SETTLED THROUGH JOINT CONSULTATION (*July 13, 1970*) 447
WE DON'T DEMAND FOREIGNERS RECOGNIZE THE IDEOLOGY OF THE CHINESE PEOPLE (*December 6, 1970*) 448
IF NIXON IS WILLING TO COME, I AM READY TO HOLD TALKS WITH HIM (*December 18, 1970*) 449
THE QUESTION OF WAR BETWEEN CHINA AND THE U.S. DOESN'T EXIST AT PRESENT (*February 21, 1972*) 451
SOVIET POLICY IS A FEINT TO THE EAST AND ATTACK IN THE WEST (*July 10, 1972*) 452
SETTLEMENT OF THE QUESTION OF RESTORATION OF DIPLOMATIC RELATIONS BETWEEN CHINA AND JAPAN STILL DEPENDS ON THE GOVERNMENT OF THE LIBERAL DEMOCRATIC PARTY (*September 27, 1972*) 453
ON THE QUESTION OF THE DIFFERENTIATION OF THE THREE WORLDS (*February 22, 1974*) 454
TALK WITH EDWARD HEATH (*May 25, 1974*) 455
NOTES 459
POSTSCRIPT 498

ADOPT AN ANTI-JAPANESE FOREIGN POLICY*

(*July 1937-May 1941*)

I

Adopt an anti-Japanese foreign policy. Accord the Japanese imperialists no advantages or facilities, but on the contrary confiscate their property, repudiate their loans, weed out their lackeys and expel their spies. Immediately conclude a military and political alliance with the Soviet Union and closely unite with the Soviet Union, the country which is most reliable, most powerful and most capable of helping China to resist Japan. Enlist the sympathy of Britain, the United States and France for our resistance to Japan, and secure their help provided that it entails no loss of our territory or our sovereign rights. We should rely mainly on our own strength to defeat the Japanese aggressors; but foreign aid cannot be dispensed with, and an isolationist policy will only play into the enemy's hands.

(July 23, 1937)
(From *Selected Works of Mao Zedong*, Vol. II)

II

Overthrow Japanese Imperialism

Sever diplomatic relations with Japan, expel Japanese officials, arrest Japanese agents, confiscate Japanese property in China, repudiate debts to Japan, abrogate treaties signed with Japan and take back all Japanese Conces-

---

* These are excerpts from five articles written by Mao Zedong: "Policies, Measures and Perspectives for Resisting the Japanese Invasion," "For the Mobilization of All the Nation's Forces for Victory in the War of Resistance," "The Identity of Interests Between the Soviet Union and All Mankind," "On Policy" and "Administrative Program for the Shaanxi-Gansu-Ningxia Border Region."

sions.

Fight to the finish in defense of northern China and the seacoast.

Fight to the finish for the recovery of Beiping, Tianjin and northeastern China.

Drive the Japanese imperialists out of China.

Oppose all vacillation and compromise.

Adopt an Anti-Japanese Foreign Policy

Conclude anti-aggression alliances and anti-Japanese pacts for mutual military aid with all countries that are opposed to Japanese aggression, provided that this entails no loss of our territory or of our sovereign rights.

Support the international peace front and oppose the front of aggression of Germany, Japan and Italy.

Unite with the worker and peasant masses of Korea and Japan against Japanese imperialism.

(August 25, 1937)

(From *Selected Works of Mao Zedong*, Vol. II)

III

It is obvious that China's foreign policy must be one of resistance to Japanese aggression. This policy means primarily relying on our own efforts, while not ignoring any possibility of securing help from abroad. Now that the imperialist world war has broken out, foreign help is coming chiefly from three sources: (1) the socialist Soviet Union, (2) the people of the capitalist countries, and (3) the oppressed nations in the colonies and semi-colonies. These are our only reliable sources of help. Anything else that might be called foreign help, even if it might become available, can only be regarded as supplementary and temporary. Of course, China should try to obtain such supplementary and temporary foreign help, but must never depend too much on it or consider it reliable. China should maintain strict neutrality toward the belligerents in the imperialist war and not join either side. To maintain that China should join the Anglo-French imperialist war front is a capitulator's view, which is harmful to the War of Resistance as well as to the independence and liberation of the Chinese nation, and it should be flatly rejected.

(September 18, 1939)

(From *Selected Works of Mao Zedong*, Vol. II)

IV

The Communist Party opposes all imperialism, but we make a distinction between Japanese imperialism which is now committing aggression against China and the imperialist powers which are not doing so now, between German and Italian imperialism which are allies of Japan and have recognized "Manchukuo"[1] and British and U.S. imperialism which are opposed to Japan, and between the Britain and the United States of yesterday which followed a Munich policy[2] in the Far East and undermined China's resistance to Japan, and the Britain and the United States of today which have abandoned this policy and are now in favor of China's resistance. Our tactics are guided by one and the same principle: to make use of contradictions, win over the many, oppose the few and crush our enemies one by one. Our foreign policy differs from that of the Kuomintang. The Kuomintang claims, "There is only one enemy and all the rest are friends"; it appears to treat all countries other than Japan alike, but in fact it is pro-British and pro-American. On our part we must draw certain distinctions, first, between the Soviet Union and the capitalist countries, second, between Britain and the United States on the one hand and Germany and Italy on the other, third, between the people of Britain and the United States and their imperialist governments, and fourth, between the policy of Britain and the United States during their Far Eastern Munich period and their policy today. We build our policy on these distinctions. In direct contrast to the Kuomintang our basic line is to use all possible foreign help, subject to the principle of independent prosecution of the war and reliance on our own efforts, and not, as the Kuomintang does, to abandon this principle by relying entirely on foreign help or hanging on to one imperialist bloc or another.

(December 25, 1940)
(From *Selected Works of Mao Zedong*, Vol. II)

V

Subject to the principle of respecting China's sovereignty and observing the laws of the government, any foreigner is allowed to travel, participate in anti-Japanese work, or carry out industrial, cultural and religious activities in the border regions. The governments of the border regions should sincerely extend protection to all who come to the border regions under the oppression of foreign governments as a result of their revolutionary actions, regardless of whether they came from a suzerain or a colony.

(May 1, 1941)
(From *Selected Works of Mao Zedong*, Vol. II)

SPEECH AT THE YAN'AN ANTI-AGGRESSION MEETING

(February 11, 1938)

Comrades:

The anti-aggression meeting held today is, in its significance, not only of Yan'an, but the whole nation, as similar meetings have been held nationwide in recent days, all with the objective of combating wars of aggression. This meeting is not just a China one, but of world significance. Tomorrow a world anti-aggression meeting will be held in London with representatives from scores of countries, marking the beginning of an unprecedented great world struggle. At present, the aggressors of the world have formed a front to undermine world peace, while the opposers to aggression are uniting the majority of the world's peoples to safeguard world peace against aggressive wars. These are the two opposite fronts that are combating each other worldwide. History has never before witnessed such a great world movement, a movement mobilizing all parts of the world. Now is the time for the good people, the majority of people worldwide, to square accounts with the bad people, who are a small minority.

As China's fate today hangs in the balance, an unprecedented unity has emerged all over the nation, great as never before in the history of China. We have set the foundation for our great national unity and are now expanding and developing it. Although we have lost some battles and territory, such great unity is of unrivaled strength, and with the support of the world's people, including the Japanese people, we are confident of defeating the Japanese aggressors. At present, there are three anti-aggression united fronts: the Chinese united front, the world united front, and the united front in Japan, where a wide range of the masses do not approve of their government's invasion of China and are forming an anti-aggression front. The three share the same objective: to act in unison to combat the war of aggression waged by the Japanese imperialists. Some people say that the anti-aggression movement of today will eventually fail, as did all such movements in China in the past scores of years. This is wrong. Today's situation differs from that of the past mainly because not only is there a national anti-aggression united front, but also this united front coincides with the world's anti-aggression united front, which is unprecedented in history, and moreover with the equally unprecedented internal contradictions in Japan, and the united front of the Japanese people. These historical features never existed before, but happen to prevail. That is the ground for us to say that the lost battles in China are temporary, and that China's War of Resistance will assuredly win final victory. With the three united fronts consolidating and expanding day by day, like the newly risen sun, the final victory surely belongs to us, and pessimism is groundless.

Therefore, our meeting today in the city of Yan'an is of nationwide and worldwide significance. All Chinese people refusing to be slaves of a foreign power, regardless of party affiliation, belief, sex or age, are uniting to strive for an identical objective. People throughout the world who love peace and hate war are uniting for the same purpose. So are a wide spectrum of the people within Japan. To combat aggression is our common objective, and it is also the general orientation in present-day world politics. The tremendous force of a united people all over China, all over the world and all over Japan will undoubtedly weaken the aggressors' strength bit by bit and bring them to final destruction. Therefore we say with firm confidence that China is bound to defeat the aggressors and that a new China will inevitably be founded as long as we continue to do our best.

(From *Selected Writings of Mao Zedong*, Vol. II)

FIGHTING FOR PERPETUAL PEACE*

(*May 1938*)

The protracted nature of China's anti-Japanese war is inseparably connected with the fight for perpetual peace in China and the whole world. Never has there been a historical period such as the present in which war is so close to perpetual peace. For several thousand years since the emergence of classes, the life of mankind has been full of wars; each nation has fought countless wars, either internally or with other nations. In the imperialist epoch of capitalist society, wars are waged on a particularly extensive scale and with a peculiar ruthlessness. The first great imperialist war of 20 years ago was the first of its kind in history, but not the last. Only the war which has now begun comes close to being the final war, that is, comes close to perpetual peace of mankind. By now one-third of the world's population has entered the war. Look! Italy, then Japan; Abyssinia,[3] then Spain, then China. The population of the countries at war now amounts to almost 600 million, or nearly a third of the total population of the world. The characteristics of the present war are its uninterruptedness and its proximity to perpetual peace. Why is it uninterrupted? After attacking Abyssinia, Italy attacked Spain, and Germany joined in; then Japan attacked China. What will come next? Undoubtedly Hitler[4] will fight the great powers. "Fascism means war"[5]—this is perfectly true. There will be no interruption in the development of the present war into a world war; mankind will not be able to avoid the calamity of war. Why then do we say the present war is near to perpetual peace? The present war is the result of the development of the general crisis of world capitalism which began with World War I; this general crisis is driving the capitalist countries into a new war and, above all, driving the fascist countries into new war adventures. This war, we can foresee, will not save capitalism, but will hasten its collapse. It will be greater in scale and more ruthless than the war of 20 years ago, all nations will inevitably be drawn in, it will drag on for a very long time, and

---

* These are excerpts from "On Protracted War," a series of lectures delivered by Mao Zedong at the Yan'an Association for the Study of the War of Resistance Against Japan.

mankind will suffer greatly. But, owing to the existence of the Soviet Union and the growing political consciousness of the people of the world, great revolutionary wars will undoubtedly emerge from this war to oppose all counter-revolutionary wars, thus giving this war the character of a struggle for perpetual peace. Even if later there should be another period of war, perpetual world peace will not be far off. Once man has eliminated capitalism, he will attain the era of perpetual peace, and there will be no more need for war. Neither armies, nor warships, nor military aircraft, nor poison gas will then be needed. Thereafter and for all time, mankind will never again know war. The revolutionary wars which have already begun are part of the war for perpetual peace. The war between China and Japan, two countries which have a combined population of over 500 million, will take an important place in this war for perpetual peace, and out of it will come the liberation of the Chinese nation. The liberated new China of the future will be inseparable from the liberated new world of the future. Hence our War of Resistance Against Japan takes on the character of a struggle for perpetual peace.

History shows that wars are divided into two kinds, just and unjust. All wars that are progressive are just, and all wars that impede progress are unjust. We Communists oppose all unjust wars that impede progress, but we do not oppose progressive, just wars. Not only do we Communists not oppose just wars, we actively participate in them. As for unjust wars, World War I is an instance in which both sides fought for imperialist interests; therefore the Communists of the whole world firmly opposed that war. The way to oppose a war of this kind is to do everything possible to prevent it before it breaks out and, once it breaks out, to oppose war with war, to oppose unjust war with just war, whenever possible. Japan's war is an unjust war that impedes progress, and the peoples of the world, including the Japanese people, should oppose it and are opposing it. In our country the people and the government, the Communist Party and the Kuomintang, have all raised the banner of righteousness in the national revolutionary war against aggression. Our war is sacred and just, it is progressive and its aim is peace. The aim is peace not just in one country but throughout the world, not just temporary but perpetual peace. To achieve this aim we must wage a life-and-death struggle, be prepared for any sacrifice, persevere to the end and never stop short of the goal. However great the sacrifice and however long the time needed to attain it, a new world of perpetual peace and brightness already lies clearly before us. Our faith in waging this war is based upon the new China and the new world of perpetual peace and brightness for which we are striving. Fascism and imperialism wish to perpetuate war, but we wish to put an end to it in the not too distant future.

The great majority of mankind should exert their utmost efforts for this purpose. The 450 million people of China constitute one quarter of the world's population, and if by their concerted efforts they overthrow Japanese imperialism and create a new China of freedom and equality, they will most certainly be making a tremendous contribution to the struggle for perpetual world peace. This is no vain hope, for the whole world is approaching this point in the course of its social and economic development, and provided that the majority of mankind work together, our goal will surely be attained in several decades.

(From *Selected Works of Mao Zedong*, Vol. II)

THE PRINCIPAL TASKS OF THE WORLD'S YOUTH IN ASSISTING CHINA'S WAR OF RESISTANCE AGAINST JAPAN*

(July 2, 1938)

Speaking of the principal tasks of the world's youth to help China in its War of Resistance Against Japan, I think, first of all, the World Federation of Students should make the majority of the youth and students in the world understand the necessity to oppose Japan jointly and help China and also enable them to comprehend that such work is closely related to their own interests, since peace is indivisible and global aggression by the fascists is the enemy of world peace. Second, students are bridge to the people; through them we can make people of all nationalities understand the necessity to oppose Japan and help China, as well as how such work relates to their own interests. As for the specific methods of assistance, they may use spoken or written propaganda to persuade people and governments to render us material assistance, put Japan under a boycott or refuse to sell any materials to Japan—right up to organizing international anti-Japanese volunteers who would come to China at proper times to participate in the war, and so on and so forth.

You represent extensive international student bodies coming to visit China and have brought us broad sympathy. All the Chinese people are grateful to you. On behalf of the Chinese Communist Party and the Chinese people, I extend my respects to you. We hope, after your return, you will present the true picture of China's Great War of Resistance Against Japan to the world's students and people. We shall always unite with you to fight for the freedom and equality of China and for everlasting peace and happiness in the world.

(From *Selected Writings of Mao Zedong*, Vol. II)

---

* These are excerpts from Mao Zedong's talks with a delegation from the World Federation of Students in Yan'an.

PRIMARILY RELYING ON OUR OWN EFFORTS, WHILE NOT SLACKENING IN SEEKING FOREIGN HELP*

(October 1938)

I

We should not neglect the work of pooling all possible foreign aid, expecting a prolonged war and acting on the principle of concentrating all efforts on combating the Japanese imperialists. Therefore, our current tasks include the following: First, firmly oppose the proposal by some people to follow the so-called German-Italian line, because it is in reality a step toward ready capitulation to the enemy. Second, seek an increase in material aid from the democratic countries and the Soviet Union, while making every endeavor to push for execution by nations of a League of Nations' resolution on sanctions against Japan. Third, set up some offices to record systematically all atrocities committed by the enemy troops, compiling them into documents and reports to be disseminated abroad, so as to arouse the whole world to stand for punishment of the Japanese fascists. Fourth, organize international propaganda teams composed of representatives of all parties and people's organizations to four countries to evoke the sympathies of peoples and governments as a supplement to our government's diplomatic activities. Fifth, protect all nationals of sympathizing countries and their peaceful activities, such as commerce and missionary work, in China. Sixth, pay attention to safeguarding the interests of overseas Chinese and promote their efforts to encourage campaigns to resist Japanese aggression and aid China.

We should strive to accomplish the above tasks no matter how much aid each country provides us, not excluding no increase in aid for the moment or

---

* The three sections selected here are excerpts from the report "On the New Stage," presented by Mao Zedong to the Enlarged Sixth Plenary Session of the Sixth Central Committee of the Communist Party of China.

even a possible partial decrease, and whether the League of Nations' resolution remains nice words. In case the War of Resistance is protracted, we should formulate our foreign policy on long-term plans for future help instead of immediate interests. It is necessary to have such foresight.

II

China is closely linked with the outside world; the Sino-Japanese war is part of the world war; and victory in China's War of Resistance Against Japan cannot be isolated from that in the world war. Some foreign aid may temporarily be reduced in the new war situation, upgrading the importance of China's own efforts. At no time should China abandon self-reliance as its fundamental standpoint. Nonetheless, China is not isolated and cannot be isolated, for China's relationship with the whole world is also our standpoint, and a necessary one. Neither do nor can we advocate a closed-door policy, and long ago China could no longer close her door. Now a world imperialist power has by war broken into all of China, so the entire Chinese people are concerned about the relationship between the world and China and, in particular, about changes in the current situation in Europe.

III

Everybody knows that in the past all democratic countries aided China to some extent, mainly because their people sympathized with China, while the Soviet Union was more active in helping us. Now that the Japanese aggressors have made penetrating offensives, contradictions between Britain, the United States, France and the Soviet Union on the one hand and Japan on the other have intensified. Attempting to maintain business as usual in Japanese-occupied regions, and to alleviate Japan's threat to Southeast Asia, Britain likely wishes to reach some compromise with Japan by applying in the East its policy of appeasement in the West. But a full compromise is difficult, at least for the time being. This is a result of the Japanese policy of monopolization; there is a certain difference between issues of East and West in the current situation. While the Japanese offensives have deepened the contradictions between Japan and the United States, the friendship between the Soviet Union and China is growing, and there is the possibility of a closer relationship among China, the United States and the Soviet Union. However, we must not forget, first, that capitalist countries differ from socialist ones; second, that the governments of capitalist countries differ from their people; and, last but not least, that the current situation differs from that in the future, so we must not place too high hopes on the former. We should try to obtain from the capitalist countries as much help as possible; such help, within limits, is not only a possibility but a fact, yet too-high hopes will be inappropriate. Support of foreign help to the Chinese national liberation movement will come mainly from the future of the anti-fascist movement of the progressive countries and the broad masses of the world's people. Such is the foundation on which we should place our policy of primarily relying on our own efforts, while not slackening in seeking foreign help.

(From *Liberation*, No. 57, published in Yan'an)

THE RELATIONSHIP BETWEEN THE WAR OF RESISTANCE AND FOREIGN AID —PREFACE TO THE ENGLISH TRANSLATION OF *ON PROTRACTED WAR*

(January 20, 1939)

    Friends in Shanghai are translating my *On Protracted War* into English, news that certainly pleases me, because China's great War of Resistance is a matter of concern not only to China and the East, but also to the whole world. The peoples of democratic countries, such as Britain, the United States and France, including progressives in all walks of life, have every sympathy for China's War of Resistance and oppose the Japanese imperialists' invasion of China; only some diehard cabals oppose China's fighting the war. Some of these diehards are just obstinate by nature, having taken the side of the Japanese warlords from the very beginning; others are too pessimistic to support China, misunderstanding the inexorable law that governs China's War of Resistance, a law under which Japan is doomed to lose and China is bound to win after an arduous course. There are probably many such people. It is, of course, my hope that my book may clarify the truth of this matter for them. As for the majority who sympathize with China's War of Resistance, perhaps some of them are still similarly unclear about the true state of the war, and although they sympathize with us, they feel depressed. Such depression mingled with sympathy particularly calls for our careful explanation. This little book of mine, written in May 1938, is meant to last for a long time, as its arguments cover the whole span of the Sino-Japanese war. As for the credibility of the arguments in the book, they have been proved true by all our past experiences during the War of Resistance and will be proved to be so again by future experience. Since the fall of Wuhan and Guangzhou the war has been proceeding toward a new stage—favorable to China but not to Japan —a stage that can be regarded as a stalemate between the enemy and us. A new situation is about to appear, in which the enemy is forced to end its strategic offensive and shift to strategic consolidation, while we, having persisted in resistance and grown in strength, conclude our strategic retreat (that is, of the main force, not the guerrillas) and move to a strategic parity. In this new stage our one and only task is to prepare for our counteroffensive, a time-consuming preparation perhaps, but to this we are to devote all our courage and energy, for we will and assuredly can throw the Japanese imperialists out of China. In the great War of Resistance, China must basically rely on herself to defeat the enemy, and there is no doubt that the forces in China, now that they are called into action, will not only become invincible, but also subdue the enemy and drive him away. In the meantime, however, we need the assistance of foreign aid. Our enemy is the whole world's enemy, China's War of Resistance is the world's war of resistance. The view of an isolated war has been proved wrong by history. There are still some people in democratic countries, such as Britain and the United States, who hold an isolationist view. They don't know that Britain, the United States and other countries would not be able to rest in peace if China were defeated. Their wrong view is most inappropriate. At present the hard truth is that aiding China means aiding themselves. So I hope this book will evoke some sympathy in English-speaking countries, for both the interests of China and the interests of the whole world. China is waging the war with much difficulty, yet the flames of war are threatening these world powers, so not a single country is able to stand clear of them. We agree to President Roosevelt's[6] call to safeguard democracy, but firmly oppose Chamberlain's[7] policy of concessions to the fascist countries of the West. Toward Japan, too, Chamberlain has so far shown a cowardly attitude. I hope the citizens of Britain and the United States will stir themselves and urge their governments to adopt a new policy against the war of aggression, for the sake of both China and their own countries.

(From *Selected Writings of Mao Zedong*, Vol. II)

INTERVIEW WITH *A NEW CHINA DAILY*[8] CORRESPONDENT ON THE NEW INTERNATIONAL SITUATION

(September 1, 1939)

Correspondent: What is the significance of the German-Soviet Treaty of Nonaggression?[9]

Mao Zedong: The German-Soviet Treaty of Nonaggression is the result of the growing socialist strength of the Soviet Union and the policy of peace persistently followed by the Soviet government. The treaty has shattered the intrigues by which the reactionary international bourgeoisie represented by Chamberlain[7] and Daladier[10] sought to instigate a Soviet-German war, has broken the encirclement of the Soviet Union by the German-Italian-Japanese anti-Communist bloc, strengthened peace between the Soviet Union and Germany, and safeguarded the progress of socialist construction in the Soviet Union. In the East it deals a blow to Japan and helps China; it strengthens the position of China's forces of resistance to Japan and deals a blow to the capitulators. All this provides a basis for helping the people throughout the world to win freedom and liberation. Such is the full political significance of the German-Soviet Treaty of Nonaggression.

Question: Some people do not realize yet that the German-Soviet Treaty of Nonaggression is the result of the breakdown of the Anglo-French-Soviet talks, but think that the German-Soviet treaty caused the breakdown. Will you please explain why the Anglo-French-Soviet talks failed?

Answer: The talks failed purely because the British and French governments were insincere. In recent years the reactionary international bourgeoisie, and primarily that of Britain and France, have consistently pursued the reactionary policy of "nonintervention" toward aggression by fascist Germany, Italy and Japan. Their purpose is to connive at wars of aggression and to profit by them. Thus Britain and France flatly rejected the Soviet Union's repeated proposals for a genuine front against aggression; standing on the side-lines, they took a "noninterventionist" position and connived at German,

Italian and Japanese aggression. Their aim was to step forward and intervene when the belligerents had worn each other out. In pursuit of this reactionary policy they sacrificed half of China to Japan, and the whole of Abyssinia, Spain, Austria and Czechoslovakia to Italy and Germany.[11] Then they wanted to sacrifice the Soviet Union. This plot was clearly revealed in the recent Anglo-French-Soviet talks. They lasted for more than four months, from April 15 to August 23, during which the Soviet Union exercised the utmost patience. But, from start to finish, Britain and France rejected the principle of equality and reciprocity; they demanded that the Soviet Union provide safeguards for their security, but refused to do likewise for the Soviet Union and the small Baltic states, so as to leave a gap through which Germany could attack, and they also refused to allow the passage of Soviet troops through Poland to fight the aggressor. That is why the talks broke down. In the meantime, Germany indicated her willingness to stop her activities against the Soviet Union and abandon the so-called Anti-Comintern Pact[12] and recognized the inviolability of the Soviet frontiers; hence the conclusion of the German-Soviet Treaty of Nonaggression. The policy of "non-intervention" pursued by international and primarily Anglo-French reaction is a policy of "sitting on top of the mountain to watch the tigers fight," a downright imperialist policy of profiting at others' expense. This policy was initiated when Chamberlain took office, reached its climax in the Munich agreement[2] of September last year and finally collapsed in the recent Anglo-French-Soviet talks. From now on the situation will inevitably develop into one of direct conflict between the two big imperialist blocs, the Anglo-French bloc and the German-Italian bloc. As I said in October 1938 at the Sixth Plenary Session of the Sixth Central Committee of our Party, "the inevitable result of Chamberlain's policy will be like 'lifting a rock only to drop in on one's own toes'." Chamberlain started with the aim of injuring others only to end up by ruining himself. This is the law of development which governs all reactionary policies.

Question: In your opinion, how will the present situation develop?

Answer: The international situation has already entered a new phase. The one-sided situation in the second imperialist war which has existed for some time, in other words, the situation in which, as a result of the policy of "nonintervention," one group of imperialist states attacks while another sits tight and looks on, will inevitably be replaced by a situation of all-embracing war as far as Europe is concerned. The second imperialist war has entered a new stage.

In Europe, a large-scale imperialist war is imminent between the German-Italian and the Anglo-French imperialist blocs which are contending for domination over the colonial peoples. In this war, each of the belligerents will brazenly declare its own cause to be just and that of its opponents unjust in order to delude people and win the support of public opinion. Actually this is a swindle. The aims of both sides are imperialist, both are fighting for the domination of colonies and semi-colonies and for spheres of influence, and both are waging a predatory war. At present, they are fighting over Poland, the Balkans and the Mediterranean littoral. This war is not at all a just war. The only just wars are non-predatory wars, wars of liberation. Communists will in no circumstances support any predatory war. They will, however, bravely step forward to support every just and non-predatory war for liberation, and they will stand in the forefront of the struggle. With Chamberlain and Daladier practicing intimidation and bribery, the social-democratic parties affiliated to the Second International are splitting up. One section, the reactionary upper stratum, is following the same old disastrous road as in the First World War and is ready to support the new imperialist war. But another section will join with the Communists in forming a popular front against war and fascism. Chamberlain and Daladier are following in the footsteps of Germany and Italy and are becoming more and more reactionary, taking advantage of the war mobilization to put the state structure in their countries on a fascist footing and to militarize the economy. In short, the two big imperialist blocs are feverishly preparing for war and millions of people are facing the danger of mass slaughter. Surely all this will arouse movements of resistance among the masses. Whether in Germany or in Italy, Britain or France, or anywhere else in Europe or the world at large, if the people do not want to be used as imperialist cannon-fodder, they will have to rise up and oppose the imperialist war in every possible way.

Besides these two big blocs, there is a third bloc in the capitalist world, headed by the United States and including a number of Central and South American countries. In its own interests, this bloc will not enter the war for the time being. In the name of neutrality, U.S. imperialism is temporarily refraining from joining either of the belligerents, so as to be able to come on the scene later and contend for the leadership of the capitalist world. The fact that the U.S. bourgeoisie is not yet prepared to discard democracy and a peace-time economy at home is favorable to the world peace movement.

Badly hit by the German-Soviet treaty, Japanese imperialism is facing a future beset with still greater difficulties. Two factions within Japan are fighting over foreign policy. The militarists are contemplating an alliance with Germany and Italy for the purpose of gaining exclusive control of China, invading Southeast Asia and expelling Britain, the United States and France from the East; on the other hand, one section of the bourgeoisie would prefer to make concessions to Britain, the United States and France in order to concentrate on plundering China. At present, there is a strong tendency toward a compromise with Britain. The British reactionaries will offer Japan the joint partition of China plus financial and economic help, in return for which Japan will have to serve as the watchdog of British interests in the East, suppress the Chinese national liberation movement and contain the Soviet Union. Therefore, whatever happens, Japan's basic aim of conquering China will never change. The possibility that Japan will launch large-scale frontal military offensives in China may not be very great, but it will step up its political offensive to "use Chinese to subdue Chinese"[13] and its economic plundering of China to "sustain" the war by means of war,"[14] while keeping up its frantic "mopping-up" campaigns[15] in the occupied areas; moreover, it will work through Britain to force China to surrender. At a favorable moment it will propose an Eastern Munich and, with some relatively big concessions as bait, will try to coax and bully China into accepting its terms for surrender, so as to attain its aim of subjugating China. No matter what cabinet changes the Japanese ruling class may make, this imperialist aim will remain unchanged until the Japanese people rise in revolution.

Outside the capitalist world there is a world of light, the socialist Soviet Union. The German-Soviet treaty enables the Soviet Union to give greater help to the world movement for peace and to China in her resistance to Japan.

This is my appraisal of the international situation.

Question: In these circumstances, what are the prospects for China?

Answer: There are two possibilities. One is perseverance in resistance, unity and progress, which would mean national rejuvenation. The other is compromise, a split and retrogression, which would mean national subjugation.

In the new international situation, as Japan comes up against increased difficulties and China firmly refuses to compromise, the stage of strategic retreat will end for us and that of strategic stalemate will begin. The latter stage is one of preparation for the counteroffensive.

However, stalemate along the front means the reverse of stalemate in the enemy's rear; with the emergence of a stalemate along the front lines, the struggle behind the enemy lines will become intense. Thus the large-scale "mopping-up" campaigns the enemy has been conducting in the occupied areas—mainly in northern China—since the fall of Wuhan will not only continue but will be intensified from now on. Furthermore, since the enemy's main policy at present consists in his political offensive to "use Chinese to subdue Chinese" and in his economic aggression for "sustaining the war by means of war," and since a Far Eastern Munich is the objective of British policy in the East, the danger of the surrender of the greater part of China and of an internal split will increase enormously. China is still far weaker than the enemy, and unless the whole country unites in an arduous struggle, it will not be able to build up strength for the counteroffensive.

Therefore, the most serious task for our country is still perseverance in the war, and there must be no slackening.

Beyond any doubt, China must on no account miss the present opportunity or make a wrong decision but must take a firm political stand.

In other words: First, firm adherence to the stand of resistance to Japan and opposition to any moves toward compromise. Determined blows must be struck at all the open or undercover Wang Jingweis. China must firmly reject any blandishments, whether from Japan or from Britain, and must never take part in an Eastern Munich.

Second, firm adherence to the stand of unity and opposition to any moves toward a split. Strict vigilance must be maintained against such moves whether they stem from the Japanese imperialists, from other foreign countries, or from the capitulators at home. All internal friction harmful to the War of Resistance must be sternly checked.

Third, firm adherence to the stand of progress and opposition to any retrogression. Whether in the military, political, financial or economic sphere, or in party affairs, or in the field of culture and education, or in the mass movement, every theory, every institution, every measure harmful to the war must be re-examined and effectively changed to serve the War of Resistance.

If all this is done, China will be able effectively to build up her strength for the counteroffensive.

From now on the whole country must make "preparation for the counteroffensive" its over-all task in the War of Resistance.

Today, it is necessary on the one hand earnestly to sustain our defense along the front lines and vigorously to help the fighting behind the enemy lines and on the other to institute political, military and other reforms and build up tremendous strength, so that when the moment comes, the whole might of the nation can be thrown into a large-scale counteroffensive for the recovery of our lost territories.

(From *Selected Works of Mao Zedong*, Vol. II)

THE QUESTION OF WAR AND REVOLUTION*

(*July 13, 1940*)

(1) The Soviet Union's noninvolvement in war

When the outbreak of war between two groups of imperialist countries cannot be prevented, the people will rise up to oppose the war, whereas the Soviet Union will simply not get involved in it. This plan of noninvolvement is the result of the struggle of the Soviet Union over the past 20 years, of peoples of the world supporting the Soviet Union, of the Soviet Union's flexibly making use of the contradictions among the imperialist countries, as well as the greatest victory of the global strategy of the proletariat, because it has not only defended the Soviet Union, but ensured the triumph of world revolution.

This triumph was achieved in the conclusion of two agreements: the German-Soviet and the Soviet-Finnish agreements.[16] Our task in the future is to strengthen this triumph.

(2) The two imperialist alignments

The so-called two imperialist alignments, or two united fronts, by no means signify there are no contradictions and struggles among the allies of both sides. Contradictions and struggles do exist, and, moreover, they are rather serious. For example, there are contradictions and struggles among the U.K., the U.S. and France, also among these three countries and other lesser countries; as well as among Germany, Italy and Japan, also among these three countries and other lesser countries.

Nor do they signify that each alignment is fixed and unchangeable. On the contrary, they are unfixed and changeable, and changes have already taken place.

On the one hand, there have been the changes in northern Europe, the Netherlands, Belgium, and the Balkan Peninsula and the great change in

---

* This is part of the main points of Mao Zedong's conclusion made at the meeting of senior cadres in Yan'an during the discussions of the "Decisions of the Central Committee of the Communist Party of China on the Present Situation and the Policy of the Party."

France, all showing a weakening of the alignment. This is the U.K.-U.S.-France alignment.

On the other hand, there is a strengthening of another alignment.

That is the Germany-Italy-Japan alignment. This has resulted in a present state of imbalance.

Japan was once pro-British and American; now it is pro-German and Italian. This is because a fascist faction is going to replace the British-American faction inside Japan.

Neither side has a durable treaty of alliance, such as between the U.S. and U.K.-France, between U.K.-France and northern Europe, between them and the Netherlands and Belgium, as well as between Germany-Italy and Japan.

These are so-called internal contradictions, struggles and changes within the alignments. There will be further contradictions, struggles and changes in future.

Despite all these, Germany, Italy and Japan want to break the status quo, and, in the meantime, the so-called democratic countries (including the Netherlands and Belgium) want to maintain the status quo. Both sides have their common interests, so they are able to form some sort of united front, each gathering several tens of or over ten countries. So far as geographical position, economic strength and naval force are concerned, the U.K. and the U.S. are still stronger, whereas Germany, Italy and Japan are superior because of Germany's victories in the war and its occupation of vast territories.

No matter whether East or West, the struggle of the two imperialist alignments is no longer limited to the continents, but has shifted to the sea. There will be tremendous conflicts in future, as no decisive battle has yet been fought.

If the U.K. were subdued, U.S. naval hegemony would still remain. The U.S. practices the Monroe Doctrine plus cosmopolitanism, i.e., "What is mine is mine, and what is yours is also mine." It will by no means give up its interests in the Atlantic and Pacific oceans.

Germany and Italy are weaker in naval power, and this condition would remain the same even after the surrender of France. Germany, Italy and Japan will be unable to take over the colonies of the U.K., France, the Netherlands and Belgium without destroying the U.S. and British navies.

It is the Versailles-Washington system on the one hand and opposition to this system in an attempt to set up a new Versailles and new Pacific system on the other. The struggle has not yet concluded.

This means that there are still contradictions among the imperialist countries that can serve the cause of revolution. Hence we must make use of them. The Soviet Union, India, China, and all other proletarian and oppressed nations must make use of them.

The present world is in an epoch of great turbulence and changes, not an epoch of "peace" and "capitalist stability," which ended long ago and will never be able to emerge again.

If one fails to see this, it is because one has incorrectly estimated the following points:

1. An overestimation of the counterrevolution

a. Contradictions among the imperialist countries have developed, instead of abated, owing to the war.

b. The bourgeoisie of various countries and the capitalist system no longer enjoy the trust of the people.

c. The social democratic party has lost the people's trust.

d. The destructive nature of war.

2. An underestimation of revolutionary forces

a. The existence of the Soviet Union.

b. The existence of the Chinese revolution.

c. The upsurge of revolutionary movements in India.

d. The existence of the Communist Parties in Europe and other countries.

(3) The inevitability of revolution

1. The triumph of Germany and Italy over the U.K. and France is equal to smashing two imperialist shackles, whereas the new imperialist shackles may be smashed at the moment of or before being used. The capitalist front can possibly be broken through at three places—Europe, India and China. This is equal to basically breaking the whole capitalist front.

2. It is impossible to expect an isolated October Revolution in Europe. It must be the October Revolution in addition to the Soviet Red Army. But such an opportunity has not yet come.

3. Instead of carrying out world revolution, the present conditions are the eight-hour working system of the Soviet Union and the forthcoming maturity of the situation of world revolution. We still have to make use of the imperialist wars and we are now on the eve of world revolution.

(From *Selected Writings of Mao Zedong*, Vol. II)

ON THE INTERNATIONAL UNITED FRONT AGAINST FASCISM*

(*June 23, 1941*)

On June 22 the fascist rulers of Germany attacked the Soviet Union. This is a perfidious crime of aggression not only against the Soviet Union but against the freedom and independence of all nations. The Soviet Union's sacred war of resistance against fascist aggression is being waged not only in its own defense but in defense of all the nations struggling to liberate themselves from fascist enslavement.

For Communists throughout the world the task now is to mobilize the people of all countries and organize an international united front to fight fascism and defend the Soviet Union, defend China, and defend the freedom and independence of all nations. In the present period, every effort must be concentrated on combating fascist enslavement.

For the Chinese Communist Party the tasks throughout the country are as follows:

1. Persevere in the National United Front Against Japan, persevere in Kuomintang-Communist cooperation, drive the Japanese imperialists out of China, and by these means assist the Soviet Union.

2. Resolutely combat all the anti-Soviet and anti-Communist activities of the reactionaries among the big bourgeoisie.

3. In foreign relations, unite against the common foe with everybody in Britain, the United States and other countries who is opposed to the fascist rulers of Germany, Italy and Japan.

(From *Selected Works of Mao Zedong*, Vol. III)

---

* This inner-Party directive was written by Mao Zedong for the Central Committee of the Communist Party of China.

WELCOME, COMRADES-IN-ARMS OF THE U.S. MILITARY OBSERVATION GROUP*

(August 15, 1944)

The U.S. Military Observation Group dispatched by the General Headquarters of the U.S. Armed Forces in China, Burma and India (i.e., General Stilwell's[17] headquarters) has now arrived in Yan'an. This is the most exciting major event since the start of China's War of Resistance. We should like to extend our warm welcome to all members of the observation group from afar!

In receiving the comrades-in-arms of the U.S. Military Observation Group, we cannot help thinking of the brilliant achievements scored by the United States in the anti-fascist world war and the American people's great spirit of readily taking up cudgels for a just cause and bearing sacrifices. In Europe, Africa and Asia there are heroic American officers and men ready to lay down their lives on the battlefield, bleeding and fighting for the liberation of the people under the fascist iron heel. On our China's battlefield of resistance to the Japanese invaders, American soldiers are fighting shoulder to shoulder with our people and becoming our closest comrades-in-arms. On this occasion of welcoming the friends of the U.S. Military Observation Group, we should like to express our heartfelt thanks to the U.S. government, the American people, the American officers and men in the navy, the army and the air force, and their wise leader, President Roosevelt.[6]

The arrival of the comrades-in-arms of the U.S. Military Observation Group in Yan'an has a great significance for victory in the War of Resistance Against Japan. Over the past seven years nearly 500,000 troops of the Eighth Route and New Fourth armies and over 80 million liberated people have been fighting bravely on three major battlefields behind enemy lines in northern, central and southern China. For a long time the battlefields behind enemy lines have been the most important ones in China's War of Resistance. It is there that we have taken on five sixths of all the Japanese and their puppet

---

* This article is the main part of an editorial of Yan'an's *Liberation Daily*, finalized by Mao Zedong.

troops in China; nearly all the major cities in China have been under siege by the Eighth Route and New Fourth armies; and most of the enemy-occupied coastlines have come under our control. This situation remains unknown to friends in allied countries.

Past information received by the governments and peoples of the allied countries about China's War of Resistance is completely otherwise. Their impressions have been that the Kuomintang was the main force in the war in China, that the Kuomintang played the greatest part in the War of Resistance, that the Kuomintang resisted the majority of the Japanese and their puppet troops, and that the Kuomintang should naturally be the major force to rely on in future counteroffensives against the Japanese invaders. Even now such impressions remain unchanged and dominant in the minds of the majority of the officials and citizens of the allied countries.

The reason for such deception, flying completely in the face of truth, is the policy of fraud and blockade adopted by the Kuomintang rulers. They have deceived foreigners by saying how the Kuomintang exerted itself in combating the Japanese, whereas for five and a half years since October 1938, they have basically followed a policy of "doing nothing but sit on top of the mountain to watch the tigers fight"; up to now this policy remains unchanged in most of the theaters of operation except for Hunan and Burma. Again they have deceived foreigners by saying that the Communist Party not only "combated no Japanese," but always "tried to sabotage the War of Resistance and endangered the nation." In actuality, it is just this Communist Party that took on five sixths of the Japanese and their puppet troops, while the Kuomintang, shouting every day about the "superior interests of the nation," faced no more than one sixth of the enemy troops. Since the Communist Party allegedly "combated no enemy," "sabotaged the War of Resistance," and "endangered the nation," the Kuomintang should long ago have called for large numbers of foreigners and Chinese to visit the Communist regions in order to check that what the Kuomintang gentlemen said were not lies. But they never did so. Instead, they sealed those areas like an iron bucket. For more than five years they banned, first, the Communist Party from issuing battlefield reports; second, the border region newspapers from circulating in other areas; third, any visit by Chinese and foreign journalists and, last, any crossing in and out of the border regions. In a word the Kuomintang is free to fabricate, vilify, abuse, rumormonger and mudsling all over, while the Communist Party and the Eighth Route and New Fourth armies are forbidden to release even a bit of their true conditions to the world. The difficulties and hardships the journalist delegation[18] had to overcome before they were able to travel to the border regions show clearly how the Kuomintang rulers racked their brains trying to vilify us on the one hand and ban people from visiting us on the other, proving themselves self-contradictory.

Facts speak louder than words, however, and truth is superior to all. The day would come when foreigners and Chinese saw clearly, and now that has happened, though gradually, as the Chinese and Foreign Journalist Delegation and the U.S. Military Observation Group visited Yan'an one after the other after breaking through the Kuomintang's blockade line. This issue is concerned with 450 million Chinese people combating the Japanese invaders to liberate all of China, with which of the two propositions and two lines in China is right, and with the allied countries defeating their common enemy and establishing a lasting peace. The Kuomintang said, "The disputes between the Kuomintang and the Communist Party are the private affairs of China," which is nothing but a fig leaf for the crimes committed by the Kuomintang in the War of Resistance. It has now become the public opinion of both Chinese and foreigners that this dirty leaf should be thrown into a latrine.

As for the Kuomintang's ineffective fighting in the war, its corruption and its incompetence, they have been conclusion of both foreign and Chinese public opinion for over half a year, but as for the Communist Party's true situation, the majority of foreigners and Chinese in the great rear area do not yet have a clear understanding, owing to the long-time counterrevolutionary propaganda and blockade policy of the Kuomintang. Nevertheless, things are changing. Foreign public opinion for more than half a year has shown the beginning of such a change. The arrival of the journalist delegation and the observation group in Yan'an will open up a new stage.

Thanks to the coverage of the foreign journalists visiting Yan'an, foreigners will gradually know the truth about the Communist Party of China, the Eighth Route and New Fourth armies and the anti-Japanese base areas, as well as their importance in supporting the war of resistance of the allied countries.

Now not only the Foreign Journalist Delegation, but also the U.S. Military Observation Group has arrived in Yan'an. We believe that the comrades-in-arms of the group will surely observe the situation here carefully and keenly and make plans for close cooperation of the two sides to defeat the Japanese invaders. It has already proved difficult for the Kuomintang to shut out the truth from the masses for long.

We wish success for the work of the U.S. Military Observation Group. We hope that such success will help the U.S. supreme command understand that the Communist Party of China has from the beginning persisted in the policies unity of in the War of Resistance and of democracy, and appreciate the strength of the Communist-led forces of resistance in the rear of the enemy, and that it will, on the basis of such understanding and appreciation, decide on a correct policy. We hope also that such success will promote unity between China and the United States, the two great allies, and speed up the final defeat of the Japanese invaders.

(From *Liberation Daily*, August 15, 1944, Yan'an)

A LETTER TO U.S. PRESIDENT ROOSEVELT

(*November 10, 1944*)

Yan'an
November 10, 1944

Your Excellency President Roosevelt,[6]

I feel honored to host your representative, General Hurley.[19] Over three days we have deliberated harmoniously all matters of vital importance to unite all the people of China and all military forces to defeat Japan and rebuild China. I proposed an agreement[20] in this regard.

In the spirit and orientation of the agreement is the objective that we, the Communist Party of China and the Chinese people, have pursued in a united front to combat Japan over the past eight years. It has been our consistent wish to reach agreement with Chairman Chiang to promote the welfare of the Chinese people. With the help of General Hurley, we now have hope that this objective will come true, and with great pleasure I appreciate your representative's outstanding talent and sympathy for the Chinese people.

The Central Committee of our Party has unanimously adopted the text of the agreement and is prepared to give it full support and make it come true. I have been authorized by the Central Committee of our Party to sign the agreement, as witnessed by General Hurley.

In the name of our Party, our army and the Chinese people, I now ask General Hurley to convey the agreement to you. Your Excellency Mr. President, I also wish to thank you for the great effort you have devoted to the unity of China in order to defeat Japan and to the realization of the possibility of a unified and democratic China.

The peoples of China and the United States have a history and tradition of deep friendship. I sincerely hope your effort and success will enable the two great Chinese and American nations always to advance hand in hand in defeating the Japanese aggressors, rebuilding lasting world peace and establishing a democratic China.

Mao Zedong
Chairman of the Central
Committee of the Communist
Party of China
(From the original manuscript)

THE PRESENT INTERNATIONAL SITUATION AND THE FUNDAMENTAL PRINCIPLE OF THE FOREIGN POLICY OF THE COMMUNIST PARTY OF CHINA*

(April 24, 1945)

What is the present international situation?

The present military situation is that the Soviet Army is attacking Berlin, and the allied forces of Britain, the United States and France are attacking the Hitlerite[4] remnants in coordination with this offensive, while the Italian people are launching uprisings. All this will eliminate Hitler once and for all. After Hitler is wiped out, the defeat of the Japanese aggressors will not be far distant. Contrary to the predictions of the Chinese and foreign reactionaries, the forces of fascist aggression will undoubtedly be overthrown and the people's democratic forces will undoubtedly triumph. The world will unquestionably take the road of progress and not the road of reaction. Of course, we must remain very much on the alert and reckon with the possibility of certain temporary or perhaps even serious twists and turns in the course of events; in many countries there are still strong reactionary forces which begrudge the people at home and abroad their unity, progress and liberation. Anyone who loses sight of this possibility will make political mistakes. The general trend of history, however, is already clearly decided and will not change. This is bad only for the fascists and for the reactionaries of all countries who are in fact their helpers, but it is a blessing for the people and for the organized democratic forces in all countries. The people, and the people alone, are the motive force in the making of world history. The Soviet people have built up great strength and become the main force in the defeat of fascism. It is their efforts, plus those of the people in the other anti-fascist allied countries, which

---

* These are excerpts from "On Coalition Government," the political report made by Mao Zedong to the Seventh National Congress of the Communist Party of China.

are making the destruction of fascism possible. War has educated the people and it is the people who will win the war, win the peace and win progress.

This new situation is very different from that in World War I. The Soviet Union was not yet in existence then and the people were not politically awakened as they are in many countries today. The two world wars represent two entirely different epochs.

This does not mean that there will be no more struggles after the defeat of the fascist aggressor countries, the end of World War II and the establishment of international peace. The remnant forces of fascism which are still widespread will certainly continue to make trouble, while within the camp now fighting fascist aggression there are forces which oppose democracy and oppress other nations, and they will continue to oppress the people in various countries and in the colonies and semi-colonies. Therefore, after international peace is established, there will still be numerous struggles over the greater part of the world—between the anti-fascist masses and the remnants of fascism, between democracy and anti-democracy, between national liberation and national oppression. The people will achieve the most extensive victory only through long and sustained efforts, when the remaining forces of fascism, the anti-democratic forces and all the imperialist forces are overcome. To be sure, that day will not come very quickly or easily, but come it surely will. Victory in the anti-fascist Second World War will pave the way for the victory of the people in their post-war struggles. A stable and lasting peace will be ensured only when victory is won in these struggles.

The Communist Party of China agrees with the Atlantic Charter[21] and with the decisions of the international conferences of Moscow, Cairo, Teheran and the Crimea,[22] because these decisions all contribute to the defeat of the fascist aggressors and the maintenance of world peace.

The fundamental principle of the foreign policy advocated by the Chinese Communist Party is as follows: China shall establish and strengthen diplomatic relations with all countries and settle all questions of common concern, such as coordination of military operations in the war, peace conferences, trade and investment, on the basic conditions that the Japanese aggressors must be completely defeated and world peace maintained, that there must be mutual respect for national independence and equality, and that there must be promotion of mutual interests and friendship between states and between peoples.

The Chinese Communist Party fully agrees with the proposals of the Dumbarton Oaks conference and the decisions of the Crimea conference on the establishment of an organization to safeguard international peace and security after the war. It welcomes the United Nations Conference on International Organization in San Francisco. It has appointed its own representative on China's delegation to this conference in order to express the will of the Chinese people.[23]

We hold that the Kuomintang government must cease its hostility toward the Soviet Union and speedily improve Sino-Soviet relations. The Soviet Union was the first country to renounce the unequal treaties and sign new, equal treaties with China. At the time of the Kuomintang's First National Congress called by Dr. Sun Yat-sen in 1924 and the subsequent Northern Expedition, the Soviet Union was the only country to help China's war of liberation. When the anti-Japanese war broke out in 1937, the Soviet Union was again the first country to help China against the Japanese aggressors. The Chinese people are grateful to the Soviet government and people for this help. We believe that no final and thorough settlement of the problems of the Pacific is possible without the participation of the Soviet Union.

We ask the governments of all the allied countries, and of the United States and Britain in the first place, to pay serious attention to the voice of the Chinese people and not to impair friendship with them by pursuing foreign policies that run counter to their will. We maintain that if any foreign government helps the Chinese reactionaries and opposes the Chinese people's democratic cause, it will be committing a gross mistake.

The Chinese people welcome the steps taken by many foreign governments in renouncing their unequal treaties and concluding new, equal treaties with China. However, we maintain that the conclusion of equal treaties does not in itself mean that China has actually won genuine equality. Genuine and actual equality is never the gift of foreign governments, but must be won mainly by the Chinese people through their own efforts, and the way to win it is to build a new-democratic China politically, economically and culturally; otherwise there will be only nominal and not actual independence and equality. That is to say, China can never win genuine independence and equality by following the present policy of the Kuomintang government.

We consider that, after the defeat and unconditional surrender of the Japanese aggressors, it will be necessary to help all the democratic forces of the Japanese people to establish their own democratic system so that Japanese fascism and militarism may be thoroughly wiped out, together with their political, economic and social roots. Unless the Japanese people have a democratic system, it will be impossible thoroughly to wipe out Japanese fascism and militarism and impossible to ensure peace in the Pacific.

We consider the decision of the Cairo conference regarding the independence of Korea to be correct. The Chinese people should help the Korean people to win liberation.

We hope that India will attain independence. For an independent and democratic India is not only needed by the Indian people but is essential for world peace.

As regards the Southeast Asian countries—Burma, Malaya, Indonesia, Vietnam and the Philippines—we hope that after the defeat of the Japanese aggressors their people will exercise their right to establish independent and democratic states of their own. As for Thailand, she should be treated like the fascist satellite states in Europe.

(From *Selected Works of Mao Zedong*, Vol. III)

THE REACTIONARY COUNTERCURRENT WILL BE SWEPT AWAY*

(June 11, 1945)

The U.S. government's policy of supporting Chiang Kai-shek against the Communists shows the brazenness of the U.S. reactionaries. But all the scheming of the reactionaries, whether Chinese or foreign, to prevent the Chinese people from achieving victory is doomed to failure. The democratic forces are the main current in the world today, while reaction is only a countercurrent. The reactionary countercurrent is trying to swamp the main current of national independence and people's democracy, but it can never become the main current. Today, there are still three major contradictions in the old world, as Stalin pointed out long ago: first, the contradiction between the proletariat and the bourgeoisie in the imperialist countries; second, the contradiction between the various imperialist powers; and third, the contradiction between the colonial and semi-colonial countries and the imperialist metropolitan countries.[24] Not only do these three contradictions continue to exist but they are becoming more acute and widespread. Because of their existence and growth, the time will come when the reactionary anti-Soviet, anti-Communist and anti-democratic countercurrent still in existence today will be swept away.

(From *Selected Works of Mao Zedong*, Vol. III)

---

* These are excerpts from "The Foolish Old Man Who Removed the Mountains," Mao Zedong's concluding speech at the Seventh National Congress of the Communist Party of China.

ON THE DANGER OF THE HURLEY POLICY*

(*July 12, 1945*)

It has become increasingly obvious that the policy of the United States toward China as represented by its ambassador Patrick J. Hurley[19] is creating a civil war crisis in China. Sticking to its reactionary policies, the Kuomintang government has lived on civil war ever since it was set up 18 years ago; only at the time of the Xi'an Incident[25] in 1936 and of the Japanese invasion south of the Great Wall in 1937 was it forced to abandon its nation-wide civil war for a time. Since 1939, however, civil war on a local scale has again been waged without interruption. "Fight the Communists first" is the mobilization slogan used by the Kuomintang government among its own people, while it relegates resistance to Japan to a secondary place. At present all its military dispositions are focused not on resisting the Japanese aggressors but on "recovering lost territory" from China's Liberated Areas and on wiping out the Chinese Communist Party. This situation must be taken into serious account in our struggle both for victory in the War of Resistance and for peaceful construction after the war. The late President Roosevelt[6] did take it into account and consequently, in the interests of the United States, refrained from adopting a policy of helping the Kuomintang to undertake armed attacks on the Chinese Communist Party. When Hurley visited Yan'an as Roosevelt's personal representative in November 1944, he expressed agreement with the Chinese Communist Party's plan for the abolition of the Kuomintang one-party dictatorship and the establishment of a democratic coalition government. But later he changed his tune and went back on what he had said in Yan'an. This change was crudely revealed in his statement in Washington on April 2. In the interim, according to the selfsame Hurley, the Kuomintang government represented by Chiang Kai-shek seems to have turned into the Beauty and the Chinese Communist Party into the Beast, and he flatly declared that the United States would cooperate with Chiang Kai-shek only and not with the Chinese Communist Party. This, of course, is not just Hurley's personal view

---

* This is a commentary written by Mao Zedong for the Xinhua News Agency.

but that of a whole group of people in the U.S. government. It is a wrong and dangerous view. At this juncture Roosevelt died, and Hurley returned to the U.S. embassy in Chongqing in high spirits. The danger of the China policy of the United States as represented by Hurley is that it is encouraging the Kuomintang government to be still more reactionary and aggravating the civil war crisis. If the Hurley policy continues, the U.S. government will fall irretrievably into the deep stinking cesspool of Chinese reaction; it will put itself in the position of antagonizing the hundreds of millions of awakened and awakening Chinese people and will become a hindrance to the War of Resistance in the present and to world peace in the future. Isn't it clear that this would be the inevitable result? A section of U.S. public opinion is worried about the China policy of the Hurley type with its dangers and wants it changed, because as far as China's future is concerned, it sees clearly that the forces of the Chinese people who demand independence, freedom and unity are irresistible and are bound to burst forth and supplant foreign and feudal oppression. We cannot yet say whether or when the U.S. policy will be changed. But one thing is certain. If the Hurley policy of aiding and abetting the reactionary forces in China and antagonizing the Chinese people with their immense numbers continues unchanged, it will place a crushing burden on the government and people of the United States and plunge them into endless trouble. This point must be brought home to the people of the United States.

(From *Selected Works of Mao Zedong*, Vol. III)

WE MUST NOT STOP CRITICIZING THE U.S. POLICY OF SUPPORTING CHIANG KAI-SHEK AGAINST THE COMMUNISTS*

(July 30, 1945)

Not long ago the U.S. embassy tried to advise us not to criticize Chiang Kai-shek. Now they have stopped doing so, but turned around to advise us not to criticize Hurley.[19] The U.S. press, so often criticizing foreign heads of state, carried sharp criticism of Chiang Kai-shek last year, so why can't we Chinese criticize Hurley? Once Hurley criticized the Communist Party of China, putting Chinese Communists on a par with the warlords, and referring to the entire Party in his criticism, so why can't the Communist Party criticize him? In our criticism we draw a clear distinction between the U.S. government and the American people, between persons in the U.S. government who decide China policy and other staff, and between wrong policies of the U.S. government and its correct ones. We shall stop criticizing the U.S. government once it changes its current policy of supporting Chiang Kai-shek against the Communists; otherwise, there is no chance that our criticism will end. Please explain the above to those who are concerned.

(From the original manuscript)

---

*This is the major part of a telegram from Mao Zedong to Xu Bing and Zhang Ming (Liu Shaowen).

WE MUST NOT BELIEVE THE "NICE WORDS" OF THE IMPERIALISTS, NOR BE INTIMIDATED BY THEIR BLUSTER*

(*August 13, 1945*)
These are excerpts from a speech delivered by Mao Zedong at a meeting of cadres in Yan'an, entitled "The Situation and Our Policy After the Victory in the War of Resistance Against Japan."

On what basis should our policy rest? It should rest on our own strength, and that means regeneration through one's own efforts. We are not alone; all the countries and people in the world opposed to imperialism are our friends. Nevertheless, we stress regeneration through our own efforts. Relying on the forces we ourselves organize, we can defeat all Chinese and foreign reactionaries. Chiang Kai-shek, on the contrary, relies entirely on the aid of U.S. imperialism, which he looks upon as his mainstay. The trinity of dictatorship, civil war and selling out the country has always been the basis of his policy. U.S. imperialism wants to help Chiang Kai-shek wage civil war and turn China into a U.S. dependency, and this policy, too, was set long ago. But U.S. imperialism while outwardly strong is inwardly weak. We must be clear-headed, that is, we must not believe the "nice words" of the imperialists nor be intimidated by their bluster. An American once said to me, "You should listen to Hurley and send a few men to be officials in the Kuomintang government."[26] I replied: "It is no easy job to be an official bound hand and foot; we won't do it. If we become officials, our hands and feet must be unfettered, we must be free to act, that is, a coalition government must be set up on a democratic basis." He said, "It will be bad if you don't." I asked him, "Why bad?" He said, "First, the Americans will curse you; secondly, the Americans will back Chiang Kai-shek." I replied: "If you Americans, sated

---

* These are excerpts from a speech delivered by Mao Zedong at a meeting of cadres in Yan'an, entitled "The Situation and Our Policy After the Victory in the War of Resistance Against Japan."

with bread and sleep, want to curse people and back Chiang Kai-shek, that's your business and I won't interfere. What we have now is millet plus rifles, what you have is bread plus cannon. If you like to back Chiang Kai-shek, back him, back him as long as you want. But remember one thing. To whom does China belong? China definitely does not belong to Chiang Kai-shek, China belongs to the Chinese people. The day will surely come when you will find it impossible to back him any longer." Comrades! This American was trying to scare people. Imperialists are masters at this sort of stuff, and many people in the colonial countries do get scared. The imperialists think that all people in the colonial countries can be scared, but they do not realize that in China there are people who are not afraid of that sort of stuff. In the past we have openly criticized and exposed the U.S. policy of aiding Chiang Kai-shek to fight the Communists; it was necessary, and we shall continue to do so.

(From *Selected Works of Mao Zedong*, Vol. IV)

WHILE THE PROSPECTS OF THE WORLD ARE BRIGHT, THE ROAD HAS TWISTS AND TURNS*

(*October 17, 1945*)

The world after World War II has a bright future. This is the general trend. Does the failure of the meeting of the Council of Foreign Ministers in London[27] mean that a third world war is about to break out? No. Just think, how is it possible for a third world war to break out right after the end of World War II? The capitalist and the socialist countries will yet reach compromises on a number of international matters, because compromise will be advantageous.[28] The proletariat and the people of the whole world are firmly opposed to an anti-Soviet and anti-Communist war. In the past 30 years two world wars have been fought. Between World War I and II there was an interval of more than 20 years. In the half million years of human history, it is only in the last 30 years that world wars have been fought. After World War I the world made great progress. After World War II the world is sure to make even faster progress. Following World War I the Soviet Union was born and scores of Communist Parties were founded—they did not exist before. After the end of World War II the Soviet Union is much stronger, the face of Europe is changed, the political consciousness of the proletariat and the people of the world is much higher and the progressive forces throughout the world are more closely united. Our China is also undergoing rapid and drastic change. The general trend of China's development is certainly for the better, not for the worse. The world is progressing, the future is bright and no one can change this general trend of history. We should carry on constant propaganda among the people on the facts of world progress and the bright future ahead so that they will build their confidence in victory. At the same time, we must tell the people and tell our comrades that there will be twists

---

* These are excerpts from "On the Chongqing Negotiations," a report made by Mao Zedong to a meeting of cadres in Yan'an.

and turns in our road. There are still many obstacles and difficulties along the road of revolution. The Seventh Congress of our Party[29] assumed that the difficulties would be many, for we preferred to assume there would be more difficulties rather than less. Some comrades do not like to think much about difficulties. But difficulties are facts; we must recognize as many difficulties as there are and should not adopt a "policy of nonrecognition." We must recognize difficulties, analyse them and combat them. There are no straight roads in the world; we must be prepared to follow a road which twists and turns and not try to get things on the cheap. It must not be imagined that one fine morning all the reactionaries will go down on their knees of their own accord. In a word, while the prospects are bright, the road has twists and turns. There are still many difficulties ahead which we must not overlook. By uniting with the entire people in a common effort, we can certainly overcome all difficulties and win victory.

(From *Selected Works of Mao Zedong*, Vol. IV)

SOME POINTS IN APPRAISAL OF THE PRESENT INTERNATIONAL SITUATION*

(*April 1946*)

1. The forces of world reaction are definitely preparing a third world war, and the danger of war exists. But the democratic forces of the people of the world have surpassed the reactionary forces and are forging ahead; they must and certainly can overcome the danger of war. Therefore, the question in the relations between the United States, Britain and France and the Soviet Union is not a question of compromise or break, but a question of compromise earlier or compromise later. "Compromise" means reaching agreement through peaceful negotiation. "Earlier or later" means several years, or more than ten years, or even longer.

---

* This document was written to counter a pessimistic appraisal of the international situation at the time. In the spring of 1946, imperialism headed by the United States of America, together with the reactionaries in various countries, was daily intensifying its anti-Soviet, anti-Communist and anti-popular activities and trumpeting that "war between the United States and the Soviet Union is inevitable" and that "the outbreak of a third world war is inevitable." In these circumstances, since some comrades overestimated the strength of imperialism, underestimated the strength of the people, feared U.S. imperialism and feared the outbreak of a new world war, they showed weakness in the face of the armed attacks of the U.S.-Chiang Kai-shek reactionary gang and dared not resolutely oppose counter-revolutionary war with revolutionary war. In this document Mao Zedong was combating such erroneous thinking. He pointed out that if the forces of the people throughout the world waged resolute, effective struggles against the forces of world reaction, they could overcome the danger of a new world war. At the same time, he pointed out that it was possible for the imperialist countries and the socialist countries to reach compromise on certain issues but that such compromise "does not require the people in the countries of the capitalist world to follow suit and make compromises at home," and that "the people in those countries will continue to wage different struggles in accordance with their different conditions." This document was not made public at the time and was circulated only among some leading comrades of the Central Committee. It was distributed at the meeting of the Central Committee of the Communist Party of China in December 1947. Since the comrades present unanimously agreed with its contents, the full text was later included in "A Circular on the Decisions Made at the Central Committee Meeting of December 1947," issued by the Central Committee in January 1948.

2. The kind of compromise mentioned above does not mean compromise on all international issues. That is impossible so long as the United States, Britain and France continue to be ruled by reactionaries. This kind of compromise means compromise on some issues, including certain important ones. But there will not be many such compromises in the near future. There is, however, a possibility that the trade relations of the United States, Britain and France with the Soviet Union will expand.

3. Such compromise between the United States, Britain and France and the Soviet Union can be the outcome only of resolute, effective struggles by all the democratic forces of the world against the reactionary forces of the United States, Britain and France. Such compromise does not require the people in the countries of the capitalist world to follow suit and make compromises at home. The people in those countries will continue to wage different struggles in accordance with their different conditions. The principle of the reactionary forces in dealing with the democratic forces of the people is definitely to destroy all they can and to prepare to destroy later whatever they cannot destroy now. Face to face with this situation, the democratic forces of the people should likewise apply the same principle to the reactionary forces.

(From *Selected Works of Mao Zedong*, Vol. IV)

TALK WITH THE AMERICAN CORRESPONDENT ANNA LOUISE STRONG*[30]

(August 6, 1946)

Strong: Do you think there is hope for a political, a peaceful settlement of China's problems in the near future?

Mao: That depends on the attitude of the U.S. government. If the American people stay the hands of the American reactionaries who are helping Chiang Kai-shek fight the civil war, there is hope for peace.

Strong: Suppose the United States gives Chiang Kai-shek no help, besides that already given,[31] how long can Chiang Kai-shek keep on fighting?

Mao: More than a year.

Strong: Can Chiang Kai-shek keep on that long, economically?

Mao: He can.

Strong: What if the United States makes it clear that it will give Chiang Kai-shek no more help from now on?

Mao: There is no sign yet that the U.S. government and Chiang Kai-shek have any desire to stop the war within a short time.

Strong: How long can the Communist Party keep on?

Mao: As far as our own desire is concerned, we don't want to fight even

---

* This very important statement on the international and domestic situation was made by Mao Zedong not long after the conclusion of World War II. Here, Mao Zedong put forward his famous thesis, "All reactionaries are paper tigers." This thesis armed the people of our country ideologically, strengthened their confidence in victory and played an exceedingly great role in the People's War of Liberation. Just as Lenin considered imperialism a "colossus with feet of clay," so Mao Zedong regards imperialism and all reactionaries as paper tigers; both have dealt with the essence of the matter. This thesis is a fundamental strategic concept for the revolutionary people. Since the period of the Second Revolutionary Civil War, Mao Zedong has repeatedly pointed out: strategically, with regard to the whole, revolutionaries must despise the enemy, dare to struggle against him and dare to seize victory; at the same time, tactically, with regard to each part, each specific struggle, they must take the enemy seriously, be prudent, carefully study and perfect the art of struggle and adopt forms of struggle suited to different times, places and conditions in order to isolate and wipe out the enemy step by step.

for a single day. But if circumstances force us to fight, we can fight to the finish.

Strong: If the American people ask why the Communist Party is fighting, what should I reply?

Mao: Because Chiang Kai-shek is out to slaughter the Chinese people, and if the people want to survive they have to defend themselves. This the American people can understand.

Strong: What do you think of the possibility of the United States starting a war against the Soviet Union?

Mao: There are two aspects to the propaganda about an anti-Soviet war. On the one hand, U.S. imperialism is indeed preparing a war against the Soviet Union; the current propaganda about an anti-Soviet war, as well as other anti-Soviet propaganda, is political preparation for such a war. On the other hand, this propaganda is a smoke-screen put up by the U.S. reactionaries to cover many actual contradictions immediately confronting U.S. imperialism. These are the contradictions between the U.S. reactionaries and the American people and the contradictions of U.S. imperialism with other capitalist countries and with the colonial and semi-colonial countries. At present, the actual significance of the U.S. slogan of waging an anti-Soviet war is the oppression of the American people and the expansion of the U.S. forces of aggression in the rest of the capitalist world. As you know, both Hitler[4] and his partners, the Japanese warlords, used anti-Soviet slogans for a long time as a pretext for enslavement of the people at home and aggression against other countries. Now the U.S. reactionaries are acting in exactly the same way.

To start a war, the U.S. reactionaries must first attack the American people. They are already attacking the American people—oppressing the workers and democratic circles in the United States politically and economically and preparing to impose fascism there. The people of the United States should stand up and resist the attacks of the U.S. reactionaries. I believe they will.

The United States and the Soviet Union are separated by a vast zone which includes many capitalist, colonial and semi-colonial countries in Europe, Asia and Africa. Before the U.S. reactionaries have subjugated these countries, an attack on the Soviet Union is out of the question. In the Pacific the United States now controls areas larger than all the former British spheres of influence there put together; it controls Japan, that part of China under Kuomintang rule, half of Korea, and the South Pacific. It has long controlled Central and South America. It seeks also to control the whole of the British Empire and Western Europe. Using various pretexts, the United States is making large-scale military arrangements and setting up military bases in many countries. The U.S. reactionaries say that the military bases they have set up and are preparing to set up all over the world are aimed against the Soviet Union. True, these military bases are directed against the Soviet Union. At present, however, it is not the Soviet Union but the countries in which these military bases are located that are the first to suffer U.S. aggression. I believe it won't be long before these countries come to realize who is really oppressing them, the Soviet Union or the United States. The day will come when the U.S. reactionaries find themselves opposed by the people of the whole world.

Of course, I do not mean to say that the U.S. reactionaries have no intention of attacking the Soviet Union. The Soviet Union is a defender of world peace and a powerful factor preventing the domination of the world by the U.S. reactionaries. Because of the existence of the Soviet Union, it is absolutely impossible for the reactionaries in the United States and the world to realize their ambitions. That is why the U.S. reactionaries rabidly hate the Soviet Union and actually dream of destroying this socialist state. But the fact that the U.S. reactionaries are now trumpeting so loudly about a U.S.-Soviet war and creating a foul atmosphere, so soon after the end of World War II, compels us to take a look at their real aims. It turns out that under the cover of anti-Soviet slogans they are frantically attacking the workers and democratic circles in the United States and turning all the countries which are the targets of U.S. external expansion into U.S. dependencies. I think the American people and the peoples of all countries menaced by U.S. aggression should unite and struggle against the attacks of the U.S. reactionaries and their running dogs in these countries. Only by victory in this struggle can a third world war be avoided; otherwise it is unavoidable.

Strong: That is very clear. But suppose the United States uses the atom bomb? Suppose the United States bombs the Soviet Union from its bases in Iceland, Okinawa and China?

Mao: The atom bomb is a paper tiger which the U.S. reactionaries use to scare people. It looks terrible, but in fact it isn't. Of course, the atom bomb is a weapon of mass slaughter, but the outcome of a war is decided by the people, not by one or two new types of weapon.

All reactionaries are paper tigers. In appearance, the reactionaries are terrifying, but in reality they are not so powerful. From a long-term point of view, it is not the reactionaries but the people who are really powerful. In Russia, before the February Revolution[32] in 1917, which side was really strong? On the surface the tsar was strong, but he was swept away by a single gust of wind in the February Revolution. In the final analysis, the strength in Russia was on the side of the Soviets of Workers, Peasants and Soldiers. The tsar was just a paper tiger. Wasn't Hitler once considered very strong? But history proved that he was a paper tiger. So was Mussolini,[33] so was Japanese imperialism. On the contrary, the strength of the Soviet Union and of the people in all countries who loved democracy and freedom proved much greater than had been foreseen.

Chiang Kai-shek and his supporters, the U.S. reactionaries, are all paper tigers too. Speaking of U.S. imperialism, people seem to feel that it is terrifically strong. Chinese reactionaries are using the "strength" of the United States to frighten the Chinese people. But it will be proved that the U.S. reactionaries, like all the reactionaries in history, do not have much strength. In the United States there are others who are really strong—the American people.

Take the case of China. We have only millet plus rifles to rely on, but history will finally prove that our millet plus rifles is more powerful than Chiang Kai-shek's aeroplanes plus tanks. Although the Chinese people still face many difficulties and will long suffer hardships from the joint attacks of U.S. imperialism and the Chinese reactionaries, the day will come when these reactionaries are defeated and we are victorious. The reason is simply this: the reactionaries represent reaction, we represent progress.

(From *Selected Works of Mao Zedong*, Vol. IV)

REPUDIATE THE TRAITOROUS FOREIGN POLICY*

(October 10, 1947)

Repudiate the traitorous foreign policy of Chiang Kai-shek's dictatorial government, abrogate all the treasonable treaties and repudiate all the foreign debts contracted by Chiang Kai-shek during the civil war period. Demand that the U.S. government withdraw its troops stationed in China, which are a menace to China's independence, and oppose any foreign country's helping Chiang Kai-shek to carry on civil war or trying to revive the forces of Japanese aggression. Conclude treaties of trade and friendship with foreign countries on the basis of equality and reciprocity. Unite in a common struggle with all nations which treat us as equals.

(From *Selected Works of Mao Zedong*, Vol. IV)

---

* This is one of the eight chief policies of the Chinese People's Liberation Army and hence also of the Chinese Communist Party, announced in the "Manifesto of the Chinese People's Liberation Army" drafted by Mao Zedong.

THE STRENGTH OF THE WORLD ANTI-IMPERIALIST CAMP HAS SURPASSED THAT OF THE IMPERIALIST CAMP*

(December 25, 1947)

When the reactionary Chiang Kai-shek clique launched the country-wide civil war against the people in 1946, the reason they dared take this risk was that they relied not merely on their own superior military strength but mainly on the U.S. imperialists with their atom bombs, whom they regarded as "exceptionally powerful" and "matchless in the world." On the one hand, they thought U.S. imperialism could meet their military and financial needs with a stream of supplies. On the other hand, they wildly speculated that "war between the United States and the Soviet Union is inevitable" and that "the outbreak of a third world war is inevitable." This dependence on U.S. imperialism is the common feature of the reactionary forces in all countries since World War II. It reflects the severity of the blows world capitalism received in World War II; it reflects the weakness of the reactionary forces in all countries, their panic and loss of confidence; and it reflects the might of the world revolutionary forces—all of which makes reactionaries in all countries feel that there is no way out except to rely on U.S. imperialist support. But, in fact, is U.S. imperialism after World War II as powerful as Chiang Kai-shek and the reactionaries of other countries imagine? Can it really pour out a stream of supplies for them? No, that is not so. The economic power of U.S. imperialism, which grew during World War II, is confronted with unstable and daily shrinking domestic and foreign markets. The further shrinking of these markets will cause economic crises to break out. The war boom in the United States of America was only temporary. The strength of the United States of America is only superficial and transient. Irreconcilable domestic and international contradictions, like a volcano, menace U.S. imper-

---

* This is part of "The Present Situation and Our Tasks," a report delivered by Mao Zedong to a meeting of the Central Committee of the Communist Party of China.

ialism every day. U.S. imperialism is sitting on this volcano. This situation has driven the U.S. imperialists to draw up a plan for enslaving the world, to run amuck like wild beasts in Europe, Asia and other parts of the world, to muster the reactionary forces in all countries, the human dregs cast off by their peoples, to form an imperialist and anti-democratic camp against all the democratic forces headed by the Soviet Union, and to prepare for war in the hope that in the future, at a distant time, some day, they can start a third world war to defeat the democratic forces. This is a preposterous plan. The democratic forces of the world must and certainly can defeat this plan. The strength of the world anti-imperialist camp has surpassed that of the imperialist camp. It is we, not the enemy, who are in the superior position. The anti-imperialist camp headed by the Soviet Union has already been formed. The socialist Soviet Union is free from crises, in the ascendant and cherished by the world's broad masses; its strength has already surpassed that of the imperialist United States, which is seriously menaced by crises, on the decline and opposed by the world's broad masses. The People's Democracies in Europe are consolidating themselves internally and are uniting with each other. In the European capitalist countries the people's anti-imperialist forces are developing, with those in France and Italy taking the lead. Within the United States, there are people's democratic forces which are getting stronger every day. The peoples of Latin America are not slaves obedient to U.S. imperialism. In the whole of Asia a great national liberation movement has arisen. All the forces of the anti-imperialist camp are uniting and forging ahead. The Communist and Workers' Parties of nine European countries have established their Information Bureau and issued a call to the people of the world to rise against the imperialist plan of enslavement.[34] This call to battle has inspired the oppressed people of the world, charted the course of their struggle and strengthened their confidence in victory. It has thrown world reaction into panic and confusion. All the anti-imperialist forces in the countries of the East, too, should unite together, oppose oppression by imperialism and by their domestic reactionaries and make the goal of their struggle the emancipation of the more than 1,000 million oppressed people of the East. We certainly should grasp our own destiny in our own hands. We should rid our ranks of all impotent thinking. All views that overestimate the strength of the enemy and underestimate the strength of the people are wrong. If everyone makes strenuous efforts, we, together with all the democratic forces of the world, can surely defeat the imperialist plan of enslavement, prevent the outbreak of a third world war, overthrow all reactionary regimes and win lasting peace for mankind. We are soberly aware that on our way forward there will still be all kinds of obstacles and difficulties and that we should be prepared to deal with the maximum resistance and desperate struggle by all our enemies, domestic and foreign. But so long as we can grasp the science of Marxism-Leninism, have confidence in the masses, stand closely together with the masses and lead them forward, we shall be fully able to surmount any obstacle and overcome any difficulty. Our strength will be invincible. This is the historic epoch in which world capitalism and imperialism are going down to their doom and world socialism and people's democracy are marching to victory. The dawn is ahead, we must exert ourselves.

(From *Selected Works of Mao Zedong*, Vol. IV)

THE DANGER OF A WORLD WAR MUST AND CERTAINLY CAN BE OVERCOME*

(*September 8, 1948*)

Regarding appraisal of the international situation. An appraisal of the international situation was made at the meeting[35] last December. There had been no consensus then within the Party, nor even in the Central Committee. There are two propositions: One is that there will be either peace or war; the other, that the danger of war exists, but its outbreak is not probable. The view as to the danger of war is identical, but it differs as to whether there will be peace or war. The first proposition holds that the world people's strength is not enough to prevent war, while the second maintains that the Soviet Union and the world's people can mobilize enough strength to prevent a war. Since the U.S.-British reactionaries have not fully prepared for war, we can work against time for its prevention; thus it is our task to mobilize the world people's forces for this purpose. The post-World War II situation being different from that after World War I, there is greater possibility for war prevention. The German and Japanese fascists have been defeated in World War II, and it is not easy to revive them. The U.S.-British reactionaries are indeed preparing for war, and the danger of war exists. Nevertheless, as the world's democratic forces, headed by the Soviet Union, have become stronger than the reactionary forces (as Molotov[36] and Zhdanov[37] said, though some comrades in our Party, those in the middle in particular, are still unclear about it), and continue to grow, the danger of war must and certainly can be overcome, only it is conditioned on our effort. War will certainly be prevented if we are given 10 to 15 years to work toward it. We should not see the alternative as either compromise or split, but sooner or later, compromise, as can be seen in the recent Berlin question.

In talking about compromise, we do not mean compromise on all issues (for instance, a compromise on the resolution to eliminate colonies is impos-

---

* This is part of a report by Mao Zedong at a meeting of the Political Bureau of the Central Committee of the Communist Party of China.

sible), but compromise is likely on some issues, international rather than domestic issues, and only on some, including some important ones. In 1947 the Soviet Union, the United States and Britain reached a peace agreement with Italy, Romania, Hungary, Bulgaria and Finland. A peace agreement with Germany, Austria and Japan, though rather difficult to reach, will be concluded in the end. Britain and France are likely to develop commerce and trade with the Soviet Union, but this is less probable between the United States and the Soviet Union.

Middle-of-the-roaders think that since the Soviet Union has compromised with the United States, Britain and France on the basis of democratic principles, we can also compromise with the Kuomintang, but to my mind, it should not be put in such a way. The Soviet Union follows a policy of noninterference in the internal affairs of other nations, and the Atlantic Charter[21] also acknowledges the right of every people to choose a political system for their own state. It is not Chiang Kai-shek's system that the Chinese people will choose. In the struggle of the Soviet Union and all democratic forces against reactionary forces, compromise on the basis of democratic principles is the result of that struggle. Then, is it true that people of every country must compromise with the reactionaries? We say no. Supposing Chiang Kai-shek were compelled to follow our practice, to disband fascist organizations, to discard local tyrants and evil gentry, and to allow us to strengthen our military forces and carry out our agrarian reform, wouldn't that be wonderful? But Chiang Kai-shek, being a reactionary, will not agree. Since olden days, reactionaries have dealt with democratic forces on two principles: One, exterminate immediately all that can be exterminated; the other, wait for a future opportunity to exterminate what cannot be exterminated right now. Britain has now taken the initial step to exterminate Communists within the government, but remains patient about exterminating Communists in society. In dealing with the reactionaries, we should reciprocate the same two principles; we are now implementing the first one.

These are the three estimations concluded in the meeting of last December. World peace and no warfare for the Soviet Union are of considerable benefit to people of the whole world. Chiang Kai-shek wishes that a third world war will break out, and so do some people in our Party. If the people of the Soviet Union and Eastern European countries can devote themselves to peaceful production for 10 to 15 years, and if the Soviet Union can improve its productivity and increase its annual steel output to 60 million tons, nobody will even dare think of warfare. Three years have elapsed, and there are only 12 years to go. That is how the international environment stands.

(From the meeting minutes)

REVOLUTIONARY FORCES OF THE WORLD UNITE, FIGHT AGAINST IMPERIALIST AGGRESSION!*

(November 1948)

At this time, when the awakened working class and all genuine revolutionaries of the world are jubilantly celebrating the 31st anniversary of the Great October Socialist Revolution of the Soviet Union, I recall a well-known article by Stalin, written in 1918 on the first anniversary of that revolution. In that article Stalin said:

> The great world-wide significance of the October Revolution chiefly consists in the fact that:
>
> 1) It has widened the scope of the national question and converted it from the particular question of combating national oppression in Europe into the general question of emancipating the oppressed peoples, colonies and semi-colonies from imperialism;
>
> 2) It has opened up wide possibilities for their emancipation and the right paths toward it, has thereby greatly facilitated the cause of the emancipation of the oppressed peoples of the West and the East, and has drawn them into the common current of the victorious struggle against imperialism;
>
> 3) It has thereby erected a bridge between the socialist West and the enslaved East, having created a new front of revolutions against world imperialism, extending from the proletarians of the West, through the Russian revolution, to the oppressed peoples of the East.[38]

History has developed in the direction pointed out by Stalin. The October Revolution has opened up wide possibilities for the emancipation of the peoples of the world and opened up the realistic paths toward it; it has created

---

* This article was written by Mao Zedong in commemoration of the 31st anniversary of the October Revolution for the organ of the Information Bureau of the Communist and Workers' Parties of Europe, *For a Lasting Peace, for a People's Democracy*. It appeared in the 21st issue of the publication in 1948.

a new front of revolutions against world imperialism, extending from the proletarians of the West, through the Russian revolution, to the oppressed peoples of the East. This front of revolutions has been created and developed under the brilliant guidance of Lenin and, after Lenin's death, of Stalin.

If there is to be revolution, there must be a revolutionary party. Without a revolutionary party, without a party built on the Marxist-Leninist revolutionary theory and in the Marxist-Leninist revolutionary style, it is impossible to lead the working class and the broad masses of the people in defeating imperialism and its running dogs. In the more than 100 years since the birth of Marxism, it was only through the example of the Russian Bolsheviks in leading the October Revolution, in leading socialist construction and in defeating fascist aggression that revolutionary parties of a new type were formed and developed in the world. With the birth of revolutionary parties of this type, the face of the world revolution has changed. The change has been so great that transformations utterly inconceivable to people of the older generation have come about amid fire and thunder. The Communist Party of China is a party built and developed on the model of the Communist Party of the Soviet Union. With the birth of the Communist Party of China, the face of the Chinese revolution took on an altogether new aspect. Is this fact not clear enough?

The world revolutionary united front, with the Soviet Union at its head, defeated fascist Germany, Italy and Japan. This was a result of the October Revolution. If there had been no October Revolution, if there had been no Communist Party of the Soviet Union, no Soviet Union and no anti-imperialist revolutionary united front in the West and in the East led by the Soviet Union, could one conceive of victory over fascist Germany, Italy, Japan and their running dogs? If the October Revolution opened up wide possibilities for the emancipation of the working class and the oppressed peoples of the world and opened up realistic paths toward it, then the victory of the anti-fascist Second World War has opened up still wider possibilities for the emancipation of the working class and the oppressed peoples of the world and has opened up still more realistic paths toward it. It will be a very great mistake to underestimate the significance of the victory of World War II.

Since the victory of World War II, U.S. imperialism and its running dogs in various countries have taken the place of fascist Germany, Italy and Japan and are frantically preparing a new world war and menacing the whole world; this reflects the utter decay of the capitalist world and its fear of imminent doom. This enemy still has strength; therefore, all the revolutionary forces of each country must unite, and the revolutionary forces of all countries must likewise unite, must form an anti-imperialist united front headed by the Soviet Union and follow correct policies; otherwise, victory will be impossible. This enemy has a weak and fragile foundation, he is disintegrating internally, he is alienated from the people, he is confronted with inextricable economic crises; therefore, he can be defeated. It will be a very great mistake to overestimate the enemy's strength and underestimate the strength of the revolutionary forces.

Under the leadership of the Communist Party of China, tremendous victories have now been won in the great Chinese people's democratic revolution directed against the frenzied aggression of U.S. imperialism in China and against the traitorous, dictatorial and reactionary Kuomintang government that has been slaughtering the Chinese people by civil war. During the two years from July 1946 to June 1948, the People's Liberation Army led by the Communist Party of China beat back the attacks of 4,300,000 troops of the reactionary Kuomintang government and went over from the defensive to the offensive. During those two years of fighting (not including developments since July 1948), the People's Liberation Army captured and wiped out 2,640,000 Kuomintang troops. China's Liberated Areas now cover 2,350,000 square kilometers, or 24.5 percent of the country's 9,597,000 square kilometers; they have a population of 168 million, or 35.3 percent of the country's 475 million; and they contain 586 cities and towns, or 29 percent of the 2,009 in the whole country. Because our Party has resolutely led the peasants to carry out the reform of the land system, the land problem has been thoroughly solved in areas with a population of about 100 million, and the land of the landlords and old-type rich peasants has been more or less equally distributed among the peasants, primarily among the poor peasants and farm laborers. The membership of the Communist Party of China has grown from 1,210,000 in 1945 to 3,000,000 today. The task of the Communist Party of China is to unite the revolutionary forces of the whole country to drive out the aggressive forces of U.S. imperialism, overthrow the reactionary rule of the Kuomintang and establish a united, democratic people's republic. We know that there are still many difficulties ahead. But we are not afraid of them. We believe that difficulties must be and can be overcome.

The radiance of the October Revolution shines upon us. The long-suffering Chinese people must win their liberation, and they firmly believe they can. Always isolated in the past, China's revolutionary struggle no longer feels isolated since the victory of the October Revolution. We enjoy the support of the Communist Parties and the working class of the world. This point was understood by Dr. Sun Yat-sen, forerunner of the Chinese revolution, who established the policy of alliance with the Soviet Union against imperialism. On his death-bed he wrote a letter to the Soviet Union as part of his testament. It is the Chiang Kai-shek bandit gang of the Kuomintang that is betraying Sun Yat-sen's policy, standing on the side of the imperialist counterrevolutionary front and opposing the people of their own country. But before long, people will witness the complete destruction of the whole reactionary regime of the Kuomintang by the Chinese people. The Chinese people are brave, so is the Communist Party of China, and they are determined to liberate all China.

(From *Selected Works of Mao Zedong*, Vol. IV)

WE SHOULD INCLUDE A DIRECT U.S. MILITARY INTERVENTION IN OUR BATTLE PLAN*

(January 8, 1949)

In our battle plan we have all along taken into account the possibility of direct U.S. military occupation of some of China's coastal cities and the United States fighting with us. We should not yet discard such calculation lest we become at a loss in such an eventuality. But the stronger and more determined the Chinese people's revolutionary forces are, the less the possibility of a direct U.S. military intervention, and collaterally maybe the less U.S. financial and arms aid to the Kuomintang. Over the past year, especially the last three months, this point has been proved by the vacillation and certain changes in the attitude of the U.S. government. We must continue to point out and rectify the wrong view among the Chinese people and in our Party that overestimates the strength of U.S. imperialism.

(From the original manuscript)

---

* These are excerpts from "The Present Situation and the Party's Tasks in 1949," an inner-Party directive drafted by Mao Zedong for the Central Committee of the Communist Party of China.

NO INTERFERENCE IN CHINA'S INTERNAL AFFAIRS IS PERMISSIBLE BY ANY FOREIGN COUNTRY OR THE UNITED NATIONS*

(January 19, 1949)

I

Foreign Relations. We shall not recognize the embassies, legations and consulates together with their diplomatic establishments and personnel, of the capitalist countries that have been recognized by the Kuomintang government, until and unless formal diplomatic relations are established by the People's Republic of China with those countries, but treat their personnel only as foreign nationals, whom we should effectively protect. The military attachés of these countries should be treated in the same way as those diplomatic personnel. However, the U.S. military attachés should be kept under military observation and allowed no freedom, since they have given direct help to the Kuomintang in waging the civil war. As for the embassies and consulates of the Soviet Union and the New Democracies, and their diplomatic establishments and personnel, we should adopt a fundamentally different attitude toward them, since their foreign policies differ basically from those of the capitalist countries. Nevertheless, since our people's state has not yet established formal diplomatic relations with them, or with any other foreign countries up to now, we shall maintain only informal diplomatic contacts with their diplomatic establishments in China and with their military attachés.

---

* These two paragraphs were added by Mao Zedong to the CPC Central Committee's "Instruction on the Work of Foreign Affairs" after he went over it.

II

Last and most important, no interference in China's internal affairs is permissible by any foreign country or the United Nations. Since China is an independent nation, all matters within the boundaries of China should be settled by the Chinese people themselves and the People's Government. We must utterly reject any foreigners' suggestion for foreign governments to mediate in China's civil war.

(From the original manuscript)

SYSTEMATICALLY AND COMPLETELY DESTROY IMPERIALIST DOMINATION IN CHINA*

(*March 5, 1949*)

Old China was a semi-colonial country under imperialist domination. Thoroughly anti-imperialist in character, the Chinese people's democratic revolution has incurred the bitter hatred of the imperialists who have done their utmost to help the Kuomintang. This has aroused the Chinese people to even deeper indignation against the imperialists and deprived them of their last shred of prestige among the Chinese people. At the same time the whole imperialist system is very much weakened after World War II, while the strength of the world anti-imperialist front headed by the Soviet Union is greater than ever before. In these circumstances, we can and should adopt a policy of systematically and completely destroying imperialist domination in China. This imperialist domination manifests itself in the political, economic and cultural fields. In each city or place where the Kuomintang troops are wiped out and the Kuomintang government is overthrown, imperialist political domination is overthrown with it, and so is imperialist economic and cultural domination. But the economic and cultural establishments run directly by the imperialists are still there, and so are the diplomatic personnel and the journalists recognized by the Kuomintang. We must deal with all these properly in their order of urgency. Refuse to recognize the legal status of any foreign diplomatic establishments and personnel of the Kuomintang period,

---

* This is part of a report by Mao Zedong to the Second Plenary Session of the Seventh Central Committee of the Communist Party of China. Before and after this session, Mao Zedong set forth two important principles for China's foreign affairs: "set up another kitchen" and "clean up the house before inviting the guests." On April 30, 1952, in addressing a meeting of Chinese envoys to foreign countries, Zhou Enlai explained that "setting up another kitchen" means nonrecognition of the old diplomatic relations between the Kuomintang government and foreign countries, and establishment of new diplomatic relations with foreign countries on a new basis. He added, "The imperialists want to retain some of their privileges in China.... We need to clean up our 'house' before establishing diplomatic relations, 'clean up the house before inviting the guests'."

refuse to recognize all the treasonable treaties of the Kuomintang period, abolish all imperialist propaganda agencies in China, take immediate control of foreign trade and reform the customs system—these are the first steps we must take upon entering the big cities. When they have acted thus, the Chinese people will have stood up in the face of imperialism. As for the remaining imperialist economic and cultural establishments, they can be allowed to exist for the time being, subject to our supervision and control, to be dealt with by us after country-wide victory. As for ordinary foreign nationals, their legitimate interests will be protected and not encroached upon. As for the question of the recognition of our country by the imperialist countries, we should not be in a hurry to solve it now and need not be in a hurry to solve it even for a fairly long period after country-wide victory. We are willing to establish diplomatic relations with all countries on the principle of equality, but the imperialists, who have always been hostile to the Chinese people, will definitely not be in a hurry to treat us as equals. As long as the imperialist countries do not change their hostile attitude, we shall not grant them legal status in China. As for doing business with foreigners, there is no question; wherever there is business to do, we shall do it and we have already started; the businessmen of several capitalist countries are competing for such business. So far as possible, we must first of all trade with the socialist and people's democratic countries; at the same time we will also trade with capitalist countries.

(From *Selected Works of Mao Zedong*, Vol. IV)

PROTECT THE LIVES AND PROPERTY OF FOREIGN NATIONALS*

(*April 25, 1949*)

Protect the lives and property of foreign nationals. It is hoped that all foreign nationals will follow their usual pursuits and observe order. All foreign nationals must abide by the orders and decrees of the People's Liberation Army and the People's Government and must not engage in espionage, act against the cause of China's national independence and the people's liberation, or harbor Chinese war criminals, counterrevolutionaries or other law-breakers. Otherwise, they shall be dealt with according to law by the People's Liberation Army and the People's Government.

(From *Selected Works of Mao Zedong*, Vol. IV)

---

* This is one of the eight points of a covenant to be abided by all announced in the "Proclamation of the Chinese People's Liberation Army" drafted by Mao Zedong.

WE MAY CONSIDER ESTABLISHING DIPLOMATIC RELATIONS WITH THE UNITED STATES AND BRITAIN IF THEY SEVER TIES WITH THE KUOMINTANG*

(April 28, 1949)

We should stress the importance of educating our troops to protect American and British nationals (and nationals of other foreign countries) and the ambassadors, ministers, consuls and other diplomatic personnel of all foreign countries, in the first place, American and British diplomats. The U.S. side has, through a third party, requested the establishment of diplomatic relations with us, and Britain, too, is eager to do business with us. We think we can consider establishing diplomatic relations with the United States and Britain if they sever relations with the Kuomintang. Deng, Rao, Chen and Liu[39] please pay attention to this matter.

(From the original manuscript)

---

* This is part of a telegram to Deng Xiaoping, Liu Bocheng and Chen Yi, written by Mao Zedong for the Military Commission of the Central Committee of the Communist Party of China.

ON THE OUTRAGES BY BRITISH WARSHIPS[40]
—STATEMENT BY THE SPOKESMAN OF THE GENERAL HEADQUARTERS OF THE CHINESE PEOPLE'S LIBERATION ARMY*

(*April 30, 1949*)

We denounce the preposterous statement of the warmonger Churchill.[41] In the British House of Commons on April 26, Churchill demanded that the British government should send two aircraft carriers to the Far East for "effective power of retaliation." What are you "retaliating" for, Mr. Churchill? British warships together with Kuomintang warships intruded into the defense area of the Chinese People's Liberation Army and fired on the People's Liberation Army, causing no less than 252 casualties among our loyal and gallant fighters. Since the British have trespassed on Chinese territory and committed so great a crime, the People's Liberation Army has good reason to demand that the British government admit its wrongdoing, apologize and make compensation. Isn't this what you should do, instead of dispatching forces to China to "retaliate" against the Chinese People's Liberation Army? Prime Minister Attlee's statement is also wrong.[42] Britain, he said, has the right to send her warships into China's Yangtze River. The Yangtze is an inland waterway of China. What right have you British to send in your warships? You have no such right. The Chinese people will defend their territory and sovereignty and absolutely will not permit encroachment by foreign governments. Attlee said that the People's Liberation Army "would be prepared to allow the ship [the *Amethyst*] to proceed to Nanjing but only on condition that she should assist the People's Liberation Army to cross the Yangtze." Attlee lied. The People's Liberation Army gave no permission to the *Amethyst* to

---

* This statement was drafted by Mao Zedong for the spokesman of the General Headquarters of the Chinese People's Liberation Army. It expressed the solemn stand of the Chinese people who fear no threats and resolutely oppose imperialist aggression; it also set forth the foreign policy of the new China which was soon to be established.

proceed to Nanjing. The People's Liberation Army does not want the armed forces of any foreign country to help it cross the Yangtze or to do anything else. On the contrary, the People's Liberation Army demands that Britain, the United States and France quickly withdraw their armed forces—their warships, military aircraft and marines stationed in the Yangtze and Huangpu rivers and other parts of China—from China's territorial inland waters, seas, land and air and that they refrain from helping the enemy of the Chinese people to wage civil war. The Chinese People's Revolutionary Military Commission and the People's Government have so far not established diplomatic relations with any foreign government. The Chinese People's Revolutionary Military Commission and the People's Government will protect those foreign nationals in China who are engaged in legitimate pursuits. They are willing to consider the establishment of diplomatic relations with foreign countries; such relations must be based on equality, mutual benefit, mutual respect for sovereignty and territorial integrity and, first of all, on no help being given to the Kuomintang reactionaries. They will tolerate no act of intimidation by any foreign government. A foreign government which wishes to consider establishing diplomatic relations with us must sever relations with the remnant Kuomintang forces and withdraw its armed forces from China. Attlee complained that the Communist Party of China, having no diplomatic relations with foreign countries, was unwilling to have contacts with the old diplomatic personnel of foreign governments (consuls recognized by the Kuomintang). Such complaints are groundless. In the past few years, the governments of the United States, Britain, Canada, etc. have helped the Kuomintang to oppose us. Can Mr. Attlee have forgotten this? Can it also be that Mr. Attlee does not know which country gave the Kuomintang the *Chongqing*, the heavy cruiser[43] which was recently sunk?

(From *Selected Works of Mao Zedong*, Vol. IV)

POINTS OF ATTENTION FOR HUANG HUA IN HIS TALK WITH JOHN LEIGHTON STUART*

(*May 10, 1949*)

(1) Huang Hua[44] may meet with John Leighton Stuart[45] for the purpose of detecting the intentions of the U.S. government. (2) At the meeting Huang Hua is to listen more to Stuart's remarks and make few comments of his own, any comments to be based on Li Tao's statement.[46] (3) In your telegram the sentence "Empty words are of no avail, and the United States is required first to do more things beneficial to the Chinese people" is defective; you should, in accordance with Li Tao's statement, say that no foreign country is allowed to interfere in China's internal affairs, that in the past the United States has interfered in China's internal affairs by helping the Kuomintang wage the civil war, and that this policy must stop. Instead of generally asking the United States to do more things beneficial to the Chinese people, you should say that if the U.S. government will consider the establishment of diplomatic relations with us, it must stop all its actions helping the Kuomintang and sever its ties with the remaining reactionary forces of the Kuomintang. The way you put it may give Americans the impression that the Chinese Communist Party also wishes to get U.S. aid. Our demand now is that the United States stop its help to the Kuomintang, sever its ties with the remaining forces of the Kuomintang and never again interfere in China's internal affairs; it is not asking the United States to do "things beneficial to the Chinese people," not to mention "more things beneficial to the Chinese people." The last quotation seems to imply that the U.S. government has already done some things beneficial to the Chinese people, but not quite enough, so it is necessary to ask it to do "more." This is where the inappropriateness lies. (4) In talking with Stuart, you should state that the talk is informal, because the two sides have not yet established diplomatic relations. (5) Prior to the talk, the Municipal Party Committee should have a discussion with Huang Hua. (6) If Stuart assumes a friendly

---

* This is a telegram sent in reply to the Nanjing Municipal Committee of the Communist Party of China and written by Mao Zedong for the Party Central Committee.

attitude in the talk, Huang Hua should reciprocate with proper friendliness, but not show excessive enthusiasm; a solemn and polite attitude should be adopted. (7) Huang Hua should not reject Stuart's wish as conveyed by Fu Jingbo,[47] of continuing to be ambassador for negotiations with us and for revision of the commercial treaty.

(From the original manuscript)

THE CHINESE PEOPLE WISH TO HAVE FRIENDLY COOPERATION WITH THE PEOPLE OF ALL COUNTRIES*

(June 15, 1949)

This is a victory for the people of all China, and also a victory for the peoples of the whole world. The whole world, except the imperialists and the reactionaries in various countries, is elated and inspired by this great victory of the Chinese people. The struggle of the Chinese people against their own enemies and the struggles of the peoples of the world against their own enemies have the same meaning. The people of China and the peoples of the world have all witnessed the fact that the imperialists have directed the Chinese reactionaries ruthlessly to oppose the Chinese people by means of a counter-revolutionary war and that the Chinese people have triumphantly overthrown the reactionaries by means of a revolutionary war.

Here, I think it is necessary to call people's attention to the fact that the imperialists and their running dogs, the Chinese reactionaries, will not resign themselves to defeat in this land of China. They will continue to gang up against the Chinese people in every possible way. For example, they will smuggle their agents into China to sow dissension and make trouble. That is certain; they will never neglect these activities. To take another example, they will incite the Chinese reactionaries, and even throw in their own forces, to blockade China's ports. They will do this as long as it is possible. Furthermore, if they still hanker after adventures, they will send some of their troops to invade and harass China's frontiers; this, too, is not impossible. All this we must take fully into account. Just because we have won victory, we must never relax our vigilance against the frenzied plots for revenge by the imperialists and their running dogs. Whoever relaxes vigilance will disarm himself politically and land himself in a passive position. In view of these circumstances,

---

* These are excerpts from Mao Zedong's address to a preparatory meeting for the New Political Consultative Conference.

the people all over the country must unite to smash resolutely, thoroughly, wholly and completely every plot against the Chinese people by the imperialists and their running dogs, the Chinese reactionaries. China must be independent, China must be liberated, China's affairs must be decided and run by the Chinese people themselves, and no further interference, not even the slightest, will be tolerated from any imperialist country.

The Chinese revolution is a revolution of the broad masses of the whole nation. Everybody is our friend, except the imperialists, the feudalists and the bureaucrat-capitalists, the Kuomintang reactionaries and their accomplices. We have a broad and solid revolutionary united front. This united front is so broad that it includes the working class, the peasantry, the urban petty bourgeoisie and the national bourgeoisie. This united front is so solid that it possesses the resolute will and the inexhaustible capacity to defeat every enemy and overcome every difficulty. The epoch we are living in is an epoch in which the imperialist system is heading for total collapse, the imperialists have fallen inextricably into crisis and, no matter how they continue to oppose the Chinese people, the Chinese people will always have a way to win final victory.

At the same time, we proclaim to the whole world that what we oppose is exclusively the imperialist system and its plots against the Chinese people. We are willing to discuss with any foreign government the establishment of diplomatic relations on the basis of the principles of equality, mutual benefit and mutual respect for territorial integrity and sovereignty, provided it is willing to sever relations with the Chinese reactionaries, stops conspiring with them or helping them and adopts an attitude of genuine, and not hypocritical, friendship toward People's China. The Chinese people wish to have friendly cooperation with the people of all countries and to resume and expand international trade in order to develop production and promote economic prosperity.

(From *Selected Works of Mao Zedong*, Vol. IV)

UNITE WITH THOSE NATIONS OF THE WORLD WHICH TREAT US AS EQUALS AND WITH THE PEOPLES OF ALL COUNTRIES*

(June 30, 1949)

The vanguard of the Chinese proletariat learned Marxism-Leninism after the October Revolution and founded the Communist Party of China. It entered at once into political struggles and only now, after a tortuous course of 28 years, has it won basic victory. From our 28 years' experience we have drawn a conclusion similar to the one Sun Yat-sen drew in his testament from his "experience of 40 years"; that is, we are deeply convinced that to win victory, "we must arouse the masses of the people and unite in a common struggle with those nations of the world which treat us as equals." Sun Yat-sen had a world outlook different from ours and started from a different class standpoint in studying and tackling problems; yet, in the 1920s he reached a conclusion basically the same as ours on the question of how to struggle against imperialism.

Twenty-four years have passed since Sun Yat-sen's death, and the Chinese revolution, led by the Communist Party of China, has made tremendous advances both in theory and practice and has radically changed the face of China. Up to now the principal and fundamental experience the Chinese people have gained is twofold:

(1) Internally, arouse the masses of the people. That is, unite the working class, the peasantry, the urban petty bourgeoisie and the national bourgeoisie, form a domestic united front under the leadership of the working class, and advance from this to the establishment of a state which is a people's democratic dictatorship under the leadership of the working class and based on the alliance of workers and peasants.

(2) Externally, unite in a common struggle with those nations of the world which treat us as equals and with the peoples of all countries. That

---

* These are excerpts from Mao Zedong's article "On the People's Democratic Dictatorship."

is, ally ourselves with the Soviet Union, with the People's Democracies and with the proletariat and the broad masses of the people in all other countries, and form an international united front.

"You are leaning to one side." Exactly. The 40 years' experience of Sun Yat-sen and the 28 years' experience of the Communist Party have taught us to lean to one side, and we are firmly convinced that in order to win victory and consolidate it we must lean to one side. In the light of the experiences accumulated in these 40 years and these 28 years, all Chinese without exception must lean either to the side of imperialism or to the side of socialism. Sitting on the fence will not do, nor is there a third road. We oppose the Chiang Kai-shek reactionaries who lean to the side of imperialism, and we also oppose the illusions about a third road.[48]

"You are too irritating." We are talking about how to deal with domestic and foreign reactionaries, the imperialists and their running dogs, not about how to deal with anyone else. With regard to such reactionaries, the question of irritating them or not does not arise. Irritated or not irritated, they will remain the same because they are reactionaries. Only if we draw a clear line between reactionaries and revolutionaries, expose the intrigues and plots of the reactionaries, arouse the vigilance and attention of the revolutionary ranks, heighten our will to fight and crush the enemy's arrogance can we isolate the reactionaries, vanquish them or supersede them. We must not show the slightest timidity before a wild beast. We must learn from Wu Song[49] on Jingyang Ridge. As Wu Song saw it, the tiger on Jingyang Ridge was a man-eater, whether irritated or not. Either kill the tiger or be eaten by him —one or the other.

"We want to do business." Quite right, business will be done. We are against no one except the domestic and foreign reactionaries who hinder us from doing business. Everybody should know that it is none other than the imperialists and their running dogs, the Chiang Kai-shek reactionaries, who hinder us from doing business and also from establishing diplomatic relations with foreign countries. When we have beaten the internal and external reactionaries by uniting all domestic and international forces, we shall be able to do business and establish diplomatic relations with all foreign countries on the basis of equality, mutual benefit and mutual respect for territorial integrity and sovereignty.

"Victory is possible even without international help." This is a mistaken idea. In the epoch in which imperialism exists, it is impossible for a genuine people's revolution to win victory in any country without various forms of help from the international revolutionary forces, and even if victory were won, it could not be consolidated. This was the case with the victory and consolidation of the great October Revolution, as Lenin and Stalin told us long ago. This was also the case with the overthrow of the three imperialist powers in World War II and the establishment of the People's Democracies. And this is also the case with the present and the future of People's China. Just imagine! If the Soviet Union had not existed, if there had been no victory in the anti-fascist Second World War, if Japanese imperialism had not been defeated, if the People's Democracies had not come into being, if the oppressed nations of the East were not rising in struggle and if there were no struggle of the masses of the people against their reactionary rulers in the United States, Britain, France, Germany, Italy, Japan and other capitalist countries—if not for all these in combination, the international reactionary forces bearing down upon us would certainly be many times greater than now. In such circumstances, could we have won victory? Obviously not. And even with victory, there could be no consolidation. The Chinese people have had more than enough experience in this regard. This experience was reflected long ago in Sun Yat-sen's death-bed statement on the necessity of uniting with the international revolutionary forces.

"We need help from the British and U.S. governments." This, too, is a naive idea in these times. Would the present rulers of Britain and the United States, who are imperialists, help a people's state? Why do these countries do business with us and, supposing they might be willing to lend us money on terms of mutual benefit in the future, why would they do so? Because their capitalists want to make money and their bankers want to earn interest to extricate themselves from their own crisis—it is not a matter of helping the Chinese people. The Communist Parties and progressive groups in these countries are urging their governments to establish trade and even diplomatic relations with us. This is goodwill, this is help, this cannot be mentioned in the same breath with the conduct of the bourgeoisie in the same countries. Throughout his life, Sun Yat-sen appealed countless times to the capitalist countries for help and got nothing but heartless rebuffs. Only once in his whole life did Sun Yat-sen receive foreign help, and that was Soviet help. Let readers refer to Dr. Sun Yat-sen's testament; his earnest advice was not to look for help from the imperialist countries but to "unite with those nations of the world which treat us as equals." Dr. Sun had experience; he had suffered, he had been deceived. We should remember his words and not allow ourselves to be deceived again. Internationally, we belong to the side of the anti-imperialist front headed by the Soviet Union, and so we can turn only to this side for genuine and friendly help, not to the side of the imperialist front.

(From *Selected Works of Mao Zedong*, Vol. IV)

CAST AWAY ILLUSIONS, PREPARE FOR STRUGGLE*

(*August 14, 1949*)

It is no accident that the U.S. State Department's White Paper on U.S. relations with China and Secretary of State Acheson's Letter of Transmittal to President Truman[50] have been released at this time. The publication of these documents reflects the victory of the Chinese people and the defeat of imperialism, it reflects the decline of the entire world system of imperialism. The imperialist system is riddled with insuperable internal contradictions, and therefore the imperialists are plunged into deep gloom.

Imperialism has prepared the conditions for its own doom. These conditions are the awakening of the great masses of the people in the colonies and semi-colonies and in the imperialist countries themselves. Imperialism has pushed the great masses of the people throughout the world into the historical epoch of the great struggle to abolish imperialism.

Imperialism has prepared the material as well as the moral conditions for the struggle of the great masses of the people.

The material conditions are factories, railways, firearms, artillery, and the like. Most of the powerful equipment of the Chinese People's Liberation Army comes from U.S. imperialism, some comes from Japanese imperialism and some is of our own manufacture.

The British aggression against China in 1840[51] was followed by the wars of aggression against China by the Anglo-French allied forces,[52] by France,[53] by Japan,[54] and by the allied forces of the eight powers (Britain, France, Japan, tsarist Russia, Germany, the United States, Italy and Austria);[55] by the war between Japan and tsarist Russia on Chinese territory;[56] by Japan's war of aggression against China in China's northeast, which began in 1931;[57] by Japan's war of aggression against all China, which began in 1937 and lasted

---

* This article and the one that follows, "Farewell, Leighton Stuart!" were two among the commentaries written by Mao Zedong for the Xinhua News Agency on the U.S. State Department's White Paper and Dean Acheson's Letter of Transmittal.

eight long years; and, finally, by the latest war of aggression against the Chinese people, which has gone on for three years, waged to all appearances by Chiang Kai-shek but in reality by the United States. As stated in Acheson's Letter, the United States in this last war has given the Kuomintang government material aid to the value of "more than 50 percent" of the latter's "monetary expenditures" and "furnished the Chinese armies" (meaning the Kuomintang armies) with "military supplies." It is a war in which the United States supplies the money and guns and Chiang Kai-shek supplies the men to fight for the United States and slaughter the Chinese people. All these wars of aggression, together with political, economic and cultural aggression and oppression, have caused the Chinese to hate imperialism, made them stop and think, "What is all this about?" and compelled them to bring their revolutionary spirit into full play and become united through struggle. They fought, failed, fought again, failed again and fought again and accumulated 109 years of experience, accumulated the experience of hundreds of struggles, great and small, military and political, economic and cultural, with bloodshed and without bloodshed —and only then won today's basic victory. These are the moral conditions without which the revolution could not be victorious.

To serve the needs of its aggression, imperialism created the comprador system and bureaucrat-capital in China. Imperialist aggression stimulated China's social economy, brought about changes in it and created the opposites of imperialism—the national industry and national bourgeoisie of China, and especially the Chinese proletariat working in enterprises run directly by the imperialists, those run by bureaucrat-capital and those run by the national bourgeoisie. To serve the needs of its aggression, imperialism ruined the Chinese peasants by exploiting them through the exchange of unequal values and thereby created great masses of poor peasants, numbering hundreds of millions and comprising 70 per cent of China's rural population. To serve the needs of its aggression, imperialism created for China millions of big and small intellectuals of a new type, differing from the old type of *literatus* or scholar-bureaucrat. But imperialism and its running dogs, the reactionary governments of China, could control only a part of these intellectuals and finally only a handful, such as Hu Shi,[58] Fu Sinian[59] and Qian Mu;[60] all the rest got out of control and turned against them. Students, teachers, professors, technicians, engineers, doctors, scientists, writers, artists and government employees, all are revolting against or parting company with the Kuomintang. The Communist Party is the party of the poor and is described in the Kuomintang's widespread, all-pervasive propaganda as a band of people who commit murder and arson, who rape and loot, who reject history and culture, renounce the motherland, have no filial piety or respect for teachers and are impervious to all reason, who practice community of property and of women and employ the military tactics of the "human sea"—in short, a horde of fiendish monsters who perpetrate every conceivable crime and are unpardonably wicked. But strangely enough, it is this very horde that has won the support of several hundred million people, including the majority of the intellectuals, and especially the student youth.

Part of the intellectuals still want to wait and see. They think: the Kuomintang is no good and the Communist Party is not necessarily good either, so we had better wait and see. Some support the Communist Party in words, but in their hearts they are waiting to see. They are the very people who have illusions about the United States. They are unwilling to draw a distinction between the U.S. imperialists, who are in power, and the American people, who are not. They are easily duped by the honeyed words of the U.S. imperialists, as though these imperialists would deal with People's China on the basis of equality and mutual benefit without a stern, long struggle. They still have many reactionary, that is to say, anti-popular, ideas in their heads, but they are not Kuomintang reactionaries. They are the middle-of-the-roaders or the right-wingers in People's China. They are the supporters of what Acheson calls "democratic individualism." The deceptive maneuvers of the Achesons still have a flimsy social base in China.

Acheson's White Paper admits that the U.S. imperialists are at a complete loss as to what to do about the present situation in China. The Kuomintang is so impotent that no amount of help can save it from inevitable doom; the U.S. imperialists are losing grip over things and feel helpless. Acheson says in his Letter of Transmittal:

> The unfortunate but inescapable fact is that the ominous result of the civil war in China was beyond the control of the government of the United States. Nothing that this country did or could have done within the reasonable limits of its capabilities could have changed that result; nothing that was left undone by this country has contributed to it. It was the product of internal Chinese forces, forces which this country tried to influence but could not.

According to logic, Acheson's conclusion should be, as some muddle-headed Chinese intellectuals think or say, to act like "the butcher who lays down his knife and at once becomes a Buddha" or "The robber who has a change of heart and becomes a virtuous man," that is, he should treat People's China on the basis of equality and mutual benefit and stop making trouble. But no, says Acheson, trouble-making will continue, and definitely so. Will there be any result? There will, says he. On what group of people will he rely? On the supporters of "democratic individualism." Says Acheson:

> ... ultimately the profound civilization and the democratic individualism of China will reassert themselves and she will throw off the foreign yoke. I consider that we should encourage all developments in China which now and in the future work toward this end.

How different is the logic of the imperialists from that of the people! Make trouble, fail, make trouble again, fail again ... till their doom; that is the logic of the imperialists and all reactionaries the world over in dealing with the people's cause, and they will never go against this logic. This is a Marxist law. When we say "imperialism is ferocious," we mean that its nature will never change, that the imperialists will never lay down their butcher knives, that they will never become Buddhas, till their doom.

Fight, fail, fight again, fail again, fight again ... till their victory; that is the logic of the people, and they too will never go against this logic. This is another Marxist law. The Russian people's revolution followed this law, and so has the Chinese people's revolution.

Classes struggle, some classes triumph, others are eliminated. Such is history, such is the history of civilization for thousands of years. To interpret history from this viewpoint is historical materialism; standing in opposition to this viewpoint is historical idealism.

The method of self-criticism can be applied only within the ranks of the people; it is impossible to persuade the imperialists and the Chinese reactionaries to show kindness of heart and turn from their evil ways. The only course is to organize forces and struggle against them, as in our People's War of Liberation and the agrarian revolution, to expose the imperialists, "irritate" them, overthrow them, punish them for offenses against the law and "allow them only to behave themselves and not to be unruly in word or deed."[61] Only then will there be any hope of dealing with imperialist foreign countries on the basis of equality and mutual benefit. Only then will there be any hope that those landlords, bureaucrat-capitalists, members of the reactionary Kuomintang clique and their accomplices, who have laid down their arms and surrendered, can be given education for transforming the bad into the good and be transformed, as far as possible, into good people. Many Chinese liberals —the old-type democratic elements, i.e., the supporters of "democratic individualism," whom Truman, Marshall,[62] Acheson, Leighton Stuart[45] and the like count on and have been trying to win over—often find themselves in a passive position and are often wrong in their judgements on the U.S. rulers, on the Kuomintang, on the Soviet Union and also on the Communist Party of China. The reason is precisely that they do not look at, or disapprove of looking at, problems from the standpoint of historical materialism.

It is the duty of progressives—the Communists, members of the democratic parties, politically conscious workers, the student youth and progressive intellectuals—to unite with the intermediate strata, middle-of-the-roaders and backward elements of various strata, with all those in People's China who are still wavering and hesitating (these people will waver for a long time to come and, even after they have once become steady, will waver again as soon as they meet difficulties), give them sincere help, criticize their wavering character, educate them, win them over to the side of the masses, prevent them from being pulled over by the imperialists and tell them to cast away illusions and prepare for struggle. Let no one think that there is no more work to do now that victory is won. We still have to work, to do a great deal of patient work, before we can truly win these people over. When they are won over, imperialism will be entirely isolated, and Acheson will no longer be able to play any of his tricks.

The slogan, "Prepare for struggle," is addressed to those who still cherish certain illusions about the relations between China and the imperialist countries, especially between China and the United States. On this matter, they are still passive, their minds are still not made up, they are still not determined to wage a long struggle against U.S. (and British) imperialism because they still have illusions about the United States. There is still a very wide, or fairly wide, gap between these people and ourselves on this question.

The publication of the U.S. White Paper and Acheson's Letter of Transmittal is worthy of celebration, because it is a bucket of cold water and a loss of face for those who have ideas of the old type of democracy or democratic individualism, who do not approve of, or do not quite approve of, or are dissatisfied with, or are somewhat dissatisfied with, or even resent, people's democracy, or democratic collectivism, or democratic centralism, or collective heroism, or internationalist patriotism—but who still have patriotic feelings and are not Kuomintang reactionaries. It is a bucket of cold water particularly for those who believe that everything American is good and hope that China will model herself on the United States.

Acheson openly declares that the Chinese democratic individualists will be "encouraged" to throw off the so-called "foreign yoke." That is to say, he calls for the overthrow of Marxism-Leninism and the people's democratic dictatorship led by the Communist Party of China. For this "ism" and this system, it is alleged, are "foreign," with no roots in China, imposed on the Chinese by the German, Karl Marx (who died 66 years ago), and the Russians,

Lenin (who died 25 years ago) and Stalin (who is still alive); this "ism" and this system, moreover, are downright bad, because they advocate the class struggle, the overthrow of imperialism, etc.; hence they must be got rid of. In this connection, it is alleged, "the democratic individualism of China will reassert itself" with the "encouragement" of President Truman, the backstage Commander-in-Chief Marshall, Secretary of State Acheson (the charming foreign mandarin responsible for the publication of the White Paper) and Ambassador Leighton Stuart who has scampered off. Acheson and his like think they are giving "encouragement," but those Chinese democratic individualists who still have patriotic feelings, even though they believe in the United States, may quite possibly feel this is a bucket of cold water thrown on them and a loss of face; for instead of dealing with the authorities of the Chinese people's democratic dictatorship in the proper way, Acheson and his like are doing this filthy work and, what is more, they have openly published it. What a loss of face! What a loss of face! To those who are patriotic, Acheson's statement is no "encouragement" but an insult.

China is in the midst of a great revolution. All China is seething with enthusiasm. The conditions are favorable for winning over and uniting with all those who do not have a bitter and deep-seated hatred for the cause of the people's revolution, even though they have mistaken ideas. Progressives should make use of the White Paper to explain things to all these persons.

(From *Selected Works of Mao Zedong*, Vol. IV)

FAREWELL, LEIGHTON STUART!

(*August 18, 1949*)

It is understandable that the date chosen for the publication of the U.S. White Paper was August 5, a time when Leighton Stuart[45] had departed from Nanjing for Washington but had not yet arrived there, since Leighton Stuart is a symbol of the complete defeat of the U.S. policy of aggression. Leighton Stuart is an American born in China; he has fairly wide social connections and spent many years running missionary schools in China; he once sat in a Japanese gaol during the War of Resistance; he used to pretend to love both the United States and China and was able to deceive quite a number of Chinese. Hence, he was picked out by George C. Marshall,[62] was made U.S. ambassador to China and became a celebrity in the Marshall group. In the eyes of the Marshall group he had only one fault, namely, that the whole period when he was ambassador to China as an exponent of their policy was the very period in which that policy was utterly defeated by the Chinese people; that was no small responsibility. It is only natural that the White Paper, which is designed to evade this responsibility, should have been published at a time when Leighton Stuart was on his way to Washington but had not yet arrived.

The war to turn China into a U.S. colony, a war in which the United States of America supplies the money and guns and Chiang Kai-shek the men to fight for the United States and slaughter the Chinese people, has been an important component of the U.S. imperialist policy of world-wide aggression since World War II. The U.S. policy of aggression has several targets. The three main targets are Europe, Asia and the Americas. China, the center of gravity in Asia, is a large country with a population of 475 million; by seizing China, the United States would possess all of Asia. With its Asian front consolidated, U.S. imperialism could concentrate its forces on attacking Europe. U.S. imperialism considers its front in the Americas relatively secure. These are the smug over-all calculations of the U.S. aggressors.

But in the first place, the American people and the peoples of the world do not want war. Secondly, the attention of the United States has largely been absorbed by the awakening of the peoples of Europe, by the rise of the People's Democracies in Eastern Europe, and particularly by the towering presence of the Soviet Union, this unprecendentedly powerful bulwark of peace bestriding Europe and Asia, and by its strong resistance to the U.S. policy of aggression. Thirdly, and this is most important, the Chinese people have awakened, and the armed forces and the organized strength of the people under the leadership of the Communist Party of China have become more powerful than ever before. Consequently, the ruling clique of U.S. imperialism has been prevented from adopting a policy of direct, large-scale armed attacks on China and instead has pursued a policy of helping Chiang Kai-shek wage the civil war.

U.S. naval, ground and air forces did participate in the war in China. There were U.S. naval bases in Qingdao, Shanghai and Taiwan. U.S. troops were stationed in Beiping, Tianjin, Tangshan, Qinhuangdao, Qingdao, Shanghai and Nanjing. The U.S. air force controlled all of China's air space and took aerial photographs of all China's strategic areas for military maps. At the town of Anping near Beiping, at Jiutai near Changchun, at Tangshan and in the Eastern Shandong Peninsula, U.S. soldiers and other military personnel clashed with the People's Liberation Army and on several occasions were captured.[63] Chennault's air fleet took an extensive part in the civil war.[64] Besides transporting troops for Chiang Kai-shek, the U.S. air force bombed and sank the cruiser *Chongqing*,[43] which had mutinied against the Kuomintang. All these were acts of direct participation in the war, although they fell short of an open declaration of war and were not large in scale, and although the principal method of U.S. aggression was the large-scale supply of money, munitions and advisers to help Chiang Kai-shek wage the civil war.

The use of this method by the United States was determined by the objective situation in China and the rest of the world, and not by any lack of desire on the part of the Truman[65]-Marshall group, the ruling clique of U.S. imperialism, to launch direct aggression against China. Moreover, at the outset of its help to Chiang Kai-shek in waging the civil war, a crude farce was staged in which the United States appeared as mediator in the conflict between the Kuomintang and the Communist Party; this was an attempt to soften up the Communist Party of China, deceive the Chinese people and thus gain control of all China without fighting. The peace negotiations failed, the deception fell through and the curtain rose on the war.

Liberals or "democratic individualists" who cherish illusions about the United States and have short memories! Please read Acheson's[66] own words:

> When peace came the United States was confronted with three possible alternatives in China: (1) it could have pulled out lock, stock and

barrel; (2) it could have intervened militarily on a major scale to assist the nationalists to destroy the Communists; (3) it could, while assisting the Nationalists to assert their authority over as much of China as possible, endeavor to avoid a civil war by working for a compromise between the two sides.

Why didn't the United States adopt the first of these policies? Acheson says:

> The first alternative would, and I believe American public opinion at the time so felt, have represented an abandonment of our international responsibilities and of our traditional policy of friendship for China before we had made a determined effort to be of assistance.

So that's how things stand: the "international responsibilities" of the United States and its "traditional policy of friendship for China" are nothing but intervention against China. Intervention is called assuming international responsibilities and showing friendship for China; as to non-intervention, it simply won't do. Here Acheson defiles U.S. public opinion; his is the "public opinion" of Wall Street, not the public opinion of the American people.

Why didn't the United States adopt the second of these policies? Acheson says:

> The second alternative policy, while it may look attractive theoretically and in retrospect, was wholly impracticable. The Nationalists had been unable to destroy the Communists during the ten years before the war. Now after the war the Nationalists were, as indicated above, weakened, demoralized, and unpopular. They had quickly dissipated their popular support and prestige in the areas liberated from the Japanese by the conduct of their civil and military officials. The Communists on the other hand were much stronger than they had ever been and were in control of most of North China. Because of the ineffectiveness of the Nationalist forces which was later to be tragically demonstrated, the Communists probably could have been dislodged only by American arms. It is obvious that the American people would not have sanctioned such a colossal commitment of our armies in 1945 or later. We therefore came to the third alternative policy....

What a splendid idea! The United States supplies the money and guns and Chiang Kai-shek the men to fight for the United States and slaughter the Chinese people, to "destroy the Communists" and turn China into a U.S. colony, so that the United States may fulfill its "international responsibilities" and carry out its "traditional policy of friendship for China."

Although the Kuomintang was corrupt and incompetent, "demoralized and unpopular," the United States nevertheless supplied it with money and guns and made it fight. Direct armed intervention was all right, "theoretically." It also seems all right "in retrospect" to the rulers of the United States. For direct armed intervention would really have been interesting and it might "look attractive." But it would not have worked in practice, for "it is obvious that the American people would not have sanctioned" it. Not that the imperialist group of Truman, Marshall, Acheson and their like did not desire it—they very much desired it—but the situation in China, in the United States and in the world as a whole (a point Acheson does not mention) did not permit it; they had to give up their preference and take the third way.

Let those Chinese who believe that "victory is possible even without international help" listen. Acheson is giving you a lesson. Acheson is a good teacher, giving lessons free of charge, and he is telling the whole truth with tireless zeal and great candor. The United States refrained from dispatching large forces to attack China, not because the U.S. government didn't want to, but because it had worries. First worry: the Chinese people would oppose it, and the U.S. government was afraid of getting hopelessly bogged down in a quagmire. Second worry: the American people would oppose it, and so the U.S. government dared not order mobilization. Third worry: the people of the Soviet Union, of Europe and of the rest of the world would oppose it, and the U.S. government would face universal condemnation. Acheson's charming candor has its limits and he is unwilling to mention the third worry. The reason is he is afraid of losing face before the Soviet Union, he is afraid that the Marshall Plan[67] in Europe, which is already a failure despite pretences to the contrary, may end dismally in total collapse.

Let those Chinese who are short-sighted, muddle-headed liberals or democratic individualists listen. Acheson is giving you a lesson; he is a good teacher for you. He has made a clean sweep of your fancied U.S. humanity, justice and virtue. Isn't that so? Can you find a trace of humanity, justice or virtue in the White Paper or in Acheson's Letter of Transmittal?

True, the United States has science and technology. But unfortunately they are in the grip of the capitalists, not in the hands of the people, and are used to exploit and oppress the people at home and to perpetrate aggression and to slaughter people abroad. There is also "democracy" in the United States. But unfortunately it is only another name for the dictatorship of the bourgeoisie by itself. The United States has plenty of money. But unfortunately it is willing to give money only to the Chiang Kai-shek reactionaries, who are rotten to the core. The United States, it is said, is and will be quite willing to give money to its fifth column in China, but is unwilling to give it to the ordinary run of liberals or democratic individualists, who are much too bookish and do not know how to appreciate favors, and naturally it is even more unwilling to give money to the Communists. Money may be given, but only conditionally. What is the condition? Follow the United States. The Americans have sprinkled some relief flour in Beiping, Tianjin and Shanghai to see who will stoop to pick it up. Like Jiang Taigong fishing, they have cast the line for the fish who want to be caught. But he who swallows food handed out in contempt will get a bellyache.[68]

We Chinese have backbone. Many who were once liberals or democratic individualists have stood up to the U.S. imperialists and their running dogs, the Kuomintang reactionaries. Wen Yiduo[69] rose to his full height and smote the table, angrily faced the Kuomintang pistols and died rather than submit. Zhu Ziqing,[70] though seriously ill, starved to death rather than accept U.S. "relief food." Han Yu[71] of the Tang Dynasty wrote a "Eulogy of Bo Yi," praising a man with quite a few "democratic individualist" ideas, who shirked his duty toward the people of his own country, deserted his post and opposed the people's war of liberation of that time, led by King Wu. He lauded the wrong man. We should write eulogies of Wen Yiduo and Zhu Ziqing who demonstrated the heroic spirit of our nation.

What matter if we have to face some difficulties? Let them blockade us! Let them blockade us for eight or ten years! By that time all of China's problems will have been solved. Will the Chinese cower before difficulties when they are not afraid even of death? Lao Zi said, "The people fear not death, why threaten them with it?"[72] U.S. imperialism and its running dogs, the Chiang Kai-shek reactionaries, have not only "threatened" us with death but actually put many of us to death. Besides people like Wen Yiduo, they have killed millions of Chinese in the last three years with U.S. carbines, machine-guns, mortars, bazookas, howitzers, tanks and bombs dropped from aeroplanes. This situation is now coming to an end. They have been defeated. It is we who are going in to attack them, not they who are coming out to attack us. They will soon be finished. True, the few problems left to us, such as blockade, unemployment, famine, inflation and rising prices, are difficulties, but we have already begun to breathe more easily than in the past three years. We have come triumphantly through the ordeal of the last three years, why can't we overcome these few difficulties of today? Why can't we live without the United States?

When the People's Liberation Army crossed the Yangtze River, the U.S. colonial government at Nanjing fled helter-skelter. Yet His Excellency Ambassador Stuart sat tight, watching wide-eyed, hoping to set up shop under a new signboard and to reap some profit. But what did he see? Apart from the People's Liberation Army soldiers marching past, column after column, and the workers, peasants and students rising in hosts, he saw something else—the Chinese liberals or democratic individualists turning out in force, shouting slogans and talking revolution together with the workers, peasants, soldiers and students. In short, he was left out in the cold, "standing all alone, body and shadow comforting each other."[73] There was nothing more for him to do, and he had to take to the road, his briefcase under his arm.

There are still some intellectuals and other people in China who have muddled ideas and illusions about the United States. Therefore we should explain things to them, win them over, educate them and unite with them, so they will come over to the side of the people and not fall into the snares set by imperialism. But the prestige of U.S. imperialism among the Chinese people is completely bankrupt, and the White Paper is a record of its bankruptcy. Progressives should make good use of the White Paper to educate the Chinese people.

Leighton Stuart has departed and the White Paper has arrived. Very good. Very good. Both events are worth celebrating.

(From *Selected Works of Mao Zedong*, Vol. IV)

THE CHINESE PEOPLE HAVE STOOD UP!*

(September 21, 1949)

Fellow Delegates, we are all convinced that our work will go down in the history of mankind, demonstrating that the Chinese people, comprising one quarter of humanity, have now stood up. The Chinese have always been a great, courageous and industrious nation; it is only in modern times that they have fallen behind. And that was due entirely to oppression and exploitation by foreign imperialism and domestic reactionary governments. For over a century our forefathers never stopped waging unyielding struggles against domestic and foreign oppressors, including the Revolution of 1911 led by Dr. Sun Yat-sen, our great forerunner in the Chinese revolution. Our forefathers enjoined us to carry out their unfulfilled will. And we have acted accordingly. We have closed our ranks and defeated both domestic and foreign oppressors through the People's War of Liberation and the great people's revolution, and now we are proclaiming the founding of the People's Republic of China. From now on our nation will belong to the community of the peace-loving and freedom-loving nations of the world and work courageously and industriously to foster its own civilization and well-being and at the same time to promote world peace and freedom. Ours will no longer be a nation subject to insult and humiliation. We have stood up. Our revolution has won the sympathy and acclaim of the people of all countries. We have friends all over the world.

Our revolutionary work is not completed, the People's War of Liberation and the people's revolutionary movement are still forging ahead and we must keep up our efforts. The imperialists and the domestic reactionaries will certainly not take their defeat lying down; they will fight to the last ditch. After there is peace and order throughout the country, they are sure to engage in sabotage and create disturbances by one means or another and every day and every minute they will try to stage a come-back. This is inevitable and beyond all doubt, and under no circumstances must we relax our vigilance.

---

* This is the major part of the opening address delivered by Mao Zedong at the First Plenary Session of the Chinese People's Political Consultative Conference.

Our state system, the people's democratic dictatorship, is a powerful weapon for safeguarding the fruits of victory of the people's revolution and for thwarting the plots of domestic and foreign enemies for restoration, and this weapon we must firmly grasp. Internationally, we must unite with all peace-loving and freedom-loving countries and peoples, and first of all with the Soviet Union and the New Democracies, so that we shall not stand alone in our struggle to safeguard these fruits of victory and to thwart the plots of domestic and foreign enemies for restoration. As long as we persist in the people's democratic dictatorship and unite with our foreign friends, we shall always be victorious.

The people's democratic dictatorship and solidarity with our foreign friends will enable us to accomplish our work of construction rapidly. We are already confronted with the task of nation-wide economic reconstruction. We have very favorable conditions: a population of 475 million people and a territory of 9,600,000 square kilometers. There are indeed difficulties ahead, and a great many too. But we firmly believe that by heroic struggle the people of the country will surmount them all. The Chinese people have rich experience in overcoming difficulties. If our forefathers, and we also, could weather long years of extreme difficulty and defeat powerful domestic and foreign reactionaries, why can't we now, after victory, build a prosperous and flourishing country? As long as we keep to our style of plain living and hard struggle, as long as we stand united and as long as we persist in the people's democratic dictatorship and unite with our foreign friends, we shall be able to win speedy victory on the economic front.

An upsurge in economic reconstruction is bound to be followed by an upsurge of cultural development. The era in which the Chinese people were regarded as uncivilized is now ended. We shall emerge in the world as a nation with an advanced culture.

Our national defense will be consolidated and no imperialists will ever again be allowed to invade our land. Our people's armed forces must be maintained and developed with the heroic and long-tested People's Liberation Army as the foundation. We will have not only a powerful army but also a powerful air force and a powerful navy.

Let the domestic and foreign reactionaries tremble before us! Let them say we are no good at this and no good at that. By our own indomitable efforts we the Chinese people will steadily advance to our goal.

(From *People's Daily*, September 22, 1949)

THE CHINESE GOVERNMENT'S PRINCIPLE FOR ESTABLISHMENT OF DIPLOMATIC RELATIONS WITH FOREIGN COUNTRIES*

(*October 1, 1949*)

The Central People's Government Council of the People's Republic of China, having taken office today in the capital and unanimously made the relevant decisions, proclaims the formation of the Central People's Government of the People's Republic of China and acceptance of the Common Program of the Chinese People's Political Consultative Conference[74] as the administrative policies of the Government.... At the same time, the Central People's Government Council proclaims to the governments of all other countries that this Government is the sole legal government representing all the people of the People's Republic of China. This Government is prepared to establish diplomatic relations with any foreign government which is willing to observe the principles of equality, mutual benefit and mutual respect of territorial integrity and sovereignty.

(From *People's Daily*, October 2, 1949)

---

* These are excerpts from the "Proclamation of the Central People's Government of the People's Republic of China" delivered by Mao Zedong at the inaugurating ceremony of the People's Republic of China.

CAPITALIST COUNTRIES MUST NEGOTIATE WITH US TO ESTABLISH DIPLOMATIC RELATIONS WITH CHINA*

(December 19, 1949)

Regarding the Burmese government's request to establish diplomatic relations with us, we should in our reply telegram ask whether it is willing to sever diplomatic relations with the Kuomintang, and at the same time ask it to send a responsible representative to Beijing to negotiate establishing Sino-Burmese diplomatic relations, whose decision will depend on results of the negotiations. Such a negotiating procedure is fully necessary and applicable to all capitalist countries. If a capitalist country declares publicly its wish to establish diplomatic relations with us, we should also ask it by telegram to send a representative to China to negotiate establishing diplomatic relations, and at the same time we can publish the gist of the telegram in a news dispatch, thus keeping the initiative in our hands. What are your views on the matter?

(From the original manuscript)

---

* This is the main part of Mao Zedong's telegram to Liu Shaoqi and Zhou Enlai sent during his visit to the Soviet Union.

ANSWERS TO QUESTIONS OF A TASS CORRESPONDENT

(January 2, 1950)

Xinhua, Beijing, January 2—According to Tass, Moscow, January 2, Chairman Mao Zedong of the Central People's Government of the People's Republic of China gave an interview to a Tass correspondent, during which he answered the following questions:

Question: How is the state of affairs in China at present?

Answer: Military affairs in China are proceeding well. At the present time the Communist Party of China and the Central People's Government of the People's Republic of China are going over to peaceful economic reconstruction.

Question: Mr. Mao Zedong, how long are you going to stay in the U.S.S.R.?

Answer: I intend to stay for several weeks. The length of my stay in the U.S.S.R. will partly depend on the time needed for the settlement of questions of interest to the People's Republic of China.

Question: Could you tell me what questions you are considering?

Answer: Among these questions are first of all the existing Treaty of Friendship and Alliance between China and the U.S.S.R.,[75] the question of Soviet loans to the People's Republic of China, the question of trade and trade agreement between our two countries and others.

Besides, I intend to visit several districts and cities of the Soviet Union in order to become better acquainted with the economic and cultural development in the Soviet State.

(From *People's Daily*, January 3, 1950)

ZHOU ENLAI TO GO TO THE SOVIET UNION FOR PARTICIPATION IN NEGOTIATIONS AND SIGNING OF TREATY*

(January 1950)

I

To the Central Committee:
(1) There is an important development in the work here in the last couple of days. Comrade Stalin has agreed for Comrade Zhou Enlai to come to Moscow and signing of a new Sino-Soviet treaty of friendship and alliance[76] and agreements on a loan, trade and civil aviation respectively. It was decided yesterday (January 1) to publish my talk with the TASS correspondent, which is carried in the newspapers today (January 2) and which you must have received. This evening at 8:00 Comrades Molotov[36] and Mikoyan[77] came and asked about my views on the Sino-Soviet treaty and other matters. I set forth three options: (A) to sign a new Sino-Soviet treaty of friendship and alliance. There is much merit in doing so. With Sino-Soviet relations codified in a new treaty, the Chinese workers, peasants, intellectuals and left-wing national bourgeoisie would all be elated, and the right-wing national bourgeoisie could be isolated. Internationally, it would give us greater political capital to deal with the imperialist countries and to review the treaties signed in the past between China and various imperialist countries. (B) To issue a simple communique through the news agencies of our two countries stating merely that the authorities of the two countries, having exchanged views on the old Sino-Soviet Treaty of Friendship and Alliance,[75] reached agreement on important issues. No details will be mentioned, in effect putting off the matter for a few years. In this case Chinese Foreign Minister Zhou Enlai would not have to come here, of course. (C) To sign a statement containing essential elements

---

* These are two telegrams to the Central Committee of the Chinese Communist Party from Mao Zedong who was on visit in the Soviet Union.

of the relation between our two countries, but not a treaty. In this case, too, Zhou Enlai would not have to come. After listening to my elaboration of the pros and cons of these three options, Comrade Molotov immediately said that option A is preferable and that Zhou should come. At this, I asked again whether the old treaty would be replaced with a new treaty. Comrade Molotov said yes. Then we began to figure out the date for Zhou Enlai to arrive and that for signing the treaty. I said my telegram would reach Beijing on January 3, Zhou Enlai would need five days for preparations, he would leave Beijing on January 9 and, after an eleven-day train journey, and arrive in Moscow on January 19. From the 20th to the end of January, about ten days would be used to negotiate and sign the treaty and various agreements. In early February Zhou Enlai and I could leave for China. Then we discussed my sightseeing and decided that I would pay homage at the Lenin Mausoleum, tour Leningrad and Gorki City, and visit an ordnance factory, the metro (these two items were proposed by Comrades Molotov and Mikoyan) and a collective farm. Also discussed was my meeting with other Soviet leading comrades for conversation. (To date, I have not gone out alone to call on any of them.)

(2) Upon receiving this telegram, please make all preparations in five days' time. I hope Enlai, bringing with him the trade minister and other necessary assistants and the requisite documents, will depart Beijing on January 9 for Moscow by train (not by air), leaving Comrade Dong Biwu[78] acting as Premier of the Government Administration Council. This should not be made public until Zhou arrives in Moscow.

(3) Is the above feasible? Are five days enough for preparations, or will one or two more days be needed? Is it necessary to ask Li Fuchun[79] or some other comrades to come to lend assistance? Please consider all these questions and reply by telegram.

Mao Zedong
11:00 p.m. January 2, 1950

II

To the Central Committee:

My telegram of 11:00 p.m. yesterday must have reached you already. Comrade Enlai's leaving the country to come to the Soviet Union should be formally approved at a meeting of the Government Administration Council, where a report should be submitted, noting that the purpose of the trip is to negotiate and sign a new Sino-Soviet treaty of friendship and alliance (There may be some changes from the old treaty on the question of Lüshun-Dalian harbors,[80] although the specifics are to be negotiated. The objective of defense against possible aggression by Japan and its allies and recognition of the independence of Outer Mongolia remain the basic spirit of the new treaty.), a loan agreement (we have asked for a total of 300 million US dollars, to be paid in several years; we did not ask for more, because in the next few years it is better to borrow less than more), a civil aviation agreement (this is conducive to establishing our own aviation industry), and a trade agreement (defining the scope of barter with the Soviet Union is helpful in defining our direction of developing production and in concluding trade agreements with other foreign countries). In addition, a discussion to be attended by all members of the Central Government currently in Beijing should be convened, at which a similar report should be submitted. At both meetings it should be pointed out that this move will place our People's Republic in a more advantageous position, so that the capitalist countries will have to accept what we have defined, and that it will help us compel other countries to recognize China unconditionally, abrogate the old treaties and conclude new ones, so that the capitalist countries will not dare act recklessly.

Mao Zedong
4:00 a.m. January 3, 1950
(From the original manuscript)

APPROVAL OF A STATEMENT REPUDIATING THE LEGAL STATUS OF THE FORMER KUOMINTANG GOVERNMENT'S REPRESENTATIVE AT THE U.N. SECURITY COUNCIL*

(January 7, 1950)

At 1:00 a.m. today (January 7) Vishinsky[81] came and talked about three things: .... (3) He suggested that our Foreign Ministry send a statement to the United Nations Security Council to repudiate the legal status of the former Kuomintang government's representative, Chiang Ting-fu. Vishinsky said if China issues such a statement, the Soviet Union is ready to take action to the effect that if Chiang Ting-fu remains in the Security Council as the representative of China (it is said he could even assume chairmanship of the Security Council this year), the Soviet Union will refuse to attend Security Council meetings. Vishinsky asked my views on this matter. I indicated immediately that China's Foreign Ministry can issue such a statement, adding that my telegram in this connection can reach Beijing on January 7 and that the statement in the name of Foreign Minister Zhou Enlai could be dispatched on the 8th or 9th of January. I asked Vishinsky whether copies of the statement need to be sent to member states of the Security Council, the Soviet Union, Britain, the U.S., France, etc., besides the U.N. Security Council and the Secretary-General. He answered in the affirmative, adding that the Soviet Union can act on the basis of the telegram from China and that he was asking my views in his capacity as Foreign Minister. I have given him a formal consent. Please act promptly upon receiving this telegram, so that the telegram containing the statement may be dispatched before Enlai's departure. Besides sending telegrams to the U.N. Secretary-General and Security Council, telegrams including the telegram to the U.N. should also be dispatched to the Foreign

---

* This is the main part of a telegram to Zhou Enlai and the Party's Central Committee from Mao Zedong who was on visit in the Soviet Union.

Ministries of the Soviet Union, Britain, the U.S., France, etc. Please tell me how this matter is handled and whether you can manage to dispatch them on January 9.

(From the original manuscript)

ON CHINA'S SENDING REPRESENTATIVES TO THE UNITED NATIONS AND SOME OTHER MATTERS*

(*January 13, 1950*)

(1) I agree to your telegram of January 13 on implementing the order on requisition of foreign military barracks and getting prepared for the United States to withdraw all its old consulates in China.

(2) I agree to the Shanghai Military Control Commission's directly taking over or requisitioning the materiel left in Shanghai by the U.S. Economic Cooperation Administration.[82]

(3) On the question of taking over the assets in Hong Kong left by the bogus regime, please decide on measures proposed by the Foreign Ministry and the Central Financial and Economic Committee.[83] I do not have specific views on this matter.

(4) Vishinsky[81] came for discussion this evening and suggested that China cable the United Nations about sending her own representatives to the U.N. to replace the Kuomintang representatives. In view of the fact that there is now intense struggle in the Security Council over the question of Kuomintang representation, with the Soviet Union supporting our statement for expelling the Kuomintang representative and the majority of countries including the U.S. and Britain against expulsion, a further expression of China's attitude is necessary, but another telegram could be dispatched a week later. I expressed agreement with his suggestion. The Central Committee please consider who should head the Chinese delegation to the U.N., and let me know by telegram; a decision will be taken after consultation with Enlai upon his arrival here.

(From the original manuscript)

---

* This is the main part of a telegram to Liu Shaoqi from Mao Zedong who was on visit in the Soviet Union.

IN REFUTATION OF DEAN ACHESON'S SHAMELESS FABRICATIONS*

(*January 19, 1950*)

Xinhua, Beijing, January 20—Hu Qiaomu, director of the Press Administration of the Central People's Government, in a statement to a correspondent of Xinhua News Agency, refuted the shameless fabrications of U.S. Secretary of State Dean Acheson.

Director Hu Qiaomu stated: U.S. Secretary of State Dean Acheson has manufactured a string of fabrications in his lengthy speech at the American National Press Club on January 12. The officials of American imperialism with Acheson and his kind as representatives have day by day become political charlatans of the lowest caliber who cannot live without resorting to the most shameless fabrications. This indicates the extent to which U.S. imperialist system has degenerated spiritually. Acheson's speech was filled with fabrications disguising the realities of the U.S. aggressive policy. For instance, he said, "Our interests have been parallel to the interests of the people of Asia." When referring to China he said that "there was no conflict but parallelism" between American interests and the interests of the people of China, and "from the time of the announcement of the Open Door Policy through the Nine-Power Treaty to the very latest resolution of the General Assembly of the United Nations, we have stated that principle and we believe it." Every word here is a lie. To bore into China by all possible means and turn China into an American colony—this is the basic policy of the United States. Helping Chiang Kai-shek with six billion American dollars in the last few years to butcher several million Chinese people—this is the so-called no conflict but parallelism between American interests and the interests of the people of China.

Director Hu Qiaomu went on to say, "These are not the most shameless

---

* This article was written by Mao Zedong when he was on visit in the Soviet Union, and was published as an interview given by Hu Qiaomu, director of the Press Administration of the Central People's Government.

fabrications of Acheson. The most shameless ones are those he made on Sino-Soviet relations.

Acheson said:

> The Soviet Union is detaching the northern areas of China from China and attaching it to the Soviet Union. This process is complete in Outer Mongolia. It is nearly complete in Manchuria and I am sure that in Inner Mongolia and in Xinjiang there are very happy reports coming from Soviet agents to Moscow. This is what is going on. It is the detachment of these whole areas, vast areas—populated by Chinese —detachment of these areas from China, and their attachment to the Soviet Union. That the Soviet Union is taking four northern areas of China is the single most significant, most important fact in the relations of any foreign power with Asia. What does that mean for us? Something very very important.

The allegations on Sino-Soviet relations made by the U.S. State Department have their own history. "The assertion of Soviet assistance to the Chinese Communist Party is groundless"—this was often said by the gentlemen of the U.S. State Department before 1948. This was because at that time these gentlemen thought that there appeared to be still hope for the American war gamble in China. "The Soviet Union attempts to control China"—this allegation was made by the U.S. State Department in 1949 in its White Paper on the China question. This was because at that time the gentlemen of the U.S. State Department felt that they would soon lose all their stakes in China. "The Soviet Union has occupied the four northern areas of China"—this allegation was made on January 12, 1950. This was because the United States had completely lost in its gamble on the mainland of China and only Taiwan was left on which it seems they still contemplate certain designs. Thank god, before the sweeping drive of the Chinese people and the Chinese People's Liberation Army, the U.S. imperialists have now no better means than that of manufacturing such fabrications. Fabrications and slanders of low intelligence such as that the Chinese Communist Party is a lackey of the Soviet Union and that the Soviet Union has annexed, is annexing or will annex China, will only evoke the indignation of the Chinese and Soviet peoples and strengthen the friendly cooperation between China and the Soviet Union. Apart from this there will be no other result.

The system of imperialism which is rotten to the core and full of contradictions displays itself in such an interesting way that two days later than Acheson's speech of low intelligence, i.e., on January 14, 1950, a resounding smack was given to Acheson by Angus Ward, former U.S.

consul-general at Shenyang, who was arrested, tried and deported by the People's Government of China.

According to a January 14 Washington dispatch of Tass:

> The recently returned United States consul-general at Shenyang, Ward, conferred with State Department officials in Washington. Afterward he said in response to press questions that he had not seen any evidence of Soviet control over Manchuria except that the Soviet Union had exercised treaty rights in connection with the joint control of the railroad. He said he had not observed any indications of Soviet efforts to incorporate Manchuria.... In response to the question whether the Communist authorities in Manchuria are under the close control of Beijing, he replied that all Communist governments exercise highly centralized control and as far as he knew, Manchuria is part of Communist China.

People can see for themselves what has happened in the Western hemisphere. One person says, Manchuria is being detached by the Soviet Union. Another says, no such thing was seen. Both these persons are no other than well-known officials of the U.S. State Department.

(From *People's Daily*, January 21, 1950)

PREREQUISITES TO THE ESTABLISHMENT OF DIPLOMATIC RELATIONS BETWEEN CHINA AND BRITAIN*

(February 8, 1950)

As the British chargè d'affaires Hutchinson is expected to arrive in Beijing soon, please tell the Foreign Ministry that, in broaching the initial procedures for the establishment of diplomatic relations to Hutchinson when he calls after arrival, it should right away tell him that the most important thing is the relationship between Britain and the remnants of the Chiang kai-shek reactionaries. If diplomatic relations are to be established between Britain and the Central People's Government of the People's Republic of China, Britain should not at the same time carry on any diplomatic intercourse with the Kuomintang government. Regrettably, in the Security Council and other bodies of the United Nations the British representatives have continued to recognize Kuomintang representation as legitimate and refused to accept the representatives of the People's Republic of China—this is a prerequisite issue for the establishment of Sino-British diplomatic relations that has to be resolved. Secondly, clarification must be made on the attitude of the British-Hong Kong government toward the Kuomintang government's official representatives and establishments and all their state assets in Hong Kong, as this and similar matters are also issues relating to severance of relations with the Kuomintang government. See how Hutchinson responds. As to the question of taking back the British barracks, this may not be brought up for the time being.

(From the original manuscript)

---

* This is part of a telegram to Liu Shaoqi from Mao Zedong who was on visit in the Soviet Union.

THE GREAT SIGNIFICANCE OF THE CONCLUSION OF THE SINO-SOVIET TREATY AND AGREEMENTS*

(*April 11, 1950*)

I

We have before now pointed out that the two basic conditions for consolidating the victory of the revolution are the carrying through of the people's democratic dictatorship and the unity with international friends. The recently signed Sino-Soviet treaty[76] and agreements have codified the friendship between the two great countries—China and the Soviet Union. They ensure for us a reliable ally, facilitate our freely carrying out of national reconstruction, and enable us jointly to cope with possible imperialist aggression and achieve world peace.
(From *People's Daily*, April 13, 1950)

II

An important task completed by the Central People's Government of the People's Republic of China since its establishment has been the conclusion of the Sino-Soviet Treaty. This is of great significance for our country, and people all over China have expressed their opinions about it. Many comrades present here today have spoken unanimously of its great significance. However, in what circumstances did we conclude this treaty? In the circumstances of having defeated one of our enemies, i.e. the domestic reaction: we have defeated the reactionaries of the Chiang Kai-shek clique, who are supported by foreign

---

* These are excerpts from a speech by Mao Zedong at the Sixth Meeting of the Central People's Government Council.

reactionaries. We have also expelled the latter beyond the bounds of China, basically expelled them. But reactionaries still exist in the world in the form of foreign imperialism. Our domestic situation is still difficult, and so we need friends.... Our relations, our friendship, with the Soviet Union ought to be modified, that is, fixed legally by means of a treaty, so as to form an alliance.... If the imperialists prepare to attack us we shall have someone to help us. This treaty is a treaty of patriotism. Comrades have just now mentioned this point. It is correct. As it is also an internationalist treaty, it is one of internationalism. Premier and concurrently Foreign Minister Zhou Enlai and many council members present have aired their views. All are very good. Since no one else has anything to say, let us take a vote now, that is, to approve this treaty.

(From the manuscript revised by Mao Zedong)

REPLY ON RECEIVING THE CREDENTIALS PRESENTED BY INDIAN AMBASSADOR TO CHINA KAVALAM M. PANIKKAR

(*May 20, 1950*)

Mr. Ambassador:

I take great pleasure in receiving the credentials of the President of the Republic of India presented by you, and thank you, Mr. Ambassador, for your greetings.

Between our two countries, China and India, which have a common boundary, there are long-standing, close relations in both history and culture; and in recent centuries they have undertaken similar long and courageous struggles to free themselves from national adversity. There exist between our peoples a profound understanding, sympathy and concern. The present formal establishment of diplomatic relations between China and India will not only further develop and consolidate the friendship which already exists between our peoples, but the concomitant sincere cooperation of the peoples of these two great Asian countries will greatly contribute to the lasting peace of Asia and the world.

I warmly welcome your assuming the post of the first Ambassador Extraordinary and Plenipotentiary of the Republic of India to the People's Republic of China, and am ready to render assistance to your work in strengthening the cooperation between our two countries.

I wish strength and prosperity to your country and people, and good health to the head of your state.

(From *People's Daily*, May 21, 1950)

A NEW WORLD WAR CAN BE AVERTED*

(June 6, 1950)

The present international situation is favorable to us. The world front of peace and democracy headed by the Soviet Union is stronger than it was last year. The people's movement for peace and against war has made headway in all countries. The national liberation movements to throw off the yoke of imperialism have greatly expanded, and the emerging mass movements of the Japanese and the German people against U.S. occupation and the growing people's liberation struggles of the oppressed nations in the East are especially noteworthy. At the same time, contradictions have developed between the imperialist countries, primarily between the United States and Britain. Quarrels among the different groups of the U.S. bourgeoisie and of the British bourgeoisie have also increased. In contrast, there is strong unity between the Soviet Union and the People's Democracies and among the latter. The new treaty between China and the Soviet Union,[76] which is of great and historic significance, has strengthened the friendly relations between the two countries; it enables us to carry on our national reconstruction more freely and more speedily and at the same time promotes the mighty struggle of the people of the world for peace and democracy and against war and oppression. The threat of war from the imperialist camp still exists, and so does the possibility of a third world war. However, the forces fighting to check the danger of war and prevent the outbreak of a third world war are growing rapidly, and the level of political consciousness of most of the world's people is rising. A new world war can be averted, provided the Communist Parties of the world continue to unite all possible forces for peace and democracy and help their further development. The war rumors spread by the Kuomintang reactionaries are designed to deceive the people, they are groundless.

(From *People's Daily*, June 13, 1950)

---

* These are excerpts from Mao Zedong's written report, "Fight for a Fundamental Turn for the Better in the Nation's Financial and Economic Situation," to the Third Plenary Session of the Seventh Central Committee of the Communist Party of China.

DEFEAT ANY PROVOCATION OF U.S. IMPERIALISM*

(June 28, 1950)

The Chinese people affirmed long ago that the affairs of the various countries of the world should be run by the peoples of the respective countries themselves, and the affairs of Asia should be run by the peoples of Asia themselves and not by the United States. The United States' aggression in Asia will only arouse the extensive and resolute resistance of the peoples of Asia. On January 5 this year Truman still stated that the United States would not interfere in Taiwan. Now he himself proves that that statement was false,[84] and that he has torn to shreds all the international agreements under which the United States has undertaken not to interfere in China's internal affairs. This open exposure by the United States of its true imperialist features is beneficial to the people of China and the peoples of Asia. U.S. intervention in the internal affairs of Korea, the Philippines, Vietnam and other countries is wholly unjustified. The sympathy of all Chinese people and the broad masses of the world's people is on the side of the victims of aggression and most certainly not on the side of U.S. imperialism. They will neither be bribed by imperialism, nor cowed by it. Imperialism is outwardly strong but inwardly feeble, because it has no support among the people. People throughout China and the world, unite and prepare adequately to defeat any provocation of U.S. imperialism!

(From *People's Daily*, June 29, 1950)

---

* This is Mao Zedong's speech at the Eighth Meeting of the Central People's Government Council.

ON THE DECISION TO SEND VOLUNTEERS TO FIGHT IN KOREA*

(*October 2, 1950*)

(1) We have decided to send part of our troops, in the name of volunteers, to Korea to fight against the armed forces of the United States and its lackey Syngman Rhee[85] and to aid the Korean comrades. We deem this essential. If all of Korea were occupied by the Americans and the Korean revolutionary forces suffered a fundamental defeat, the U.S. aggressors would grow more rampant, which would run counter to the interests of the whole of the East.

(2) We deem that since we decide to dispatch Chinese troops to fight against the Americans in Korea, then first, this must be capable of resolving the problem, i.e., be prepared to wipe out and drive away the aggressor troops of the U.S. and other countries in Korea, and second, as Chinese troops (though sent in the name of volunteers) will fight American troops in Korea, we should be prepared for the U.S. declaring a state of war with China and at least using its air force to bomb a number of big cities and industrial bases in China and its navy to attack our coastal regions.

(3) The first of the two above questions is whether the Chinese troops will be able to annihilate the U.S. troops in Korea, thus effectively solve the Korean issue. If only our troops can wipe out the U.S. troops in Korea, mainly their Eighth Army (a veteran army with combat capability), then though the second question (the U.S. declaring war on China) may still remain a grave one, the situation will become favorable to the revolutionary front and China. In other words, with the Korean issue concluded in fact with victory over the U.S. armed forces (in form the issue may not yet be concluded with the United States for a considerably long time refusing to acknowledge Korean victory), even if the United States has declared war against China, that war probably will not be very large in scale, nor a prolonged one. In our view, the most disadvantageous scenario would be Chinese troops failing to annihilate large

---

* This is the main part of a telegram from Mao Zedong to J. V. Stalin.

numbers of the U.S. troops in Korea, resulting in a stalemate of troop confrontation, while the United States would have entered a state of war against China openly, thus frustrating China's plan of economic reconstruction, which has already begun, and causing dissatisfaction among the Chinese national bourgeoisie and some other people (who are very afraid of war).

(4) In the present circumstances we have decided to move from October 15[87] 12 divisions (five or six are not sufficient), which have previously been mustered in southern Manchuria,[86] and into appropriate areas in northern Korea (not necessarily up to the 38th Parallel[88]). On the one hand, these troops will fight enemy troops that dare to attack areas north of the 38th Parallel, initially only fighting defensive battles, annihilating small contingents of enemy troops and sizing up all aspects of the situation. On the other hand, we are awaiting the arrival of Soviet weaponry for reequipment of our troops with a view to going over to the counteroffensive in cooperation with the Korean comrades and wiping out the U.S. aggressor troops.

(5) According to our knowledge, each U.S. army (composed of two infantry divisions and one mechanized division) is equipped with 1,500 pieces of artillery of various types, including tank guns and AA guns, with calibers ranging from 7 cm to 24 cm. Our army (composed of three divisions) has only 36 such heavy guns. The enemy has control of the air, while the first batch of the Chinese Air Force now undergoing training will be able to go into operation with some 300 combat aircraft only in February 1951. Therefore, at the present moment our troops do not have the certainty of annihilating a whole U.S. army in one campaign. However, since the decision has already been taken to fight the Americans, we should be prepared, when the U.S. high command concentrates a whole army to fight a campaign against us on the battlefield, to counter the enemy with a military strength four times as strong (i.e., countering one enemy army with four of our armies) and with firepower one-and-a-half to two times as strong (i.e., countering the 1,500 pieces of enemy artillery of over 7-cm caliber with 2,200 to 3,000 pieces of our artillery of similar caliber), and should have the certainty of annihilating one enemy army thoroughly and completely.

(6) In addition to the above-mentioned 12 divisions, we are moving 24 divisions from areas south of the Yangtze River and from the Shaanxi-Gansu area along the Longhai, Tianjin-Pukou and Beining railway lines as the second and third batches of forces for aiding Korea, to be put into operation one by one next spring and summer in view of the evolving situation.

(From the original manuscript)

ORDER TO ORGANIZE THE CHINESE PEOPLE'S VOLUNTEERS

(October 8, 1950)

To Peng, Gao, He, Deng, Hong, Xie[89] and other leading comrades of the Chinese People's Volunteers at all levels:

1. In order to assist the Korean people's war of liberation against the attacks of U.S. imperialism and its running dogs, thereby safeguarding the interests of the people of Korea, China and the other countries in the East, I hereby order to change the Northeastern Border Defense Army into the Chinese People's Volunteers, march speedily to Korea and join the Korean comrades in fighting the aggressors and winning a glorious victory.

2. The Chinese People's Volunteers will have under its command the 13th Army with its subordinate 38th, 39th, 40th and 42nd Corps, and the Frontier Defense Artillery Headquarters with its subordinate 1st, 2nd and 8th Divisions. The above units must complete their preparations promptly and await orders to set off.

3. Comrade Peng Dehuai is appointed Commander and concurrently Political Commissar of the Chinese People's Volunteers.

4. The Chinese People's Volunteers will have the Northeast Administrative Area as their general rear base, and all rear work, supplies and matters in connection with assistance to Korean comrades are to be under the management and direction of, and to be guaranteed by, Comrade Gao Gang, Commander and concurrently Political Commissar of the Northeast Military Area.

5. While in Korea, the Chinese People's Volunteers must show fraternal love and respect for the people, the People's Army, the Democratic Government, the Workers' (Communist) Party and the other democratic parties of Korea and for Comrade Kim Il Sung, the leader of the Korean people, and strictly observe military and political discipline. This is a most important political basis for ensuring the fulfilment of your military task.

6. You must fully anticipate various possible and inevitable difficulties and

be prepared to overcome them with great enthusiasm, courage, care and stamina. At present, the general international and domestic situation is favorable to us, not to the aggressors. So long as you comrades are firm and brave and are good at uniting with the local people and at fighting the aggressors, final victory will be ours.

Mao Zedong
Chairman of the Chinese People's
Revolutionary Military Commission
October 8, 1950, Beijing
(From the manuscript revised by Mao Zedong)

OUR TROOPS SHOULD AND MUST ENTER KOREA TO JOIN THE FIGHTING*

(October 13, 1950)

(1) Consultations with comrades of the Political Bureau have resulted in the consensus that it is advantageous for our troops to move into Korea. In the first stage our troops can single out the puppet troops[90] as our target of attack. Our troops are certain of victory in dealing with the puppet troops and can open up base areas in the vast mountainous regions of Korea north of the Wonsan-Pyongyang line, thereby heartening the Korean people. In the first stage, with the wiping out of several divisions of the puppet troops, the situation in Korea will take a turn to our advantage.

(2) Our adoption of the above-mentioned positive policy is extremely advantageous to China, Korea, the East and indeed the world as a whole. Conversely, if we do not send our troops and let the enemy press forward to the banks of the Yalu River, the arrogance of the domestic and international reactionaries will be inflated, causing disadvantages to all concerned, first of all to northeast China, with the entire northeast border-guard forces pinned down and the electrical power of southern Manchuria[86] brought under enemy control.

In short, we deem that we should and must join the fighting in Korea. Participation will be most advantageous, while nonparticipation will be detrimental.

(From the original manuscript)

---

* These are excerpts from a telegram from Mao Zedong to Zhou Enlai, who was then visiting the Soviet Union.

NO ROOM FOR SAY BY ANY FOREIGN COUNTRY IN THE MATTER OF CHINESE TROOPS ENTERING TIBET*

(*October 28, 1950*)

Zhou[91] and Ministry of Foreign Affairs:

Shen Jian's reply is quite correct,[92] though his attitude should have been stronger. He should have said that Chinese troops must reach all places in Tibet that should be reached, and that there is no room for say by any foreign country in this matter, whether the local government of Tibet is willing to negotiate or not and whatever the outcome of the negotiations might be.

Mao Zedong
October 28
(From the original manuscript)

---

* These are comments Mao Zedong wrote on the report submitted by Yuan Zhongxian, Chinese ambassador to India, regarding Indian Deputy Foreign Secretary Krishna Menon's talk with Shen Jian, political counselor of the Chinese embassy in India, on the question of Tibet.

THE CHINESE PEOPLE'S VOLUNTEERS SHOULD CHERISH EVERY HILL, EVERY RIVER, EVERY TREE AND EVERY BLADE OF GRASS IN KOREA*

(January 19, 1951)

The Korean Workers' Party and People's Army headed by Comrade Kim Il Sung have achieved great successes during the past five years of struggle in Korea. Resolutely opposed to imperialism and feudalism, they have founded a people's political regime to serve the people, formed the courageous People's Army and established friendly relations with the Soviet Union, China and other people's states. Now they are waging a heroic struggle against the U.S. invaders and the Syngman Rhee bandit army. Therefore, all Chinese People's Volunteers in Korea must conscientiously learn from the Korean comrades, and whole-heartedly support the Korean people, the government of the Democratic People's Republic of Korea, the Korean People's Army, the Korean Workers' Party and Comrade Kim Il Sung, the leader of the Korean people. The Chinese and Korean comrades should unite as closely as brothers, go through thick and thin together, stick together in life and death and fight to the end to defeat their common enemy. The Chinese comrades must regard Korea's cause as their own, and the commanders and fighters must be educated to cherish every hill, every river, every tree and every blade of grass in Korea and not take a single needle or thread from the Korean people, just the way we think and do in our own country. This is the political basis for victory. So long as we act this way, final victory will be assured.

(From the original manuscript)

---

* This paragraph was added by Mao Zedong in looking over the draft of a report to be dilivered by Peng Dehuai, commander and political commissar of the Chinese People's Volunteers, to a joint meeting of senior officers of Chinese and Korean armies.

CONGRATULATORY SPEECH AT INDIA'S NATIONAL DAY PARTY HOSTED BY THE INDIAN AMBASSADOR TO CHINA

(January 26, 1951)

The Indian nation is a great nation, and the Indian people is an excellent people. For thousands of years, excellent friendship has existed between the two nations and peoples of China and India. Today, in celebrating the National Day of India, we hope that the two nations of China and India will continue to unite to strive for peace. People all over the world need peace, only a few people want war. India, China, the Soviet Union and all other peace-loving countries and people, unite to strive for peace in the Far East and the whole world. Greetings on the National Day of India and best wishes to the Indian people and your President.

(From *People's Daily*, January 27, 1951)

THE WORLD FROM NOW ON MUST BE A WORLD THAT BELONGS TO THE PEOPLE*

(*October 23, 1951*)

The great struggle to resist U.S. aggression and aid Korea is going on and must go on until the U.S. government is willing to come to a peaceful settlement. We have no intention of encroaching on any country; we are only opposing imperialist aggression against our country. As everyone knows, the Chinese people would not be fighting U.S. forces if they had not occupied our Taiwan, invaded the Democratic People's Republic of Korea and pushed on to our northeastern borders. But since the U.S. aggressors have attacked us, we cannot but raise the banner of anti-aggression. This is absolutely necessary and perfectly just, and the whole nation understands that it is so. To press on with this struggle, which is essential and just, we must continue to stiffen our efforts in resisting U.S. aggression and aiding Korea and must increase production and practice economy to support the Chinese People's Volunteers. This is the central task of the Chinese people today and accordingly the central task of our present meeting.

We have long affirmed that the Korean question should be settled by peaceful means, and this is still our position. If the U.S. government is willing to settle the question on a fair and reasonable basis instead of sabotaging and obstructing the progress of negotiations in various underhand ways as it has done in the past, it will be possible for the Korean armistice negotiations to succeed; otherwise it will be impossible.

In the two years since the founding of the People's Republic of China, we have won great victories in all fields of work. We have won these victories by relying on all the forces that can be united. Within the country, we have relied on the solid unity of all the ethnic groups, democratic classes, democratic parties, people's organizations and patriotic democrats under the leadership of the working class and the Communist Party. Internationally, we have relied

---

* This is part of Mao Zedong's opening address to the Third Session of the First National Committee of the Chinese People's Political Consultative Conference.

on the solid unity of the camp of peace and democracy headed by the Soviet Union and on the profound sympathy of the peace-loving people throughout the world. Hence our great victories in all spheres of work, which were not what our enemies had expected. Our enemies thought that since the new-born People's Republic of China was faced with a lot of difficulties and since on top of that they were launching a war of aggression against us, we would not be able to overcome our difficulties or deal counterblows to the aggressors. Contrary to their expectation, we have proved able to overcome our difficulties, deal counterblows to the aggressors and win great victories. Our enemies are short-sighted, they fail to see the strength of our great domestic and international unity and fail to realize that the founding of the People's Republic of China has once and for all put an end to the days when the Chinese people could be bullied by foreign imperialists. Nor do they realize that the birth of the socialist Soviet Union, the People's Republic of China and the People's Democracies, the solid unity between the two great countries of China and the Soviet Union based on the Treaty of Friendship, Alliance and Mutual Assistance,[76] the solid unity of the entire camp of peace and democracy and the profound sympathy of the peace-loving people of the world for this great camp have ended for good the era in which imperialism could dominate the world. Our enemies fail to see all this and still want to bully the People's Republic of China and dominate the world. But, comrades, I can say with confidence that their design is crazy, and futile, and impossible of achievement. Contrary to their thinking, the People's Republic of China will brook no bullying, the great peace camp headed by the Soviet Union will brook no encroachment, and the peace-loving people of the world will not be taken in. Comrades, the victory of the great October Socialist Revolution of the Soviet Union has assured the prospect of victory of the people of the world, and today this prospect has developed and reinforced with the founding of the People's Republic of China and the People's Democracies. It is true that, in the historical period following World War I and the October Revolution in Russia, three imperialist powers—Germany, Italy and Japan—made attempts to dominate the world; this happened before the founding of the People's Republic of China and the People's Democracies. But what came of it? Didn't the attempts of the three imperialist powers prove to be crazy and futile? Didn't the results turn out to be the opposite of what they wanted? Didn't the imperialists who aimed at domination get struck down themselves? Today things are entirely different; the great People's Republic of China has been founded, the People's Democracies have been established, the level of political consciousness of the people of the world has been raised, the struggle for national liberation has been surging ahead all over Asia and in North Africa, the strength of the imperialist bloc as a whole has been drastically weakened and, what is of vital importance, the strength of the Soviet Union, our closest ally, has been greatly enhanced. In these circumstances, isn't the outcome quite predictable if any imperialist power tries to follow in the footsteps of the three aggressors, Germany, Italy and Japan? In a word, the world from now on must be a world that belongs to the people, with the people of each country governing themselves, and definitely not a world where imperialism and its lackeys can continue to ride roughshod. I hope that the people of our country will do a good job of uniting themselves, uniting with our ally the Soviet Union, uniting with all the People's Democracies and uniting with all nations and peoples of the world that sympathize with us, and continue to advance to victory in the struggle against aggression, to victory in building our great country, to victory in the defense of a lasting world peace. Comrades, I am confident that, so long as we do all this, victory will decidedly be ours.

(From *People's Daily*, October 24, 1951)

SUCCESS OF THE KOREAN ARMISTICE NEGOTIATIONS HINGES ON WHETHER THE U.S. GOVERNMENT IS SINCERE*

(February 14, 1952)

We will not encroach on any country. The struggle waged by the Chinese People's Volunteers in Korea is for the purpose of repulsing the acts of aggression of the U.S. imperialists advancing toward our borders. In the armistice negotiations between the two belligerent sides, held at Kaesong and then Panmunjong since July last year, the representatives of the Korean People's Army and the Chinese People's Volunteers have made greatest efforts to promote the success of the negotiations. Had it not been for the deliberate procrastination of the American side, the negotiations would have succeeded long ago. The success or failure of future negotiations still hinges on whether the U.S. government is sincere about resolving the Korean question peacefully. If the U.S. government is sincere, as we are, about resolving the Korean question by peaceful means, then it will be possible for the armistice negotiations to succeed.

(From the original manuscript)

---

* This is a paragraph added by Mao Zedong to the draft of a speech to be delivered by Zhou Enlai at a meeting in commemoration of the second anniversary of the signing of the Sino-Soviet Treaty of Friendship, Alliance and Mutual Assistance.

TELEGRAM TO J. V. STALIN IN CELEBRATION OF THE SEVENTH ANNIVERSARY OF VICTORY IN THE WAR OF RESISTANCE AGAINST JAPAN

(September 2, 1952)

To Generalissimo Stalin:

On the occasion of the seventh anniversary of victory in the War of Resistance Against Japan, please accept the warm congratulations and heartfelt thanks of myself, the Chinese People's Liberation Army and the entire people of China to you and to the armed forces and people of the Soviet Union.

The Soviet Union rendered great assistance to the Chinese people in the War of Resistance Against Japan, and by annihilating the Japanese Kwantung Army, which was the main force of Japan, the Soviet armed forces helped the Chinese people win final victory in the War of Resistance. The fraternal assistance extended to the Chinese people by the Soviet Union in the course of China's rehabilitation and reconstruction has helped the speedy consolidation and growth of the strength of the Chinese people.

Now, at a time when Japanese militarism is being revived and Japanese forces of aggression are reemerging, the unbreakable friendly alliance between China and the Soviet Union is a powerful guarantee for deterring new aggression by Japan and any other countries colluding with Japan in acts of aggression and for safeguarding peace in the East and the world as a whole.

Long live the unbreakable and great friendship between the People's Republic of China and the Union of Soviet Socialist Republics!

Mao Zedong
Chairman of the Central People's Government
of the People's Republic of China
September 2, 1952
(From *People's Daily*, September 3, 1952)

FIGHT ON UNTIL U.S. IMPERIALISM IS WILLING TO GIVE UP*

(February 7, 1953)

The struggle to resist U.S. aggression and aid Korea should be strengthened. As U.S. imperialism insists on detaining Chinese and Korean POWs, sabotaging the armistice negotiations, and attempting vainly to expand its war of aggression in Korea, the struggle to resist U.S. aggression and aid Korea must continue to be strengthened. We are for peace, but so long as U.S. imperialism does not give up its arrogant and unreasonable demands and its schemes to expand aggression, the determination of the Chinese people is to fight on together with the Korean people. This is not because we are warlike. We are willing to stop fighting immediately and leave other matters to be resolved in the future. However, U.S. imperialism is not willing to do so. Well, then, fighting has to continue. We are prepared to fight as many years as U.S. imperialism wants to fight, fight on until U.S. imperialism is willing to give up, or until complete victory is won by the Chinese and Korean peoples.

(From the news release in *People's Daily*, February 8, 1953)

---

* These are excerpts from the speech by Mao Zedong at the Fourth Meeting of the First National Committee of the Chinese People's Political Consultative Conference.

TELEGRAM TO THE CONGRESS OF INDIANS IN SOUTH AFRICA

(*May 28, 1954*)

To Mr. Kazalia and Mr. Mistri,
Joint Honorary Secretaries,
Congress of Indians in South Africa:

On behalf of the people of China, I should like to express our full support to the just position of the nonwhite people in South Africa (including Indians and other Asian and African people) in fighting for their democratic rights and against racial discrimination and racial oppression. I wish the congress success in the cause of uniting the Indians and all the people in South Africa, white and nonwhite, for peace, freedom, democracy and progress.

Mao Zedong
May 28, 1954, Beijing
(From *People's Daily*, May 29, 1954)

ON THE INTERMEDIATE ZONE, PEACEFUL COEXISTENCE, SINO-BRITISH AND SINO-U.S. RELATIONS*

(*August 24, 1954*)

The People's Government, democratic parties and mass organizations of China all welcome your visit to China and regard you as friends. Please feel at home here. It is very good that you have come to China to see for yourselves.

There must be many areas where we still lack mutual understanding. However, since the beginning of World War II Sino-British relations have radically changed, although this does not mean that there are no disputes and differences of opinion between us, nor that there is no difference between the social systems of our two countries. In the past Japan dominated China. That was quite a few years ago. After the war with Japan the United States replaced Japan and helped Chiang Kai-shek to bully us. In those two periods of time Britain changed its attitude toward China. There are not many fundamental disputes between us, are there? This is a basic point.

Our relations with France are similar. In the past the problem was that of the Japanese, now it is the American. We too have an ocean beside us, called the Pacific Ocean, yet the Pacific Ocean is by no means pacific. There are some questions we do not understand. For instance, Australia signed a treaty[93] with the United States, alleging that its purpose was to oppose the Communist Party and that we were out to commit aggression against Australia, so it was necessary for Australia to conclude such a treaty with the United States and New Zealand for joint opposition against communism. The hue and cry of anti-communism has been quite loud, especially in the recent past. It is alleged that the Chinese have committed a great crime, mainly in driving out a very good guy called Chiang Kai-shek, who is said to be the nicest guy possessing

---

* These are excerpts from Mao Zedong's talk with a delegation of the British Labour Party.

perfect virtue and the whole truth. This is the "bad thing" we are supposed to have done. I have read an article written by Mr. Bevan,[94] in which he says the Americans have invented a new kind of logic—the Chinese have committed aggression against themselves.

The Americans allege that we have committed a big crime, and the issue is not yet resolved even now. On the question of whether Chiang Kai-shek is a good man or a bad man, there are two views. In the eyes of the United States, Chiang Kai-shek is better than we are. Your view is somewhat different, for you have long refused to recognize Chiang Kai-shek. That is why I say we do not have fundamental divergences. On the question of Japan we do not have a fundamental divergence either, as this question is today out of the control of Britain. So we are very pleased to meet you.

There is another point I should like to make. That is, so-called anti-communism is not an entirely true thing. As I see it, the United States is using anti-communism as a pretext to attain its own ulterior motives, firstly to occupy the intermediate zone stretching from Japan to Britain. Situated in North America, the United States is on the other side of this intermediate zone, while the Soviet Union and China are on this side of the zone. The objective of the United States is to occupy the countries in this vast intermediate zone, bully them, control their economies, establish military bases on their territory, and see to it that they are increasingly weakened—with Japan and Germany included among them.

You ask if there can be peaceful coexistence between us and your socialism. I think, yes. Then a question arises: Can there be coexistence only with this kind of socialism, and not with other things? Nonsocialist things, such as capitalism, imperialism, feudal kingdoms, etc.? I think the answer is also yes; only one condition is needed, i.e., both sides must be willing to coexist. Why? Because we think that different social systems can coexist peacefully.

There can also be cooperation between us. First of all, there will not be any war between us. Why fight a war? Not only would we not fight a war with the Labour Party, we would not fight a war with the Conservative Party either.

You ask how the international situation is likely to evolve. In my view, the present international situation is good; there have been some changes after the Geneva Conference.[95] Some people criticized you, saying that coming to China you would walk into a trap. It was mainly Americans that said so. I think you would be well advised not to listen to them. History is measured in periods of years; one should not take transitory talk as a criterion, and should not listen too much to such talk. China is a backward country just beginning to change her face; economically and culturally she lags behind the Western countries. But she is beginning to change and has already attained the conditions for change. For an agricultural country like China to change into an industrialized country, several decades are needed, help from others is needed, and, first of all, a peaceful environment is needed. It is difficult to get things done if you have to fight frequent wars, and the maintenance of a large number of troops would hamper economic development. If you agree, we will continue to work for a peaceful international environment. I think this is also a need for Britain and France. Our country is still very poor and it would be good if we could have peace for several decades. Do you agree? If you do, let us conclude a treaty—a no-war pact for several decades. Of course, I do not mean for this treaty to be signed this afternoon. Let us oppose whoever wishes to make war. We have no assets other than the common people. Great numbers of people and a vast expanse of territory—these are our two assets. As for modernizing the country, it will take a great deal of time and energy. Countries like China and the Soviet Union rely mainly on domestic markets, not on markets abroad. This does not mean that we do not want links and trade with other countries. On the contrary, links and trade are needed and isolation is not what we want. Two basic conditions make our cooperation fully possible. One, both of us want peace and are not willing to fight wars. Two, each country is engaged in its own national reconstruction and so needs to do business. Peace and trade, on these two points at least we can agree. Isn't that so?

In my view, our British Labour Party friends do not properly understand the Soviet Union. Britain is a big country, and so is the Soviet Union. When these two countries are not on good terms, problems in world peace crop up. The question is not for China to move away from the Soviet Union, but for Britain to move closer to the Soviet Union. My advice is for you to move closer to the Soviet Union. This is our suggestion. Why is it that you dislike the Soviet Union so much?

China, the Soviet Union, Britain and all other countries should move closer to one another. Defrost one's views, and things will improve. How about that? Let me repeat. This includes the United States as well. We hope the United States will also adopt a policy of peaceful coexistence. If a big country like the United States does not want peace, we shall not have tranquillity, nobody will have tranquillity. Britons are in a better position to do such persuasion, for the abuses between us and Americans are rather heated. In my view, not the majority, but a small number of Americans are against China.

Why is China not allowed to join the Southern-Asian Treaty[96]? We are ready to join, but they do not want us to. What's wrong with China, the Soviet Union, Britain, the United States and France all joining it?

The Americans have acted unseemly. They are supporting Chiang Kai-shek in harassing our mainland almost every day. So you would do well to advise the Americans to call off their Seventh Fleet. Those few ships are easy to handle—call them off, and off they will go. The Americans are going against the international trend and against the trend of history. They are only a minority of the Americans, such as J. F. Dulles[97] and his ilk. We hope our friends in the Labour Party will try to persuade the Americans to do the following:

(1) Withdraw the Seventh Fleet and refrain from meddling in the affairs of Taiwan, because Taiwan is part of China's territory.

(2) Do not go in for SEATO, which runs counter to the trend of history. Rather, if a pact is to be concluded, let it be a pact of collective peace.

(3) Do not arm Japan. Though arming Japan is directed against China and the Soviet Union, it will eventually harm the United States itself and the countries in southwest Pacific. This is "lifting a rock only to have one's own feet crushed." Such a possibility exists.

(4) Do not arm Germany. Arming will lead to no good. It will likely be another case of "lifting a rock only to have one's own feet crushed."

Let us all disarm. We can do without our troops. Let us—China, the Soviet Union, Britain and France, these Asian and European countries—initiate this matter and put forward this suggestion to the United States.

(From the verbatim record)

APPLICATION OF THE FIVE PRINCIPLES OF PEACEFUL COEXISTENCE[98] SHOULD BE EXTENDED TO STATE RELATIONS AMONG ALL COUNTRIES*

(*October 1954*)

All Countries in the East Have Been Bullied by Western Imperialist Powers

(*October 19, 1954*)

Historically, all of us, peoples of the East, have been bullied by Western imperialist powers. Though located in the East, Japan was also an imperialist power that bullied other Eastern countries. Now, however, even Japan is being bullied. China was bullied by Western imperialist powers for over 100 years. Your country was bullied even longer, for more than 300 years. Now, the Japanese people are also being oppressed. Therefore, we, peoples of the East, have instinctive feelings of solidarity and for protecting ourselves. Ambassador Raghavan[99] has served in China for a few years, and he surely understands the Chinese people's patriotism and their feelings for the Indian people and the people of the other countries in the East. In spite of differences in our ideologies and social systems, we have an overriding common point, that is, all of us have to cope with imperialism. Prime Minister Nehru should not think China has attained complete independence and has no problems. We still face very big problems. Taiwan is still in the hands of the United States and Chiang Kai-shek. We have over 30 islands that are only a few kilometers off the coast of our mainland, and three of them are fairly big. These islands are all occupied

---

* These are excerpts from Mao Zedong's talks with Indian Prime Minister Jawaharlal Nehru on four occasions.

by the U.S. and Chiang Kai-shek forces, so that our vessels cannot pass through, nor can foreign vessels. American airplanes fly to the air over our interior and air-drop special agents. These special agents form groups of seven to ten persons and are equipped with radio sets. To date, scores of such groups of special agents have been air-dropped in our interior provinces. In Sichuan and in parts of Qinghai adjacent to Tibet, American airplanes have air-dropped not only special agents, but also weapons to aid the bandits there. All this shows that a small number of people in the U.S. authorities are bent on harming us whenever they have the opportunity to do so.

Besides, as is known to Prime Minister Nehru, China is not an industrialized country, but an agricultural country. The level of our industrial development is lower than that of India. It will take us another 10 to 20 years' effort to achieve some tangible results. At present the imperialist powers still look down upon us. Our two countries are in a similar plight, and this is the common plight of countries in the East. I have read Prime Minister Nehru's speech of the 29th of last month, and found the sentiments he expressed similar to ours.

The welcome shown by the peoples of our countries to the leaders of our countries on mutual visits illustrates that they place emphasis on our common point rather than the differences in our ideologies and social systems.

Application of the Five Principles of Peaceful Coexistence should be extended to the state relations among all countries. As pointed out by Prime Minister Nehru in his speech of the 29th last month, countries should be committed to the Five Principles and assume obligations accordingly. If a country says one thing, but acts otherwise, there is justification to censure that country, which is in the wrong in the eyes of the people. The problem is that some big powers refuse to commit themselves or conclude agreements on the Five Principles, as our countries have done. No one knows what they have in mind. To my knowledge, the United States and Britain also say that they want peace and will not interfere in the internal affairs of other countries. However, if we want to issue a statement with them in accordance with the Five Principles, they are unwilling.

It is inconceivable that any country would march its troops into the United States. There is alleged U.S. fear of losing the places it has occupied in various parts of the world. However, I seem to have heard that the United States is against British and French colonialism. The alleged U.S. fear is excessive. It has advanced its defense lines to South Korea, Taiwan and Indochina, which are so far from the United States and so close to us. This makes our sleep uneasy.

In doing things the United States does not care whether others can tolerate them. For instance, in rigging up SEATO,[96] it did not bother to consult China and India. There are many countries in Asia, yet it consulted only three countries, Pakistan, Thailand and the Philippines.

Prime Minister Nehru has said that SEATO is a U.S. reaction to the Geneva Agreements. This is quite right. The Geneva Conference[95] did some good, so the United States tried to sabotage it.

Anthony Eden proposed that a Locarno Pact[100] for Asia be concluded. Later on, however, he gave up the idea and accepted SEATO instead. Such a big power should not have been so timid. Our two countries are not afraid. When the United States invited India to the Manila Conference, India had the courage to stay away. On the question of restoration of China's status in the United Nations, India has the courage to cast an affirmative vote, while big powers like Britain and France are so timid. Let us propose that they hand over their big-power status to us. All right?

Britain often asserts that it is China that does not recognize Britain, but we have told them that it is Britain that does not recognize China. We have advised Britain to follow the example of India, and if that is done, Britain can establish formal diplomatic relations with China. Some Scandinavian countries, for example Norway, also had the courage to vote for restoration of China's status in the United Nations; we have therefore established formal diplomatic relations with Norway.

Australia has expressed fear of us, alleging that Communists will commit aggression against it. But we do not even have the ships—how can we reach there? In joining the Manila Pact, Australia asserted it was for defense purposes. However, when we proposed to that country an agreement on the Five Principles, on mutual nonaggression and noninterference, Australia declined.

I have two points of doubt:

First, the United States is shouting anti-communist slogans, and it is in fact opposed to the Communist Parties. But is it really afraid of the Chinese Communist Party? China has only a few worn-out guns; what we have are only people, farming and handicrafts. As I see it, the United States is not really afraid of the Chinese Communist Party, but is using this as a pretext for ulterior purposes.

Second, why is it that countries like Britain, France and Australia follow the United States, while India, Indonesia, Burma and some Scandinavian countries do not necessarily follow the United States? I think this is because countries like Britain, France and Australia have tied their interests to the

American locomotive, and they have to obey when the United States issues an order, whereas India, Indonesia, Burma and some Scandinavian countries have not tied their interests to the American locomotive, or have only loose ties, so these countries do not have to follow the United States.

Cooperation Between Countries Must Be Mutually Beneficial

(October 21, 1954)

On the question of cooperation, experience has shown us that cooperation, whether between persons, political parties or countries, has to be mutually beneficial and should not be detrimental to any party. If any party's interests are hurt, cooperation cannot be sustained. That is why one of our Five Principles is equality and mutual benefit.

Mencius, one of the sages of ancient China, said, "Ununiformity is the nature of things."[101] That is to say, diversity is the reality of the world. Marxism also recognizes diversity, which differs from the view of metaphysics.

Countries, especially friendly countries, should not guard against each other. The mutual vigilance between China and the United States is not a good thing.

We Should Work Together to Prevent War and Win a Lasting Peace

(October 23, 1954)

We do not agree with the past allegations of Hitlerite Germany. One of the allegations of Hitlerite Germany and Japan was that they were "have-not" countries; and they wanted to snatch things from the "have" countries. Japan was truly the "yellow peril" in the past, ten years ago.

We in China need peace, a peace of at least several decades, to develop our national production and improve the people's standard of living. We do not want war. It would be very good if such an environment of peace were created. We can cooperate with anyone who supports the goal of peace. Undoubtedly, India supports it, and so do Indonesia and Burma.

I think Thailand does not believe that China would launch a massive attack against it. We want to have good relations with it, but the Thai government seems rather strange, paying no heed to us.

The Philippines says it is afraid of our aggression, yet when we expressed our wish to build good relations with it, it declined. We have indicated that since there is fear of aggression, we should make friends, and issue a statement on mutual nonaggression, as China and India have done. Again it has declined and refuses to recognize the existence of China. We cannot comprehend why this is so. The only reason is that it heeds the United States and follows its tracks—it does whatever the United States says.

Regarding the United States, there is a question we did not finish discussing last time, and that is the question of war. Prime Minister Nehru has said that the United States wants war, that it wants to reap greater benefits by means of war. Whether war can bring benefits is a question that merits study. We can examine which countries benefited from the two world wars. It can be said that the two world wars brought benefits to three categories of countries and were harmful to all other countries.

In the first category is U.S. imperialism, which benefited from the two world wars and grew.

The second category encompasses countries established after the world wars and led by the Communist Parties and working class.

The third category encompasses oppressed nations and countries that are not led by Communist Parties, but by patriotic organizations or parties. Countries such as India, Indonesia, Burma, Syria and Egypt belong to this category.

To go in for war, one has to mobilize the people, subject them to tension, and teach them how to fight. But when the people are banded together, revolution occurs. That was the case with the Chinese revolution, and that was also the case with the Indian revolution. The independence of both our countries is an outcome of World War II. Had it not been for World War II, it would have been very difficult to win independence.

Other countries have been weakened by the war, for instance, Germany, Italy and Japan. Though among the winning countries, Britain and France have also been weakened. In China, as Japan and Chiang Kai-shek were both weakened, we were able to stand up. Moreover, with the weakening of Britain, countries such as India, Burma and Egypt have stood up. With the weakening of France, Vietnam and Syria have stood up. And with the weakening of the Netherlands, Indonesia has stood up.

If another war is to be waged, it is not yet known what exactly is in the minds of the U.S. military clique. Their past experience is that they benefited and grew from the two world wars, and they may hope to have even greater benefit and growth from another war. This line of thinking is based on their experience, but this is only one aspect of past experience. The other aspect is that a number of countries were founded after the two world wars—countries led by Communist Parties or patriotic parties. If a new world war is launched, I do not think the United States can necessarily benefit, and problems may emerge in the United States itself. If another world war is fought, the bulk or whole of West Asia and Africa and the whole of Latin America will shake off imperialism.

The people's revolutionary forces emerge only when the time is opportune. If an opportunity had not been provided for the Bolsheviks by World War I, the Russian October Revolution would have encountered difficulties. In China we had fought for 22 years, yet not until the final few years did we win victory. Not until the end of World War II did we have the opportunity to stand up. These are cases of countries led by Communist Parties.

As for countries led by patriotic parties, we can see instances in Southeast and West Asia. People tend to hold differing views. But to my mind, it will not pay for the United States to fight another big war, as that will plunge the whole world or the greater part of the world into a state of revolution. It is not alarmist talk when I say so; it is based on the actual state of affairs following the two world wars. If another world war is unleashed, I don't think the United States can gain any benefits; war can only diminish the areas under U.S. domination.

With respect to weaponry, the United States thinks that since it has atom bombs, heavy artillery and a strong navy and air force, it can rely on these. In my view, though there have been changes in weaponry, apart from inflicting more casualties there is no fundamental difference. In ancient times, cold weapons, such as swords and spears, were used. Then hot weapons, such as rifles, machine-guns, artillery, etc., were used. Now atom bombs have been added. The basic difference is that cold weapons inflicted fewer casualties, hot weapons more, and atom bombs still more. There has been no difference except in the number of casualties. In the past, both belligerent parties had cold and hot weapons in their possession, and now both the Soviet Union and the United States have atom bombs. The changes in weaponry can inflict greater numbers of casualties—that is all.

If a third world war is fought, the number of casualties will be not tens of millions, but hundreds of millions. China so far has no atom bombs, and I do not know whether India has them. We have begun research in this connection, yet atom bombs require financial input. We may not have one for some time to come.

If a third world war is fought, casualties will be inflicted on both sides. That will strike a balance. The ultimate factor deciding the outcome of a war will still be men—who handle the weapons, what the combatants wielding the weapons regard as most advantageous, and who are better at fighting. The first two elements are of primary importance. As regards the quantity of weapons, both the Congress Party of India and the Communist Party of China had no weapons at the very beginning, but now both of us have them.

Another point comes from experience. In both world wars the defenders succeeded and the attackers were defeated. In World War I the German armed forces advanced to Paris in the west and approached Petrograd in the east. But in the end the invaders failed. In World War II the invaders, Germany, Italy and Japan, were all defeated, and the defensive side won victory, though some countries on the side of defense, such as Britain and France, were weakened by the war.

We can thus draw the conclusion that another world war should not be fought, and lasting peace should be maintained. The outcome of another world war will not be in the interest of the aggressors.

Your analysis and mine, though similar in some areas and different in others, have reached an identical conclusion. In analyzing the United States, Prime Minister Nehru has said that, on the one hand, the United States has benefited from the war, but, on the other hand, it has encountered difficulties. This is a very good analysis. As for the implements of warfare, we can roughly identify three stages, namely, arrows and spears, then artillery, and then atom bombs. Prime Minister Nehru says that these weapons differ in quality. That is true. When I talked about weaponry just now, I was only referring to the outcome of wars.

Whatever weapons are used, in whatever period of time a war is fought, and no matter whether it is local or global in scale, the outcome of wars is always one side destroying the other. Of course, there are also wars that end in a draw and a kind of peace, such as the wars relating to the 38th Parallel[88] and the 17th Parallel[102]; in these wars no party fundamentally defeated another party. In the majority of cases, however, there are invariably a winning side and a losing side, with the latter's strength destroyed to a greater extent. By strength is meant not only effective strength, but also material strength.

Therefore, in the final analysis, victory is determined by the extent to which the overall strength has been destroyed.

Of course, here I am referring to the final outcome of wars. The outcome of World War II was that all the German armed forces were annihilated, while the armed forces of the Soviet Union, instead of being destroyed, fought on to Berlin. All the forces of Germany, Italy and Japan were disarmed. Prime Minister Nehru's perception is that a third world war would plunge the whole world into a period of chaos. That is possible. Atom bombs will bring destruction not only to humans, but also to material things. Will many countries be devoid of governments? I do not think so. As long as humans survive, there will be governments. When one government is destroyed, another will come into being. Human beings invariably find a way out, and those who survive will try to live on. It has also to be taken into account that people today have changed a great deal from those of the past, that their consciousness for winning liberation and independence has been enhanced enormously. This is the case with all countries, including the United States.

In a word, it is best that no war be fought. If we could act as chief's-of-staff for Eisenhower,[103] he would listen to us instead of being besieged by his advisers. Prime Minister Nehru is in a better position than we to do this work. If we did it, Eisenhower would say that we were frightening him with revolution and that he was not afraid of revolution. I think that, not only war, even a tense situation will benefit and at the same time harm those who create tension. I wish to ask: Which is more advantageous—to let people feel safe, or to make people live in tension every day? A tense situation would awaken the people and make them prepare to resist pressure. That is conducive to revolution.

Evidently, there is no tension between China and India. Our two countries do not wage psychological warfare, nor are we on the alert against each other —unlike the state of affairs between China and the United States and between the Soviet Union and the United States.

Having been in China for a few days already, Prime Minister Nehru must be aware of our situation. We are now implementing the Five-Year Plan, and our socialist transformation has just begun. If a war should break out, our entire plan would be upset. Our funds have all been put in reconstruction. If a war should break out, our economic and cultural plans would have to halt, and a war plan would have to be drawn up to cope with the war. That would delay the process of China's industrialization. However, it would be difficult to destroy China completely or to sink China to the ocean floor by bombing. The Chinese people will live on forever. The same would be true of India.

Tens of million years ago there was a giant animal, namely, the dinosaur, which became extinct in the glacial epoch. Later, however, other animals emerged, and finally the human race came into being, though relics of the glacial epoch can be seen in China even now.

In short, we should make joint efforts to prevent war and to preserve a lasting peace.

All Issues Between Countries That Can Cause Suspicion or Hamper Cooperation Should Be Resolved

(October 26, 1954)

About 2,000 years ago the Chinese poet Qu Yuan wrote these two verses: "A great sorrow it is to bid adieu; / A great joy it is to make friends new."[104]

I remember telling Prime Minister Nehru at a dinner party about our feelings toward India, saying that China and India do not need to be on the alert against each other. We have no apprehension that India would harm us.

I asked whether our countries' Prime Ministers and concurrent Foreign Ministers could correct themselves if they had a slip of the tongue. I think they can correct themselves, but this applies only to our two countries and not to some other countries, which perhaps would seize on our errors in speech, as we would seize on theirs. There is a Chinese saying—"to seize somebody's pigtail." But China and India do not seize each other's pigtail—we are not on the alert against each other, and it does not matter if a slip of the tongue occurs.

India is a promising nation, a great nation. I have heard from our Ambassador Yuan Zhongxian[105] that the people in southern India practice intensive farming and utilize all the land that can be utilized—somewhat like the situation in the areas around Chengdu of our country. Every piece of good news from India makes us happy. When India gets better, the world will benefit.

I am very glad to have had these several rounds of talks together, which have enabled us to exchange views. Meanwhile, Prime Minister Nehru has had talks with Premier Zhou Enlai. The diplomatic work between our two countries is easy to do; there is no need to quarrel. Between friends there are sometimes differences and sometimes quarrels—quarreling until faces turn red. This kind of quarrel, however, is different in nature from our quarrel with John Foster Dulles.[97]

With this visit Prime Minister Nehru must be aware that China is truly in need of friends. Ours is a new China, still weak, though called a big country. We are faced with a strong opponent, the United States, which is bent on fixing us whenever it has the opportunity. Therefore, we need friends, and Prime Minister Nehru must have felt this already. I think India is also in need of friends; this can be seen from the talks we have just had, from our cooperation over the last years, and from the welcome accorded Premier Zhou Enlai during his visit to India and the sincere talks held during that visit.

Prime Minister Nehru advocates the establishment and expansion of zones of peace and hopes that countries that stand for peace will continually increase. To establish and expand zones of peace is a very good idea, with which we agree. To attain this goal, it is necessary to remove certain factors that are likely to cause suspicion or hamper cooperation. The Sino-Indian Agreement relating to Tibet[106] is conducive to the removal of factors causing suspicion or hampering cooperation. It is very good, too, that we have jointly announced the Five Principles. The question of overseas Chinese should also be solved in an appropriate manner, lest some countries assert that we wish to utilize overseas Chinese to make trouble. If overseas Chinese retain their status as foreign nationals, they should not take part in the political activities of the country in which they reside. If they have acquired the nationality of the residing country, they should abide by the laws of that country. Overseas Chinese should also observe the laws of the country in which they reside.

We should try to resolve all issues that can cause suspicion or hamper cooperation. By so doing, equality and mutual benefit, as contained in the Five Principles, can be realized. Cooperation should not harm any of the participating parties. If it does, it cannot last long and is bound to break up. That is true of all cooperation, whether between friends, countries, or political parties. Cooperation has to be beneficial; otherwise, who will join in it?

(From the verbatim record)

THE FIVE PRINCIPLES OF PEACEFUL COEXISTENCE[98] ARE A LONG-TERM POLICY*

(*December 1954*)

We Should Promote Understanding in the Course of Cooperation

(*December 1, 1954*)

Chairman Mao Zedong (hereinafter referred to as *Mao*): We are pleased to see Prime Minister U Nu, Madame Nu and the other friends from Burma. The Chinese people, too, are very glad to see you, for our two countries are neighbors with close relations—friendly countries of long standing.

Were there wars between China and Burma in history? Probably very few —isn't that so?

Prime Minister U Nu (hereinafter referred to as *Nu*): Only two wars—one during the reign of Kublai Khan[107] of the Yuan Dynasty, the other in the Qing Dynasty. There has never been a war, however, with the Hans of China.

Mao: In both wars the Chinese were in the wrong. It was China that invaded you.

In past history Korea and Vietnam suffered the most wrong from China; Burma suffered relatively less. From now on our two countries should coexist in peace.

Nu: Thank you.

Mao: We hope there will be no wars in the world; that would be best.

Nu: Frankly speaking, we have fears of big countries. However, Premier Zhou Enlai's visit to Burma greatly removed such fears among the Burmese. This is a point I am very happy to report to Chairman Mao.

---

* These are excerpts from Mao Zedong's talks with Burmese Prime Minister U Nu on two occasions.

Mao: With more contacts and familiarity between us, we can live together even better. It is only natural that two countries do not know each other well enough for a period of time. We should enhance our mutual understanding in the course of cooperation. We in China are truly in need of a peaceful environment, as we have a lot of things that remain to be done.

Nu: I fully agree with what the Chairman has just said.

Mao: Our domestic problems should and can be resolved in our own country. What we need is international cooperation and assistance. For instance, the question of our big population can be solved by means of developing our production. We are against Hitler's[4] past assertion that a big population should seek expansion and snatch things from abroad. Again, our land problem. We are solving it by land distribution, setting up of cooperatives and reclaiming of barren land. I have discussed all these with Prime Minister Nehru. We are now practicing a planned economy—something we had not done before. This is not easy work and is fraught with difficulties.

Nu: One of the purposes of my visit is to study how you implement the plan.

Mao: Our First Five-Year Plan has been implemented for nearly two years. The achievements have not been great, but some achievements have been scored.

Nu: We also have a plan, but not much progress has been made, owing to rebellion in our country.

Mao: Take your time. The economic levels of our two countries are about the same, being both mainly agricultural countries. Countries such as China, Burma, India and Indonesia are currently at similar economic levels. All of us hope to transform our countries into industrialized ones.

Nu: This is our hope, too.

Mao: This is long-term work and cannot be accomplished in a short time. We need a peaceful environment and we need friends. Therefore, we are very happy to meet Prime Minister U Nu.

Nu: The attitude of China toward Burma has been consistently correct. If the Chinese government had taken advantage of the presence of Kuomintang troops in Burma,[108] that might face the Burmese government with many difficulties. But the Chinese government has never taken advantage of that and has instead shown sympathy with the difficulties of the Burmese government. On behalf of the government and people of Burma, I wish to express our thanks to the Chairman for this correct and friendly attitude of the Chinese government.

Mao: We understand your difficulties. We know that the continued presence of Kuomintang troops in Burma is because you have difficulties and not that you intentionally allow them to stay in Burma. We shall never use the Kuomintang troops' presence in Burma as an excuse to undermine the peaceful relations between our two countries.

Nu: Thank you.

Mao: The Kuomintang troops in Burma are not many. We are not afraid of them. The harassment they can make is rather limited.

Nu: Though they are few in number, if the government of the People's Republic of China had not adopted an attitude of sympathy toward us, they might have led to a second Korea or a second Indochina. That was our worry in the past. However, thanks to the Chinese government's sympathetic attitude toward us, no dispute whatsoever has occurred.

Mao: We have issued strict orders to our people in the border areas to confine themselves to defensive measures and never take even one step across the boundary. However, the objective of the United States is different from yours. The United States has been using the Kuomintang troops in Burma to bully China and Burma. Thailand has not been so friendly to us; still, if possible, we should very much like to establish relations and develop good relations with Thailand.

Nu: Has the Chinese government taken any steps to establish friendly relations with Thailand—like the friendly relations between China and Burma?

Mao: We have discussed this matter with Prime Minister Nehru, and we also hope that Prime Minister U Nu would render indirect help in this connection. I do not know what could prompt Thailand to improve relations with us.

Nu: On December 26 Prime Minister Nehru and I will pass through Bangkok on our way to Indonesia to attend a meeting of the Colombo Conference participants.[109] Taking the opportunity of our sojourn in Bangkok we shall convey the opinion of the Chinese government to the prime minister and other members of the government of Thailand.

Mao: That will be very good.

Nu: We shall raise this matter with the prime minister and other members of the government of Thailand.

Mao: Thailand has said it is afraid of China's aggression. In keeping with what we have done with India and Burma, we can, on the basis of the Five Principles, issue a joint statement with Thailand to affirm mutual nonaggression and peaceful coexistence. Anyone who commits aggression will be in the wrong.

The joint statement issued by the prime ministers of China and Burma[110] laid down the Five Principles governing our mutual relations. One of the principles is noninterference in each other's internal affairs; another is equality and mutual benefit. What is noninterference in each other's internal affairs? It means that a country's internal disputes should be handled by that country itself, and no other countries should meddle in or take advantage of such a domestic dispute. A country should recognize only the government of another country chosen by the people themselves. Therefore, Burma has recognized our government and we have recognized Prime Minister U Nu's government. A country can have only one government. Whether or not a country will in future have another government is an affair of that country and none of our business. Whether or not China will in future have another government is China's affair and not the business of other countries. This is our principle.

The national boundary between our two countries is rather long, with some sections still undefined. Among the minority peoples in the border areas of our two countries some are ethnically identical and are quite likely to visit one another; it is also quite likely that those who are dissatisfied with their government might flee to the other country. We shall never utilize those who have fled over to harm the interests of the Burmese government. This is noninterference in each other's internal affairs and also mutual benefit, because mutual benefit should rule out doing harm to each other. Now that both of our countries are for cooperation, we should not harm each other; otherwise cooperation cannot proceed well. For any doubts remaining evidence should be found to ascertain whether our actions are mutually beneficial or mutually harmful. Evidence can be found in the course of our cooperation. In the last five years we have gained a better understanding of each other than we had at the beginning, and it can be said that relations between our two countries have progressed. For instance, we now have a trade agreement, which we did not have. In future, our cooperation should further advance.

We know what is on your minds. You are afraid our Yunnan Province will be harmful to you.

Nu: Yes, very much afraid. That is why I suggested to Premier Zhou that he and I visit Yunnan together. Regrettably, this time our airplane is not capable of flying over the mountain ranges of Yunnan.

Mao: There is still some divergence between our thinking and your thinking. You are very much afraid because you do not understand the real situation. We know the situation very well. We have enjoined our people there to be friendly to Burma and not make trouble. We have made preparations for Prime Minister U Nu to return to Burma via Yunnan. However, the trip cannot be made by air; instead, automobiles will have to be used. That will take about four days. The only drawback is that the roads are not so good. We have made the preparations, and Prime Minister U Nu can have a look around there.

Nu: Let me make the trip next time.

Mao: Don't think Yunnan is a mysterious place. It is not mysterious at all. Burma once proposed opening a consulate in Kunming. I know your purpose is to take a look at Yunnan, to observe what is going on there. This can be done and indeed should be done. You may go there to see for yourselves, to see whether what we are doing there is friendly to you or covertly harmful to you. It would not be good for us not to allow you to look around there. For our part, we can find a place in Burma to set up our consulate.

Nu: You are welcome.

Mao: Let this matter be discussed by both prime ministers. Both of you should find ways to ease the tension in that area.

We should find ways to resolve questions pending between our two countries. That will enhance our mutual confidence. We may not be able to resolve some of the questions now, for instance, the boundary question, but they should also be resolved in future. They may be left to be solved later on. In short, we must see to it that no interest of either side be harmed.

Prime Minister U Nu earlier mentioned a Colombo Conference. When will it be held?

Nu: On the 28th of December.

Mao: Is it a conference to discuss matters relating to peace and to the Asian-African Conference?[111]

Nu: Yes, it is.

Mao: We are greatly interested in the Asian-African Conference. Prime Minister Nehru has told us that the purposes of the Asian-African Conference are to expand the zone of peace and to combat colonialism. We think these are very good purposes, and we support such a conference. We hope to attend this conference if that is agreeable to the other countries.

Nu: All Asian and African countries will be invited to attend this conference. Incidentally, what will China think if countries such as the Philippines and Thailand are invited?

Mao: We think they should be invited. It does not matter that we have no diplomatic relations with these two countries. The Geneva Conference[95] was attended by the United States, too.

Premier Zhou Enlai: Japan should also be invited, but Chiang Kai-shek should not be invited.

Nu: I can say with some degree of certainty that some countries will suggest that Chiang Kai-shek be invited, but Prime Minister Nehru and I will oppose that.

Mao: There seem to be some difficulties! Still, we hope that China will be invited. Only, there mustn't be a situation, as suggested by some people, where China is invited to the United Nations and at the same time Chiang Kai-shek is kept there. In that case it would be difficult for China to attend, for the question of Taiwan is China's internal affair and Taiwan is a part of China. We shall feel honored if we can attend the Asian-African Conference.

The conference is aimed at promoting the cooperation of Asian-African countries; it will therefore be greatly beneficial to world peace. In the past there was in Asia an aggressor country, Japan, but Japan has changed in its status—into a semi-occupied country—and it is in a difficult position. The Chinese people no longer hate Japan so much and are now friendly to that country. If Japanese militarism should reemerge, we would have fears. Countries such as Burma and Indonesia would probably have similar feelings. However, the present reality is that Japan is under semi-occupation and the Japanese nation is under oppression.

Besides, there are the few Asian countries that have joined SEATO,[96] who hold views different from ours. Still, we hope to persuade those countries to establish friendly relations with us.

Nu: This idea is very good.

Mao: If Thailand is willing, we can establish friendly relations with that country and commit ourselves to mutual nonaggression and noninterference in internal affairs in accordance with the Five Principles. There are three million overseas Chinese in Thailand, many of whom are opposed to the Chinese government. If diplomatic relations are established between China and Thailand, should the Chiang Kai-shek elements be driven out of Thailand? I don't think that will be necessary, so long as they do not intrude into our territory. There are also some Chiang Kai-shek elements among the overseas Chinese in Burma, who still fly the flag of Chiang Kai-shek and refuse to fly our national flag.

We constantly enjoin the overseas Chinese to abide by the laws of the country in which they reside. Since they live in the residing country, they should be law-abiding and should not take part in any unlawful activities in the residing country. We have frequently carried out such educational work, enjoining the overseas Chinese to abide by the law and to maintain good relations with the government and people of the residing country. It is all the more important to foster good relations in countries where there are many overseas Chinese, as the governments of these countries have the suspicion that we will utilize overseas Chinese to make trouble. It will take some time to prove whether we have been educating the overseas Chinese to be law-abiding or covertly instigating them to oppose the governments of the countries in which they reside.

In various countries there could be unlawful political activities or revolutions, but those are their internal affairs, in which overseas Chinese should not participate. The question of nationality has also to be clarified, whether one holds Chinese nationality or a foreign nationality, and there should be no dual nationality.

Nu: During Premier Zhou's visit in Rangoon I raised this question with him. He said that this question was beyond his authority and he had to consult with his colleagues upon return to China. Having heard Chairman Mao's remarks on dual nationality today, I am very pleased.

Mao: We are ready to resolve this question with a number of countries. At present, talks are going on with Indonesia to solve the question in accordance with the principles just mentioned. As we are for peace and cooperation, we should resolve issues between us through negotiation.

Nu: That is also what we hope.

Mao: Let you two prime ministers discuss the relevant details! Prime Minister U Nu should make contact with people in our society, personages of our democratic parties and leading officials of our government. You are welcome to visit whatever places you may wish to go in China.

Nu: Thank you. We hope that someday Chairman Mao can spare some time to visit our country.

Mao: Thank you. It is also my hope to visit various countries in the world. I am a rustic man of China who has seldom been abroad. I shall certainly be very pleased if I have an opportunity to visit Burma. My knowledge is rather limited, and it would be a very good thing if I could visit Burma to increase my knowledge.

Each nation has its special features and strong points for us to learn from. Both Premier Zhou and Ambassador Yao Zhongming[112] have said to me that Bruma has many things worthy of our learning. They have told me that the Burmese are better than us at growing grains, and we are ready to learn how grains are grown in Burma.

Nu: That will be very good.

Mao: Between nations there should be exchanges of strong points.

Countries Should Be Equal, Irrespective of Size

(December 11, 1954)

Chairman Mao Zedong (hereinafter referred to as *Mao*): Prime Minister U Nu has probably already seen that it is our policy to be friendly with your country. The Five Principles represent a major development, yet more work needs to be done in pursuance of them. We should take steps to give concrete expression to the Five Principles and should not let them become abstract principles merely to be talked about. At present, there are two different attitudes internationally: One is to merely talk; the other is to achieve concrete implementation. Britain and the United States also talk about peaceful coexistence, but they merely talk, and if they are asked to truly act on peaceful coexistence, they will desist. We are not like that. We deem that the Five Principles are a long-term policy, not an expediency. The Five Principles are suited to the conditions of China, which needs a lasting peaceful environment. The Five Principles are also suited to the conditions of your country and the overwhelming majority of countries in Asia and Africa. To us, stability is preferable. There should be stability within our countries as well as internationally.

I know Prime Minister U Nu has had extended discussions with Chairman Liu Shaoqi on Burma's internal situation. We wish you peace in your country. As to how specifically to attain domestic peace, that is a matter for you to handle by yourselves. It would not be appropriate for us to express an attitude toward this specific question.

The question of the Communist Party is not confined to one country; it is a global question in the sense that there are Communist Parties in most countries. Therefore, it is up to each country to handle this question.

In your country there are political parties, organizations and individuals unfriendly to China, as there are in other countries, such as India and Indonesia. But it is not for us to interfere—to tell those parties, organizations and individuals that they should not oppose us. In each country there are usually several kinds of parties. We cannot express opposition to any of those parties or support any of them. In solving questions we can only deal with the government of a given country. We hope you can understand why we adopt such an attitude.

Prime Minister U Nu (hereinafter referred to as *Nu*): This is quite correct, and any other attitudes are not correct. I fully agree with the views of

Chairman Mao.

Mao: Both the Burmese people and the Chinese people have seen the steps we have taken, for instance, the Five Principles and the questions already resolved as stated in the communiqué on the Prime Ministers' talks.[113] Between our two nations, two governments and two peoples we do not differentiate the political parties, but we have jointly attained an initial solution to our common problems.

In China, too, there are various political parties and organizations. These parties are different; they are not on the same footing, the difference consisting of the leading and the led. All the democratic parties of China acknowledge the leadership of the Chinese Communist Party. There are also in China various organizations, including those of the workers and even those of capitalists. However, the Burmese government, Prime Minister U Nu and Burmese ambassador U Hla Maung can only treat all the Chinese political parties equally and cannot express satisfaction with one party and dissatisfaction with another. Otherwise, dissatisfaction would arise in some parties.

The same is true with our relations with Burma. If we were to express, in the name of our government, an attitude toward any party in Burma, we would offend that party and some ordinary people.

Since we have broached this question, we should like to say that we wish Burma peace domestically. Prime Minister U Nu has said that the Burmese civil war has become a heavy burden. I do not know whether or not you could hold talks among yourselves, to see whether a compromise could be reached. If that could be done, Burma could concentrate her energy entirely on reconstruction. We would be glad to see that. My personal suggestion is to start with some informal talks among yourselves, to have a try, and not to block avenues completely. It would be best to start with informal, exploratory talks. If the talks can get you closer to one another, so much the better. If not, the issue can be put aside for the time being, and there will be opportunities to resume the talks.

Our ways with Tibet may be of some reference value to you. We are prepared to talk and consult with the local government of Tibet for a fairly long period of time. We do not insist on immediate social reforms in Tibet. If after consultations they say alright, we can carry out a little reform; if they say no, we can refrain from pursuing it for the time being. Of course, our experience is only for your reference, because the domestic conditions of our two countries differ. Each country should address her problems in light of her own national conditions.

Here, a few words may be said about revolution. It has been very rare in history for a revolution to win victory in a country by relying on the assistance of foreign countries or political parties of other countries. The East European countries won, because during the fight against Nazi Germany the armed forces of the Soviet Union occupied those countries. Otherwise, it would have been impossible for them to win victory by relying on foreign assistance or on the export of revolution by foreign countries. It is in this sense that we maintain revolution cannot be exported. This, however, does not mean that the revolution in a given country can be immune from foreign influence. The independence of countries such as Burma, India, Indonesia, Pakistan and Ceylon[114] was not entirely free from foreign influence, but the independence of Burma was not won because of any foreign countries' help in human, material and financial resources.

We have seen a different case in Guatemala, in Central America, where there is interference by the United States, which helped the opposition party to organize troops in another country to fight their way into Guatemala, while the U.S. ambassador instigated from within Guatemala. We shall never do such a thing. We shall never organize troops in Yunnan border areas to fight into Burma, with Ambassador Yao Zhongming instigating from within Burma. Ambassador Yao will never do such a thing. If he did, we would definitely dismiss him at once from his office.

There are some radical elements among the overseas Chinese in Burma, and we enjoin them not to interfere in Burma's internal affairs. We educate them in abiding by the law of the residing country and not contacting the political parties that oppose the Burmese government with armed force. We do not organize a Communist Party among the overseas Chinese; all previous party branches have been disbanded. We have done the same in Indonesia and Singapore. We have enjoined the overseas Chinese in Burma not to participate in Burma's internal political activities and to take part only in some activities permitted by the Burmese government, such as celebrations, but not other activities. If they did otherwise, it would place us in an awkward position and make it difficult to get things done.

We have adopted the same policy toward the three million overseas Chinese in Thailand. Thailand is not friendly to us and the reason does not lie with us. We truly desire to establish good relations with Thailand. China and Thailand being so close geographically, it stands to reason that the two countries should have good relations. Foreign newspapers suspect us of aggressive intentions against Thailand or setting up a so-called Free Thailand by establishing a minority autonomous region of the Dais. There are three hundred thousand people of the Dai ethnic group in our Yunnan Province, and they have organized themselves into an autonomous region.[115] Similarly, there are in Guangxi more than seven million people of the Zhuang ethnic group, and they have also organized themselves into an autonomous region. We have scores of such minority autonomous regions, such as those of the Koreans and Mongols. We are preparing to set up an autonomous region in Tibet. We have many different national minorities in China, but their total population is less than forty million. We have no intention of setting up a so-called Free Thailand, or of invading Thailand. Those allegations do not square with the facts. We have not conceived such ideas, or made such preparations, or acted in such a way.

We very much want to establish diplomatic relations with Thailand—to have mutual recognition with it. If Thailand so wishes, she is also qualified to establish a consulate at Kunming.

Thailand has expressed fear of aggression by us. Burma, too, had such fears. However, Burma has chosen to have good relations with us and come to see whether we are really going to commit aggression against Burma. Thailand does not even bother to come to see for herself. If Thailand sets up a consulate at Kunming, they may visit our Dai autonomous region to see for themselves.

I hope Prime Minister U Nu will convey our thinking to the authorities of Thailand.

Nu: I have already promised Premier Zhou. I shall stop overnight in Bangkok and meet with the Thai prime minister. I shall tell him not only that the Chinese premier has expressed readiness to establish diplomatic relations with Thailand, but furthermore, China's wish is sincere; this is what I have discovered during my visit in China. I hope Prime Minister Nehru will fully support my remarks.

Mao: We have discussed this matter with Prime Minister Nehru, but not in such detail and not at such great length. I hope Prime Minister U Nu will convey what we have said today to Prime Minister Nehru. We shall be very glad if both you and Prime Minister Nehru discuss this matter with the authorities of Thailand, so that relations like those between China and Burma can be established between China and Thailand.

Nu: I shall try my best to do so.

Mao: Now I should like to say a few words on the question of big countries and small countries. In our view, there should be no discrimination between big and small countries. We are opposed to big countries having special rights, as that would place big countries and small countries on an unequal footing. It is the logic of imperialists that big countries are superior and small countries inferior. No matter how small a country may be, having a population of only several hundred thousand or even tens of thousands, it should be entirely equal in status to a country with a population of several hundred million.

This is a matter of basic principle, not empty talk. Since they are equal, big countries should not harm small countries, exploit them economically, oppress them politically, impose on them their own will, policy or ideology. Since they are equal, mutual courtesy should be extended; a big country should not behave like the patriarch of a feudal family and look upon other countries as its nephews or juniors. In criticizing U.S. behavior in Guatemala, Mr. Attlee[116] said that the United States behaved like the father of a Medieval family, picking a woman he liked for wife of his son. The relationship between countries, irrespective of size, should be equal, democratic and friendly and a relationship of mutual help and mutual benefit, not a relationship of inequality or one mutually detrimental.

The current situation in North and South America is like that in a Medieval family, with the United States as the patriarch and the other countries as its nephews or juniors. We don't want this kind of relationship in Asia. Japan wanted to behave that way in the past, purporting to practice coexistence and coprosperity, but in reality trying to subject others to exploitation and aggression.

China and Burma have had relations for five years already. Let us see in another five years, another five years of coexistence and cooperation, whether we are merely talking about them or are implementing them in earnest.

Your attitude is very good in that if you have something to say or if you have doubts or dissatisfaction, you speak your mind. In future, there may yet crop up between our two countries some questions, some doubts or dissatisfaction. Let us hope that both of us will speak up, so that measures may be taken to resolve the questions. In this way, our relations can be further improved and our friendly cooperation enhanced.

Nu: Frankly speaking, in the past we did not dare to speak our mind, lest we might be mistaken as stooges of Britain or the United States, or reported to you as such by our opposition parties. However, after meeting each other and with our mutual understanding enhanced through discussions, we are now no longer afraid of speaking our mind. This is one of the greatest achievements of my current visit to China. Yesterday, while talking with Premier Zhou at his home, I told this to my friend, Premier Zhou.

I even went so far yesterday as to request Premier Zhou to release the American fliers. Normally, I would not do such a thing, nor should I do it, as this smacked of interference in internal affairs. However, as Premier Zhou and I have developed a very good mutual understanding, I brought this matter up without leading to any misunderstanding on the part of Premier Zhou. This has made me very happy.

Mao: They will be released at some points but not now. We do not kill foreign offenders, though Chinese committing the same offense would be sentenced to death. Nevertheless, we must act according to law, as they have offended against the law.

Ours is a big country in terms of its big population and vast territory, but ours is not yet a strong country. Prime Minister U Nu, having visited our automobile factory, knows that so far we are not able to manufacture a complete car or airplane, so in what sense is our country strong? However weak our country may be, we will never allow the United States to impose its will upon us. In Yan'an we never yielded to pressure. During the War of Liberation, we arrested the Americans who had intruded into our areas for espionage. No matter how strong the United States may be, no matter how much steel it can produce or how many automobiles and airplanes it can manufacture, we shall never yield to its pressure. Toward friendly countries, our attitude is to treat them as brothers. Toward countries that oppress us, so long as they continue their oppression we shall not yield, not even for a day.

The airplanes used by the American spies were shot down within our territory, in northeast China, but the United States asserted that the men were POWs. The real POWs were the twenty thousand Korean and Chinese captured, detained and handed over to Syngman Rhee[85] and Chiang Kai-shek. This is utterly unreasonable and infuriating.

Countries like ours have suffered many wrongs. Countries in Asia and Africa have for many years been bullied by imperialist powers, mainly Britain, the United States, France, Germany and Japan. We are still suffering wrongs. The day will come when we shall have genuine independence, when we shall have built up our country; then we shall be able to suffer fewer wrongs.

Yours is by no means a small country. You have a population of nearly twenty million, more than double the population of Australia. Your country's land area is also rather large, nine to ten times that of Ceylon. Your country is rich in various resources, and your people are industrious and intelligent. You can, step by step, accomplish various undertakings, such as automobile manufacture and iron and steel production. Your country has bright prospects, and we wish to see your country prosper.

Nu: Thank you.

Mao: If all the Asian and African countries become prosperous, then the hegemony of a few big powers cannot work. The population of the whole of Asia is more than half of the world's population. Moreover, Asia is a good place with two oceans—the Pacific Ocean and the Indian Ocean.

Nu: The conditions of Burma are unique. It would be very good if the Chinese Communist Party could send some impartial observers to Burma to study the conditions there. We shall not only be pleased to receive them, but also offer them all facilities. They can study on the spot the position of the Burmese government and the Burmese people's feelings about the rebels.

Mao: It would be inappropriate for us to send an observer team to Burma; that would make a bad impression on the outside world. Our ambassador and consuls can conduct some research on the basis of press reports and public documents. They should not get in direct touch with the opposition parties, but they can get indirect knowledge of the opposition parties through the legal political parties. In doing such research, our embassy is doing what the Burmese embassy is doing here. We cannot intervene in your internal disputes.

Nu: As you would be coming to Burma at our invitation, not against our will, that would not constitute interference in our internal affairs. If we make a request, you can even send troops to us, and that will not be interference in internal affairs either.

Mao: It cannot be said sweepingly that whatever is desired by the government is not interference in internal affairs. Four different situations are possible:

First, in the case of allied countries, to oppose aggression and fight a common enemy, troops of one allied country can move into the territory of another. That is not interference in internal affairs.

Second, in the case of one country's establishing military bases in another country, providing aid or loans with military or political strings attached, or establishing religious bodies in another country to conduct espionage—all these are acts of interference in internal affairs.

Third, in matters falling within the scope of purely domestic affairs, such as ethnic conflicts or strife between political parties, if any foreign country intervenes, that will also constitute interference in internal affairs.

Fourth, foreign professors or experts sent at the invitation of the host country—that is not interference in internal affairs, but a kind of mutual assistance.

The above-mentioned second and third situations constitute cases of interference in internal affairs, because they encroach on the national interests of another country.

If we were to send an observer team to Burma to study the ethnic conflicts or political party disputes there, though the Burmese government might regard this as noninterference, the other Burmese ethnic groups or political parties would hold different views on this, and other countries would not have a favorable opinion of this either.

Nu: I did not foresee this point. Then I shall refrain from putting forward my suggestion.

Mao: When I made some suggestions to Prime Minister U Nu, I did so not in my capacity as a government worker, but as a Party worker. I am not only chairman of the People's Republic of China, but also chairman of the Chinese Communist Party, so I was making suggestions in my capacity as chairman of the Chinese Communist Party to U Nu, president of the Antifascist People's Freedom League of Burma.

Chairman Liu Shaoqi and I have both told Prime Minister U Nu about some of China's experience. That was an exchange of views between friends. Whether or not the Burmese government acts accordingly is entirely up to the Burmese government to decide in light of its own conditions. Whether or not the Burmese government has better relations with a particular political party will never be made a condition in our doing business with Burma.

Nu: I regard the suggestions made by Chairman Mao and Chairman Liu as suggestions from elder brothers to a younger brother. Elder brothers are more experienced than a younger brother. When I believe that those who give me suggestions are honest, sincere and dedicated to their people, I shall listen to their suggestions with the humbleness of a younger brother toward his elder brothers.

Mao: Ours is not a relationship between elder and younger brothers, but brothers born in the same year, same month, same day and same hour. In fact, Burma attained independence in 1948—one year earlier than we did.

Nu: I am most happy to have had the opportunity for these talks. There was a time when I wondered what kind of people I would meet in China and was afraid of meeting people like Hitler, who would smite the table and shout while speaking. Now I have found that my fears were entirely groundless. I feel very happy for having had these sincere talks.

Mao: Everybody starts with lack of understanding and ends with a better understanding. That is only natural.

(From the verbatim record)

GREETING THE FIFTH ANNIVERSARY OF THE SIGNING OF THE SINO-SOVIET TREATY OF FRIENDSHIP, ALLIANCE AND MUTUAL ASSISTANCE*

(February 12, 1955)

To Comrade K. Y. Voroshilov
President of the Presidium of the Supreme Soviet of the USSR
Comrade N. A. Bulganin
Chairman of the Council of Ministers of the USSR
Comrade V. M. Molotov
First Vice-Chairman of the Council of Ministers and Minister of Foreign Affairs of the USSR

On the occasion of the fifth anniversary of the signing of the Sino-Soviet Treaty of Friendship, Alliance and Mutual Assistance,[76] on behalf of the Chinese people and the Government of the People's Republic of China, we wish to extend our warm greetings to you and, through you, to the great Soviet people and the Government of the Soviet Union.

During the last five years the all-round cooperation between China and the Soviet Union in political, economic and cultural fields has scored extensive development, and the government and people of the Soviet Union have extended comprehensive, systematic and meticulous assistance to the Chinese people, who are engaged in socialist construction. The Soviet Government has successively helped China establish or expand 156 large industrial enterprises, dispatched a large number of outstanding experts to assist China in national reconstruction, provided China with loans on favorable terms, transferred back to China, free of charge, all the assets of the Chinese Changchun Railway, once jointly managed by China and the Soviet Union, as well as assets taken over from Japanese hands by the Soviets in 1945 in northeast China, sold to

---

* This is a telegram jointly sent by Mao Zedong, Liu Shaoqi and Zhou Enlai to the leaders of the Soviet Union.

China the Soviet shares in the Sino-Soviet joint ventures, and decided to put entirely at China's disposal the naval base at Lüshun Port, once jointly used by China and the Soviet Union, and the equipment in that naval base area. Recently, the Soviet Government has proposed scientific, technological and industrial assistance to China to promote research in the peaceful uses of atomic energy. Such friendly cooperation and sincere assistance have greatly helped promote the development of our national reconstruction and demonstrated to the whole world the great vitality of this new type of relationship between countries. The Government of the People's Republic of China and the Chinese people deeply appreciate the supreme value of this fraternal friendship. On behalf of the Government of the People's Republic of China and the Chinese people, we wish to express heartfelt gratitude to the Government and people of the Soviet Union for their great assistance.

The consolidation and development of friendship and alliance between China and the Soviet Union have had an immeasurable impact guaranteeing the security of our two countries and safeguarding peace in the Far East and the world as a whole. The policy of peace pursued by China and the Soviet Union has prompted and helped bring about the armistice in Korea and the restoration of peace in Indochina, eased to a certain degree the tense international situation, and rejoiced all peace-loving countries and peoples. The Chinese people warmly support the struggle waged by the Soviet Union for the establishment of a collective security system in Europe and against the rearming of West Germany. Both China and the Soviet Union are ready to establish normal relations with Japan and actively support the Japanese people in taking the path of independent development and international cooperation. The sincere cooperation between China and the Soviet Union is not only in the interests of the people of our two countries, but also those of the peace-loving countries and peoples of Asia, Europe and the whole world; it is a reliable guarantee of peace in the Far East and in the world.

The aggressive circles of the United States and their followers are pushing everywhere a policy of war and creating international tension. Currently the United States is carrying out acts of aggression and war provocations[117] against China in the Taiwan area, which constitute a grave menace to China's security and have aroused the just condemnation of peace-loving countries and peoples all over the world. The Chinese people's struggle to liberate their own territory, Taiwan, is a cause of justice. Causes of justice can never be blocked by any force. In the new tense international situation Sino-Soviet friendship and alliance will assuredly play its important role more and more in opposing aggression and defending peace.

The Sino-Soviet Treaty of Friendship, Alliance and Mutual Assistance is a great treaty of peace and is symbolic of the great friendship between China and the Soviet Union. Facts in the last five years have proved the great role of the treaty in promoting world peace and human progress. Life and experience in future will increasingly demonstrate the great strength and dazzling brilliance of this treaty.

May the great friendship between China and the Soviet Union grow with each passing day in the interests of the common prosperity of the Chinese and Soviet peoples and consolidation of peace in the Far East and in the world as a whole.

Long live the eternal and unbreakable friendship between the peoples of China and the Soviet Union!

Mao Zedong, Chairman of
the People's Republic of China
Liu Shaoqi, Chairman of the Standing
Committee of the NPC of the PRC
Zhou Enlai, Premier of the State Council
and Minister of Foreign Affairs of the PRC
Beijing, February 12, 1955
(From *People's Daily*, February 14, 1955)

ORDER ON TERMINATION OF THE STATE OF WAR BETWEEN THE PEOPLE'S REPUBLIC OF CHINA AND GERMANY

(April 7, 1955)

In view of the fact that Hitlerite Germany had unleashed a fascist war of aggression, destroying world peace, and had supported Japan in its war of aggression against China, on December 9, 1941, China proclaimed a state of war with Germany. After the annihilation of the Hitlerite aggressors, the Potsdam Conference[118] of 1945 decided that Germany should evolve into a peaceful, democratic and unified country and on the approach to concluding a peace treaty with Germany.

However, because of the policy continually pursued by the United States, Britain and France of dividing Germany, reviving militarism in Western Germany and bringing it into their aggressive military bloc, Germany still remains divided and a peace treaty with Germany has not yet been concluded. Currently, the United States, Britain and France are actively trying, through the implementation of the Paris Protocol,[119] to further obstruct the peaceful reunification of Germany and the conclusion of a peace treaty with Germany, thus gravely menacing the peace and security of Europe.

The People's Republic of China resolutely supports the struggles waged by the German Democratic Republic, all the German people, the Soviet Union and all peace-loving countries and peoples for the peaceful reunification of Germany, the conclusion of a peace treaty with Germany, the collective security of Europe and world peace. At the same time, in the interests of the Chinese people and all the German people and in accordance with the resolution adopted by the Standing Committee of the First National People's Congress of the People's Republic of China at its Ninth Meeting on April 7, 1955, I hereby declare:

(1) That the state of war between the People's Republic of China and Germany is now terminated and peaceful relations should be established between the two countries.

(2) That termination of the state of war between the People's Republic of China and Germany does not change the international obligations of Germany, nor does this affect the rights to which the People's Republic of China is entitled and the obligations which it has assumed under the relevant international agreements relating to Germany.

Mao Zedong
Chairman of the People's Republic of China
April 7, 1955
(From *People's Daily*, April 9, 1955)

CHINA AND PAKISTAN SHOULD BECOME GOOD FRIENDS*

(*April 27, 1955*)

Both China and Pakistan are countries in the East. There are many common points among Eastern countries, as all of them have been oppressed by Western countries. Among the countries in Asia and Africa only Japan is an industrialized country, but now it is in a difficult position. The recent Asian-African Conference[111] was a success, its participating countries basically united. The communiquè of the conference was adopted not by a majority vote, but by consensus. Between China and Pakistan there has never been war, nor are there any disputes. Trade is going on. China and Pakistan should therefore become good friends.

If the Asian-African Conference had not been sponsored by the five Colombo countries[109] but by China, it could not have been held. Those people believed in you, not in us, for ours is a country in which the Communist Party is in power. But we Communists are not like what the United States has depicted—people with disheveled hair, green faces and long teeth, fiendish creatures with three heads and six arms. We are reasonable people. As you have accepted U.S. military aid, India is afraid and we too are afraid. Ambassador Ahmed says that Pakistan will never use such military aid against India or other countries. It is good to have such assurance. Besides, your country has signed the Manila Pact.[96] We are not afraid of Pakistan, Thailand or the Philippines, or even Britain and Australia, but the United States. Now we understand that when Pakistan joined the Manila Treaty bloc, it did so for fear of aggression from China. I hope you will gradually understand that China will not commit aggression against others. I also hope that misunderstandings between our two countries will be cleared up and relations between us will be improved. We have already established diplomatic and trade relations with Pakistan. Though diplomatic relations have not yet been established with Thailand and the

---

* These are excerpts from Mao Zedong's talk with Sultan-uddin Ahmed, Pakistan's ambassador to China.

Philippines, we hope our relations with those countries can also be improved. Premier Zhou Enlai had some contact with representatives of those countries during the Asian-African Conference.

China is ready to live together in peace with all countries, including the United States. In his statement Premier Zhou Enlai expressed our readiness to sit down to negotiations with the Americans. During the Asian-African Conference we talked about the Taiwan question to the five Colombo countries and Thailand and the Philippines. All questions should be resolved through negotiation, and it is not good to resort to fighting.

I hope Mr. Ambassador will soon settle down in Beijing and work for improvement of relations between our two countries; you can contact the Ministry of Foreign Affairs if you have any difficulties. For our part, we shall enjoin the Chinese envoy and all the embassy staff in Pakistan to develop good relations with the government of Pakistan.

(From the verbatim record)

THE UNITED STATES, THOUGH FRIGHTFUL, IS NOT SO FRIGHTFUL*

(*April 29, 1955*)

Our assessment of the United States can be put this way: frightful, yet not frightful. The United States has some atom bombs in its hands. If one says it is not frightful, then what is the point of organizing the peace movement? In reality, however, the United States is not frightful. At present the United States has deployed one million out of its three million armed forces in its military bases established in the vast intermediate zone, stretching from Tokyo to London, with those forces bogged down, unable to move. This does not seem to be a posture for fighting a war. The United States is pursuing a policy of force; if war should ever break out, the intermediate zone would be doomed first. However, the people in this vast intermediate zone—1.4 billion on the Asian and African continents alone as well as the people in Europe—are all our allies in opposing U.S. aggression. Therefore, we have much work to do domestically and internationally, and in the end the United States will certainly be isolated. Those in other countries who support the U.S. war policy will also be increasingly isolated. They may be found in almost every country, and I think that persons like Chiang Kai-shek can be found in Britain, too.

Now the question is: peace or war? If a war should break out, the capitalist system would be finished earlier; if there should be no war, they can live for more years.

We call U.S. imperialism a paper tiger; it still clamors disbelief. It can be said that if a war should break out, then in the early stage of the war the United States may in appearance be an iron tiger; however, it will eventually change into a paper tiger. As U.S. imperialism does not enjoy popular support and is opposed by the people, it can only be something that has the form of an iron tiger but the substance of a paper tiger. That was also the case with Hitler,[4] though U.S. imperialism has greater components of a paper tiger. U.S.

---

* These are excerpts from Mao Zedong's talk with Harry Pollitt, chairman of the British Communist Party.

forces are everywhere unwelcome. Having a total of three million armed personnel, the United States has deployed 1.5 million abroad in various parts of the world, thereby bogging down its own strength and becoming incapable of fighting. It seems what the United States is after at present is just occupying some places, and not necessarily to unleash war right away. If there is a peace of 50 years, we shall be able to carry out ten five-year plans. In the course of the 50 years the people of the countries controlled by the United States, no longer able to tolerate it, will rise to shake off U.S. control. However, if U.S. imperialism really chooses to fight, we are not afraid either. We do not want to fight. But if the United States should come over fighting, then we shall mop it up. Asia, Africa and Europe can certainly do such mopping up. If fighting should start, these three continents will speak as one voice. As we have the strength, we are not afraid of imperialism.

We should exert effort to prevent the outbreak of a war. If war cannot be prevented, let us prepare to fight for several years and to sweep the war out of our three continents. World War I lasted only four years; World War II lasted five to six years. If a third world war should break out, let us prepare to fight for ten years. In the entire history of humankind only two world wars have been fought. World War I ended with the emergence of the Soviet Union, and World War II ended with the emergence of People's Democracies with a total population of 800 million. Since World War II, two types of new countries have emerged. The first type encompasses China and the other People's Democracies; the second type includes newly independent or semi-independent countries, such as India, Burma and Indonesia. Therefore, one can draw a conclusion without waiting for future events; namely, if a third world war should break out, that war would mean the end of the capitalist world. If some maniacs should unleash a world war, that would be nothing terrific; it is imperialism that is doomed to extinction.

(From the summary of the talk)

PEACE IS THE BEST*

(May 26, 1955)

There is no barrier between us. We are for good on your behalf, because what is good for you is also good for us. We hope you will become strong, prosperous and developed, that will be good for us as well as for world peace. The Asian and African countries have just held a conference in Bandung[111]; all the countries participating in the conference should become strong and prosperous, including Japan. In the past Japan did not behave well, but it is now being bullied, too. It will be good if all the countries being bullied by imperialism become strong and prosperous.

Thanks to the initiative and sponsorship of the five Colombo countries[109] and the chairmanship of the President and Prime Minister of Indonesia, the Bandung Conference was a success. China attended the conference as one of the Asian-African countries and, in that capacity, contributed her share of effort. China has always been ready to develop friendly cooperation with all other countries, and China did not go to the conference to do anything bad. Because of the attitude adopted by China, countries not friendly to China, such as Japan, the Philippines and Thailand, could get along with us during the conference—relations were passable, with no great difficulties. There were, of course, many bickerings, but there were common points, too. Those countries have one thing in common with us, namely, they face the same difficulty of being bullied by the U.S. imperialist power. The economy of Thailand is also under-developed. Japan, though more advanced than we are, also faces economic difficulties. This is the case, generally speaking. Of course, there are individual exceptions. Thus, in general, we have certain common points politically and economically. The recent Asian-African Conference is perhaps the first of its kind ever held by Asian and African countries.

Owing to their prolonged aggression for several hundred years, the Western countries have developed a complex of looking down upon the

---

* These are excerpts from Mao Zedong's talk with Ali Sastroamidjojo, Prime Minister of Indonesia.

backward countries in Asia and Africa. They call us colored people making a distinction according to skin color, like calling some metals nonferrous or colored metals. But we, the colored metals, will expand. Of course, we shall not commit aggression against others. But colored metals are more valuable, because they include gold, silver, copper and tin.

A nation that has not only survived but developed over the centuries must have its strong points. Otherwise it is incomprehensible. The Western powers assert that our nations are inferior, then how can our nations have survived and developed?

We can get along very well discussing with each other. We have had conversation with Prime Minister Nehru and Prime Minister U Nu respectively, and now we are having a conversation with you, Prime Minister Sastroamidjojo. As friends, we can get along very well. In the face of the Western countries, our common concern is to unite and protect ourselves, not to calculate against or harm each other. Our relationship should be one of mutual benefit, not mutual harm. Not only commercially and culturally, but politically we should cooperate; the Bandung Conference is a case in point. We should see that all our countries make progress every year. We should help one another and try to solve some difficult problems that can be solved. Each of our countries has its own difficult problems and, through mutual help, we should try to solve these problems. For this purpose, steps need to be taken to remove misunderstandings and obstacles between our countries and increase mutual understanding. For instance, between China and India there used to be a question concerning Tibet; between China and Burma there are the overseas Chinese question and the boundary question; between China and Indonesia there is also a question regarding the overseas Chinese. With countries not on very good terms with us we shall also take concrete steps to solve some questions. In the case of countries such as Thailand and the Philippines we have the same idea, i.e., if only there is the possibility, efforts should be made to develop good relations with them. We have discussed the question of Thailand with Prime Minister Nehru and Prime Minister U Nu respectively and requested them to help us in persuading Thailand. Thailand has said it is afraid that we may send our troops to attack it, but how can one attack others indiscreetly? Thailand is also afraid of our minority autonomous district of the Dais;[115] we have made it clear that Thailand can accredit a consul to Kunming to see whether we are going to attack it. In Bandung Premier Zhou talked about this with the Thai foreign minister for the same purpose of improving relations. If possible, I hope Mr. Prime Minister will speak on our behalf when you meet leaders of Thailand and the Philippines and tell them that China wants to have friendly relations with their countries.

Even in the case of the Western countries, if only they are willing, we are ready to cooperate with them. We are ready to solve pending questions by peaceful means. Fighting is always bad; it especially cannot bring good to Western countries, which has been proved by history. Though war inflicts material and human losses on both warring parties, history has proved that the political outcome of war is not to the advantage of the Western countries. Following World War I Soviet Russia got rid of old bonds; following World War II China and a number of other countries won liberation. World War II brought two outcomes: First, countries such as China, Poland, and Czechoslovakia came into being—countries with the Communist Party at the helm of state affairs. Second, in countries such as Indonesia, India, Burma and many other Asian and African countries movements led by nationalists made their respective countries independent or near independent. Great changes have also taken place in Egypt since World War II, and such is the case with many other countries in the Near East and Middle East. Though the United States emerged stronger than before, the camp of the Western countries as a whole has been weakened.

Several years ago all of us now present here would have been outlaws. We were then branded "unlawful elements," "rebels" or "bad men." Now the situation has changed. All of us have driven away those so-called good men. You have driven out the Japanese and Dutch; we have driven away the Japanese, Americans and Chiang Kai-shek. Those guys used to allege that we were very bad. Prime Minister Nehru, Prime Minister U Nu and Prime Minister Sastroamidjojo were all imprisoned for a long time. We can try to convince the Western countries by citing this chapter of history. They claimed that they were most powerful. Then why was it that after World War II we were able to win independence? This is strong historical evidence; it is neither fabrication nor bluffing. Over the past several hundred years the Western countries tried to frighten us. In the end, however, were we frightened by them or were they frightened by us? The conclusion is therefore that it is best not to fight a third world war; if it should break out, its outcome would not be disadvantageous to Asian and African countries, but to the Western countries; if they should say this is bluffing let them say so; but our remarks are well grounded, based on the historical experience of the two world wars. In view of this we say that questions should be solved through negotiation—let us have a try. In fact, the Korean war and the Indochinese war were both solved in the end through negotiation, so the Taiwan question can also be solved through negotiation. We made this clear during the Bandung Conference, and this point should be driven home to the Western countries. The Western countries may refuse to listen, as their views are biased, thinking they have more iron and steel, money and atom bombs. Are we afraid of these? A little, but not much. When we say we are a little afraid, that is because weapons invariably kill people. Our people do not wish to suffer losses, so we want no war. Those things in the hands of the Western countries will not surpass the people's strength, because the people have vitality. There are in Western countries many kings or magnates, such as an oil king, steel king, and automobile king. History has proved that domineering kings do not fare well in the end. Hitler,[4] Mussolini,[33] Tojo[120] and Chiang Kai-shek were all domineering kings for some time. Emperors used to live in this very room, but they are all gone. Kings possessed a lot of things, while the people went empty-handed. I believe that at the very beginning of their struggle our Indonesian friends had practically nothing. When we first started our struggle, we were bare-handed, while our opponents were armed to the teeth. But the bare-handed people succeeded in wiping out those armed to the teeth. History of the last millennia shows that the more things decaying personages possess, the sooner they fall. Hence the conclusion: Peace is the best.

As far as atom bombs are concerned, we Asian-African countries are the "proletarians," because we do not have even a single atom bomb. It is hoped that countries rich in such "magic treasures" will handle them wisely; if they use them indiscreetly, the outcome will not necessarily be to their advantage. For our part, we do not have even one atom bomb, so how can we commit aggression against others? Is it not dangerous to commit aggression with two fists against those who have atom bombs? Yet they have branded us "aggressors," asserting that the Chinese are fond of aggression. According to them, we have, first, "invaded" China's mainland and are now going to "invade" the Jinmen and Mazu islands; second, in Korea Kim Il Sung "invaded" up to the 38th Parallel[88] and then China helped him, and, third, Ho Chi Minh also "invaded" up to the 17th Parallel.[102] Those who vilify us seem to be very peace-loving guys. We have, moreover, heard that the Dutch assert that Indonesia is going to "invade" West Irian.[152]

Mr. Prime Minister has said that Indonesia wants to make peaceful use of its own rich resources. To this, I agree fully. Having such enormous quantities of valuable resources, Indonesia has very bright prospects. Though Japan is relatively more developed, it lacks natural resources, and Indonesia can certainly surpass Japan one day. The population of Indonesia and that of Japan are about the same size, but Indonesia is larger than Japan in area, with good climatic conditions and particularly rich resources. After a number of years a new Indonesia, stronger than Japan, will emerge. Of course, Indonesia is making peaceful use of its resources, and this will be in the interest of others too.

The Chinese people fully support the Indonesian people in defending their own country. We believe that similarly the Indonesian people support the Chinese people in defending China. We see no conflicts of interest between our two countries; we can only find areas in which the two countries can cooperate with mutual benefit.

There are good prospects for the solidarity of Asian and African countries, and the Bandung Conference is the first step. In future we should exert common effort, continue our work, unite and promote peace. Even if a war threatens, we can put it off. We should strive for a peaceful environment for as long as possible, and this is possible and hopeful. If the United States is also willing to sign a peace treaty, let it be a peace treaty valid for 100 years, if 50 years is not enough; we can agree to any length of time. It is not known whether the United States would agree or not. The main problem now lies with the United States. I believe you would have no objection.

(From the verbatim record)

HISTORY AND CURRENT REALITY DEMAND THAT WE UNITE AND COOPERATE*

(*June 30, 1955*)

The Yugoslavians are heroic people who have waged heroic struggles, and your party has also waged heroic struggles. Now your country has won liberation, and so have the other East European countries, China, North Korea, and the half of Vietnam under the leadership of Chairman Ho Chi Minh. All this is a contribution to humankind, and this makes the imperialists unhappy. When we quarrel among ourselves, the imperialists are happy. Recently the leading comrades of the Soviet Union and Yugoslavia have held talks, following initiative on both parties. The Soviet delegation was accorded a warm welcome by the people of your country, and following the talks your two countries issued a joint statement, which made us and all the progressive people of the world very happy.

It is a very good thing that diplomatic relations have now been established between our two countries. Your country recognized ours very early. Since the founding of our People's Republic, you have always supported us; there has been no change in your consistent position. There is a reason why we delayed establishing diplomatic relations with you, and that was because we hoped to act together with the Soviet Union in improving relations with your country. We thought that it would be better for China to follow the Soviet Union in establishing relations with Yugoslavia, so the establishment of diplomatic relations between our two countries was delayed for a few years. In view of the international environment, it is more appropriate that now our diplomatic relations are established.

The people of China have friendly feelings for the Yugoslav people; Comrade Ambassador can see this for yourself in China.

Now the stalemate in Soviet-Yugoslav relations has been resolved. It is the international development that have prompted this resolution and promoted

---

* These are excerpts from Mao Zedong's talk with V. Popovic, ambassador of Yugoslavia to China.

the improvement in Soviet-Yugoslav relations. This is in the interest of international peace and socialism and in conformity with Marxism-Leninism. This does not mean that your two countries' views are now identical. However, when there is agreement on major issues, matters will be easier to handle.

Recently I received Comrade Tito's[121] letter, introducing you to serve as Yugoslav ambassador to China. I was delighted to receive this letter, as it was correspondence not only between states, but also between comrades. On the 27th of this month Comrade Tito received the Chinese ambassador to Yugoslavia and expressed friendly sentiments. I am very thankful for this, and I request that you convey my thanks to Comrade Tito. Yugoslavia's relations with the Soviet Union and other relevant countries can still be improved. We have heard that Comrade Tito is preparing to visit Moscow shortly; is this news true? [*Popovic*: It is true.] This will be a very good thing. History and current reality demand that we unite and cooperate. We have time; we do not have to hurry. Maybe there are still some discordant matters; however, things will get better by and by. We should stress our common points. Where views differ, talks can be held without haste, and discussions can be conducted. If agreement cannot be reached, the differing views can be put aside to await future talks; they should not be allowed to hinder relations. This is a beneficial approach.

Our People's Republic was founded only recently and is still backward. Our national reconstruction which has just started will take a very long time. We need the help of the Communist Parties and people of all other countries. You need help, and so do we. If you find any shortcomings on our part, please do not hesitate to let us know, and we can exchange views.

(From the verbatim record)

REESTABLISHMENT OF DIPLOMATIC RELATIONS BETWEEN CHINA AND ITALY IS BENEFICIAL TO BOTH SIDES*

(October 3, 1955)

We appreciate very much your efforts to promote reestablishment of diplomatic relations between China and Italy; this is beneficial to both sides. As to difficulties, there is only one point, namely, we ask Italy to sever relations with Chiang Kai-shek, and we are opposed to the U.S. move to create "two Chinas." Take the case of our relations with Britain. Only after Britain severed most of its relations with Chiang Kai-shek, did we agree to mutual recognition. However, Britain maintained its recognition of Chiang Kai-shek in the United Nations, and that was why we agreed to only "semidiplomatic relations" with Britain—accrediting only a chargè d'affaires mutually. Italy is not yet a member state of the United Nations, so the question of its recognition of the Kuomintang in the United Nations does not arise. However, the United States is exerting pressure on Italy to refrain from recognizing People's China. If the Italian government can resist this pressure, we can at once establish diplomatic relations. Presumably, this would take some time.

Some countries are not friendly toward the Chinese people, yet once normal relations are established, we are ready to do business with them. We are willing to establish normal relations with Italy, as this would be in the interest of the people of both our countries.

I can cite the cases of India, Burma, Indonesia, Pakistan, Sweden, Denmark, Norway and Switzerland—all these countries severed relations with Chiang Kai-shek before establishing normal relations with China. Britain has chosen to leave a "tail issue" pending in the United Nations; when we raised this question, the British found it difficult to provide an answer.

Our art troupe is currently giving performances in Italy. Can Italy also

---

* These are excerpts from Mao Zedong's talk with Pietro Nenni, Vice-Chairman of the World Peace Council, Chairman of the National Peace Council of Italy and General Secretary of the Socialist Party of Italy.

organize an art troupe to visit China? Various ways of contact can be explored and tried. Delegations sent by Italy to China may include some capitalists, to let them see for themselves. If the Italian government agrees, China can also send delegations to Italy. Our contact with Japan has been more frequent; currently there are over 200 Japanese delegates visiting China.

We are now engaged in work that was never undertaken in the past. To do our work better, we rely on our own efforts, but we need help from friends as well. We warmly welcome your visit to China.

(From the verbatim record)

ON SINO-JAPANESE RELATIONS AND THE QUESTION OF A WORLD WAR*

(*October 15, 1955*)

A warm welcome to all of you. We are all colored people, who are looked down upon by others, and whose biggest "shortcoming" is being colored. Some people like "colored metals," or nonferrous metals, but dislike colored people. In my view, colored people are like colored metals which are precious, and colored people are at least as valuable as white people. Both colored people and white people are human beings; both are first-class, not second-class—the second class being animals, not humans. All humans in the world, whatever the color of their skin, are equal. Now our two nations are equal; we are two great nations. Yours is a very good nation. I think it will not be easy for anyone to bully the Japanese. In many areas you are wiser than we are; yours is an industrialized country, while ours is still an agricultural country, and we are exerting effort.

In calling on the host, guests indicate their good opinion of the host, and so the host should thank the guests. Today our guests come from a neighboring country; coming from next door, they are very close neighbors. When Japanese friends come to China, come from your homes in Japan to our homes to have a look, we should express our thanks. In future we should have more contact with one another. In the world there is no instance in which only one side thanks the other side; if that were the case, it would not be good. There should be mutual benefit, mutual help and mutual gratitude.

Our two countries face a common problem, that is, there is a country that is weighing heavily on us. You think China is now independent, don't you? China is not yet completely independent, just like you; you too is not completely independent, and this is our common point. Our Taiwan is not yet liberated; the United States has stretched its hands very far. It has seized our Taiwan, and it has seized Japan, the Philippines and South Korea. It wants to

---

* These are excerpts from Mao Zedong's talk with a visiting delegation of Japanese Diet members.

seize this vast land of Asia. This cannot last long. This land is our land, and affairs here should be managed by our peoples. Now we demand that the United States let go and withdraw its hands. Thereafter, we can shake hands. The United States is bullying us; it refuses to recognize China, asserting that China cannot be regarded as a country. We recognize the United States, but it refuses to recognize us. This has got you implicated, so that you find it difficult to recognize us. In fact, the majority of the Japanese people recognize us; only the American hands make you feel it is not yet time for recognition. This matter has to be resolved one day. Japan, the United States and other countries will have to recognize us one day. We are not impatient. Do you think we shall be unable to eat and sleep simply because you refuse to recognize us? We shall, as always, eat and sleep well. You may refuse to recognize us for 100 years, but in the 101st year you will have to recognize us.

The hand weighing over our heads must be pushed away. The hand over the heads of the Chinese people, the Japanese people, the Filipinos, the South Koreans and all other oppressed nations will be pushed away one day. On this point, we know and allow for your difficulty and we do not blame you for failing to establish diplomatic relations with us. In the past, when you recognized Chiang Kai-shek, our Foreign Ministry did blame you, but we sympathize with the whole Japanese nation. The Chinese people wish to see you grow stronger to push away the American hand. We have butted the United States in the belly. We butted it during the War to Resist U.S. Aggression and Aid Korea; when the United States was attempting to cross the Yalu River into our country, we pushed it back to the 38th Parallel.[88] That was also in the interest of Japan. Now, regarding our Taiwan, the day will come when we push the United States away from Taiwan. That will be in your interest as well as in our interest. We hope every struggle you wage will take your national independence one step forward and also advance your nation's rights one step. That would be in our interest as well as in your interest, and so we should also thank you. To attain independence is one's own obligation. Sino-Japanese relations should be improved without delay. In the past, ordinary Chinese did not like the Japanese; now we like you very much and are pleased to see people from Japan. Is this because then you gained and now you lose? No, then you did not gain, and now you do not lose. Your nation's struggle to regain independence is developing year by year and day by day; this is noticeable. Your achieving independence will have an impact on many other countries.

There is no tension between our two countries. What is your feeling? Perhaps before you came to China you had a little tension in your mind, when you thought that China was a Communist country, and communism was good according to some people and bad according to others. Would China show you courtesy? Would you be welcome here? Would you be faced with many accusations? I think possibly you had such speculations before you came. Now you can see for yourselves, as you have been in China for more than ten days. You may look for a longer time to see whether the Chinese people are friendly to you and whether they will bring accusations against you. We have not put to you any harsh terms, and there is nothing here to feel tense about. Don't feel tense. Too much tension is not good for life; it is better to ease international tensions. Moreover, although the social systems of our two countries are not the same, this should not prejudice our mutual respect and friendship. The debts of the past are not an obstacle, nor is the present difference in social systems. Let bygones be bygones; what matters is mainly the future.

Each nation in the world is moving forward; each has its strong points. If a nation has no strong points, it will become extinct. As both of us are colored peoples, it is only natural that we should respect each other. China has many shortcomings; she is still economically and culturally backward. In this regard you are better than we are. It took you only a few decades to change your country from an agricultural to an industrialized one, and you have therefore many things we can learn from. Ours is still an agricultural country, and we are now exerting efforts to change this state of backwardness—to change from an agricultural country into an industrialized one and from a culturally backward country into a country with modern culture. In this respect you, as friends, can criticize us, express your views and point out our shortcomings. This is not interference in internal affairs. Questions of interference in internal affairs are matters for your foreign minister and our foreign minister to worry about. In this case our foreign minister would not have objections—whatever opinions you may have in this respect, please speak your mind. I am sorry to say that I lag behind you; you are more knowledgeable about China, while I am not knowledgeable about your country—I am a backward element. I hope someday I shall have the opportunity to learn—to take a look around in Japan and to express the friendship of the Chinese people. The earth is revolving really fast; it seems the sun sets soon after it rises. I hope to take a look at some other countries too, even the United States, and to express there the friendship of the Chinese people. However, this hope cannot be realized now.

The affairs of each country should be managed by that country itself. This is a truism. The affairs of the United States should be managed by that country itself; they are none of our business. But now the United States is meddling too much. Your nation committed a grave mistake in the past. However, you have derived a blessing from a bane—having laid down that burden, you now have the initiative. You are now qualified to criticize the Americans, as well as the French, Dutch, Belgians, Portuguese and British. You are now in a very good position. It is not fortuitous that your country attended the Bandung Conference.[111] Your attitude at the Bandung Conference was good, and now you are free from a burden. China also committed mistakes; all the past governments were corrupt, those of the Qing Dynasty, of the Northern Warlords and of Chiang Kai-shek were all corrupt governments, with the result that China today is still a backward agricultural country. We give great attention to this question, knowing that things went wrong in this connection in China. We have lifted our heads and are also qualified to criticize others. We are making efforts to overcome our backwardness in industry. Our agricultural production level was very low—much lower than yours—and is now beginning to improve. We still have many shortcomings. We still have too many flies, and it is no good to be boastful. I hope you will maintain your present advantageous position and manage well your own affairs; then your prospects will be bright. Every victory of yours is helpful to us, and deserves our thanks. Now the Americans are committing no end of mistakes. They discriminate against the Japanese nation, enslave the Japanese people, and slaughter our people, too. This is an issue. Our two countries need mutual support, with you helping us and us helping you, without reservation. Between our two countries there should be no trouble-making—we do not make trouble in your affairs, nor you in ours. Let each of us manage our own affairs in an environment of mutual friendship. That will be in our interest as well as yours.

The so-called major issues of the world are issues concerning liberation, independence, democracy, peace, friendship, and human progress. There is a Chinese saying that the momentum of history was ever thus: "Prolonged division leads to reunification, and prolonged unification leads to division"; it appears at the very beginning of the Chinese novel *Three Kingdoms*. That was another mistake China committed in the past, for with endless alternation of division and unification, nothing could be accomplished. I may say here that peace and friendship will be the basic aspects of future world trends and a world war is undesirable. It is not necessary that we shall get frightened by war. The dropping of atom bombs is frightful to anyone, to the Japanese and Chinese alike. Therefore, it is best to have no war and to make every effort to avert a war. What if others insist on unleashing a war? If they want to fight, dropping an atom bomb over your head, then an enormous hole will be created, with the bomb going downward from China and coming out of an enormous hole somewhere in the United States. The earth is not very big; to my knowledge it has a diameter of only 25,100 Chinese *li*, that is, 12,550 kilometers. What is there to boast of in drilling this hole? If that really happens, I think things will not be fine for them. You have no colonies, nor do we, so both of us are not afraid of losing something. Hence, in unleashing a new world war they will only land themselves in a disadvantageous position. They are very much afraid of communism. World War I ended with the emergence of the Soviet Union, and World War II ended with the emergence of many countries guided by communism. Historically, communism has emerged in countries as an outcome of world wars. When there was fighting, the people got into a state of tension, which compelled them to seek a way out. No one at the time of his birth was told by his mother to go for communism—my mother never told me to go for communism. One was driven by circumstances to go for communism—having been driven repeatedly, one had to join the Liangshan rebels. In addition, there are countries that are not communist, but are countries of national independence, such as India, Indonesia and some other Asian and African countries, that also emerged as an outcome of the world war. I have discussed this reasoning with Prime Minister Nehru by saying that India and Indonesia emerged as an outcome of the last world war. I was not spreading falsehoods. Such are the consequences of the two world wars. If you do not believe, you can do some investigation; the Soviet Union does exist, another country called the People's Republic of China does exist, and other independent countries, such as India, do exist in the world. So you can in no way say I was lying. Though I am not a historian, history is clearly there. Of course, it would be better not to have world wars.

They may assert, "You are using communism to frighten us, threaten us and subvert us." No, we are not threatening them; we only want no new world war. If there is no world war, their pursuits can continue, and communism can come later. If they insist on fighting and actually unleash a war, then the world's people will again be placed under tension and most of them will go communist. If you do not believe me, let us have a bet. If, as an outcome of another world war, 70 to 80 percent of the world's people do not go communist, I shall stop eating, leaving all my food for you to enjoy. This is not a wager with you, but a wager with the United States. For evidence, there are the outcomes of the two world wars.

Sino-Japanese relations have a very long history. Humankind lived in peace for hundreds of thousands of years. Though our ancestors had quarrels and fights, those episodes can and should be forgotten. As those were unpleasant episodes, what is the point of keeping them in mind?

World War II changed the relations between our two countries. As I said earlier, your country is now in an advantageous position, with reason and justice on your side. In the past your country owed debts to others; that is over and now someone owes you debts. Now you have much political capital and we also have the political capital to ask for payment of the debts the United States owes us. I have full confidence to say that the United States owes us debts. Now you feel at ease, as distinct from your position during World War II. You are on just grounds now, aren't you? As you have formally apologized for the debts you incurred in the past, it is not reasonable to ask for your payment of those debts. You cannot be asked to apologize everyday, can you? It is not good for a nation to constantly feel guilty, and we can understand this point. We are your friends, and you can see clearly that the Chinese people treat you not as enemies but as friends. To speak frankly, we should try by all means to make the United States withdraw its hands. It is entirely unjustifiable that the United States has stretched its hands so far. You Japanese can resolve this issue after a number of years.

We should help each other, complement each other's deficiencies, live together in peace and friendship, carry out cultural exchanges, and establish normal diplomatic relations (which cannot be done through compulsion). The question of war criminals has been raised a bit too early. Let normal diplomatic relations be resumed, then a solution to this question can be sought as soon as possible. The reason is very simple: We do not need to detain those war criminals. What good is there to detain them? In Japan, however, some people tend to twist political issues into technical questions, asserting that as there is now no fighting between China and Japan, why the state of war between the two countries? But legally, China and Japan are still in a state of war. It is very good that you have given resumption of Sino-Japanese relations top priority. The interests of the people demand that normal diplomatic relations between our two countries be established as soon as possible. Cultural exchanges can be conducted right now. A Japanese song and dance ensemble came to China, and I had the pleasure of watching the performance, which was very good. Their visit helped to promote understanding between our two peoples and was also helpful to us artistically. We can learn from each other's strong points to make up for deficiencies and help each other.

(From the verbatim record)

OUR WISH IS TO PROMOTE FRIENDSHIP BETWEEN CHINA AND THAILAND*

(December 1955 and February 1956)

I

China can trade with Thailand. Thailand wants to sell several hundred thousand tons of rice to China, and we can buy it. In addition, we can buy some rubber from Thailand. What do you need from us? You need steel and iron—we have these. If you need light industrial products, we have them too. As for daily necessities, you should set up your own factories to produce them. We can help you build light-industry factories. At present we can help you build cotton textile factories, paper mills and sugar refineries. For these you can barter rice and rubber. If you so need, we can also send technical personnel to help you in designing those factories, after whose completion they will return to China and hand over to you the entire factories.

I am thankful for the greetings from Prime Minister Marshal Piblu Songgram, Police-General Nai Phol and Nai Nuan. We hope that all parties concerned will cooperate and unite; we also hope that Pibul Songgram and Nai Phol will unite. We in China do not have secrets—we do not behave in one way in front of people and in another way behind their back. We are open and aboveboard, and do not go in for double-dealing. You can find this out when you have the opportunity of visiting India or Burma. With more contact with China and with the passage of time you can understand this by yourselves.

Will China commit aggression against your country? You can wait and see for eight or ten years. You can see whether China respects you and treats you as brothers. Wait and see for a number of years, and you will see clearly.

---

* These are excerpts from Mao Zedong's two talks: the first one with Thai representatives Anphon and others, and the second one with the visiting delegation of the People of Thailand for Promoting Friendship with China.

Another thing: you can wait and see whether we are reasonable. Some people say that Communists are unreasonable, unfaithful, irascible and difficult to make friends with because of past loggerheads. You can also wait and see. Although the United States has had the severest quarrels with us, yet we are willing to make friends with it, but it is unwilling. What can be done when we are willing, but the United States is unwilling? We can only wait.

You need to act with caution, as the United States could be ruthless. You should take care. When you proposed that you would come to China secretly, we agreed as soon as we understood your difficulties. We should both proceed slowly and step by step in improving Sino-Thai relations. It is desirable that Pibul Songgram and Nai Phol unite, as their unity is in the interest of Thailand. The United States wishes to see discord and quarreling in your midst. In inciting one faction against another, the United States aims to fish in troubled waters. It is very good that you have come to China at this time, and you may come again if there is another opportunity. If you so wish, we can also send people to visit your country, but we would not do so if you found it inconvenient. If because of our visit the United States created trouble and caused you difficulty, our people could refrain from going. In your country we shall not talk about communism; we shall talk only about peaceful coexistence, friendship and trade. We never incite anyone to oppose his government. Prime Minister U Nu used to fear we might incite the Burmese Communist Party to oppose his government; we have said to him that we recognize only his government and that there cannot be two governments simultaneously in any country. In your country, too, there are Communists, but we shall never incite them to oppose your government.

There are overseas Chinese in Thailand. Those who have acquired Thai nationality should be regarded as citizens of Thailand; only those who have not acquired Thai nationality are Chinese. Otherwise the presence of too many overseas Chinese might cause fears. The Communist organizations among the overseas Chinese have been disbanded in order to expel possible suspicions on the part of the government of the countries in which the overseas Chinese reside; mutual trust can thus be promoted. You can see for yourselves whether our action differ from our words. If you think words are no proof, you can wait and see the facts. With a longer period of observation you can see clearly the true state of affairs.

(December 21, 1955)
(From the verbatim record)

II

We hope to improve relations between our two countries step by step, so that diplomatic relations will be established later on. This can be done as conditions in your country permit; for our part, we can wait. Our wish is to see our two countries friendly to each other. Misunderstandings can gradually be cleared. For instance, there are fears that China might commit aggression against Thailand. In reality, it is China that is afraid of aggression, aggression by the United States. We have no fear of India or Thailand invading us, but the United States has invaded and occupied our Taiwan.[117]

As you are faced with difficulties, you need to take your time and proceed in light of realities. If necessary, you may say a few good words about the United States and a few bad words about China—this we can understand. Every country must develop its own economy and culture. The fact that your country and other countries have attained independence and made progress in their economic and cultural development is in the interest of China. The prime ministers of Pakistan, Cambodia and Ceylon[114] are scheduled to visit China in the near future. In fact, Mr. Mohammed Ali, the ex-prime minister of Pakistan, abused China and quarreled with Premier Zhou Enlai at the Bandung Conference. Prince Sihanouk[122] too quarreled with Premier Zhou. [Mao asks Premier Zhou: Did Prince Wan Waithayakon[123] quarrel with you? Zhou replies: Prince Wan Waithayakon was friendly from the very beginning.] So you quarreled little. Between China and those countries quarreling is one aspect; solidarity is another aspect. Those countries' opposition to China is different from U.S. opposition to China. Do you agree that there is a difference? I believe there is. The Japanese government also opposes us, but that is not the same as U.S. opposition to China. The same with the Philippines; it is not willing to establish diplomatic relations with China and Carlos P. Romulo[124] quarreled with Premier Zhou at the Bandung Conference. We are concerned about the predication of these countries, with whom we share a common lot, as we are all bullied by the United States. Asian and African countries are all opposed to colonialism. Indonesia resents the Netherlands; North Africa and Indochina resent France; Malaya[125] resents Britain, and so do Near East and Middle East countries. Those colonialists speak ill of us, alleging that we are grabbing their markets. However, it is not China but the United States that snatches markets in other countries. It is not China but the United States that has established military bases on foreign soil. Again, it is not China but the United States that has dispatched military advisory missions to various other countries. To sum up, first, China has not snatched the markets of other countries; second, China has not established any military bases abroad; third, China has not dispatched military advisory missions to other countries, and, fourth, China has not imposed unequal treaties on other countries with political strings attached. In actuality, China has seized their market on the territory of China and built military bases within China, thus driving away their friend, Chiang Kai-shek. The United States alleges that we have committed mistakes in snatching the market of China, in building military bases within China, and in having been impolite to Chiang Kai-shek. Now we have committed further mistakes. What are these mistakes? These allegedly are the mistake of playing host to visiting foreign friends. In the last three years 1,000 Japanese have come to visit China, including members of the Japanese Diet, and we have committed the mistake of according them hospitality. Now we have committed the mistake of playing host to you. One day this mistake will recur in our hosting visiting Americans. The president of the Chinese People's Institute of Foreign Affairs is a maker of mistakes, because he constantly plays host to foreign friends. In visiting China, you are also committing a mistake, and more people will commit the same mistake. As your country moves toward neutrality, she will be committing more mistakes, because any talk about peace and neutrality is branded by the United States as committing a mistake. Strange that this should be the right and wrong of the world.

(February 10, 1956)
(From the verbatim record)

WE WISH TO LEARN FROM ALL COUNTRIES OF THE WORLD*

(*April 10, 1956*)

Chairman Mao Zedong (hereinafter referred to as *Mao*): How long have you been in Beijing?

Ambassador J. A. Gregerson (hereinafter referred to as *Gregerson*): About three years. I like Beijing very much. I sincerely hope that relations between our two countries will develop further.

Mao: There has never been any war between our two countries. Will there be any in the future?

Gregerson: No, there won't be any.

Mao: But isn't your country a member state of NATO? If the U.S. unleashes a war, how would you act?

Gregerson: That will not happen. Our two countries will not fight against each other. The emergence of China as a world power has saved peace.

Mao: China is only a mediocre country; she has a vast territory, but she is not strong.

Gregerson: China is a very big country, having an area of 12 million square kilometers, while Denmark has an area of only some 40 thousand square kilometers.

Mao: China's land area is not that big. It would be very good indeed if every square kilometer in China were as developed as in your country.

Gregerson: In addition, China has a population of 600 million!

Mao: China will not get cocky toward other countries; if she ever does, you can criticize her.

Gregerson: Of course, that will not happen. As for Denmark, small as it is, Denmark's management of per-unit area crops is not bad. I wish to point out to the Chairman that China is sending two delegations to Denmark to study agriculture and cooperatives there.

---

* These are excerpts from Mao Zedong's talk with J. A. Gregerson, Danish ambassador to China.

Mao: We very much wish to learn from your country; we wish to learn from all countries of the world. If the United States is willing, we wish to learn from that country, too. Every country has strong points worthy of learning. We wish to learn from Iceland, too.

Gregerson: Iceland has only a fishery industry; she has very little agriculture.

Mao: The fishery industry is something worth learning.

Gregerson: I hope that after their study tour in Denmark the Chinese delegations will introduce Denmark to people here.

Mao: Such an introduction needs to be published in China's newspapers. As you have always stayed in Beijing, your knowledge of China must be limited. I think every year after May First and October First (i.e., after the spring sowing and autumn harvest) two tours can be organized for the diplomatic envoys in Beijing to see various places in China. What do you think of that?

Gregerson: That is a very good idea.

Mao: We also wish to learn from you the way you run your cooperatives.

(From the verbatim record)

THE RELATIONSHIP BETWEEN CHINA AND OTHER COUNTRIES*

(*April 25, 1956*)

We have put forward the slogan of learning from other countries. I think we have been right. At present, the leaders of some countries are chary and even afraid of advancing this slogan. It takes some courage to do so, because theatrical pretensions have to be discarded.

It must be admitted that every nation has its strong points. If not, how can it survive? How can it progress? On the other hand, every nation has its weak points. Some believe that socialism is just perfect, without a single flaw. How can that be true? It must be recognized that there are always two aspects, the strong points and the weak points. The secretaries of our Party branches, the company commanders and platoon leaders of our army have all learned to jot down both aspects in their pocket notebooks, the weak points as well as the strong ones, when summing up their experience. They all know there are two aspects to everything, why do we mention only one? There will always be two aspects, even 10,000 years from now. Each age, whether the future or the present, has its own two aspects, and each individual has his own two aspects. In short, there are two aspects, not just one. To say there is only one is to be aware of one aspect and to be ignorant of the other.

Our policy is to learn from the strong points of all nations and all countries, learn all that is genuinely good in the political, economic, scientific and technological fields and in literature and art. But we must learn with an analytical and critical eye, not blindly, and we mustn't copy everything indiscriminately and transplant mechanically. Naturally, we mustn't pick up their shortcomings and weak points.

We should adopt the same attitude in learning from the experience of the Soviet Union and other socialist countries. Some of our people were not clear

---

* This is a section from "On the Ten Major Relationships," speech by Mao Zedong at an enlarged meeting of the Political Bureau of the Central Committee of the Communist Party of China.

about this before and even picked up their weaknesses. While they were swelling with pride over what they had picked up, it was already being discarded in those countries; as a result, they had to do a somersault like the Monkey Sun Wukong. For instance, there were people who accused us of making a mistake of principle in setting up a Ministry of Culture and a Bureau of Cinematography rather than a Ministry of Cinematography and a Bureau of Culture, as was the case in the Soviet Union. They did not anticipate that shortly afterward the Soviet Union would make a change and set up a Ministry of Culture as we had done. Some people never take the trouble to analyse, they simply follow the "wind." Today, when the north wind is blowing, they join the "north wind" school; tomorrow, when there is a west wind, they switch to the "west wind" school; afterward when the north wind blows again, they switch back to the "north wind" school. They hold no independent opinion of their own and often go from one extreme to the other.

In the Soviet Union, those who once extolled Stalin to the skies have now in one swoop consigned him to purgatory. Here in China some people are following their example. It is the opinion of the Central Committee that Stalin's mistakes amounted to only 30 per cent of the whole and his achievements to 70 per cent, and that all things considered Stalin was nonetheless a great Marxist. We wrote "On the Historical Experience of the Dictatorship of the Proletariat"[126] on the basis of this evaluation. This assessment of 30 per cent for mistakes and 70 per cent for achievements is just about right. Stalin did a number of wrong things in connection with China. The "Left" adventurism[127] pursued by Wang Ming in the latter part of the Second Revolutionary Civil War period and his Right opportunism[128] in the early days of the War of Resistance Against Japan can both be traced to Stalin. At the time of the War of Liberation, Stalin first enjoined us not to press on with the revolution, maintaining that if civil war flared up, the Chinese nation would run the risk of destroying itself. Then when fighting did erupt, he took us half seriously, half sceptically. When we won the war, Stalin suspected that ours was a victory of the Tito type, and in 1949 and 1950 the pressure on us was very strong indeed. Even so, we maintain the estimate of 30 per cent for his mistakes and 70 per cent for his achievements. This is only fair.

In the social sciences and in Marxism-Leninism, we must continue to study Stalin diligently wherever he is right. What we must study is all that is universally true and we must make sure that this study is linked with Chinese reality. It would lead to a mess if every single sentence, even of Marx's, were followed. Our theory is an integration of the universal truth of Marxism-Leninism with the concrete practice of the Chinese revolution. At one time some people in the Party went in for dogmatism, and this came under our criticism. Nevertheless, there is still dogmatism today. It still exists in academic circles and in economic circles too.

In the natural sciences we are rather backward, and here we should make a special effort to learn from foreign countries. And yet we must learn critically, not blindly. In technology I think first we have to follow others in most cases, and it is better for us to do so, since that is what we are lacking at present and know little about. However, in those cases where we already have clear knowledge, we must not follow others in every detail.

We must firmly reject and criticize all the decadent bourgeois systems, ideologies and ways of life of foreign countries. But this should in no way prevent us from learning the advanced sciences and technologies of capitalist countries and whatever is scientific in the management of their enterprises. In the industrially developed countries they run their enterprises with fewer people and greater efficiency and they know how to do business. All this should be learned well in accordance with our own principles in order to improve our work. Nowadays, those who make English their study no longer work hard at it, and research papers are no longer translated into English, French, German or Japanese for exchange with other countries. This too is a kind of blind prejudice. Neither the indiscriminate rejection of everything foreign, whether scientific, technological or cultural, nor the indiscriminate imitation of everything foreign as noted above, has anything in common with the Marxist attitude, and neither in any way benefits our cause.

In my opinion, China has two weaknesses, which are at the same time two strong points.

First, in the past China was a colonial and semi-colonial country, not an imperialist power, and was always bullied by others. Its industry and agriculture are not developed and its scientific and technological level is low, and except for its vast territory, rich resources, large population, long history, *A Dream of Red Mansions* in literature, and so on, China is inferior to other countries in many respects, and so has no reason to feel conceited. However, there are people who, having been slaves too long, feel inferior in everything and don't stand up straight in the presence of foreigners. They are just like Jia Gui[129] in the opera *The Famen Temple* who, when asked to take a seat, refuses to do so, giving the excuse that he is used to standing in attendance. Here we need to bestir ourselves, enhance our national confidence and encourage the spirit typified by "scorn U.S. imperialism," which was fostered during the movement to resist U.S. aggression and aid Korea.

Second, our revolution came late. Although the Revolution of 1911 which overthrew the Qing emperor preceded the Russian revolution, there was no Communist Party at that time and the revolution failed. Victory in the people's revolution came only in 1949, some 30 years later than the October Revolution. On this account too, we are not in a position to feel conceited. The Soviet Union differs from our country in that, firstly, tsarist Russia was an imperialist power and, secondly, it had the October Revolution. As a result, many people in the Soviet Union are conceited and very arrogant.

Our two weaknesses are also strong points. As I have said elsewhere, we are first "poor" and second "blank." By "poor" I mean we do not have much industry and our agriculture is underdeveloped. By "Blank" I mean we are like a blank sheet of paper and our cultural and scientific level is not high. From the developmental point of view, this is not bad. The poor want revolution, whereas it is difficult for the rich to want revolution. Countries with a high scientific and technological level are overblown with arrogance. We are like a blank sheet of paper, which is good for writing on.

Being "poor" and "blank" is therefore all to our good. Even when one day our country becomes strong and prosperous, we must still adhere to the revolutionary stand, remain modest and prudent, learn from other countries and not allow ourselves to become swollen with conceit. We must not only learn from other countries during the period of our First Five-Year-Plan, but must go on doing so after the completion of scores of five-year plans. We must be ready to learn even 10,000 years from now. Is there anything bad about that?

(From *People's Daily*, December 26, 1976)

DO NOT BLINDLY BELIEVE THAT EVERYTHING IS GOOD IN A SOCIALIST COUNTRY*

(June 28, 1956)

You may have discussions with responsible personnel of our government departments, armed forces, Party committees and mass organizations. You can ask to meet with whomever you wish to talk with. If the persons talking with you speak only about achievements and do not speak about mistakes and shortcomings, they are not giving an account of the real conditions. People with experience will not believe their assertions. We should not blindly believe that everything is good in a socialist country. There are two aspects to everything: the good and the bad. In our society we certainly have good things, but we also have bad things; we have good people and also bad people; we have advanced things as well as backward things. It is precisely because of this that we are carrying out reforms, to reform the bad into the good. We must be prepared to find bad things; otherwise, if a problem crops up, one will think it is terrifying. In the past, the Soviet Union was believed to be free of mistakes; now that the question of Stalin has surfaced, many people are taken aback. The world is beautiful and also not so beautiful, and there are conflicts and contradictions in the world. To hope that everything is well and good is our subjective wish, but the reality is something objective. Since ancient times there have been good things and bad things in the world, and it will be like that 10,000 years hence. As there are bad things in the world, we need to work and carry out reforms. However, we can not do everything well, or our offspring will have no work to do.

We should not do anything to excess, as excessiveness invariably leads to mistakes. Stalin was basically correct and had great meritorious achievements, but he also committed very big mistakes and did many things wrong. Stalin

---

* These are excerpts from Mao Zedong's talk with Nicolae Cirroiu, ambassador of Romania to China.

erred on the side of excessiveness. The suppression of counterrevolutionaries was originally a good thing, but doing it to excess and regarding revolutionary comrades as counterrevolutionaries was a big mistake. I told the Soviet comrades that they had committed mistakes in the past and would commit mistakes in future. They were not inclined to believe this. We in China have also committed many mistakes, including grave mistakes. In our Party there have been mistakes of Chen Duxiu's Right opportunism,[130] Li Lisan's "Left" opportunism,[131] Wang Ming's "Left" opportunism,[127] Zhang Guotao's Right opportunism,[132] Wang Ming's Right opportunism,[128] and Gao Gang's Anti-Party Right Opportunism.[133] In future there certainly will be mistakes and there will be persons like Gao Gang and the others. We will try to confine the extent of mistakes, and that is possible. But it is unrealistic to deny we can commit mistakes. That will not be the situation of this world or of the earth, but of planet Mars.

(From the verbatim record)

ASIAN-AFRICAN COUNTRIES SHOULD UNITE TO SAFEGUARD PEACE AND INDEPENDENCE*

(*August 21, 1956*)

We welcome very much your visit to China. Our two countries are neighbors and friends, and we are very happy that relations between our two countries have recently become closer and have developed further. You have already seen how delighted the Chinese people are to see you.

We in China have difficulties, too. As we have been oppressed by foreign powers for over 100 years and founded the People's Republic not long ago, development is needed in industry, culture and other fields. We need help from friends. Our countries can carry on cooperation in the future.

We welcome your visit to China in order to promote mutual understanding. Smaller countries should also be respected. Cambodia regards herself as a small country, but we have received her visiting delegation as envoys of a great nation. We treat big and small countries as equals.

All Asian-African countries are now striving for independence. It has been only a little over one year since the Asian-African Conference[111] and the Bandung Spirit has spread fast and its impact is great. The Asian-African conference united big and small countries encompassing a population of 1.5 billion. Since the Egyptian incident[134] the line of demarcation between colonialism and anti-colonialism has become more pronounced. At the London Conference[135] even Japan did not side with the colonialists. Japan had not been so active at the Bandung Conference. The colonialist countries have few people and are fundamentally not frightening. With their wings clipped, they cannot fly now. Currently all Asian-African countries are striving for independence and developing their economies and cultures, and this has even influenced Latin America.

As our numerous Asian-African countries had been subjected to foreign domination, with the winning of independence we should unite to safeguard

---

* These are excerpts from Mao Zedong's talk with Prince Souvana Phuma, Prime Minister of the Kingdom of Laos.

peace and independence. It can be seen by just looking at our countries that we shall not commit aggression against other countries. There is no reason to commit aggression against others. A land has long been inhabited by its own nation; on what grounds should other nations intrude? In the past Japan was the aggressor, and now the United States is. There are still foreign bases on your soil, and our Taiwan is still occupied by others.

Your policies and principles are very good—internally you have pursued a policy of peace and democracy, and externally a policy of independence and friendship. This enables you to develop your economy in a peaceful environment. Now your civil war has ended and reconciliation has been achieved. We follow a similar policy, and we are ready to resolve the Taiwan question with Chiang Kai-shek by peaceful means. You have done very well—with the solution of internal problems, things are easier to manage.

Among those present here today on our side there are none who fought with us in the past, but there are some who quarreled with us, because they belong to various political parties. Those who fought against us also have their jobs in Beijing, with each playing an appropriate role.

Many of our principles are identical. We shall never interfere in your internal affairs, never do communist propaganda in your country, never attempt to overthrow your government—ours is a policy of friendship. Whatever system, policy and religion you choose is your own affair, in which we shall not, and should not, interfere. We shall assuredly support you on the basis of the Five Principles,[98] and this is mutually beneficial.

We are concerned about the East, not the West, as in the East there are still people like Syngman Rhee,[85] Chiang Kai-shek and Ngo Dinh Diem.[136] In the past Japan committed aggression against China; now many Japanese have contact with us. We want to have good relations with them, and we are also willing to have good relations with the United States. We have talked with the United States at Panmunjom for two years and at Geneva for a year; we believe the talks will end up well one day, and we are not impatient. Over the Taiwan question our attitude is the same, we are not impatient.

(From the verbatim record)

UNITING WITH FRATERNAL COUNTRIES AND ESTABLISHING FRIENDLY RELATIONS WITH ALL COUNTRIES*

(August 29, 1956)

I

It must be made clear that both the Chinese revolution and China's national reconstruction depend primarily on mobilizing the efforts of the Chinese people, and secondarily on seeking foreign assistance. The mentality of diffidence, thinking that we Chinese are not good at anything, that it is not we ourselves who decide China's destiny and, therefore, that everything relies on foreign assistance, is a totally erroneous mentality. Having affirmed this point, we must also affirm another point; namely, we should continue efforts to unite with the Soviet Union and all the other fraternal countries and to unite with all fraternal parties, people's revolutionary parties and the broad masses of the people around the world, winning their sympathy and assistance. It will be equally erroneous if we do not affirm this point.

II

Our foreign policy is based on the Five Principles of Peaceful Coexistence.[98] To ease international tension and support the anti-colonialist national liberation movement, our government and people have done a great deal of useful work. We should do more in the future to unite and develop all world forces for peace in the interest of a lasting world peace and thus also in

---

* These two paragraphs were added by Mao Zedong while going over the draft text of the Central Committee's Political Report to the Eighth National Congress of the Communist Party of China.

the interest of our national reconstruction. In the interest of peace and reconstruction, we are ready to establish friendly relations with all other countries in the world, including the United States. We are convinced that this will eventually be achieved one day.

(From the original manuscript)

THE CHINESE PEOPLE SUPPORT EGYPT'S RECOVERY OF THE SUEZ CANAL*

(*September 17, 1956*)

We are very pleased to see Egyptians; there are no barriers between us. Egypt has done an extremely good thing.[134] All the people of China support Egypt; the peoples of Africa, Asia, Latin America and indeed of the whole world support Egypt. At least 80 percent of people around the world support Egypt; only a few countries oppose Egypt, and a few others have remained neutral.

As I see it, the United States also approves of Egypt's recovery of the Suez Canal. It will not help Britain recapture the canal from the hands of Egypt, for that would not be in its interest. The United States has its own objectives. To that country, it does not make much difference whether the Suez Canal is in the hands of Britain and France or in the hands of Egypt. From the very beginning it does not expect to have the Dulles Plan[137] implemented. What the United States wants is to use this opportunity to drive Britain and France out of the Middle East, so as to establish its own sphere of influence there. The Soviet Union, the Arab states, India and the Colombo countries[109] all support Egypt. With the Soviet Union standing by, Britain, the United States and France do not dare act rashly. This time Egypt has ingeniously made use of the contradictions among the imperialist countries, those between the imperialist and socialist countries, and those between the imperialist countries and the nationalist independent countries. You might also make use of the contradictions between the governments and the people of the imperialist countries, as they are not homogeneous internally.

The king of your country[138] did bad things and was therefore overthrown by the people, but he is still an Egyptian. Now that all the people of Egypt are united, as are all the Arab peoples and all Asian-African peoples, he should also show some patriotism and refrain from making statements detrimental to

---

* These are excerpts from Mao Zedong's talk with Hassan Rajab, ambassador of Egypt to China.

Egypt, from behaving like a lackey of the imperialists. You might try to work on him. In China, though the landlords were deprived of land during the land reform, they still supported our fighting U.S. aggressors during the War to Resist U.S. Aggression and Aid Korea.

Egypt has united the 80 million Arab people to form a staunch anti-imperialist front, and Egypt stands as its advance guard. China is the advance guard of another anti-imperialist front. With your presence, the going is easier for us; if you were defeated, our going here would be tougher. In Egypt there are many foreign businesses, and in the Middle East there are many more foreign oil enterprises. It is impossible to take those businesses back all at once; things have to be done step by step. The recovery of the Suez Canal is a very good beginning. For the time being, it is better for President Nasser[139] not to go to places where security measures are inadequate, for the imperialists, having failed in their plans, are capable of resorting to all means, including assassination. Western countries are vilifying President Nasser, calling him a careerist and a Hitler and alleging that he wants to dominate the Arab world. But in our view President Nasser is a national hero of the Asian-African region and therefore is disliked by the imperialists. He has handled matters very wisely, alternating tough and soft tactics and take a very peaceable approach on some occasions. In his recent talks with the Five-Nation Committee,[140] President Nasser managed to send them back with a very gentle tone.

In China you may go to any place you want without restrictions. If you so wish, you can see our army, air force and naval units, factories, schools, villages, etc. You can talk to anyone you wish, including face-to-face talks with our workers and peasants. You can call on leaders of our democratic parties; they are very supportive of Egypt and would be delighted to have you call on them. You can also call on responsible members of our various departments and ask for any data from them that you need. Our Foreign Ministry will give you all the necessary help and facility. You might wish to study the conditions of China, which are truly worth studying. In Beijing now Egyptians are most welcome.

The Soviet Union will do its utmost to help Egypt. We in China are also ready to do what we can to help Egypt, and our assistance is without any strings attached. Whatever you need, we are willing to help to the best of our ability. If you can pay, you may do so; if you cannot, let it be; we shall provide assistance free of charge. Of course, being a country with national pride, Egypt may wish to pay back our assistance. An account may be kept for future repayment, or repayment after 100 years. Egypt is now subjected to an economic blockade by the Western powers; we understand the hardships of the Egyptian people, having weathered similar blockade. In the War to Resist U.S. Aggression and Aid Korea, China spent a lot of money and sustained heavy casualties. Now that war is no more, we can do our best to help Egypt.

(From the verbatim record)

OVERSEAS CHINESE SHOULD OBSERVE THE LAWS OF THE COUNTRY IN WHICH THEY RESIDE*

(*September 18, 1956*)

The government of China has consistently encouraged overseas Chinese to observe the laws and decrees of the country in which they reside, enjoined them not to engage in political activities, and encouraged them to contribute their human efforts and financial resources to serve the interests of the residing country. Of course, it is possible that some overseas Chinese have done something against the interests of Indonesia, but that has nothing to do with the Chinese government. If such cases occur, the Chinese government and the Indonesian government should cooperate closely to educate them. The legitimate interests of overseas Chinese, including businessmen, should be protected; however, punishment should be meted out to unscrupulous merchants who engage in illegal, fraudulent or blackmail activities. We in China punished such unscrupulous businessmen during our movements against the Three Evils [i.e., corruption, waste and bureaucracy] and the Five Evils [i.e., bribery, tax evasion, theft of state property, cheating on government contracts and stealing of classified economic information]. We have not yet established diplomatic relations with Singapore; if and when diplomatic relations are established, we can also carry on such education among the overseas Chinese there.

(From the verbatim record)

---

* These are excerpts from Mao Zedong's talk with Soekadjo Wijopranoto, ambassador of Indonesia to China.

DRAW HISTORICAL LESSONS AND OPPOSE BIG-NATION CHAUVINISM*

(*September 1956*)

We welcome you to China. We are delighted that you have come. We have received support from you and from all other fraternal parties. Of course we, too, have supported you and all other fraternal parties. Now the Marxist-Leninist Communist front is united, whether in places where victory has been won or in places where victory has not yet been won. There were times when the parties were not united. In certain respects we let you down. We went along with the views of the Information Bureau.[34] Though we did not join that bureau, it was difficult for us not to support it. In 1949, when the Information Bureau branded you butchers and Hitlerites, we did not express our attitude on the related resolution of the bureau. In 1948 we published an article criticizing you. In fact, we should not have taken such an approach, but should have consulted with you. If some of your views were wrong, we could have discussed them with you, let you make self-criticism, and avoided being in such a hurry. Conversely, if you have a disagreement with us, you can also take this approach, the approach of consultation and persuasion. Indeed, to criticize the party of a foreign country in the press is seldom successful. This incident was a profound historical lesson for the international communist movement. You suffered a wrong, but to the international communist movement it was a lesson derived from a mistake, which should be fully understood.

When you recognized New China, we did not respond, nor did we object. Of course we could not, and should not, object, and objection would be irrational. Even when the British imperialists recognized our state, we did not object; on what grounds, then, could we object to the recognition of China by you—a socialist country?

There was a reason why we did not respond to your recognition; namely, the Soviet friends did not wish to see us establishing diplomatic relations with

---

* These are excerpts from Mao Zedong's talk with a delegation of the League of Communists of Yugoslavia.

you. Then, one might ask: Wasn't China an independent country? Of course, she was. Being independent, why should China listen to them? Well, comrades, at that time, when the Soviet Union put forward that opinion, it was difficult for us to disagree. At that time there was the allegation that there were two "Titos" in the world, one in Yugoslavia, the other in China. Of course, no resolution was passed to the effect that Mao Zedong was a Tito. I said to the Soviet comrades, "You suspected me of being a 'half-Tito'"; but now they do not admit this. When did they remove that label of "half-Tito"? The label was removed only when we dealt blows to U.S. imperialism in the War to Resist U.S. Aggression and Aid Korea.

In the past Wang Ming's line was in effect Stalin's line, which caused the loss of 90 percent of our forces in our base areas and 100 percent of our underground forces in Kuomintang-controlled areas. This was mentioned in Comrade Liu Shaoqi's Report to the Eighth National Congress of our Party. Why didn't we point out publicly that Wang Ming's line was Stalin's line? There was a reason too. The Soviet Union could criticize Stalin, but it would not be so good for us to criticize him. We should maintain good relations with the Soviet Union. Maybe, after some time, this point can be made public. World affairs are always like this, facts are facts. In the past many wrong things were done by the Third International,[141] which was possible in its initial and last periods, but no good in its quite long middle period. It was good when Lenin was alive, and relatively good when Dimitrov[142] was in charge. The first time Wang Ming's line ruled for four years in the Chinese Party, and it caused the greatest damage to the Chinese revolution. Wang Ming is now recuperating in Moscow, and we shall again elect him a member of the Party's Central Committee. He is a teacher, a professor for our Party, a priceless treasure that no amount of money can buy. He has taught our whole Party that it will never do to follow his line.

That was the first time we suffered on Stalin's account.

The second time was during the War of Resistance Against Japan. Wang Ming, who had personal access to Stalin, spoke Russian and was skilled in flattering Stalin, was sent back to China by Stalin. Previously he pushed a "Left" opportunist line; this time he pushed a Right opportunist line. In cooperating with the Kuomintang, he "put on cosmetics and delivered himself" and advocated obedience to the Kuomintang in all matters. He put forward his Six-Point Program, which overthrew the Ten-Point Program[143] of our Party's Central Committee, and opposed the establishment of anti-Japanese base areas and the maintenance of our own troops, thinking that with Chiang Kai-shek at the helm all will be right with the world. We corrected that erroneous line. Chiang Kai-shek also helped us correct Wang Ming's wrong line. While Wang Ming "put on cosmetics and delivered himself," Chiang Kai-shek "slapped him in the face and threw him out of the gate." Chiang Kai-shek proved to be China's greatest teacher, teaching the entire Chinese people and all our Party members. While Wang Ming taught with words, Chiang Kai-shek taught with machine-guns.

The third time was at the end of World War II and after the surrender of Japan. Stalin had a conference with Roosevelt[6] and Churchill,[144] and decided on giving the whole of China to the United States and Chiang Kai-shek. At that time Stalin did not support us Chinese Communists materially or morally —especially morally—but supported Chiang Kai-shek. That decision was made at the Yalta Conference[145]. It was told Tito by Stalin, and the conversation is recorded in Tito's autobiography.

With the dissolution of the Communist International we had greater freedom. Prior to that, we had begun to criticize opportunism, unfold our rectification movement and criticize the Wang Ming line. Our rectification movement was in effect a criticism of the errors of Stalin and of the Third International in their guidance on the Chinese revolution, though we did not mention a word about Stalin and the Third International. Maybe they will be mentioned in the near future. We did not name them for two reasons. First, since we in China listened to them, we should be held responsible. Why did we heed them? Why did we go ahead committing mistakes of "Left" and Right opportunism? There were two types of Chinese: One type was the doctrinaires, who obeyed what Stalin said; the other type was the Chinese who refused to obey and criticized the doctrinaires. Second, we did not wish to see unpleasant developments in Sino-Soviet relations. As the Third International did not make a self-criticism of these mistakes and the Soviet Union did not mention them, if we started to criticize them, they will fall out with us.

The fourth time was when I was labeled a half-Tito or a quasi-Tito. Not only in the Soviet Union but also in other socialist and nonsocialist countries a considerable number of people doubted whether the Chinese revolution was a genuine revolution.

Maybe you do not quite understand why Stalin's portraits are still displayed in China. The comrades in Moscow have informed us that they will no longer display Stalin's portraits, and in parades, only the portraits of Lenin and current leaders will be carried. Of course, they have not asked us in China to do the same. We find it rather difficult. The Chinese people in general do not know of Stalin's four mistakes as mentioned above, nor does the whole Party membership. Your situation is different, as your experiences are known to all your people and indeed to the whole world. Our Party members do know the mistakes of the two erroneous lines of Wang Ming, but our people do not know that those erroneous lines originated in Stalin's mistakes. As for Stalin's mistakes of not allowing the Chinese revolution to proceed and of suspecting me of being a half-Tito, they are known only to members of our Party Center.

We think it is beneficial to the socialist movement to accept and support the Soviet Union as its center. You may disagree to this. When Khrushchev[146] criticized Stalin, your whole nation welcomed it, but we were different, our people felt dissatisfied. Therefore, it will not do not to display Stalin's portraits in China. In the past, our paraders used to carry the portraits of Marx, Engels, Lenin and Stalin, plus the portraits of several Chinese—Mao Zedong, Liu Shaoqi, Zhou Enlai and Zhu De—and portraits of the leaders of fraternal parties. Now we have adopted the method of "down with all"—that is, not carrying anyone's portrait. On the occasion of the May Day this year, Comrade Popovic was in Beijing, and he did not see portraits being carried by the paraders. However, the portraits of five departed ones—Marx, Engels, Lenin, Stalin and Sun Yat-sen—and the portrait of one alive, Mao Zedong, were still hung. Well, let them be hung. You Yugoslavs may say, why you Chinese still hang Stalin's portraits when the Soviets themselves have stopped doing so.

Even now there are people who doubt whether we can build socialism and allege that we are sham Communists. What can one do about that? Having eaten their fill and slept well, those people are spreading the story that the Chinese Party is not a genuine Communist Party, that China cannot succeed in building socialism, and that it would be odd if China should succeed. Look, China is likely to become an imperialist country, the emerging fourth imperialist country along with U.S., British and French imperialism. China! China now has no industry and no capital, yet she will be terrifying after 100 years. Genghis Khan[147] revived —woe to Europe, possibly invading Yugoslavia. Beware of the "yellow peril"!

This story absolutely will not come true! The Chinese Party is a Marxist-Leninist Party and the Chinese people are peace-loving. We regard aggression as a crime, and we shall not invade even an inch of others' land or grab even a single straw of others. We are peace-loving and are Marxists.

Internationally, we are opposed to big-nation chauvinism. Though having little industry, our country is large, and some of our people tend to get cocky, or "stick up their tails." So we enjoin them: "Don't stick up your tails; behave with tails between your legs." In my childhood my mother used to enjoin me to "behave with tail between your legs." That is a good advice, which I now often give to my comrades.

Domestically, we are opposing Han-chauvinism, which is a tendency detrimental to the unity of all ethnic groups in China. Both big-nation chauvinism and Han-chauvinism are sectarianism. Big-nation chauvinists care only about the interests of their nation, but have no regard for the interests of others; and Han-chauvinists care only about the Han ethnic group, regarding the Hans as superior, thus harming the minority ethnic groups.

In the past there were people abroad who thought that China was not willing to befriend others, would separate from the Soviet Union and would become a peril. Now people in socialist countries holding such a view have become fewer since the beginning of the War to Resist U.S. Aggression and Aid Korea. The imperialists are different; the stronger China grows, the greater their fear. But they also know that China's industries are still underdeveloped, that her strength depends only on the sheer numbers of population and that therefore she is not frightening. First of all, they fear the Soviet Union; secondarily, they fear China—fearing China's politics and her influence in Asia. That is why they are always alleging that China is terrifying, is going to commit aggression, etc.

We are very prudent and cautious; we shall never get cocky or domineering, but abide by the Five Principles.[98] Having ourselves been bullied by others, we know the bitterness of being bullied. You probably have the same feeling, don't you?

China's future lies in socialism. It will take 50 to 100 years to transform China into a rich, strong country. Now there are no longer forces obstructing China's development. China is a big country with her population accounting for one quarter of the world's total, but her contribution to mankind is not commensurate to the size of her population. This situation will change, but this change will not happen in my lifetime or in that of my sons. How the country will change depends on future developments. China may commit mistakes, become corrupt, evolve from the present relatively good stage to a not-so-good stage, then again to a relatively good stage. Of course, even if it is a not-so-good stage, it will not be so dark as the days of Chiang kai-shek. It will be a dialectical process—affirmation, negation, and the negation of negation. Things will develop thus in twists and turns.

Corruption, bureaucratism, big-nation chauvinism and arrogance—these are all mistakes China may commit. Now we in China are modest and willing to learn from others. One of the reasons is that we have no capital. First, we did not originally have Marxism-Leninism, which we learned from others; second, we did not have the October Revolution, and not until 1949, 32 years after the October Revolution, did we win victory in our revolution; third, during World War II we were only a detachment in the fighting, not the main force; fourth, our country is not yet industrialized and is still mainly agricultural with some shabby handicrafts. Therefore, even if some people in China want to get cocky, or "stick up their tails," they do not yet have the capital to do so, and at most one or two meters high. But we should guard against the possibility in the future—it could be dangerous after 10 or 20 years and even more dangerous after 40 to 50 years.

Comrades, I suggest that you heed this point, too. Your level of industrialization is higher, your development is faster and, having been wronged by Stalin, you now have reason and justice on your side. All this may become a burden on your back.

Similarly, Stalin's above-mentioned four mistakes hurting us may become a burden on our back. Several decades from now, when China becomes industrialized, the possibility of her "sticking up her tail" will become greater. I request you, on your return to Yugoslavia, to tell your younger generation that if in future China should "stick up her tail," to a height of 10,000 meters, you must criticize China, keep a watch on her and, indeed, let the whole world keep a watch on her. By that time I shall have departed—gone to join Karl Marx at a congress.

In the past we let you down and so we owe you a debt. As the saying goes, he who kills shall repay with his life, and he who owes a debt shall repay money. We wrote articles to criticize you, why should we keep mum even now? Before the criticism of Stalin some matter could not be explained so clearly. That was why when I talked with Ambassador Popovic, I only said that we could not very well criticize Stalin when the Soviet Union did not; and that we could not very well establish diplomatic relations with Yugoslavia when the Soviet Union had not restored relations with Yugoslavia. Now we can speak up. About Stalin's four mistakes I have already talked with Soviet friends, with Yudin,[148] and I shall tell Khrushchev when I meet him. As you are our comrades, I have told you, too, but these cannot yet be published in the press, nor can they yet be known to the imperialists. Maybe one or two of the above-mentioned Stalin mistakes can be made public some time in the future. In this connection, our situation is not the same as yours; Tito clearly mentioned Stalin in his autobiography, because your country had severed relations with the Soviet Union.

Stalin advocated dialectical materialism, but sometimes he lacked materialism and tended to be metaphysical, writing historical materialism, but acting often on historical idealism. His extremist actions, his personal deification, his hurting others' feelings, etc., had nothing in common with materialism.

Before meeting him, I had little affection for Stalin. I did not quite like reading his works and had read mainly "The Foundations of Leninism," a long article criticizing Trotsky[149] and "Dizzy with Success." I liked even less reading his articles on the Chinese revolution. Unlike Lenin, who opened his heart to people and treated others as equals, Stalin tended to be overbearing, giving orders to others. His works invariably have such airs. When I did meet him, I disliked him even more and had quite a quarrel with him in Moscow. Stalin had a bad temper and tended to say things not quite appropriate when he got excited.

I have written articles praising Stalin, three in all.[150] One was written in Yan'an on the occasion of his 60th birthday, the second a toast I proposed in Moscow, and the third at the request of *Pravda* after Stalin's death. As a rule, I do not like to felicitate others, nor do I like others to felicitate me. But when one went to Moscow on the occasion of his birthday, what could one do other than expressing praise? Could one have disparaged him instead? Upon his death the Soviet Union needed our support, and we wanted to support the Soviet Union; therefore, that eulogistic article was written. It did not eulogize Stalin as an individual, but eulogized the Soviet Party. In writing the article in Yan'an, I put aside my personal feelings and treated Stalin as the leader of a socialist country; that article has some degree of vitality. The other two articles were written not out of my free will, but out of necessity. Such is the contradiction in human life: One is not in the mood to write, but reason tells one that one has to.

Now that Moscow has openly criticized Stalin, we are in a position to tell you all this. Today I have told you about his four mistakes, though for the sake of Sino-Soviet relations it is not yet desirable to discuss these publicly in the press. In Khrushchev's report, about Stalin's mistakes on China he mentioned only the question of a sugar refinery, so it is not yet opportune for us to make them public. Contradictions will remain.

Generally speaking, the Soviet Union has been good. It has four merits: Marxism-Leninism, the October Revolution, being the main force, and industrialization. It also has a dark side and has made some mistakes. Its achievements are primary, its mistakes secondary. As enemy forces are taking advantage of the criticism of Stalin to launch a global offensive, we should render support to the Soviet Union. It can correct its mistakes. Regarding mistakes toward Yugoslavia, Khrushchev has had them corrected. Regarding Wang Ming, the Soviets now have a better understanding, though they were not agreeable to our criticism of Wang Ming in the past. In addition, they have removed the label of "half-Tito," so that they have uncapped one and a half Titos. We are pleased that they have removed the label imposed upon Tito.

There are some among our people who are not satisfied with the current criticism of Stalin, but this criticism is good, as it serves to explode deification, take off the lid, emancipate the mind—it is in this sense a war of emancipation, so that people dare to speak up and can think over problems. This has also been a process of affirmation, negation, and the negation of negation.

Liberty, equality and fraternity used to be slogans of the bourgeoisie, and now we are fighting for these. Should the Parties be like a father and his sons, or should they be brothers? In the past they were like father and sons; now they are more like brothers, though there are vestiges of patriarchalism. This is understandable, for vestiges cannot be eliminated overnight. With the lid taken off, people can think freely and independently. Currently there is a touch of anti-feudalism in the air. With the transition from father-son relationship to a fraternal relationship, patriarchalism is opposed. In the past the ideological control was so tight that it even surpassed the practice under the rule of feudalism. Not a sentence of criticism was tolerated, while some enlightened emperors of the past did listen to criticism. I suppose in Yugoslav history you also had some emperors who tolerated a critic pointing at his nose. Capitalist society has progressed one step beyond the times of feudalism; for instance, the Republicans and the Democrats—the two U.S. political parties — can quarrel against each other.

We in the socialist countries should work out some measures. Of course, it will not do without centralism and unity, and unanimity should be maintained. Unity of will of the people is beneficial; it enables us to realize industrialization sooner and to cope with imperialism. However, it has drawbacks in that it could discourage people from speaking up. Therefore, we should provide people with opportunities to air their views. We comrades in the Politburo are considering these questions.

In my country very few people criticize me publicly, and people forgive my shortcomings and mistakes. This is because we do serve the people, and we have done some good things for the people. Although we sometimes err on the side of commandism and bureaucracy, the people feel that we have done more good things than bad; so they praise us more and criticize us little. This has led to a kind of idolatry, and when someone criticizes me, he will be opposed and blamed for disrespect for the leader. I and other comrades of the Party Center receive on average 300 letters daily from the masses, with several letters expressing criticism, but these are usually not signed or signed with a pseudonym. These letter-writers are not afraid of my retaliation, but are afraid of people around them fixing them.

You have mentioned the article "On the Ten Major Relationships." That is the result of my discussions with 34 ministers over a period of one and a half months. What ideas could I, an individual, advance? I was only summing up the views of others; it was not my creation. To manufacture anything, raw materials and factories are needed. I am no longer a good factory, but an old one needing transformation and reequipping, like factories in Britain that are in need of retrofitting. I am old, no longer able to play the leading role, but can only play a walking part. You can see that at the current Party Congress I have been playing a walking part, whereas the key actors have been Liu Shaoqi, Zhou Enlai, Deng Xiaoping and other comrades.

(From the verbatim record)

ON RESTORATION TO CHINA HER LEGITIMATE SEAT IN THE UNITED NATIONS*

(*September 30, 1956*)

Chairman Mao Zedong (hereinafter referred to as Mao): the Bandung Conference[111] was a good conference. It was wonderful. The world has changed a lot in the more than one year since the conference, hasn't it?

President Ahmed Sukarno (hereinafter referred to as Sukarno): Yes, indeed. Wherever I go people speak about the Bandung Conference.

Mao: In the past, people spoke about the Geneva Conference[95] and the Bandung Conference together. But now, the Geneva Conference and the Geneva Spirit are not mentioned much. What's left is only the Bandung Conference.

We were very glad to read the speech you made in the United States. It is remarkable to say those things in a country like that. You were speaking for all of Asia.

Sukarno: Yes, I also felt I was speaking for Asia.

Mao: In fact, you were speaking for Asia, Africa and Latin America. Did the Americans give you good hospitality?

Sukarno: In general I received a warm welcome from the Americans, but most of the leading members in the U.S. government were not pleased, for my statements were not to their liking. However, like it or not, I had to speak the facts.

Everywhere in the United States journalists asked about Indonesia's position on China's entry into the United Nations. Our answer was firm —China must join the United Nations. We also added, without representatives of the 600 million Chinese people, the United Nations will only be a stage for farces.

Mao: As you see it, which is better for China to enter the United Nations, sooner or later?

---

* This is Mao Zedong's talk with Ahmed Sukarno, President of Indonesia.

Sukarno: The sooner, the better for the United Nations.

Mao: We have thought about the alternative; that is, it may not be such a bad idea not to join.

Sukarno: Indonesia believes the sooner, the better.

Mao: Be it sooner or later, we have to prepare for either possibility.

Sukarno: It had better come sooner.

Mao: We would rather it came a bit slower.

Sukarno: I wish to know the Chairman's line of thinking.

Mao: In public, we say we wish to join. Our friends are helping us toward this. This is our right. It is unfair that representatives of 600 million people can't participate, whereas Taiwan can. As it stands, it's not we who represent Taiwan in the United Nations, but the other way around. This is inappropriate. During the negotiations in Geneva we raised this with the U.S. side, pointing out their mistake. However, it was not on the agenda of the Geneva negotiations, the topics for the Geneva negotiations being the repatriation of civilians, the lifting of the embargo, popular exchanges and, more important, the elimination of tension in the Taiwan area.

Sukarno: I hope the Chairman can explain why China is not eager to join the United Nations.

Mao: Britain, the United States and France are imperialist and colonialist countries. It would be better for us to put off granting them a legal status within China.

Sukarno: But the problem is the three imperialist countries all harbor ill intentions. They will be more rampant if there are no anti-imperialist countries in the United Nations.

Mao: We can oppose them outside the United Nations.

Sukarno: I'm still not very clear.

Mao: Britain is anxious to establish diplomatic relations with us. We thought up a formula called negotiations for the establishment of diplomatic relations, which have been going on for five years. The British have their negotiating representatives, not legal diplomats in China. The British vote for Chiang Kai-shek in the United Nations, not for us, which gives us more reason to charge them with sitting between two chairs. What we have with the British now is semiofficial diplomatic relations.

Sukarno: But the Chairman has not come to the question of the United Nations.

Mao: I'm on the reasoning.

We are also not in a hurry to establish diplomatic relations with countries like France, West Germany, etc. They are not impatient for it; neither are we.

As for how many years it will be put off, we can only wait and see. They can delay as long as they wish. It is the same with the United States.

The United States does not want to establish diplomatic relations with China now, which for us is not such a bad thing. They are calling us names every day. Our ears are used to their abuses. This brings me to the question of the United Nations. The United States doesn't want to see China in the United Nations. It will obstruct our entry.

Sukarno: This question could be tackled separately.

The establishment of diplomatic relations between China and Britain, France, West Germany and the United States and China's joining the United Nations are two different matters. The imperialist countries wish to control the United Nations. Once China is inside, it will be able to oppose their attempt.

Mao: But the question is Taiwan.

Sukarno: The Taiwan question can be put aside. Taiwan and the mainland are one; those who control the mainland should represent China.

Mao: These are your views and ours. But they are not shared by the United States and its followers.

Sukarno: The question could be solved like this: One country proposes that China join the United Nations; other countries support it. There is bound to be a fight for this. Indonesia is ready to join the fight. If the People's Republic of China joins the United Nations, the representatives of Taiwan will automatically forfeit their right.

Mao: What is needed for such a resolution to be adopted, a simple majority or a two-thirds vote?

Sukarno: A two-thirds vote. If it is passed by a two-thirds majority in the General Assembly, it can't be vetoed by the Security Council.

Mao: Can we enter the Security Council after the adoption of the General Assembly resolution? There is veto power in the Security Council, and unanimity is required among the five major powers.[151] Among the five, one major power is called the United States; another is called Chiang Kai-shek.

Sukarno: Regardless of the veto power in the Security Council, once the issue is brought up, it will give rise to a struggle, which is a good thing anyway.

Mao: We agree with you on this, but the question remains difficult to solve in the end.

Sukarno: But world opinion will be different. For instance, if a major power exercises its veto in the Security Council after a General Assembly resolution by a two-thirds majority, it would be a folly, which would certainly be resented.

Mao: Fine, this should be done as a way to struggle. But there must be only one China in the United Nations, not "two Chinas," the one China being we. So, as we said just now, we should be prepared for two possibilities. We should be ready to enter the United Nations to be with you, so that there will be one more vote.

Sukarno: What does the Chairman think about this tactic: for one China to represent the whole of China and, as a transitional measure, for Taiwan to be represented by the Taiwan clique?

Mao: No, that's not the right thing to do. We have to capitalize on the issue of Taiwan. We shall not enter the United Nations so long as there is tiny Taiwan there.

Sukarno: But this is only for a transitional stage, just like the relations between West Irian[152] and Indonesia.

Mao: West Irian doesn't represent Indonesia. On the contrary, Indonesia is represented in the United Nations, while West Irian is not.

Sukarno: I wonder if the question of China and Taiwan can be treated like that of Indonesia and West Irian, that is, for Taiwan to be regarded as territory to be recovered by China?

Mao: Is West Irian represented in the United Nations?

Sukarno: But what I suggest is only a transitional measure.

Mao: We will capitalize on this issue. We will stay outside the United Nations for 10,000 years if necessary, as long as Taiwan is represented there.

Sukarno: That is to say, when the People's Republic of China enters the United Nations, Chiang Kai-shek will have to go; there will be no place for Taiwan representatives.

Mao: That's right.

(To Ambassador Huang Zhen[153]) Has the China Beijing Opera Troupe been to perform in Indonesia? Did they perform *The Yandang Mountains* there?

Huang Zhen: Yes, they did.

Mao: In this opera there are two forces fighting each other. The conservatives are defending the city, which is besieged by the revolutionaries. In the end, the revolutionaries take the city by flying into it. A cartoon in a British newspaper on China's entry into the United Nations showed China flying into the United Nations just like the story in *The Yandang Mountains*. In other words, we have to fight our way in.

Sukarno: Member states already in the United Nations can get united in demanding that the question of China's entry into the organization be included in the agenda.

Mao: And also the expulsion of the Chiang Kai-shek representatives.

Sukarno: That should be the ultimate goal.

Mao: We won't enter as long as the Chiang Kai-shek representatives are still there. There are many ways in which we can yet capitalize on this issue.

Sukarno: I put the question like this in order to find out China's attitude.

Mao: Our attitude is clear. If, after a General Assembly resolution is adopted by a two-thirds majority, we are still kept out of the Security Council, we shall know what to fight for next. We also have the time to do it. As far as we are concerned, it would be better to wait for another five or six years. In six years' time we'll have fulfilled our Second Five-Year Plan. It would be preferable to wait 11 years; by then our Third Five-Year Plan will have been fulfilled. At present we are a weak country, not a strong one. The United States is afraid of the Soviet Union, but not of us. It knows our true strength. China is a big country, but not a strong one for we have nothing except 600 million people. It looks down on us. What's more, it has that big thing in its hands called the atom bomb, whereas we don't have even a small one. So what's the hurry?

Sukarno: The Chairman just said that the United States is not afraid of China, in fact it's not true. The United States is afraid of China. However, this is not because China is already industrialized or in possession of atom bombs.

Mao: It is our politics that they are afraid of.

Sukarno: Yes, they are afraid of China's politics and her ideology.

Mao: They fear we would spread them, to their detriment.

Sukarno: The United States does not want China in the United Nations, exactly because it is afraid of China.

Mao: The United States is a little afraid of China. To tell the truth, we are also a little afraid of the United States.

Sukarno: Australia is also a little afraid of Indonesia. It is not because Indonesia is industrialized, but if Indonesia recovers West Irian, the question of East Irian will arise.

Mao: What you say is true.

Where do you suggest we put our emphasis in our work and effort to win friends? I believe it should be the three continents of Asia, Africa and Latin America, plus the larger half of Europe. What's left is only a smaller half of Europe, half of the Americas and Oceania. They are not in favor of us, and we are prepared to wait for them for 100 years.

Sukarno: Which countries are not in favor of China?

Mao: Britain, which still votes for Chiang Kai-shek. We will not establish diplomatic relations with Britain so long as it continues to do so. If it goes on voting for Chiang Kai-shek for 100 years, for so many years we will not establish diplomatic relations, only exchange chargé d'affaires with it. France and Belgium also refuse to recognize us, and Portugal and Spain, too.

Sukarno: As I said yesterday in my speech in Ulan Bator, the majority, almost all, of the people in the world are in favor of China's entry into the United Nations. If a number of countries put forward a resolution asking the United Nations to admit China, with a condition attached saying that the United Nations must have China's participation, otherwise it will become only a stage for farces, and those countries would have to withdraw. Under such circumstances it would be folly for the United States to oppose.

Mao: We are fully in favor of this. However, they don't have to withdraw from the United Nations; they can stay in the organization to fight.

Sukarno: The struggle will be a complex one. We need to consult one another.

Mao: Of course. Finally, the struggle will end with the departure of Chiang Kai-shek. By then we shall have flown into the United Nations, and the show will be over. But we must be prepared for the second alternative; that is, we continue to be kept out for many years.

Sukarno: It is almost the same as the question of our recovering West Irian. Some people in Indonesia propose that we put the question of West Irian aside and concentrate on national reconstruction, saying that West Irian will naturally come back when we grow strong. I don't share that view. I believe we should struggle for the recovery of West Irian while we engage in reconstruction.

Mao: It is the same with the Taiwan question. On the one hand, we shall strive to grow stronger; on the other, we shall try to recover Taiwan as soon as possible. Like the question of West Irian, there are two possible timings for Taiwan's return. The first is sooner, which is of course ideal. The second is later, which is all right too. We can sleep with it. It is not going to cause insomnia.

Sukarno: But what about the morale of the people in their struggle, will it be affected?

Mao: The question is not entirely up to us. For us, of course, the sooner, the better.

Sukarno: Perhaps we should keep in mind that the morale of the people in their struggle is like a fire. It will die down without fanning.

Mao: The fire is burning all right, but there are still two possible timings —sooner or later.

Sukarno: I agree with you here. We should build our countries, on the one hand, and continue our struggle, on the other.

Mao: Sooner is certainly better, but a little later is all right, too.

Sukarno: Of course, it can't be done in a day or two.

Mao: Not in a day or two, not even in a year or two. It may take eight or ten years, or even more.

Sukarno: I agree on this. The recovery of West Irian can't be done in five or six years; it may take longer. However, when we speak to the people, we have to say that we should keep up our struggle to get West Irian back next year.

Mao: I'm 99 percent in agreement with you. We are also saying every day that we shall recover Taiwan, but we don't mention tomorrow or next year. We are saying every day we want to enter the United Nations, but we don't mention the time. We say we want to establish diplomatic relations with all countries in the world, including the United States, but we leave out the time. In doing things, the Chinese people do not specify the time. Some people jeer at us, saying the Chinese always take it easy. That's exactly our way.

Sukarno: A tactic.

Mao: No, it is actually like that. The solution of a question does not depend on us alone. It has to depend on the other side also, which has to change.

Sukarno: Who is the other side?

Mao: Britain, the United States, France, Taiwan, West Irian, and the Netherlands. The problem is their chiefs of staff are their own people, not our people. If Foreign Minister Ruslan Abdulgani were the Secretary of State of the United States, that would be fine.

Sukarno: The people in West Germany are saying the same. They say, if Adenauer[154] left the stage, the whole country would change.

Mao: If after the changes it proposed establishing diplomatic relations with us, we would have no reason to refuse.

Sukarno: The Chairman's remarks are meaningful, just as they are all truthful.

Now, let's sum up. Does China think we should raise in the United Nations the question of her entry sooner or later?

Mao: Sooner.

Sukarno: Oh, that's good.

Mao: It should be raised every year until we succeed.

Sukarno: In order to succeed, we shall have to fight. There are many advantages in raising the matter sooner. For one thing, the various countries will be obliged to make clear their positions, so that clear lines will be drawn.

Mao: Perfectly right.

It is the same with the question of the embargo imposed on us. We ask for the lifting of the embargo everyday, but a little later would be all right, too. As a matter of fact, it'd better be lifted a few years later. To tell the truth, we don't have much to export, apart from some apples, peanuts, hog bristles and soybeans.

If the embargo is not lifted, we are also able to sleep and eat properly. We can wait for another six or eleven years. By that time, the embargo should have been lifted and China recognized and admitted into the United Nations. When they come to visit China, they will be the ones to regret, for they will find that there is nothing they can do.

Sukarno: Don't they know about China's development at all?

Mao: Yes, they do, but they are self-contradictory. On the one hand, they say they have been fooled into doing what they are doing; on the other hand, they have their own difficulties, which force them to hold out against us. They can't let it go; if they do, if the dyke of the Yellow River is breached, its waters will flood. This will make them lose face. As we see it, it's fine if they recognize us sooner, but it would be better if they do so a little later. By the time they finally come to China, it will be too late for them to regret, for there will be nothing they can do. We have a second point in mind, that is, for them to lose face in front of the whole world. For it's they who refuse to recognize us, not we refusing to recognize them. Every day we propose establishing diplomatic relations with them, but they don't want to do this. It is not we who don't want to enter the United Nations, but they who won't let us. Every day we ask them to lift the embargo, but they won't. As a result, the United States is landed in an utterly passive position, with all the reasons in our hands and in those of our friends. To deal with the Americans, one has to be resourceful, one has to have two tactics, not just one. The first is to struggle resolutely, crying out every day, which is your method. The second is not to get impatient, which is not to be put in the newspapers.

Our relations with Chiang Kai-shek are just as subtle. We want to restore friendship and cooperation with him. We cooperated twice in the past; why can't there be a third time? But Chiang Kai-shek balks. He balks every day, and we keep saying every day we want to cooperate with him. This makes it difficult for our Generalissimo Chiang, with his forces disintegrating from within.

Sukarno: Nor do the American people see eye to eye with the American ruling class. There are people in the U.S. Congress who are in favor of China's entry into the United Nations.

Mao: Not the majority.

Sukarno: Nevertheless, there are already people who are in favor.

Mao: We are pleased to see people in favor. In both the political report and the resolution of the recent Eighth National Congress of the Communist Party of China we say we wish to establish diplomatic relations with all countries. However, there is no mention of the second point, which I described to you just now, in either the report or the resolution. We are good friends, so I have let you know our bottom line.

(From the verbatim record)

SPEECH AT THE BANQUET IN HONOR OF PRESIDENT SUKARNO OF INDONESIA

(*October 2, 1956*)

Your Excellency Mr. President,
Distinguished Guests from Indonesia,
Ladies and Gentlemen,

We warmly welcome President Sukarno, who is a good friend of the Chinese people, on his visit to China. We should like to express our thanks to President Sukarno for bringing to us the fraternal friendship of the 82 million people of Indonesia.

The Indonesian people are a great people. The Chinese people have the greatest respect for the Indonesian people and President Sukarno. Indonesia, having suffered 350 years under colonial rule, finally won its national independence through long and arduous struggle. At present, the Indonesian people are engaged in a brave struggle to preserve national unity, gradually eliminate the vestiges of colonialism and defend world peace. The outstanding role that President Sukarno has played in these struggles and the great achievements he made during his recent visits in Europe and America have won the unanimous praise of the Chinese people and of all who love peace and justice the world over. Indonesia's abrogation of the Round Table Conference Agreement[155] and her demand and struggle to recover West Irian[152] are just endeavors that enjoy the firm support of the Chinese people.

Indonesia's pursuance of an active foreign policy of independence is in the best interests of not only her own people but also world peace. The Bandung Conference,[111] to the success of which Indonesia made important contributions, has already had an extensive and far-reaching impact. Indonesia is playing an ever more important role in international affairs. We—the free- and independence-loving people of Asia, Africa and Latin America—are all combating colonialism. On the question of Egypt's recovering the Suez Canal Company,[134] we peace-loving people of Asia, Africa and Latin America and the whole world must continue to give our firm support to the just struggle of

Egypt. The colonialists wish to see us disunited, uncooperative and unfriendly to each other. They must be answered by our strengthened unity and enhanced friendly cooperation. The schemes of the colonialists must be thoroughly bankrupted.

The Chinese people and the Indonesian people have always been good friends. In recent years the friendship of our two peoples in our common endeavor to oppose colonialism and preserve world peace has been further strengthened. I'm convinced that the friendly cooperation between China and Indonesia, based on the principles of equality, mutual benefit and peaceful coexistence, will be further consolidated and developed in the future.

I propose we raise our glasses,

to the friendship between China and Indonesia,

to peace in Asia, Africa, Latin America and the whole world,

to the prosperity of the Republic of Indonesia and the well-being of her people,

to the health of President Sukarno,

Ganbei!

(From *People's Daily*, October 3, 1956)

IS IT RIGHT TO "LEAN TO ONE SIDE"?*

(December 8, 1956)

Now I shall speak on current affairs. As you see it, can socialism be accomplished? Perhaps you're perturbed—with seven buckets coming up and eight buckets going down—maybe socialism will fail. Maybe the socialist camp will collapse. In my view, even if socialism were to collapse, it would not be such a big thing—nothing terrifying. The most important countries in the socialist camp are the Soviet Union and China. It is correct for China to close up to the Soviet Union. But some people still doubt this principle, saying China should not stand close with the Soviet Union, but can take a neutral position between the Soviet Union and the United States, playing the role of a bridge. In our opinion, standing in the middle is not a good idea; it is not in the interests of our nation, for on one side is powerful imperialism by which China has long been oppressed. If we stand between the Soviet Union and the United States, it may look good and independent, but it can't be true independence. The United States is not to be relied on. It may give you something, but not much. Can it be imagined that the imperialists will help feed our country full? The imperialists have been oppressing Asian, African and Latin American countries for decades and centuries, never allowing them to eat their fill. The forces of the imperialist powers burned down our Yuanmingyuan and seized our Hong Kong and Taiwan. Hong Kong belongs to China. Why was it snatched away? Why could the Bandung Conference[111] unite so many Asian and African countries? Because of the aggression and oppression of imperialism. Principal among the imperialist powers is the United States. It is inappropriate to fancy that we could benefit from playing the role of a bridge between the Soviet Union and the United States. We still don't have the ability to design big factories. Who is helping us design them? The chemical, iron and steel, oil refining, tank, automobile and aircraft industries, for example—who helps us design them? Never has a single

---

* This is part of Mao Zedong's talk at a symposium of the heads of provincial delegations to the Second Congress of the National Industrial and Commercial Federation.

imperialist country given us help on this. Within our democratic parties, nonparty personages, high-level intellectuals, religious, industrial and commercial circles, even among a part of the proletariat are people who cherish the illusion that the United States will help us, and Britain will help us. No, they won't.

Is it right to "lean to one side"? By leaning to one side we side with the Soviet Union, and this leaning on one side is based on equality. We believe in Marxism-Leninism and combine the universal truth of Marxism-Leninism with the actual conditions in China, instead of uncritically copying from the experiences of the Soviet Union. It is wrong to uncritically copy from the experiences of the Soviet Union. Our transformation of capitalist industry and commerce and our cooperative movement in agriculture are different from what they have done in the Soviet Union.

(From the verbatim record)

ON SINO-AMERICAN AND SINO-SOVIET RELATIONS*

(January 27, 1957)

Now a few words about Sino-American relations. We have had Eisenhower's[103] letter to Chiang Kai-shek reproduced and distributed among you. In my view, the letter is meant chiefly to pour cold water on Chiang Kai-shek and then pump a little courage into him. The letter talks about the need to keep cool and not to be impulsive, which means not resorting to war but relying on the United Nations. That's pouring cold water. For Chiang Kai-shek has really become rather impulsive. To pump courage into Chiang Kai-shek, Eisenhower says he will continue his hard-line policy toward the Communists and pins his hopes on disturbances breaking out in our midst. In Eisenhower's view, disturbances have already occurred and the Communists cannot stop them. Well, everybody has his own way of looking at things.

I still think it preferable to put off the establishment of diplomatic relations with the United States for some years. This will be more to our advantage. The Soviet Union established diplomatic relations with the United States 17 years after the October Revolution. In 1929 a world-wide economic crisis broke out which lasted through 1933. In 1933 Hitler[4] came to power in Germany and Roosevelt[6] in the United States. And it was only then that diplomatic relations were established between the Soviet Union and the United States. It will probably be after our Third Five-Year Plan that we will establish diplomatic relations with the United States, that is, 18 years or even more from the day of liberation. We are in no hurry to take our seat in the United Nations, just as we are in no hurry to establish diplomatic relations with the United States. We adopt this policy to deprive the United States of as much political capital as possible and put it in the wrong and in an isolated position. You bar us from the United Nations and don't want to establish diplomatic relations with us; all right, but the longer you stall, the more you will be in

---

* This is part of a talk by Mao Zedong at a conference of secretaries of provincial, municipal and autonomous region Party committees.

debt to us. The longer you stall, the more you will be in the wrong and the more isolated you will become in your own country and before world opinion. Once I told an American in Yan'an, the United States can go on withholding recognition of our government for 100 years, but I doubt if it can withhold it in the 101st. One day the United States will have to establish diplomatic relations with us. When the Americans come to China then and look around, they will find it too late for regrets. For this land of China will have become quite different, with its house swept clean and the "four pests" eliminated; they won't find many friends here and they can't do much even if they spread a few germs.

Since World War II, the capitalist countries have been very unstable and in deep turmoil, with anxiety widespread among their people. There is anxiety in all countries, China included. But there is less here anyway. Look into the matter and see who is actually afraid of whom—the socialist countries or the imperialist countries, principally the United States, or the other way round. I say there is fear on both sides. The question is, which side is more afraid of the other? I'm inclined to think that the imperialists are more afraid of us. There may be some danger in making such an assessment, that is, our people may all go to bed and sleep for three days on end. So we must take two possibilities into account. In addition to the favorable possibility, there is the unfavorable one, and that is the imperialists may go berserk. They harbor evil designs and are always out to make trouble. Of course, today it is not so easy for them to start another world war, for they have to think of the consequences.

Now a few words about Sino-Soviet relations. In my view, wrangling is inevitable. Let no one imagine that there is no wrangling between Communist Parties. How can there be no wrangling in this world of ours? Marxism is a wrangling *ism*, dealing as it does with contradictions and struggles. Contradictions are always present, and where there are contradictions there are struggles. Now there are some contradictions between China and the Soviet Union. The way they think, the way they do things and their traditional habits are different from ours. So we must work on them. I always say that we should work on our comrades. Some people say, since they are Communists, they should be as good as we are, so why is such work needed? To work on people means doing united front work, working on the democratic personages, but why on Communists? It is wrong to look at the matter this way. There are different opinions inside the Communist Party itself. Some people have joined the Party organizationally, but ideologically they still need to be straightened out. And even among veteran cadres there are some who do not talk the same language as we do. Therefore, it is often necessary to have heart-to-heart talks, confer individually or collectively and hold meetings more than once to help people straighten out their thinking.

In my opinion, circumstances are more powerful than individuals, even than high officials. The force of circumstances will make it impossible for those die-hard elements in the Soviet Union to get anywhere if they continue to push their great-nation chauvinism. Our present policy is still to help them by talking things over with them face to face. This time when our delegation went to the Soviet Union,[156] we came straight to the point on a number of questions. I told Comrade Zhou Enlai over the phone that these people are blinded by their material gains and the best way to deal with them is to give them a good dressing down. What are their material gains? Nothing but 50 million tons of steel, 400 million tons of coal, and 80 million tons of petroleum. Does this amount to much? Not at all. Now at the sight of this much their heads are swelled. What Communists! What Marxists! I say multiply all that tenfold, or even a hundredfold, it still doesn't amount to much. All you have done is to extract something from the earth, turn it into steel and make some cars, planes, and what not. What is so remarkable about that? And yet you make all this such a heavy burden on your backs that you even cast away revolutionary principles. Isn't this being blinded by material gains? If one attains high office, one can be blinded by material gains too. To be the first secretary is some kind of material gain, which is also liable to swell one's head. When a man's head gets too swelled, we have to give him a good bawling out one way or another. This time in Moscow, Comrade Zhou Enlai did not stand on ceremony and took them on, and consequently they kicked up a row. This is good, straightening things out face to face. They tried to influence us and we tried to influence them. However, we didn't come straight to the point on every question, we didn't play all our cards but kept some up our sleeves. There will always be contradictions. As long as things are tolerable on the whole, we can seek common ground and reserve differences, to be dealt with later. If they insist on having their own way, sooner or later we will have to bring everything into the open.

As for us, we mustn't talk big in our external propaganda. We must always be modest and prudent and must, so to speak, tuck our tail between our legs. We must continue to learn from the Soviet Union. However, we must do it selectively, learning only what is advanced and not what is backward. In regard to what is backward there is another way of learning—just don't. As for their mistakes, we can avoid repeating them if we know about them. As for those things of theirs which are useful to us, we must learn them by all means. We shall learn what is useful from every country in the world. One should go everywhere in search of knowledge. To go to one place only would be monotonous.

(From the verbatim record)

ON A THIRD WORLD WAR AND INTERNATIONAL SOLIDARITY*

(February 27, 1957)

People all over the world are now discussing whether or not a third world war will break out. On this question, too, we must be mentally prepared and do some analysis. We stand firmly for peace and against war. But if the imperialists insist on unleashing another war, we should not be afraid of it. Our attitude on this question is the same as our attitude toward any disturbance: first, we are against it; second, we are not afraid of it. The First World War was followed by the birth of the Soviet Union with a population of 200 million. The Second World War was followed by the emergence of the socialist camp with a combined population of 900 million. If the imperialists insist on launching a third world war, it is certain that several hundred million more will turn to socialism, and then there will not be much room left on earth for the imperialists; it is also likely that the whole structure of imperialism will completely collapse.

......

To strengthen our solidarity with the Soviet Union, to strengthen our solidarity with all the socialist countries—this is our fundamental policy, this is where our basic interests lie. Then there are the Asian and African countries and all the peace-loving countries and peoples—we must strengthen and develop our solidarity with them. United with these two forces, we shall not stand alone. As for the imperialist countries, we should unite with their people and strive to coexist peacefully with those countries, do business with them and prevent a possible war, but under no circumstances should we harbor any unrealistic notions about them.

(From *People's Daily*, June 19, 1957)

---

*These two paragraphs are excerpts from "On the Correct Handling of Contradictions Among the People," a speech by Mao Zedong at the 11th Session (Enlarged) of the Supreme State Conference.

ON SOME POLICY ISSUES IN CHINA'S FOREIGN RELATIONS*

(*March, September 1957*)

I

I should also like to discuss with you some policy issues in our foreign relations.

On the question of Taiwan, there has been some change lately. The United States is trying to bring Chiang Kai-shek down. It has been cultivating a group of people to replace Chiang Kai-shek. Now we need to help Chiang Kai-shek oppose the United States. For the question is: Which is better, Chiang Kai-shek or the more pro-American forces fostered by the United States? Which is more desirable, that Taiwan remain under the semioccupation of the United States, as it is now, or come under total U.S. occupation?

Countries such as the United States and Britain are scheming to create "two Chinas" by recognizing us, on the one hand, and Taiwan, on the other. Our policy is if they recognize us, they can't recognize Taiwan. We are not upset by their nonrecognition. The later the United States recognizes us, the better, for it will give us more time to put our own things in order. If it has an embassy here, it will engage in various disruptive activities from the inside. This has been our actual policy. Externally we are having negotiations with the United States, too. The purpose is to take the offensive in diplomacy. The negotiations have been going on for more than a year. The reason they have not broken down is that each side wants to place the responsibility for disrupting the negotiations onto the other side. If the United States wishes to keep on talking, we are ready to go along, even if the negotiations last for decades. It seems they will drag on for a long time.

---

* This piece comprises Part I, excerpts from Mao Zedong's conversation with a government delegation from Czechoslovakia, and Part II, excerpts from Mao Zedong's conversation with a delegation from the National Assembly of Czechoslovakia and a delegation from the People's Council of Prague.

With Britain we shall not establish full but only half-official diplomatic relations. Our policy is to keep up with it a relationship of neither closeness nor separation.

On the question of joining international organizations such as the Olympic Committee and the organizations affiliated to the United Nations, some fraternal countries, out of kind intentions and lack of understanding of our position, have always hoped we would join these organizations. They—I don't know if you are also with them—seem to think that we are being much too leftist on the issue. Our view is, we shall not join if there are Kuomintang representatives in these organizations, for if we joined under those circumstances, it would mean recognition of "two Chinas." So we say we can rely on our cooperation with the Soviet Union and the various people's democratic countries. As a big country and with its cooperation with Asian and African countries, China can just as well develop economically and culturally without the Western countries. The United States is imposing an embargo on us. We are glad it does so. If it didn't, we should have to trade with it and with countries such as Britain, France and West Germany. However, because of our economic backwardness, we yet have nothing to trade with them. Of course, our slogan is against the embargo. We shall keep on scolding it so long as its embargo continues. This is also a diplomatic offensive. If the embargo is lifted after completion of our Second or Third Five-Year Plan, we shall have some things to trade with them, and it will be time to establish diplomatic relations.

(March 22, 1957)
(From the verbatim record)

II

The principles guiding our foreign policy are the following: first, to unite with the countries in the socialist camp; second, to establish diplomatic relations with the countries of Asia, Africa, Latin-America and Scandinavia; third, as for the major Western powers, we are now mainly waging a struggle against them, and there is no hurry to establish diplomatic relations with them. Dulles'[97] policy is the same: Americans don't want diplomatic relations with us, lest we create trouble in their country.

(September 29, 1957)
(From the verbatim record)

SPEECH AT THE BANQUET IN HONOR OF VICE-PRESIDENT SARVEPALLI RADHAKRISHNAN OF INDIA

(*September 19, 1957*)

Your Excellency Mr. Vice-President,
Comrades and Friends,

Dr. Radhakrishnan, the vice-president of the Republic of India, distinguished Indian scholar and statesman and a good friend of the Chinese people, has come on a friendly visit to China, we wish to extend to him our warm welcome. We thank him for bringing to the Chinese people the profound friendship of the great Indian people.

The Chinese nation and the Indian nation have been good friends and good neighbors since ancient times. The Five Principles of Peaceful Coexistence[98] our two countries jointly initiated have laid a new foundation for our traditional friendship and promoted its further development. Our two peoples are both engaged in national reconstruction and in efforts for world peace. For these common objectives our two countries are carrying on close and friendly cooperation. The one billion people of China and India, being united, are a great force and an important guarantee for peace in Asia and the whole world.

An important feature of our times is the upsurging national independence movement of the Asian and African countries. The colonialists are trying by all means to reverse this trend. However, as shown to the whole world by the Egyptian people last year and by the Syrian people now, all the schemes and provocations of the colonialists are doomed to disastrous defeat. The Chinese people give their firm support to the Asian and African peoples in their struggle to win and safeguard national independence.

The Chinese people have always had great respect for the industrious and wise people of India. We hail every achievement of the India people in their peaceful reconstruction. We esteem the outstanding contributions the Indian people have made to the cause of international peace. We want to give our special thanks to India for her righteous support to China in international affairs. We have no doubt that India will play an ever more important role in the world.

Now, I propose a toast

to the prosperity of the Republic of India and the well-being of the Indian people,

to the friendship between the peoples of China and India,

to world peace,

to the health of His Excellency Vice-President Radhakrishnan of the Republic of India,

to the health of President Prasad of the Republic of India,

Ganbei!

(From *People's Daily*, September 20, 1957)

A NEW TURNING POINT IN THE INTERNATIONAL SITUATION*

(*November 18, 1957*)

At present, I feel the international situation has reached a new turning point. Two winds are blowing in the world today, an east wind and a west wind. There is a Chinese saying—If the east wind is not prevailing over the west wind, the west wind must be prevailing over the east wind. I believe the current situation is characterized by the fact that the east wind prevails over the west wind. In other words, the forces of socialism are overwhelmingly superior to the forces of imperialism.

The October Revolution 40 years ago was the turning point in the whole history of mankind. How come there is now another turning point? Yes, there is. During the war against Hitler[4] there was a time, a period of one or two years, when Hitler had the upper hand. He had not only occupied a major part of Europe, but also invaded the Soviet Union, which had to give up a big stretch of land. So for a time Hitler had the upper hand. The Battle of Stalingrad[157] became the turning point from which Hitler declined. The Soviet army began its irresistible advance and, finally, took Berlin. Was that not a turning point? In my opinion, the Battle of Stalingrad was the turning point of the entire Second World War.

Last year and in the past few years the Western world was very aggressive, taking advantage of problems that occurred in our camp, particularly the Hungarian incident,[158] to discredit our camp. Dark clouds covered our skies. However, the counterrevolutionaries of Hungary were suppressed. During the Suez Canal incident[134] the warning by the Soviet Union played a role in curbing the war of aggression. The purpose of the Western mudslinging, in my view, was to "fix" the Communist Parties. In this respect, they achieved part of their aim. For instance, Howard Fast[159] of the United States, a shameful renegade of communism, left the Party. Some other Communists also deserted

---

* These are excerpts from Mao Zedong's speech at the Moscow Conference of Representatives of Communist and Workers' Parties.

their parties. The imperialists were overjoyed about it. I think we should also be glad. The renegades left. What's the harm in that?

This year, 1957, the situation is quite different. Our skies are bright all over, whereas the Western skies are overcast. We are optimistic. What about them? They are in trepidation. The ascent of the two satellites has caused them insomnia. The meeting of the Communist Parties of over 60 countries in Moscow is unprecedented, and larger than ever in scale. Yet in the socialist camp countries, the Communist Parties, and particularly among the people of the various countries, considerable people still believe that the United States is terrific. Look, it has so much steel, so many aircraft and artillery pieces. We have so much less. The numerous Western newspapers and radio stations have been boasting every day. The Voice of America and Radio Free Europe have been lauding it to the skies, creating a false appearance that has misled many people. Our job is to expose this deception. I have ten pieces of evidence to show who is actually more capable, they or we. Is it the east wind prevailing over the west wind, or the west wind over the east wind?

First, during the war against Hitler, how much steel did Roosevelt[6] and Churchill[144] have? About 70 million tons. But they still could not eat up Hitler. Nothing could be done. A way had to be found. They traveled all the way to Yalta[145] to ask for help from the Soviet Union. How much steel did Stalin have at that time? Before the war, 18 million tons. With the territories lost during the war, as Comrade Khrushchev[146] told me, steel production halved, and only nine million tons were left. They who had 70 million tons of steel came asking for help from those with only nine million tons. What were the conditions? The land east of the Elbe was designated for a Red Army offensive. That is to say, they decided, however painfully, to allow this large area to leave their system, giving it the possibility to convert to the socialist system. This example is very convincing. It shows that material resources alone are not decisive; the people are more important, and so is the system. At Yalta the question of fighting Japan was also discussed. Again, the Americans couldn't eat up Japan, and had to ask the Communists for help. Manchuria[160] in China and part of Korea were designated for a Red Army offensive. It was also decided that Japan should return half of Sakhalin Island and all the Kurile islands. That was also a painful concession, since it was for the purpose of eating up their pals—the Japanese imperialists.

Second, the Chinese revolution. When the Kuomintang was desperately beaten by us at the beginning of 1949, it cried for help from Truman,[65] begging, "My American lord, please send a few soldiers." Truman answered, "No, not a single soldier." Then the Kuomintang said, "Could you please say a few words? Say that the United States would not sit idly by if the Communists reached south of the Yangtze River." Truman said, "No, that can't be done. I can't say that, for the Communists are formidable." So finally Chiang Kai-shek had to take to his heels. He is in Taiwan now.

Third, the Korean War. At the start of the war each American division was equipped with 800 field guns, whereas every three Chinese Volunteers' divisions had only a little over 50. But what happened during actual fighting was like herding ducks. In a few weeks' time the Americans were driven back several hundred kilometers, from the Yalu River all the way to south of the 38th Parallel.[88] After that the Americans concentrated their forces for a counteroffensive. Following consultations between Comrade Kim Il Sung and us, it was decided to pull back to the 38th Parallel for a stalemate and to build our positions there. Fighting continued. The whole Korean War lasted nearly three years. American planes were swarming like wasps, while we had not a single plane at the first line. The two sides agreed to negotiate an armistice, but where to have the negotiations? They proposed a Danish ship. We proposed Kaesong in our area. They said OK. Because the negotiating site was in our area, when they came to the meeting every day, they had to fly a white flag, as they did when they went back after the meeting. Later they felt embarrassed flying a white flag every day. They said, "Let's change to a place called Panmunjom, which is situated between the battle lines of the two sides." We agreed. The negotiations went on for about a year, but the Americans still loathed to sign an agreement. So the negotiations dragged on. Finally, in 1953, we breached 21 kilometers of the American defense line at the 38th Parallel. They were scared and immediately signed the agreement. The Americans, so powerful and with so much steel, could do nothing else. On our side the war was actually fought by three countries, Korea, China and the Soviet Union. The Soviet Union supplied the weapons. But how about the enemy side? They had 16 countries.[161]

Fourth, the Vietnam War. The French were beaten out of their wits by Ho Chi Minh. One person can bear witness to this, that is, Comrade Ho Chi Minh, who is present. While the French wanted to stop, the Americans persisted, because they had more steel. What the Americans did was supply weapons to sustain the tense situation. They were not prepared to send in troops. That's how the Geneva Conference[95] came about, resulting in designating the major part of Vietnam to the Democratic Republic of Vietnam.

Fifth, the Suez Canal incident. Two imperialist powers launched an invasion, but the war lasted only a few days. When the Soviet Union spoke up, they pulled back. Of course, there was a second factor; the whole world spoke up against the Anglo-French aggression.

Sixth, Syria. The United States was all set to fight. Again, the Soviet Union said a few words and appointed a general called Konstantin Rokossovsky. After those acts by the Soviet Union, the Americans decided to be careful about fighting. The whole thing is not over yet. We still have to be on the alert for possible trouble in the future. But, anyway, war has been averted thus far.

Seventh, the two satellites that the Soviet Union has launched. How much steel does the launching country have? Fifty-one million tons. Isn't the United States said to be very powerful? "Why haven't you sent up even a potato? You have 100 million tons of steel and have been boasting so much about the Vanguard Program!"[162] It seems the Vanguard Program needs to change its name to the Rearguard Program.

From the above seven examples I think a concept can be formed: The Western world has been left behind by us. Is it close or far behind? In my opinion, and maybe I'm being a little adventuresome, I should say it has been left behind forever. Before the Soviet Union launched its man-made satellites, the socialist countries already enjoyed an overwhelming superiority over the imperialist countries in terms of popular support and population. With the Soviet satellites launched, an overwhelming superiority in the most important scientific and technological fields has been added. Some people say the Americans will catch up; they are also going to launch satellites. That's true. Comrade Khrushchev said in his report the United States would launch satellites. The question being disputed is whether it will take the Americans one, two or five years to catch up with the Soviet Union. "I don't care if it takes one, two or five years; you are left behind all the same." I suppose our Soviet comrades and Comrade Khrushchev sleep only at night, not in the daytime. Not all the people in the Soviet Union will be sleeping day and night for one, two or five years, will they? "You may catch up in one, two or five years, but the Soviet Union will be advancing at the same time." Comrades, let me talk a little about things in our country. This year we have produced 5.2 million tons of steel. In another five years, we shall have 10 to 15 million tons. In another five years, 20 to 25 million tons. In still another five years, 35 to 40 million tons. Of course, I may just be talking big, and when the next international conference convenes, you may criticize me for being subjectivistic. But I'm well founded when I say this. We have the help of many Soviet experts. The Chinese are hard-working. China is a big country in terms of political significance and population, but economically it is still a small one. The Chinese people are working hard, enthusiastic in their efforts to turn

China into a true big power. Comrade Khrushchev told us in 15 years the Soviet Union will be able to overtake the United States. I can say that in 15 years we shall probably catch up with or surpass Britain. For I've had two conversations with Comrade Pollit and Comrade Gollan[163], at which I asked them about their country. They told me Britain now produces 20 million tons of steel a year, which could possibly be increased to 30 million tons in 15 years, whereas in 15 years China will produce 40 million tons. Won't that surpass Britain? So, 15 years from now, in our camp, the Soviet Union will have surpassed the United States and China will have surpassed Britain.

In the final analysis, we should strive for 15 years of peace. By the end of that period we shall be invincible in the world, nobody will dare to fight us and the world will be able to enjoy lasting peace.

Now, there is another possibility that should be taken into account; that is, the war-mongering maniacs will drop their atom bombs and hydrogen bombs everywhere. If they drop, we shall drop too. A mess of casualties will be created. We should base our considerations on a worst-case possibility. The Political Bureau of our Party has held several meetings on this question. If war breaks out today, China has only hand-grenades, not atom bombs. But the Soviet Union has. Let's imagine the number of people that will be killed in case of war. Out of the world population of 2.7 billion, one third may be lost; it may be still more, with one half lost. It is they, not we, that want war. Once war breaks out, atom bombs and hydrogen bombs will start dropping. I have argued this question with a foreign statesman. He believes the human race will be wiped out in case of atomic war. I said, if the worst comes to the worst, half the world population is wiped out and half left, imperialism will be wiped off the earth, but the whole world will be socialized. In time, the population will be back at 2.7 billion—it is bound to be even more. China's reconstruction is not yet completed. We wish for peace. But if the imperialists insist on fighting a war, we shall have to harden our heart to fight first and do reconstruction afterward. If you keep worrying about war every day, what can you do if war actually breaks out? At the beginning, I said the east wind prevails over the west wind and war will not break out. Now I have made these supplementary explanations in case war breaks out. Thus we have reckoned with both possibilities.

I said there were ten pieces of evidence I could cite. I have already cited seven; here are three more.

The eighth is the British withdrawal from large areas in Asia and Africa.
The ninth is the Dutch withdrawal from Indonesia.
The tenth is the withdrawal of France from Syria, Lebanon, Morocco and

Tunisia. It is in a helpless situation in Algeria.

Who is stronger, the backward countries or the advanced ones? India or Britain? Indonesia or the Netherlands? Algeria or France? In my view, the imperialists are all the setting sun at six o'clock in the afternoon, whereas we are the rising sun at six in the morning. Hence the turning point. That is to say, the Western countries are left behind and we have got the upper hand. It is definitely not the west wind prevailing over the east wind, for the west wind is too weak. It is definitely the east wind prevailing over the west wind, for we are stronger.

What really counts is not the amount of steel, but primarily popular support or the lack of it. It has always been so in history. In history, it is always the weak who defeat the strong, the bare-handed who defeat the fully armed. The Bolsheviks started without even a single gun. The Soviet comrades told me that during the February Revolution[32] there were only 40,000 Party members; at the time of the October Revolution the Party membership was still only 240,000. The opening paragraph of the *History of the Communist Party of the Soviet Union (Bolsheviks), Short Course,* is a good example of dialectics: from a small group to the whole country. The Bolsheviks started as a few scattered groups, each with a few dozens of people, and, in due course, they became the leaders of the whole country. My Soviet comrades, when you revise the *History of the Communist Party of the Soviet Union*, I hope these sentences will not be deleted. It has been the same with us in China. At the beginning, there were a few scattered communist groups, each with a few dozens of members. Now we are a big Party, leading an entire country and a population of 640 million. The communist groups with a few dozens of members have grown into a party of 12 million. I say this especially for the purpose of exchanging views with comrades of the Communist Parties in capitalist countries, because they are still in a difficult situation. Some parties are very small. Some parties have members deserting in large numbers. I should say there is nothing strange about all this; it's probably a good thing. Our road forward is tortuous, rising in spirals.

I should also like to speak on the question of "paper tigers." When Chiang Kai-shek started his offensive against us in 1946, many of our comrades and the people of the country were much concerned about whether we could win the war. I myself was concerned. But we were confident of one thing. At that time an American correspondent, Anna Louise Strong, came to Yan'an. She was a woman writer who had lived in the Soviet Union for decades, was driven out of the country by Stalin, and was later rehabilitated by Comrade Khrushchev. In an interview, I discussed many questions with her, including Chiang Kai-shek, Hitler, Japan, the United States and the atom bomb. I said all allegedly powerful reactionaries are merely paper tigers. The reason is that they are divorced from the people. Look! Wasn't Hitler a paper tiger? Wasn't he overthrown? I also said that the tsar of Russia was a paper tiger, as were the emperor of China and Japanese imperialism, and see, they were all overthrown. U.S. imperialism has not yet been overthrown and it has the atom bomb, but I believe it too is a paper tiger and will be overthrown. Chiang Kai-shek was very powerful, for he had a regular army of more than four million. We were then in Yan'an. What was the population of Yan'an? Seven thousand. How many troops did we have? We had 900,000 guerrillas, all isolated by Chiang Kai-shek in scores of base areas. Yet we said that Chiang Kai-shek was only a paper tiger and that we could certainly defeat him. We have developed a concept over a long period for the struggle against the enemy, namely, strategically we should despise all our enemies, but tactically we should take them all seriously. In other words, with regard to the whole we must despise the enemy, but with regard to each specific problem we must take him seriously. If we do not despise him with regard to the whole, we shall commit opportunist errors. Marx and Engels were but two individuals, yet in those early days they declared that capitalism would be overthrown throughout the world. But with regard to specific problems and specific enemies, if we do not take them seriously, we shall commit adventurist errors. In war, battles can be fought only one by one and enemy forces can be destroyed only one part at a time. Factories can be built only one by one. Peasants can plow the land only plot by plot. The same is true even of eating a meal. Strategically, we take the eating of a meal lightly; we are sure we can manage it. But when it comes to the actual eating, it must be done mouthful by mouthful; you cannot swallow an entire banquet in one gulp. This is called the piecemeal solution and is known in military writings as destroying the enemy forces one by one.

(From documents of the Second Session of the Eighth National Congress of the Communist Party of China)

CHINA WILL NOT EXPAND OUTWARD*

(*December 14, 1957*)

Chairman Mao Zedong (hereinafter referred to as *Mao*): You are both very young, and this is of great advantage to your country.

Deputy Prime Minister U Ba Swe (hereinafter referred to as *Ba*): It is just because our country is young, and so are the leaders.

Mao: Our country is also young, but we are relatively older, because we have been engaged in guerrilla warfare for a long time. The area of Burma is not small; what is the amount of land per capita?

Deputy Prime Minister U Kyaw Nyun (hereinafter referred to as *Kyaw*): On average, one acre of cultivated land per person, but we still have a lot of reclaimable wasteland. The area of cultivated land at present is 20 million acres, which can probably be increased by 40 million.

Mao: The Chinese people have only three *mu* per capita, half what the Burmese people have. Our reclaimable land is rather scanty, but you need not be afraid that China would covet Burmese territory. Burmese territory belongs to the Burmese people. No Chinese is allowed to covet it.

I asked Prime Minister U Nu when he came to China whether anyone in Burma is afraid of China. He said some people were. I explained to him then that Burma need not be afraid of China. We are resolutely against aggression—aggression against any country.

Kyaw: We believe China in this respect. However, before Prime Minister U Nu's visit to China and his meeting with Chairman Mao, Burma was indeed a bit afraid of China, because Burma is a small country, while China is a big one. Since Premier Zhou Enlai visited Burma and we jointly initiated the Five Principles,[110] we came to understand each other. Therefore, there is no fear in Burma now.

Mao: Burma used to think of Yunnan Province as being wrapped in

---

* This is the main part of Mao Zedong's conversation with deputy prime ministers U Ba Swe and U Kyaw Nyun of Burma.

darkness, wondering how many troops China stationed there and what it was cooking against Burma. Burma was then very uneasy about us, so we suggested that Burma set up a consulate in Yunnan to observe.

Ba: It is quite natural that we had such fear, because historically big countries always bully small ones, and Burma is situated between big countries. Anyhow, our fears have now vanished.

Mao: Prime Minister Nehru also told us that some countries are afraid of China, some of the United States, and some even of India. China and India, Burma, Laos and Cambodia are friendly neighbors, so we are quite at ease in our southwest. We are also at ease in the north, because the Soviet Union, Korea and the People's Republic of Mongolia are there. What we are worried about is our east. Surely we are not afraid of Japan, the Philippines, Taiwan or Hong Kong, but of the United States, which will make use of these places to plot against us. We have a very long coastline of 12,000 kilometers, so we have to pay more attention to our maritime defense. There is no need to station many troops in our southwest.

Ba: By no means will Burma join any military bloc or become the base of any imperialist power.

Mao: China is a large country and it has a great number of things to take care of. How could we have the idea of aggression against others when we can barely manage our own affairs? Although we have a big population, we are able to meet the people's needs for food and clothing by relying on ourselves. Some Western observers, such as Attlee,[116] hold that China with too big a population will have difficulty in finding a way out. They do not know that in China it requires only one fifteenth of a hectare (one *mu*) of land to feed one person, and even one thirtieth of a hectare (half a *mu*) is enough in some places. Our population is increasing and is estimated to reach one billion by the end of the 20th century, but by then both our industry and our agriculture will have developed.

Premier Zhou Enlai: By that time every ten persons may have one hectare of land, or one and a half *mu* for each person.

Mao: That's why China will not expand outward. How nice if humans were able to invent artificial food, like the synthetic fibers for clothing at present.

Kyaw: If the synthetic fibers could be mass-produced, the land now used to grow cotton and hemp could be turned over to food crops.

Mao: How many remnants of Kuomintang troops are still in Burma?

Ba: There are a few, but they move about in the Burmese-Laotian and Burmese-Thai border areas and are difficult to locate. They flee to Laos or

Thailand when we send armed forces to pursue and attack them, and they come back to make harassment as soon as our forces have left.

Mao: Is the number less than before?

Ba: It is estimated between 1,000 to 1,500 persons, they are no longer a political organization but just a gang of bandits, who loot and plunder wherever they go. They were 12,000 to 16,000 when they numbered most.

Mao: These Chinese did great harm to the Burmese people, destroying Burmese villages. I wonder if Burma will demand compensation from China.

Kyaw: The Chinese government has nothing to do with these bad elements.

Mao: Yet we feel this way. You are helping us wipe them out, and this is mutual cooperation, because they are our common enemy.

Ba: In this regard, Thailand has given us some help, and so has China. For instance, when we sent our air force to bomb these Kuomintang troops, our planes sometimes flew over Thailand territory, and we had to apologize to Thailand from time to time. Everything is all right now, since we have arrived at an understanding with Thailand.

Mao: It would be good if Thailand could change into a country like yours. Thailand is a member state of the Southeast Asian Treaty Organization,[96] but the majority of the people of Thailand harbor no hostility against us. Some people in Thailand are afraid of our aggression. Hence someone spread the rumor that China was going to give Pridi Phanomyong, the ex-prime minister of Thailand, now seeking political asylum in China, an army of 100,000 soldiers to stage a comeback; another rumor was that China was carrying out Free Thailand activities. Of course, Thailand came to understand us later on.

Kyaw: True, Thailand had such fears of China in the beginning.

Mao: They have sent some delegations here to see what is going on, and it is better now.

Does Burma have diplomatic relations with Thailand?

Ba: Yes, since long ago. However, the improvement in relations between the two countries is a matter of recent years.

Mao: I said to Prime Minister U Nu last time that I hope Burma would help China by working on Thailand.

U Hla Maung (Burmese Ambassador to China): Prime Minister U Nu has made efforts in this respect. Pakistan is a SEATO member, but it has diplomatic relations with China. Why not Thailand?

Mao: Your observation is quite correct.

Ba: Prime Minister U Nu will go to Thailand before long.

Mao: Please tell Prime Minister U Nu that we hope he will give us further help. We are grateful for his help in the past. We believe that Thailand will improve its relations with us after a period of time, but right now it still dares not do so.

(From the verbatim record)

TELEGRAM TO KIM IL SUNG ON THE WITHDRAWAL OF THE CHINESE PEOPLE'S VOLUNTEERS FROM KOREA

(January 24, 1958)

Comrade Prime Minister Kim Il Sung,

We have received both your letters, dated December 16 and 25, 1957.

We have carefully studied the two plans put forward for the withdrawal of the Chinese People's Volunteers from Korea. We feel that it is more appropriate for the Democratic People's Republic of Korea to initiate a request for the withdrawal of foreign forces from Korea, then for the Chinese government to respond to the request of the Korean government. Therefore, we consider it better to adopt the plan proposed in your letter of December 16. Regarding this plan, we now make some specific suggestions. We have already consulted the Soviet government on these suggestions, to which they have expressed full agreement. The suggestions are now presented as follows, and we request you and the Central Committee of the Korean Workers' Party to consider whether they are appropriate.

1. The Supreme People's Council of the Democratic People's Republic of Korea would write a letter to the United Nations, which would be put forward in the United Nations by the Soviet Union, as a member of the United Nations, to press for action by the United Nations. But this method has one defect, that is it would treat the whole United Nations as our belligerent, whereas in actuality it is only a minority of U.N. members who have sent aggressive troops to form the U.N. Forces. Hence we suggest that the government of the Democratic People's Republic of Korea issue a public statement, advancing the following proposals in accordance with the basic propositions of the Korean-Chinese side on the Korean question at the 1954 Geneva Conference:

(1) The U.N. Forces and the Chinese People's Volunteers are to withdraw from Korea simultaneously;

(2) South Korea and North Korea are to conduct consultations on an equal

footing, so as to establish and develop economic and cultural relations between them and prepare for free elections in all of Korea;

(3) Within a defined period of time after the complete withdrawal of foreign forces from South Korea and North Korea, free elections are to take place throughout Korea under the supervision of an organization composed of neutral nations.

2. The Chinese government would issue a statement right after the public statement of the government of the Democratic People's Republic of Korea, supporting the latter's stand and officially expressing its readiness to consult with the government of the Democratic People's Republic of Korea on the withdrawal of the Chinese People's Volunteers in groups at set times, in the meantime demanding that the governments of countries on the side of the U.N. Forces take similar steps.

3. Subsequently, the Soviet government would issue a statement supporting the statements of the Korean and Chinese governments and stressing that the governments of countries on the side of the U.N. Forces should, like the Chinese government, respond to the demand of the government of the Democratic People's Republic of Korea; it would also propose convening a conference of all countries concerned to discuss the peaceful settlement of the Korean question.

4. During the forthcoming visit to Korea by Comrade Zhou Enlai representing the Chinese government in mid-February this year, the Korean and Chinese governments may announce in a joint communiquè that the Chinese government has obtained, through consultation, the agreement of the Chinese People's Volunteers to withdraw from Korea and that the latter have decided to do so in groups before the end of 1958. The Korean and Chinese governments may state in the joint communiquè that the withdrawal of the Chinese People's Volunteers from Korea prior to that of the U.N. Forces is for the purpose of easing tension and facilitating consultations between South and North Korea on an equal footing for the peaceful reunification of Korea. Therefore, the U.N. Forces ought to take similar actions. Meanwhile, the Chinese People's Volunteers would issue a statement to the effect that the Chinese people and the Korean people depend on each other like lips and teeth and will stand together through thick and thin, and that the withdrawal of the Chinese People's Volunteers from Korea by no means signifies disregard of the interests of the Korean and Chinese peoples, who share the same weal and woe. If Syngman Rhee[85] and the United States dare renew provocations and cross the armistice line, the Chinese People's Volunteers will, at the request of the Korean government, unhesitatingly fight once again shoulder to shoulder with

the Korean People's Army to repulse aggression.

5. We have provisionally worked out the timetable for the withdrawal of the Chinese People's Volunteers from Korea as follows:

(1) From March to April 1958, after the publication of the joint communiquè of the Korean and Chinese governments, one third of the Chinese People's Volunteers will be withdrawn and completely replaced by the Korean People's Army at the first defense line, while the remaining two thirds will be stationed at the second defense line;

(2) From July to September 1958 the second third will be withdrawn;

(3) The final third is to be withdrawn before the end of 1958.

6. Following publication of the joint communiquè of the Korean and Chinese governments, Switzerland and Sweden on the Neutral Nations Supervisory Commission[165] most likely will again ask for the abolition of the Supervisory Commission. Thereupon we can, on the ground that the U.N. Forces are not yet withdrawn, request that they leave a minimum number of persons at Panmunjom to carry out supervision. However, we must be prepared for their departure in disregard of our request.

Please study the above-mentioned points and give us a reply.

Please accept my salutation.

Mao Zedong
January 24, 1958
(From the draft of the telegram)

FROM THE SOVIET UNION'S EXPERIENCE WE SHOULD CHOOSE ONLY THE GOOD THINGS*

(*March 1958*)

Comrade [Liu] Shaoqi talked about the issue of rules and regulations at the Nanning meeting.¹⁶⁶ We have borrowed many rules and regulations from the Soviet Union, such as those on security. They are very bad rules. They have restricted the activities of our leaders, who are always surrounded by an entourage and are not allowed to see places they want to see, to eat out or to buy a pair of shoes in the street. It is good that Comrade Chen Yun¹⁶⁷ cooks for himself, but his bodyguards consider it shockingly unacceptable. This is how it is at the Ministry of Public Security. Other ministries have problems concerning rules and regulations. Many were copied from the Soviet Union and are harmful. Those rules and regulations restricted productivity, produced waste and created a bureaucracy. This was buying experience with money. As we first established our republic, we had no alternative but to copy some of the Soviet Union's rules and regulations. This is partly, but not completely, true. It is wrong to think we have no alternative but to copy the Soviet Union. In the past we had political and military dogmatism, but only a small segment of people in the Party made the mistake. The majority of people did not want to copy the Soviets rigidly. In the initial period of the Party and the Northern Expedition period our Party was relatively lively. Rigid copying did not appear until later. Rules and regulations are red tape. Everything is ritual. There are many rituals that the Central Committee does not know about, the State Council does not know about and ministers do not necessarily know about. Industry and education departments borrowed more rules and regulations from the Soviet Union than other departments. The agricultural Department borrowed some. The Central Committee is strict on this issue. Several rules and by-laws have been approved by the Central Committee and the experience of some localities in implementing these rules has been approved. Considering

---

* These are excerpts from a speech by Mao Zedong at the working conference of the Party's Central Committee in Chengdu.

actual circumstances, the rules were not copied rigidly. In agriculture there are machines to copy and persons to learn from, but in industry there are only machines to copy and in commerce even less to copy. We have copied a lot from the Soviet Union in planning, statistics, finance, capital construction procedure and management. The basic idea is to control people with rules and regulations.

We should use our own minds when we copy [foreign experience]. We must not copy mechanically, which means giving up our judgment and forgetting the lesson of dogmatism in the past. The lesson is that theory must be combined with practice. Theory comes from practice and returns to practice. This principle has not been used in economic construction. To combine the general principle of Marxism and Leninism with the practice of the Chinese revolution is materialism. The two are a unity of opposites, that is, dialectics. Copying [foreign experience] mechanically shows an ignorance of dialectics. The Soviet Union has its own ways. Its experience is one side and China's practice is another. This is the unity of opposites. In terms of the Soviet Union's experience we must choose the good things to follow and ignore the bad things. Accepting the Soviet Union's experience without taking China's actual circumstances into consideration is not choosing the good things to follow. For instance, in publishing a newspaper we would copy everything from *Pravda* without making our own judgments. It's just the way of a three-year-old child, supported everywhere, and having no ideas of its own. We should think of two ways for doing everything just to compare. This is dialectics. Otherwise, it is metaphysics. We produce several drafts when we want to choose the route for a railway line, the site of a factory or a dam at the Three Gorges. Why can't rules and regulations have more than one draft? Rules and regulations for the armed forces are also mechanical copies without independent judgment—"complete equipment" imported.

(March 9, 1958)
(From the verbatim record)

In foreign relations we must make friends with the Soviet Union, all the People's Democracies, Communist Parties and working classes. Internationalism should be adopted. Learning from the strong points of the Soviet Union and other countries is a principle, but learning has two ways: mere copying and learning creatively, or combining learning with originality. Mechanically copying the Soviet Union's rules and regulations lacks originality.

(March 10, 1958)
(From the verbatim record)

LEARN ADVANCED EXPERIENCE FROM ALL COUNTRIES IN THE WORLD*

(*April 2, 1958*)

We wish to learn from you; you began industrialization earlier than we. China is a very poor country; it can be said we have nothing at all. It is good to learn about fine things wherever they exist in the world. If there are fine things in foreign countries, why not learn from them? Will this be good or bad for us? This is about learning fine things, including the Soviet experience, we learn from their good experiences, learn things useful to us. However, sometimes we have learned things of no use to us. We can't blame this on the Soviet experts, but on ourselves. This refers to indiscriminately and mechanically copying experiences from the Soviet Union. In one case out of ten we may be wrong in our way of learning. Our watchword is to learn from advanced experience, but sometimes we have learned some experience that is not suitable for China. There is some good in this too, we can improve on the unsuitable experience until we get a more proper experience. Every country has its own characteristics, and if something doesn't suit these characteristics, it won't work.

To learn advanced experience is good for all countries. At the same time, a small part may not suit all and may be harmful if blindly applied to certain countries. Lenin told people not to copy mechanically what is written in Marxist works, and we must not even take Marxist basic principles as dogma, but as a guide to action. Communist Parties should creatively implement the Marxist principles by integrating it with the specific conditions of the different countries.

It is good now. A conference was convened in Moscow, and representatives of Communist Parties of many countries worked out a basic program.[168] What I have just mentioned is also included in the program: The universal truths of Marxism have to be integrated with the concrete conditions of

---

* This is part of Mao Zedong's conversation with a delegation from the Polish government.

different countries, and there is unity between internationalism and patriotism. For quite a long time there was not such a program. There is one now, and it has become the program accepted by the Communist Parties of all countries.

(From the verbatim record)

WITHIN THE FOUR SEAS
ALL MEN ARE BROTHERS*

(*May 16, 1958*)

This is a good document,[169] which is well worth reading. Comrade Xiaoping,[170] please get it immediately printed and distribute to all comrades participating in the conference. Things should be done according to this document, with no exception allowed, wherever there are Soviet experts. Soviet experts are good comrades and are subject to reasoning and persuasion. For any misunderstanding caused by our being unreasonable or inadequate at reasoning we have on ourselves to blame. Within the four seas all men are brothers so far as the ranks of Communists are concerned; we must regard the Soviet experts as members of our own family. After the conference we should talk more with them in compliance with the General Line,[171] respect them and assiduously and modestly learn from them. In the meantime we must do away with blind faith and down with Jia Gui![129] Jia Gui, a typical lackey, is despised by all people.

Mao Zedong
(May 16, 1958)
(From the original manuscript)

---

* Thses are comments written by Mao Zedong on the report of the leading Party group of the Second Ministry of Machine Building on relations with Soviet experts, which was printed and distributed at the Second Session of the Eighth National Congress of the Communist Party of China.

ON THE SOVIET REQUEST TO ESTABLISH A SPECIAL LONG-WAVE RADIO STATION[172] IN CHINA*

(*June 7, 1958*)

I

For Comrades Liu, Lin Biao, Xiaoping, Zhou, Zhu, Chen, Peng Zhen and Chen Yi[173] to read, and then return to Comrade Peng Dehuai:[174]

This matter can be handled as suggested here, but the money must be paid by China, not the Soviet side. For joint use.

Mao Zedong
(June 7)

In case the Soviet side applies high pressure, do not reply but put it off for some time. Or reply to them after consultations in the Party Center. For this matter, an agreement should be signed by the governments of the two countries.

Peng is requested to pay attention to Mao's comments[175] on the conversation part.

(From the original manuscript)

---

* Part I is Mao Zedong's comments on Peng Dehuai's report of June 5, 1958, presented to Mao Zedong and the CPC Central Committee; Part II is a paragraph in the record of Peng Dehuai's conversation with Soviet general military advisor Dorovanov on June 4, 1958, which was revised by Mao Zedong. The words in italics were either added or rewritten by Mao Zedong.

II

The investment for this radio center should *be borne by the Chinese side*; this is China's unshirkable responsibility. *As for the technical part, such as construction and equipment, we shall ask the Soviet comrades to help us, while all the equipment needed should be evaluated and its cost paid by us. It can be put to joint use after being set up.* An official agreement should be signed by the governments of the two countries. This is not my personal opinion, but the opinion of China.

(From the manuscript revised by Mao Zedong)

SELF-RELIANCE IS PRINCIPAL AND STRIVING FOR FOREIGN AID IS AUXILIARY*

(June 17, 1958)

This document should be distributed immediately to all comrades attending the meeting of the Military Commission. It is a very good document, worthy of being read earnestly, and it is an eye-opener. This is your own business. Where does a modernized national defense come from without modernized industry? Self-reliance is principal and striving for foreign aid is auxiliary. We must do away with superstition, independently develop industry, and agriculture, and carry out technological and cultural revolutions, break down the slavish mentality, bury dogmatism, conscientiously learn from the good experience of foreign countries and also definitely study their bad experiences to serve as a lesson. This is our line. It should be adopted on the economic front as well as completely on the military front. If those who object to this line are unable to persuade us, they should accept it. "He is like a cul-de-sac, neither able to issue orders nor willing to listen to other people."[176] Where is the outlet if you have entered an impasse?

(From the original manuscript)

---

* These are Mao Zedong's comments on the distribution of the main points of Li Fuchun's report on the Second Five-Year Plan to an enlarged meeting of the Central Military Commission of the Communist Party of China.

DO AWAY WITH SUPERSTITION ABOUT IMPERIALIST "CIVILIZATION"*

(July 12, 1958)

Welcome to you. Very few African friends have come to China. We are all Asian-African countries, participants in the Bandung Conference.[111] The three regions of Asia, Africa and Latin America used to suffer from imperialist oppression. Africa is very near Asia, with only a strip of water between them —the Suez Canal—which can be crossed at a stride.

The world belongs to the oppressed people, and there is no future for oppressors. The Western imperialists are oppressors of the people, and in countries in Asia, Africa and Latin America there are local oppressors. For instance, the Turkish government is not so good, nor is the Lebanese government. China has Chiang Kai-shek, who is not a good man either; Japan also has bad people. However, oppressors are a minority, while good people are still in the majority. This is a question of nine fingers versus one finger; even in Western countries good people are a majority. In France, likewise, good people constitute the majority, and oppressors the minority. The minority oppressors are afraid of the opposition of the good people, just as one finger, that is, the bad fellow, is afraid of the opposition of the other nine fingers, the good people.

The people are distinct from the rulers and this is very important. It requires an observation of decades or even 100 years before a clear distinction is achieved. We came to understand this after being subjected to imperialist oppression for over 100 years. In past decades the Chinese people used to think that all foreigners were wicked. It is not easy for you to understand this point, only with which can victory be won. Now that you understand this point you are close to victory. Most nations are the oppressed, only a minority are oppressors.

Western imperialists consider themselves to be civilized and call the

---

* This is part of Mao Zedong's conversation with the Youth Delegation of Black Africa.

oppressed barbarous. However, we have not occupied other people's territory, nor has Africa occupied Europe. It is Europe that has occupied Africa. Can this be called civilized? Europe is inferior to Africa; it occupies other people's territory. Isn't this rather barbarous? Imperialists occupied China, and this was very barbarous. China has never in the past or at present occupied other countries, nor will it in the future occupy the United States or Britain as colonies. Therefore, we have always been civilized, and so have you. After liberation you won't occupy France, the United States, Britain or Germany. The imperialists are prone to castigate us as being dirty, unclean and unhygienic. I don't think this is necessarily correct. We are cleaner. We must have self-confidence and despise European and American imperialism. They count for nothing.

Over a long period of time imperialists have spread the lie that they are civilized, noble-minded and hygienic. Its influence remains in the world, like the existence of a slavish mentality. We used to be slaves of imperialism, and our mentality was affected in the long run. Such mental influence still exists among some of our people. That's why we have done extensive work among the whole people to do away with this superstition. There used to be a U.S.-phobia among the Chinese people, and its influence must be done away with. Are there people in your country who suffer from France-phobia? Most probably there are, because the French have all along disseminated that kind of stuff and they must have some followers. We should gradually rid the people of such mentality.

(From the verbatim record)

TALK TO YUDIN, AMBASSADOR OF THE SOVIET UNION TO CHINA*

(*July 22, 1958*)

I was unable to sleep after you left yesterday, nor did I eat anything. I have invited you for a conversation today, to serve as a doctor, in order that I may be able to eat and sleep in the afternoon. You are very lucky, being able to eat and sleep.

Let's return to our main topic and talk about the problems we discussed yesterday. Only in this room! There is no tension between us. We have ten fingers; nine are in accord and one is not. I have said this two or three times; have you forgotten?

I have reflected on the question raised yesterday. Maybe I misunderstood; maybe I was correct, and it can be resolved through argument. It appears that the request for nuclear submarines put forward by the navy[177] can be withdrawn. I had no inkling of this question and learned of it only after asking them. Some enthusiastic people at the Navy Headquarters—the Soviet advisers—said that the Soviet Union already has nuclear submarines, which can be given to China just by requesting them via telegram.

The nuclear submarine is a sophisticated branch of science, involving classified information. We Chinese are clumsy; things may go wrong when it is given us.

The Soviet comrades won victory 40 years ago and are experienced, while we won victory only eight years ago and lack experience, and you have just raised the idea of joint operation. The question of ownership was raised long ago. Lenin proposed a lease system; however, it was to capitalists.

---

* This is the main part of Mao Zedong's talk with Ambassador Yudin of the Soviet Union to China. Yudin conveyed to Mao Zedong on July 21 the suggestion of Khruschev and the Presidium of the CPSU Central Committee for the "establishment of a joint submarine fleet" by the Soviet Union and China, and the hope for Zhou Enlai and Peng Dehuai to go to Moscow for concrete consultations. Mao Zedong immediately responded, "First of all, the principle must be made clear: Are we to operate it with your help? Or can it only be joint operation, otherwise you won't help us, thus forcing us into joint operation?"

There are still capitalists in China, but the state is under the leadership of the Communist Party. You don't trust the Chinese, only the Russians. The Russians are superior, while the Chinese are inferior, clumsy, hence the question of joint operation. Speaking of that, how about putting everything under joint operation: the army, navy and air force, industry, agriculture, culture and education? Shall we hand over to you our coastline of over 10,000 kilometers, while we ourselves engage solely in organizing guerrilla forces? You have had some success with atomic energy, so you want to control others, to enjoy the right of lease. What other argument do you have?

You used to control Lüshun and Dalian, but left later. Why did you control those places? Because China was then ruled by the Kuomintang. Subsequently you left of your own accord, because now China is under the leadership of the Communist Party.

Under Stalin's pressure two spheres of influence were defined—the northeast and Xinjiang—as well as four enterprises under joint operation.[178] They were abolished afterward at the proposal of Comrade Khrushchev.[146] We are thankful to him for this.

You, especially Stalin, have all along distrusted the Chinese, regarding them as a second Tito, a backward nation. You say the Europeans despise the Russians; I think some Russians despise the Chinese.

At the most critical junctures Stalin would not allow us to make revolution and opposed our revolution. He committed a very serious mistake on this account, just like Zinovyev.[179]

Besides, we are dissatisfied with Mikoyan.[77] He used to put on superior airs, regarding us as his sons. He was haughty and arrogant. When he came to Xibaipo the first time he assumed great airs. He did the same on subsequent visits. He tried to persuade me to visit Moscow every time he came. I asked him what for? He replied there must be something to do there. Later on, it was Comrade Khruschev who set the topic— to attend a conference and work out a document.

To celebrate the 40th anniversary of the October Revolution was our common cause. I remarked then that the relationship among so-called fraternal parties was nominal, in fact it was a father-and-son, or cat-and-mouse relationship. I talked about this to Khruschev and other comrades within a small circle. They admitted it. Such a father-and-son relationship is Asian, not European. Those present then were Bulganin,[180] Mikoyan, Kuusinen,[181] Suslov,[182] and others. You (referring to Yudin) too, eh? On the Chinese side, Deng Xiaoping[170] and I were present.

I was dissatisfied with Mikoyan's congratulatory speech at our Eighth

National Party Congress. I purposely absented myself that day to express my protest. You didn't know that many delegates were dissatisfied too. He posed as a father, prattling about China's being Russia's son.

China has her own revolutionary tradition. However, the Chinese revolution could not have been victorious without the October Revolution or Marxism-Leninism.

We should learn from the Soviet experience. We should abide by universal truths, which are the nine articles in the Moscow Declaration.[168] We should learn from all kinds of experience, correct or incorrect. Incorrect experience is Stalin's metaphysics and dogmatism. Strictly speaking, it is not entirely metaphysics, but part dialectics, with the major part metaphysics. You call it a personality cult. It is the same thing. Stalin was very fond of assuming airs.

We support the Soviet Union, but not its wrong things. We have not publicly discussed the question of peaceful transition, not in our newspapers. We have been very careful, refraining from openly criticizing you, using only the method of internal exchange of views. I had talked with you before I left for Moscow. During our stay there, Comrade Deng Xiaoping discussed five points. We are not going to discuss the question publicly either, because this would not be in the interest of Comrade Khrushchev, whose leadership should be reinforced. That we refrain from discussing our views doesn't mean that they are not the truth.

As for the relationship between our two countries, we are united as one. This has been acknowledged by our enemies even now. We have opposed anything that is of disservice to the Soviet Union. On major issues, we are opposed to attacks on the Soviet Union by imperialism and revisionism. The Soviet Union does the same.

When did the Soviets begin to trust the Chinese? It began with the Korean War. Thereupon the two countries began to close up, hence the 156 projects of Soviet aid.[183] There were only 141 projects during the life time of Stalin; Comrade Khrushchev added many items.

We keep no secrets from you. You know all about our military, political, economic and cultural matters; there are more than 1,000 Soviet experts working in our country. We trust you because your country is a socialist country and you are Lenin's descendants.

But there used to be some troubles in our relations, chiefly concerning Stalin. They happened on three occasions: First, the two Wang Ming lines. Wang Ming was Stalin's offspring. Second, he didn't allow us to make revolution and opposed our revolution. After the Third International[141] was disbanded he still issued an order, saying that if we didn't make peace with

Chiang Kai-shek and carried on civil war, the Chinese nation would face the peril of destruction. However, we have not been destroyed. Third, when I went to Moscow for the first time, Stalin, Molotov[36] and Beria[184] immediately launched an offensive against me.

Why did I ask Stalin to send a scholar here to look over my essays? Did I lack self-confidence so much that I wanted you to look over my writings? Had we nothing else to do? No, we invited you to come and see whether China represented genuine Marxism or half-genuine, half-sham Marxism.

You spoke a good word for us when you went back. Your first remark to Stalin was: "The Chinese are genuine Marxists." But Stalin still had doubts. It was not till the time of the Korean War that he changed his own view and also changed the doubts about us among the fraternal parties of Eastern Europe and other countries.

Such doubts were inevitable: "First, you opposed Wang Ming. Second, you insisted on revolution although we didn't allow it. Third, you were so cocky, coming to Moscow with the demand that Stalin conclude a treaty and that the Chinese Changchun Railway be returned to you." In Moscow Kovalyov[185] played host and Fedorenko[186] was the interpreter. I lost my temper and thumped the table. I said I had three tasks there: eating, sleeping and emptying the bowels.

An adviser in the Military Academy, giving lectures on battle examples, allowed only for those of the Soviet Union, not of China or of the Korean War, confining them to the ten major attacks of the Soviet army.

Why not let us discuss? He would not even allow ourselves to talk! We fought for 22 years, plus three years in Korea! Please tell the Military Commission to gather material about this case and hand it to Comrade Yudin if he needs it.

There are some matters we haven't talked about lest they affect Sino-Soviet relations, especially at the time of the Polish and Hungarian incidents. When Poland wanted to expel your experts, Comrade Liu Shaoqi suggested in Moscow that you withdraw some of them, and you accepted this. The Poles were glad, saying they had got freedom. At that time we could not raise the question of your experts, lest you suspect we would take the opportunity to expel them. No, we won't do that, even if ten Polands did so. We need Soviet aid.

I have advised the Poles to learn from the Soviet Union, urging them to advance the slogan "Learn from the Soviet Union" after combating dogmatism. To whose benefit would it be to learn from the Soviet Union: Poland's or the Soviet Union's? Certainly, Poland's first.

We wish to learn from the Soviet Union, but primarily we ought to take our own experiences into consideration, giving them priority.

A definite term of service could be set for some advisers. For example, no term has been set so far for the chief advisers to the military and public security departments. You have neither informed nor consulted us about changes several times. Take the case of the appointment of an ambassador —when you, Yudin, are to leave and another person is to be sent to replace you, will it do not to consult us in advance? This is the wrong way. Moreover, if your advisers sent to our public security departments just sit in their offices, what can they learn if the Chinese do not tell them anything?

I have advised you to tour various provinces, have more contact with the people, and learn more. I have talked to Comrade Yudin many times, maybe 1,000, if not 10,000, times.

The majority of the experts are basically good; only a few have shortcomings. We had shortcomings on our part, failing to brief the Soviet comrades more on our own initiative. Now we have to correct these shortcomings and adopt a forward attitude. This time we have briefed them on China's general line. If once is not enough, then twice, thrice, or even more times.

All the above words arose from the nuclear submarine "cooperative." Now we have decided to drop it and withdraw our request for nuclear submarines. Or else we would rather hand over to you all our coastline, extending from the past Lüshun and Dalian. But there mustn't be a joint undertaking: You do yours and we do ours. At any rate, we shall have our own fleet; it is not good to play second fiddle.

Circumstances will be different in case of war. Your troops can come over to our country, and our troops can also go over to your country. If the battle is fought on our territory, your troops should obey our command; if it is fought on your territory and our troops are fewer than yours, our troops should obey your command.

My words may sound disagreeable, and you may call me a nationalist, the emergence of a second Tito. Should you say so, I can well answer that you have extended Russian nationalism to the Chinese coast.

It was Comrade Khrushchev who abolished the four companies under joint operation and the base in Lüshun. When he was alive Stalin wanted to set up a canned food factory in China. I replied, "You provide us with the equipment and help us build it, and we'll give you all the products." Comrade Khrushchev praised me for my proper reply. Why now again the idea of a naval "cooperative"? How would you explain your proposal of a naval "cooperative" to the whole world and to the Chinese people? You may train Chinese to fight against imperialism while you act as advisers. Or else, we can lease Lüshun—and not only Lüshun—to you for 99 years. A "cooperative" involves a question of ownership, and it will be 50 percent by each side according to your proposal. You made me so angry yesterday that I didn't sleep a wink last night. They (referring to the other Chinese leaders present) were not angry, only me. If any mistake was committed, I did it alone.

(Zhou Enlai: This is the unanimous opinion of our Politburo.)

In case the matter is not straightened out this time, we can discuss it again, or let's discuss with you once every day. If it still won't do, I can go to Moscow to talk to Comrade Khrushchev, or we can invite Comrade Khrushchev over to Beijing in order to straighten out all the problems.

(Peng Dehuai: Soviet Defense Minister Comrade Malinovsky sent me a telegram earlier this year, asking to set up a long-wave radar observation station on the Chinese coast in order to command the submarine fleet in the Pacific Ocean. The cost would be 110 million roubles, of which the Soviet Union would shoulder 70 million and China 40 million.)

This request is similar to that for naval "cooperative," which we will be unable to explain to our people or the outside world; it is politically harmful.

(Peng: Pedroshevsky is also very rude. He is most displeased with our principles of army building and our non-use of Soviet army ordinances in individual cases. At an enlarged meeting of the Military Commission Comrade Ye Fei[198] of the Fujian Military Area pointed out that the Soviet troop training regulations, which are formulated chiefly according to conditions on the plains, are not totally suitable in Fujian, where mountains are everywhere. Pedroshevsky was displeased at hearing this, saying bluntly, "You have insulted the great military science created by the great Stalin." Thereupon the atmosphere in the conference hall became very tense.)

Some of the above matters have been mentioned before and some not. You may feel bad, since you have made so much effort to help us, yet we speak ill of you. Our relationship can be compared to that between teacher and students. Should the students express their opinions while the teacher may have some shortcomings? Yes, they should. But this does not mean to oust the teacher. The teacher remains a good teacher.

You can help us build a navy. You can be our advisers. Why did you raise the question of half-half ownership? This is a political issue. We intend to build a fleet of 200 to 300 such submarines.

Speaking of political condition, not even half a finger will be allowed. Please tell Comrade Khrushchev that if any condition is to be attached there is no longer anything for us to discuss. He may come if he agrees with me, and not come if not, as we shall have nothing to talk about. No, not even half a finger of condition will be allowed.

We can do without aid in this respect for 10,000 years. But cooperation in other respects can go on; by no means will we fall out. We shall continue consistently to support the Soviet Union. Our quarrel will be confined to our rooms.

When in Moscow I told Comrade Khrushchev that you don't have to satisfy all our demands. Your not giving us aid will compel us to make efforts ourselves. It will be a disservice to us if you satisfy all our demands.

Political cooperation is very important. If we let you down politically, it will put you in a fix; likewise, we shall be in a difficult position if you let us down.

In time of war all our military harbors and airports are at your disposal; you can come to any place in our country. In like manner, we can go to your country, go to Vladivostok. We shall return home when the war is over. We can conclude a wartime agreement on this point in advance, not wait for the outbreak of war. Moreover, it should be stipulated in the agreement that we can also go to your country. This clause must be written in, even if we do not go, as this is a matter of equality. However, this is not applicable during time of peace, when you will help us build military bases and build the army.

As for operation of a naval "cooperative," we would not have accepted it even during Stalin's lifetime. I had a row with him in Moscow.

Comrade Khrushchev abolished the "cooperatives" and restored trust. Raising the question of ownership this time suggests to me the return of Stalin's practice. Maybe I misunderstand, but I have to make myself clear.

You said yesterday that your inferior conditions made it impossible for your nuclear submarines to give full play to their strength or develop any further, whereas China's conditions were much better, with long coastline, etc. Well, you can start from Vladivostok and enter the Pacific Ocean via Sakhalin and the Kurile Islands. What excellent conditions!

I am displeased with your remarks. Kindly tell Comrade Khrushchev exactly what I have said. Don't whitewash my words so that they may be soothing to his ear. He has criticized Stalin, but now he is reviving Stalin's practice.

Differences do exist. You may disagree with us in some cases, and we in some of yours. For instance, are you so pleased with our "Contradictions Within the Ranks of the People" and the "Hundred Flowers Bloom"?

Stalin supported the Wang Ming line, which caused the loss of over 90 percent of our revolutionary forces. He did not allow us to make revolution and opposed our revolution at critical junctures. After the victory of our revolution he still didn't trust us. He was very boastful, alleging that China's victory was won under the guidance of his theory. Blind faith in Stalin must be thoroughly exploded. I am going to write an essay before I die concerning all Stalin did to China, to be published after 10,000 years.

(Yudin: The attitude of the CPSU Central Committee on the various policies of the Chinese Communist Party is: It is the affair of the Chinese comrades themselves to solve the problems of China, because they know the circumstances best. In the meantime, we consider that any comments on the policies of such a great party as the Chinese Communist Party as to whether they are correct or not would be indiscreet and arrogant.)

It can only be said that our policies are basically correct. I myself committed mistakes that resulted in defeat in war, such as the four battles of Changsha, Tucheng and others. I should be very glad if it is said that I have been basically correct, because to say that I have been basically correct would be approaching reality.

As for the building of the submarine fleet, this involves a question of principle: Whether we are to operate it ourselves with your help or a joint "cooperative" will be run must be decided in China. Comrade Krushchev may come over, since I have already gone to him in Moscow.

There should not be blind faith in anything. For example, one of your experts said on the authority of a book written by an academician that our coal of Shanxi cannot be used in coking. Thus it's all finished: We shall have no coking coal, since most of our coal resources are in Shanxi!

Soviet expert Comrade Sinin, who has worked at the Yangtze River Bridge, is a good comrade. All along he was denied the opportunity to try out his method of bridge building in your country. You let him handle neither large nor medium-sized projects, not even small ones. However, he came to China and we found that his theory quite stood to reason, so we invited him to undertake the project, as we were complete laymen any way. His experiment proved successful at once, and it became a first-class scientific achievement in the world!

I have never met Comrade Sinin, but I have talked to many leading comrades in the construction of the Yangtze River Bridge. They all reported in one voice that Sinin was a good comrade, who used to join personally in all kinds of jobs with persuasive working methods and did everything together with the Chinese comrades. The bridge was completed and the Chinese comrades learned a lot of things. Whoever among you is acquainted with him, please convey to him my best regards.

Do not create a strained atmosphere among the experts or in the relations of our two Parties and two countries. I have no such intention. Our cooperation is comprehensive and excellent. You should make this clear to the embassy staff and the experts and not say that Comrade Mao Zedong has made complaints, how terrible!

We meant to raise some of these questions a long time ago, but it was not opportune because conditions were unfavorable with the Polish and Hungarian incidents taking place and you facing difficulties politically. Such as the question of experts, we could not very well raise it at that time.

Later on, Stalin became rather agreeable. The treaty between China and the Soviet Union was signed, aid was given in the Korean War, and the 141 projects were launched. Of course, these were not his personal merits alone, but the merits of the whole CPSU Central Committee. Therefore, we do not emphasize Stalin's mistakes.

(From the verbatim record)

BIG NATIONS AND SMALL NATIONS SHOULD TREAT ONE ANOTHER AS EQUALS*

(August 16, 1958)

Big nations and small nations should treat one another as equals. There is a view that big nations cannot be offended, while small nations can be bullied at will. This is utterly fallacious. A big nation is usually composed of a number of small nations. China in ancient times was made up of around 10,000 small states, later on of 800, then seven, and finally was united into one big nation. China today still consists of many provinces. Which is stronger: the deer or the tiger? I think the tiger is not necessarily stronger than the deer. The Eight-Power Allied Expedition[55] invaded Beijing in 1900. There were some small nations among the eight powers, which yet bullied a big nation. Japan is also a small nation, but it committed aggression against us. This is because they are industrialized countries, while we are an agricultural country, in addition the government was very corrupt.

The difference of nations in size is only form. Our two countries are completely equal, like two friends. We hope you will prosper and become strong. In my opinion, this is entirely possible.

(From the verbatim record)

---

* This is part of Mao Zedong's talk with Prince Norodom Sihanouk, Prime Minister of the Kingdom of Cambodia.

FIGHT FOR NATIONAL INDEPENDENCE AND DO AWAY WITH BLIND WORSHIP OF THE WEST*

(*September 2, 1958*)

Chairman Mao Zedong (hereinafter referred to as Mao): I'm sorry to have kept you waiting. We were having a meeting, and I was unable to meet you earlier.

Mariudim (hereinafter referred to as M): It is a great honor to be received by you, no matter how long we have had to wait.

Mme. Dotere (hereinafter referred to as D): Thank you for your reception, even though our wait was a long one. Moreover, our wait has given us time to read more materials and to stay longer in China.

Mao: What materials have you read?

M and *D*: Some of your writings, including "On New Democracy."

Mao: I said in that book that after the outbreak of the Second World War it was no longer possible for more countries like Kemal Ataturk's[187] Turkey to emerge. The bourgeoisie in the colonies and semi-colonies either lined us on the imperialist front or on the anti-imperialist front. There was no other choice. But in fact this view only fits with the case of some countries, and is not applicable to India, Indonesia or the United Arab Republic. The latter are neither imperialist countries nor socialist countries; they are nationalist countries. There are quite a number of such countries in Latin America too, and there may be more in future.

D: The book "On New Democracy" is very important for a country like Brazil.

Mao: This book deals with the bourgeois-democratic revolution. Its viewpoint is generally correct; some supplement is necessary only at a few places, such as I have mentioned.

M: Can the third position of the nationalist countries be maintained for long?

---

* This is the gist of an interview given by Mao Zedong to the Brazilian journalists Mariudim and Mme. Dotere.

Mao: Nothing can be maintained permanently, neither imperialism nor socialism. This is because there will be advance to the higher level of communist society. The third position can be maintained for a fairly long period, as long as it is still necessary.

D: Is it right for the nationalist countries to adopt a position of neutrality?

Mao: Yes, it is. These countries stand neither on the imperialist side nor on the socialist side. They adopt a neutral position, without participating in either bloc. This suits their present circumstances.

D: Can they maintain normal relations with both sides at the same time?

Mao: We think they can. But the imperialist countries do not like their neutral position, because their neutrality was obtained by shaking off imperialist domination. The neutrality of the nationalist countries is a position of independence, sovereignty and freedom from control. We in the socialist camp welcome the neutral position of these countries, because it is favorable to the cause of peace and unfavorable to the imperialist plans of aggression and war. We regard as our friends the independent countries in Asia, Africa and Latin America and also those countries which have not yet achieved or are fighting for independence. We support them.

What is the population of Latin America?

M: About 100 million.

Mao: 100 million friends. The population of Brazil occupies 60 percent of that of Latin America. Yours is a big country. The population of Brazil is likely to grow. You have a vast territory, about the same area as China. There is a bright future for your country.

M: We hope China will help us industrialize.

Mao: So long as you wish we are always willing to do so. We are always willing to give a helping hand to all Asian, African and Latin American countries whenever they need one.

D: Latin America is important for the United States. The latter is retreating in defeat from different parts of the world. That is why it is putting more pressure on Latin America.

Mao: Latin America is a rear area of the United States. Countries of Asia, Africa and Latin America have all been or still are rear areas and warehouses of imperialism. Now there is rebellion in the rear, and many countries have broken away from imperialist domination.

D: The Latin American countries are beginning to do so, but with much difficulty.

Mao: They may first achieve a state of semi-independence and then gain complete independence, like many countries in Asia and Africa, some of which have won independence, some are semi-independent and fighting for complete independence, and others are still subjected to imperialist rule.

M: We wish to know, Chairman, your views on the establishment of diplomatic relations and carrying out of trade between China and Latin American countries.

Mao: If Brazil and other Latin American countries wish to establish diplomatic relations with China, we welcome them all. Doing business without establishing diplomatic relations is all right, so is the conducting of ordinary exchanges of visits without doing business. The social systems of China and Latin American countries are different, but we have many points in common. First, we both want independence. It is not only you who have the problem of independence; we have it too. We still face the Taiwan problem, and the United States is still threatening us. Even if we recover Taiwan, the U.S. menace will continue to exist. This is our major point in common. Secondly, both our economies are not developed. Your desire for economic development is pressing, and so is ours. All Asian, African and Latin American countries is facing this common historical task of fighting for national independence and developing national economies and cultures.

M: Does the U.S. embargo hurt China?

Mao: We are not adversely affected. On the contrary, it has brought us a lot of advantages.

M: Are you, Chairman, optimistic or pessimistic about the international situation?

Mao: The present international situation is excellent. It is very difficult for the Western countries to realize their aim. Their aim is to rule all places that can be ruled, but they meet resistance everywhere. The colonialist countries band together and call themselves "Western countries." Geographically speaking, Brazil is also a Western country, but politically the so-called Western countries are in fact merely the United States, Britain, France, Italy, Belgium, West Germany, the Netherlands, etc. The sun of the Western world is the setting sun in the evening, while that of Asia, Africa and Latin America is the rising sun in the morning. Imperialism is always trying to intimidate people, and sometimes raise a hand to strike others. We must not be intimidated or scared by them. Adoration of the West is a kind of blind worship, of superstition, which is shaped by history, but this blind worship is being gradually done away with. It is also a kind of superstition to describe the West as advanced. On the contrary, it is backward. Of course, the Western countries have some possessions, but no more than some steel and some atomic bombs. In fact, this is nothing terrible, because they are politically backward, corrupt and vulgar. That's why we despise them. Lenin once said something about advanced Asia and backward Europe. What Lenin meant at the time was the democratic movements in China and other Asian countries, and he foresaw that Asia would run ahead of Europe. Now, on top of the socialist camp and the national revolutionary movements in Asia, there are the national revolutionary movements in Africa and Latin America. All these are advanced, while the Western world is backward. Dulles and his ilk may not accept this remark. Perhaps they will say: "This is simply boasting. We have steel and atomic bombs, so how can we be backward?" I say: Although they possess steel and atomic bombs, they are in the hands of backward people—the monopoly capitalists. They may bluff and bluster for a short while, but they will break down in the end.

It is a major task to do away with blind worship of the West. It should be carried out everywhere, in Asia, Africa and Latin America. In our country, too, we shall continue to wipe out this blind worship. What I mean is that strategically we should despise imperialism as a paper tiger, as something of little account. But tactically and in each concrete task, we must attach importance to it and deal with it seriously. Imperialism will change from a real tiger to a half-real and half-fake tiger, and finally to a completely fake tiger, or paper tiger. This is a process of transformation of a thing to its opposite. Our task is to accelerate this process. For a time before the conclusion of this process, the tiger may live and still be able to bite people. Therefore, we must deal the tiger blow after blow and pay attention to the art of boxing, and must not be careless.

The people in the Western countries do not agree with the ways of their governments, either. When I say the United States is bad, I mean its ruling clique, while the American people are very good. Many people among them have not yet awakened, but they surely will.

D: We believe that your explanation is very helpful to Latin America.

Mao: We pay a great deal of attention to the situation of the Latin American people. We are very interested in stories such as Nixon's visit to eight Latin American countries.

M: He received a very bit "welcome" there. Dulles, too, received a similar welcome in Rio de Janeiro.

Mao: The people of Latin America are rising. They look down on Nixon and Dulles, who are but paper tigers in their eyes. Nixon and Dulles are falling behind. The Latin American people are much more capable than they.

(From the verbatim record approved by Mao Zedong.)

SPEECH ON THE INTERNATIONAL SITUATION AT THE 15TH SESSION OF THE SUPREME STATE CONFERENCE

(September 1958)

Views on the International Situation

(September 5, 1958)

With regard to the international situation, we have always cherished an optimistic view, summing it up as "the east wind prevails over the west wind."

The United States is now "running the whole show" on our stage simply by monopolizing Jinmen and Mazu islands as well as some other islands, such as Dadan, Erdan and Dongding, and I see it is quite comfortable doing so. The United States has put itself into our noose; its neck hangs in the iron noose of our Chinese people. Taiwan is also such a noose, only a bit farther away. By assuming all obligations for Jinmen and other islands, the United States will only find itself thrusting its head further into the noose. Someday, when we feel like kicking it, it will have no way to dodge, for it will be trapped by this noose.

Now I shall put forward some views, just some ways of looking at the matter, they are just for your reference, not as decisions or laws of some sort. As laws they are fixed but as thoughts they are flexible. These views can be used to analyse the international situation.

First, who fears whom more. As I see it, the Americans fear war. So do we. The point is who fears war more. This is both a view and a thought. Everybody may apply the view to his observation, for one year, two years, three years, four years, and on, to see whether the West fears the East more, or vice versa. In my judgment Dulles[97] fears us more, and Western countries such as Britain, the United States, Germany and France fear us more. Why so? This is a matter of strength, a matter of popular sentiment. Popular sentiment constitutes strength, since we have more people on our side and they have less on theirs. Among the three doctrines of communism, nationalism and imperialism, communism and nationalism are closer to each other. nationalism prevails in rather wide areas, covering three continents: Asia, Africa, and Latin America. Even if many rulers in those areas are pro-West, such as in Thailand, Pakistan, the Philippines, Japan, Turkey, and Iran, quite a few, probably a great number, of the people there are pro-East. Only the monopoly capitalists as well as those perniciously influenced by them are belligerent. The rest (the great majority but not all), except the monopoly capitalists, are not willing to fight a war. For instance, in several northern European countries the rulers, though capitalists, do not favor war. Such is the balance of forces. For truth is in the hands of the great majority, and not Dulles; those who oppose us lack confidence while we are confident. We rely on the people, whereas they try to support the reactionary rulers. This is what Dulles is now pursuing, and he is expert at backing people such as "Generalissimo Chiang," Syngman Rhee,[85] and Ngo Dinh Diem.[136] I thus put it this way: Both sides are afraid, but they fear us a bit more, so it is not possible for war to break out.

Second, the American imperialists have formed military blocs with their allies—the North Atlantic Treaty Organization,[189] the Baghdad Pact Organization,[190] and the Manila Treaty Organization,[96] but what exactly is the nature of these blocs? We say they are of an aggressive nature. It is absolutely true that they are of such a nature, but which is their target? Socialism or nationalism? In my opinion, they are launching attacks against nationalism, i.e., against Egypt, Lebanon and other weak countries in the Middle East. The time is not ripe for them to attack socialist countries, unless countries such as Hungary fail, Poland, Czechoslovakia and East Germany fall apart, and even the Soviet Union and China encounter such big trouble as to struggle on the verge of collapse. If you are crumbling, why wouldn't they attack you? Now we are standing upright, we are consolidating our position, and we are tough bones to gnaw, so they turn to those places that are easy to gnaw, places such as Indonesia, India, Burma and Ceylon,[114] wishing to bring Nasser[139] down, bring Iraq down, conquer Algeria, and so on and so forth. Latin America has now achieved great progress. Nixon, though vice-president, was so unpopular during his visits to eight Latin American countries[188] that he was spat at and stoned. A spitting reception for an American political representative is indeed a defiance of "dignity" and a disregard of "manners," indicating that to them the United States no longer counts. Since you are our adversary, you deserve spit and stones. Therefore, we should analyze these three military blocs instead of making too much of them. Though aggressive, they are not consolidated.

Third, tension. Every day we demand a relaxing of tension, for a relaxed situation benefits the world's people. Then, is it true that tension always harms us? Not exactly, in my opinion. How can tension benefit us instead of harming us? Because tension, besides evoking detriment, may serve to mobilize forces and awaken inactive strata and intermediate sections. The fear of atomic war demands a second thought. Just look at the shelling of Jinmen and Mazu islands. I did not expect the world to get so stirred up over it. Such a few shots and there was such a drastic storm and the towering smoke of gunpowder. It is because people fear war, they are afraid of disasters the United States might randomly cause. Despite the existence of so many countries in the world, only that of Syngman Rhee, without a single follower, claims to support the United States. Perhaps the Philippines could be included, but with what is called "conditional support." Take the Iraq revolution as another example. Wasn't it also caused by tension? Tension is not caused by us, but created by the imperialists. In the final analysis it will be more detrimental to them. Lenin touched upon this when referring to war, saying that war rallies people and intensifies man's mind. There is no war now, of course, but the tension of military confrontation can also mobilize positive elements, as well as set inactive strata to thinking.

Fourth, the issue of troop withdrawal from the Middle East. The United States and Britain must withdraw their troops. That the imperialists intend to hold on there, though it is not in the interest of the people, serves as an educational example for the people. It is impossible to fight against aggression without an object, a target, or an antagonist. The U.S. invaders are not only acting as antagonists, but also hanging on and refusing to clear out, which is good enough to arouse people all over the world to fight against them. Therefore, their reluctance to withdraw is not necessarily completely harmful to people, for that reluctance provides a reason for people to press them to leave: Why don't you get out?

Fifth, is it good or not that De Gaulle[191] rises to power? The French Communist Party and people should resolutely oppose De Gaulle's rise to power, vote against his constitution, and, in the meantime, prepare to fight him if the opposition fails and he succeeds in assuming power. De Gaulle will oppress the French Communist Party and the French people if he rises to power, but this will not prove harmful in both domestic and foreign affairs. In dealing with foreign affairs, this man is at odds with Britain and the United States, because he likes to argue. As he once suffered from his obedience, he wrote his memoirs, blaming Britain and the United States and praising the Soviet Union. Now it seems he would again not see eye to eye. It is very good that France would be at odds with Britain and the United States. Just like our "Generalissimo Chiang" in China, in France a teacher is of utmost necessity for the French proletarians. It would be impossible for 600 million people to learn the truth without "Generalissimo Chiang," for positive education by the Communist Party alone would not work that efficiently. Since De Gaulle enjoys the popular trust, if he were defeated now, he would still be remembered. Let him rise to power; he can remain in power for five years, six years, seven years, eight years, or as long as ten years, then he will fall from power. Once he does, there will not be a second De Gaulle. The venom of such a nature must be let out, like the venom of our Rightists, which has to be allowed out. If he is not given a chance, he will remain in the venom's danger, but no venom will bother him once it is let out.

Sixth, embargo; no business with us. How on earth could this affect us? In my opinion, the embargo will benefit us significantly; we do not think it will be of any harm to us. The embargo will considerably benefit our daily necessities as well as our construction (steel and iron smelting). We shall have to find a way out by ourselves once the embargo starts. I have forever remained grateful to He Yingqin.[192] In 1937, when the Red Army was redesignated the Eighth Route Army of the National Revolutionary Army, Kuomintang paper currency worth 400,000 yuan was paid monthly, and we depended on this paper currency after he issued it. The pay was rescinded in 1940 when anti-communism climaxed. We had to find a way out, so we issued an order that each regiment, as a unit of the army, decide on its own plan to offset the no-longer-available Kuomintang paper currency. As a result, each base area started a production movement of its own, leading to an output valued not at 400,000 yuan, four million yuan, or even 40 million yuan, but possibly at 100 to 200 million yuan, if all the base areas are included. From then on, we began to rely on our own efforts. Then who is the current He Yingqin? It is Dulles, the name thus changed. Now that they have imposed an embargo, we have to rely on ourselves, striving for the Great Leap Forward, and all will turn out to be promising when we get rid of dependence and blind faith.

Seventh, the issue of not being recognized. Does recognition benefit us or not? I say we would benefit more from not being recognized by the imperialist states than the other way around. Up to the present, there are still 40-odd countries that have not recognized us, the major reason being the stance of the United States. France, for instance, though wishing to recognize us, is not willing to take the risk, owing to the opposition of the United States. There are other such countries in Central and South America, Asia, Africa, and Europe, as well as Canada, that fear to recognize us for the same reason. Counting all the capitalist countries that have recognized us, there are 19, if you add 11 more countries in the socialist camp, that makes 30,[193] or 31, if you count Yugoslavia. As I see it, let's get along with what is available. I don't think it bad that we are not recognized. Rather, it is a good thing, urging us to make more steel, say an output of 600 or 700 million tons, and then they will have to recognize us. At that point they could still feel free not to do so, but what difference would their nonrecognition make by then?

Last point, preparation for an anti-aggression war. In my first point I explained that a war would not break out, since both sides fear war, but setting a safety coefficient for everything in this world is better than not doing so. Because a monopoly capitalist class exists in the world, we should be prepared for war in case these troublemakers run wild. This point must be driven home among cadres. First of all, we do not want war and we are opposed to it, as does the Soviet Union, but should a war break out, it would be they who launch it and we who are forced to fight back. Second, we are by no means afraid of fighting back; if they start a war, so be it. All we have now are grenades and potatoes. A war of hydrogen bombs and atomic bombs would certainly be horrifying and devour people, hence we oppose it. Nevertheless, such decision-making power is not within our grasp, and if the imperialists determine to launch a war, we shall have to be fully prepared. If there is war, there is a war, but we shall not be frightened even if half the people are lost in action. This would be an extreme instance, of course. Judging from the history of the universe, I just don't believe things would turn out so badly. I debated this issue with Nehru, who said that there would be no governments by then, as none would have been spared by the war, and there will be no governments to turn to for reconciliation. How could that be, I asked, for people would constitute another government to carry on the reconciliation when the first had been destroyed by atomic bombs. Regarding what may happen in this world, you cannot sleep unless you have taken into account the worst possible situation. The worst that can happen is people will die, so there is fear of war. But if the imperialists are determined to fight a war, and they start the war and drop atomic bombs, then they will fight whether you fear or not. Now since that is the case what is the better choice to fear or not to fear? It would be dangerous for us to be stricken with fear, day in and day out; and not be able to bring the revolutionary fervor of the cadres and people into play. In my opinion, let's steel our hearts to fight back when war breaks out and be prepared to resume our construction after it. Therefore, we must set up a people's militia. Each commune is to organize militiamen, so that every citizen is a soldier, and rifles will be allocated, totaling several million at the start and tens of millions in future. All provinces are required to manufacture light weapons, including rifles, machine-guns, hand-grenades, small mortars, and light mortars. There will be military departments in people's communes to conduct militia drill. Among the participants today are intellectuals. You intellectuals should tell your colleagues that it is not enough to hold only the shaft of a pen. Be a militiaman as well as an intellectual by holding the shaft of a pen in one hand and the barrel of a gun in the other.

The eight viewpoints above are merely thoughts, just for your reference in observing the international situation.

(From the verbatim record)

The U.S. Imperialists Are Caught in Their Own Noose[194]

(*September 8, 1958*)

I should like to resume my previous topic. I talked to you last time about a noose, didn't I? Now let's turn to the issue of how to trap warmongers such as Dulles and Eisenhower.[103] There are many instances for which the United States deserves nooses. In my judgment, where there is a military base, there is a noose. For instance, in South Korea, Japan, the Philippines and Taiwan in the East; in West Germany, France, Italy and Britain in the West; in Turkey and Iran in the Middle East; in Morocco in Africa, and so on and so forth. The United States has many military bases at each of these locations. Take Turkey for example; there are 20-odd of them. There are said to be 800 in Japan. Despite the absence of military bases in some locations other than the above, a military occupation has been maintained, as in Lebanon by the United States and in Jordan by Britain.

Now let me focus on two nooses: Lebanon and Taiwan. Taiwan is an old noose, since it has been under U.S. occupation for several years. By whom has the United States been trapped? By the People's Republic of China. In the hands of 600 million people is a noose made of steel, already around the neck of the United States. Who caused it to be "noosed"? It prepared the noose for itself, got trapped, then tossed an end of the noose to the Chinese mainland, right into our grasp. Only recently did it get trapped in Lebanon by a noose also made by itself, and again one of its ends has been tossed to the Arab people. Not only this, but the end has also reached the grasp of the majority of people in the world, for all are accusing the United States, sharing no sympathy for it. People and governments in most countries are holding this noose in their hands. Take the Middle East, for example; a conference concerning this issue has been held at the United Nations, yet the United States is not able to free itself, mainly because it is trapped in the noose held by the Arabs. It now faces two alternatives: Would an early or a later extrication yield positive results? If the former, then why did it come in the first place? Otherwise, the noose, getting tighter and tighter, might become fast, and where would it all end then? As for Taiwan, it is bound by a treaty,[117] a situation different from that of Lebanon. The situation is rather flexible in Lebanon, for there is no treaty or anything like that; the story goes that one invited the other, who readily accepted, but was noosed thereupon. With Taiwan it has concluded a treaty, a fast knot. There is no distinction here between the Democratic Party and the Republican Party, as it was Eisenhower who signed the treaty, but Truman[65] who dispatched the Seventh Fleet. Without a treaty, Truman was free to stay or leave, but Eisenhower agreed to a treaty. This was owing to the Kuomintang's fear, resulting in a demand for concluding a treaty, which the United States accepted, meanwhile noosing itself thereby.

Has it been noosed by Jinmen and Mazu islands? As I see it, yes. Why so? Aren't they telling the public that all remains uncertain at this moment, until the Communist Party fights its way there? The problem is the 110,000 Kuomintang troops, 95,000 on Jinmen and 15,000 on Mazu. Taking care of them represents class interests, class affections. Why are Britain and the United States so kind to some governments? They cannot face the dying without attempting a rescue. Today a U.S.-Chiang joint military exercise is under way under the command of Arleigh A. Burke himself, commander of the Seventh Fleet, and don't forget Smout,[195] firing heavy guns, remember? This gentleman, who displeased both the Defense Department and the State Department, also joined Arleigh Burke's command.

In a word, you have been noosed. It might be possible to get free, but only by a slow process if you take the initiative. Isn't there a policy for extrication? There was one for Korea, and now I suspect another one has been formulated for Jinmen and Mazu. You have expressed the wish to free yourselves, and public opinion has so demanded. To get free means to be unnoosed. How to do it? Just withdraw the 110,000 troops. Taiwan belongs to us, and under no circumstances will we make concessions for it is an issue of internal affairs. To negotiate with you is an issue of international affairs, and they are two cups of tea. You, the United States, have secured yourself with Chiang Kai-shek, but a chemical compound of this nature is resolvable. Take electrolytic aluminum and electrolytic copper, for example; do they not decompose once electrolyzed? An issue of internal affairs on the part of Chiang Kai-shek and an issue of foreign affairs on your part cannot be lumped together.

At present, the United States wishes to dominate four of the five continents, Australia being the exception. North America is its foremost dominance, as it is its own major location, where its troops are stationed; then come Central and South America, which are to be under its "protection" despite the absence of troops there. Also included are Europe, Africa and Asia, with the main forces in Europe and Asia. I have no idea how it is going to handle a war with so few soldiers available, but so widely dispersed. Therefore, I consider it is mainly concerned with dominating the intermediate zone. As for places like ours, I do not think it would come to do so, unless the socialist camp encountered great chaos and it was sure its presence would lead to a collapse of the Soviet Union and China. It wishes to dominate everywhere —Latin America, Europe, Africa and Asia—except for our camp. Australia is also included, bound by military treaties and obeying its orders. Which is better, its taking over these places under the banner of "anti-communism" or its taking real action to counter communism? In the latter sense, it would send troops to fight against us and the Soviet Union. No one would be that stupid. With just a few soldiers to dispatch from here to there, it had to send them from the Pacific Ocean to the Red Sea when the incident in Lebanon occurred, only to find the situation there so unfavorable that it again had to turn around and in a rush to land them in Malaya,[125] remaining quiet for 17 days nominally for "rest and recreation." Later a journalist with the troops claimed they were there to keep an eye on the Indian Ocean, provoking widespread opposition to its presence there. As soon as we started our shelling, it sent the troops back here as reinforcements. Early extrication from places such as Taiwan is in the interest of the United States, but it hangs on and refuses to clear out. So let it be noosed there; it poses nothing serious for the overall situation. We shall keep striving for the Great Leap Forward.

I might say a few more words about tension. You reckon you will benefit from the tension you have created? Not exactly so, for tension, stirring up public feeling around the world, evokes condemnation of the Americans. For the tension in the Middle East all condemn the Americans. For the tension on

Taiwan all do so again, with just a few condemning us—the Americans, Chiang Kai-shek, Syngman Rhee and perhaps a few others. Britain, a wavering element, does not participate in military actions, but has shown much political sympathy, as has been said. Haunted by the issue of Jordan, it cannot do otherwise; how could it handle matters if the Americans withdrew from Lebanon? Nehru has issued a statement basically consistent with our views, favoring turning Taiwan over to us, but hoping for a peaceful solution. Countries in the Middle East would also be pleased by the turn of events. Particularly the United Arab Republic[196] and Iraq, which have been praising us almost every day. Thanks to our action, they now feel less pressure from the Americans.

I think we can loudly proclaim to people all over the world that tensions are rather detrimental to Western countries, to the United States as well. If there is any benefit, where is it? How has the United States benefited from tension in the Middle East? How has Britain benefited from it? It has been more to the interest of the Arab countries and to Asia, Africa, Latin America and to people of other continents who love peace. Who would benefit more from the tension on Taiwan? Take our country, for example; all our country has been mobilized by now, and if some 30 to 40 million people hold demonstrations and assemblies for Middle East events, at least 300 million people will be out there, and they will be educated and tempered. The tension on Taiwan also benefits unity among the democratic parties, and with a common goal to strive for, those who have complaints, were criticized or suffering wrongs in the past will somehow be mollified. Let's proceed step by step, and with everybody performing his duty, we shall all be able to become members of the working class. Therefore, the tensions created by the imperialists have now yielded reversed results, benefiting hundreds of millions of our people and also, to my mind, the people, classes, social strata and governments of the entire peace-loving world. They have had to have second thoughts, because the United States is more likely to bare its fangs and brandish its claws. Six of its 13 aircraft carriers have come, the big one in a class described as 65,000-ton displacement, clubbing together 120 ships to form the strongest fleet. Even if you go beyond the strongest, even if you gather all four fleets here, I welcome all. That stuff of yours, even put together, is of no use anyway, and you are by no means able to land it. A characteristic of a ship is its capacity to float in water, not on land. All you can do is show the ships off here, for the more belligerent you are, the more aware people of the whole world will become of how unreasonable you are.

(From the verbatim record)

THE NECESSITY IN DIPLOMATIC STRUGGLE TO OPERATE FROM A STRATEGICALLY ADVANTAGEOUS POSITION WITH IRRESISTIBLE FORCE*

(September 19, 1958)

Comrade Enlai,

I have received your letter written the night of the 18th.[197] It is superb that we have the initiative. I felt very pleased after reading it and we shall proceed accordingly right away. Please immediately transmit your letter and my answer to Comrades Wang Bingnan and Ye Fei[198] to help them understand our new policy and strategy, which is active, offensive and justified. It is necessary to carry out our diplomatic struggle from a strategically advantageous position with irresistible force.

Mao Zedong
4:00 a.m.
September 19
Hefei
(From the original manuscript)

---

* This is Mao Zedong's answer to Zhou Enlai concerning the struggle against the United States.

JOHN F. DULLES[97] IS THE BEST TEACHER BY NEGATIVE EXAMPLE IN THE WORLD*

(October 2, 1958)

I wish all the comrades good health and unity in the struggle for the greater development of socialism and in striving for the final triumph over imperialism. Will we defeat imperialism or not? Sooner or later we will defeat it. Of course, I don't necessarily mean tomorrow morning; it may be tomorrow evening or the day after tomorrow. We will defeat it eventually, won't we? Imperialism is bound to be defeated. There are two ways to fight: militarily and nonmilitarily. Basically, we shall use nonmilitary means, peaceful means, but we are also prepared to use military means. There are a few military delegations among you. Are you prepared to fight militarily or nonmilitarily? We have all these troops. With troops, how can we not be prepared to use the gun? Of course, we are. I am answering on your behalf. But this is our last resort. We shall use it if our enemy uses this means against us.

You may criticize me for my contradictory theory. "Since it is the last means, why are you still shelling Jinmen?" This puts me in an awkward position and I find it difficult to answer. Shelling Jinmen[199] is real battle, but we are fighting a nonviolent battle on the whole. We are not at war against any foreign country. Every day the Americans ask us to cease fire. "We are not engaged in war against you. Why a cease-fire?" China has not declared war on the Americans; or fired on you. We are fighting only our Generalissimo Chiang, also known as President Chiang. Our country has a "president" named Chiang Kai-shek, who is also our old friend. We have been fighting him for quite some time, 31 years, since 1927. I do not know how many more years we shall have to fight, perhaps 70 more years, which will make it a 100-year war altogether.

It is better to have a Chiang Kai-shek, isn't it? Do you think it is good or not to have him? Without Chiang Kai-shek the Chinese people would not

---

* These are excerpts from Mao Zedong's talk with delegations from Bulgaria, Albania, Romania, Mongolia, the Soviet Union and Poland.

be able to progress, unite or arm. Marxism alone is not enough to educate the Chinese people, so besides our Marxist teachers we have invited another teacher, namely, Chiang Kai-shek. Well, this man has done a very good thing in China, and he is still doing his historical duty. He has not finished his role as a teacher. There is a great advantage in having him as a teacher. He is paid by the United States; we do not pay him a penny, yet he serves as our teacher.

Hitler[4] did such historical duty to educate the vast people of Europe and the people of the world. So did Mussolini,[33] and Japanese imperialists in the East. It is a pity that there is no longer a Hitler or a Mussolini, and some Japanese militarists no longer exist. But there is a teacher. There is Dulles. Isn't he a good teacher? The world finds things difficult to do without him and easy with him. Therefore, we often feel that Dulles is our comrade. We want to thank him. This man really knows Marxism. In the capitalist class he is relatively well informed about Marxism. Because he has stubbornly carried out the line of class struggle with little compromise. I did not say without compromise at all, because he still has some shortcomings. He is quite obstinate, but not obstinate enough. Despite his shortcomings, he remains the best teacher in the world, except for communists. The first teachers are Marxists, and the second are Dulles and Chiang Kai-shek, since he is still alive.

It seems that the people of the world have been educated about the issue of Jinmen and it is developing in our favor. It is now in our favor and it will be all the more so in future. Dulles has landed in a passive position and finds it pretty hard. People may ask him only one question: Why has he gone so far as to run affairs in Jinmen? He always compares it with Korea, alleging that the Communists are launching a Korean war again. People say it doesn't look like it, because Korea is Korea and Jinmen is Jinmen. Jinmen is as tiny as a wineglass. The whole world, except Dulles, recognizes Jinmen as China's island. The issue of Jinmen is China's internal affair, so he now finds it hard to deal with it. We shall make it more difficult for him, to keep him in the sticky situation. We shall not let him off easily or let him slip away easily. For the moment, he will probably find it quite difficult to slip away from this place.

I do not want the United States to leave Lebanon too quickly. If the United States leaves, good! It thus wants to love peace again. The United States, a thief that has never been caught before, was caught in Lebanon this time.[200] We caught Britain and France on the Suez Canal in 1956.[134] At that time the United States pretended to be a good guy, a peace lover. We caught the United States in Lebanon this time. I say that it had better stay longer there. I have consulted with Comrade Khrushchev,[146] who agreed with me. As for how long the United States should stay, how about three years? I am afraid that our friends in the Arab world will not agree; they want the U.S. to leave sooner. The United States may leave before long, because it finds things there not easy. Well, it seems I cannot attain my goal. I want to have the U.S. there a bit longer, but it wants to leave. I wonder what your observation is. It may leave Lebanon in a few months, but we can make it stay longer in another place, that is, the Taiwan Straits. The question of the Taiwan Straits is educating the whole world, especially the Chinese people who have learned a lot from it. Don't you believe it?

Good! Then, what's to be done if a war breaks out? Who wants a war? We love peace. What we are fighting now is a nonmilitary battle, not a military one. We want to punish Chiang Kai-shek. We want to thank this teacher as much as to punish and criticize him. Students may criticize the teacher—criticize him with a cannon.

(From the verbatim record)

CHINA AND THE U.S. HAVE NO WAR, SO THEY CAN HAVE NO CEASE-FIRE*

(October 1958)

I

The United States of America occupies Taiwan, the Penghu Islands and the Taiwan Straits, which is a problem involving China and the United States. It should be solved through negotiations between the two countries, and now negotiations are being held in Warsaw.[201] The Americans will have to leave some time; they cannot always stay there. It is advantageous for them to leave earlier, because it gives them the initiative. Leaving later is disadvantageous, because it is always passive. Why should a country of the eastern Pacific come to the western Pacific? The western Pacific Ocean belongs to the people of the western Pacific Ocean, just as the eastern Pacific Ocean belongs to the people of the eastern Pacific Ocean. This is common sense and the American people should know it. There is no war between the People's Republic of China and the U.S., so there is no fire to be ceased. It is ridiculous to talk about ceasing fire when there is no firing.

(October 6, 1958)
(From *People's Daily*, October 6, 1958)

---

* These are passages from "Message to Our Compatriots in Taiwan," "Order to the PLA Men on the Front Line in Fujian" and "Another Message to Our Compatriots in Taiwan" respectively—all drafted by Mao Zedong. The first and second passages were issued in the name of the Minister of National Defense, Peng Dehuai; the last was also going to be issued in his name, but publication was canceled for some reason.

II

The Americans want to lend a hand in China's civil war. They call it a cease-fire, but one cannot help laughing. Are they qualified to talk about this matter? Whom do they represent? No one. Do they represent the American people? There is no war between China and the U.S., so there is no fire to be ceased. Do they represent the Taiwan people? The Taiwan authorities have not granted them certificates of appointment. Actually, the Kuomintang leaders object to negotiations between China and the U.S. The United States is a great nation, and its people are good and honest. They don't want war, but love peace. However, some people in the U.S. government, such as Dulles[97] and his like, are not at all clever. For instance, the so-called cease-fire—isn't it lack of common sense? To recover all the territory of Taiwan, the Penghu Islands, Jinmen and Mazu and complete the unification of the motherland—this is the sacred task of the 650 million Chinese people. It is an internal affair of the Chinese people and no outsiders, not even the United Nations, have the right to interfere. All the invaders and their running dogs are doomed to be buried, and that won't be very long. They cannot escape, even if they run away to the moon. If the enemy can go there, we can go there too; anyhow, they will be brought back. In a word, victory belongs to the people all over the world. In the Jinmen sea area Americans are not allowed to convoy Kuomintang ships. If they do, fire as soon as you find them. This order is hereby issued in all earnestness!

(October 13, 1958)
(From *People's Daily*, October 13, 1958)

III

What is being negotiated in Warsaw is the matter of the Americans going away. They are dealing with us as if talking about business. They want to exchange Jinmen and Mazu for Taiwan and the Penghu Islands, thus creating two Chinas. What a sweet dream! Cease-fire, cease-fire, and cease-fire once again! We really don't know how much common sense these American officials have. It seems they have little. If they are talking about the matter on behalf of their own nation, the United States, there is no fire to be ceased, since there is no war between China and the U.S. It is clear that they cannot represent themselves. If they represent you, it is also a sham. Your leaders object to the Warsaw negotiations and mock a cease-fire. You have not entrusted the Americans as your representatives. Even if you do, we don't agree either. Why should you entrust a foreign country to be your representative for negotiations instead of holding direct negotiations between our two Chinese political parties? For such negotiations we feel shame; therefore, we don't agree. Discussed in Warsaw is the relationship between China and the United States. It will be thus for 10,000 years.

(October 13, 1958)
(From the original manuscript)

THE WESTERN WORLD WILL INEVITABLY SPLIT UP*

(November 25, 1958)

Huan Xiang's argument is right. Splitting up is the right word to describe the Western world. It is now in the process of gradual splitting, not finally split yet. It is moving in that direction and the final splitting up is unavoidable. The process may be rather long, not a matter of overnight. The so-called unity of the West is empty talk. There is unity; Dulles[97] is striving for it. But he demands "unity" under the control of the United States and under the atom bomb; he demands his partners, big and small, get closer to the United States, pay tribute and kowtow. This is the so-called unity of the United States. This situation will inevitably lead to the opposite of unity, split. Comrades, we shall see who is to prevail in today's world after all.

(From the original manuscript)

---

* These are Mao Zedong's remarks on the report to the Foreign Ministry on the splitting of the Western world sent by Huan Xiang, Chinese chargé d'affaires to the United Kingdom.

ON THE ISSUE OF WHETHER IMPERIALISTS AND ALL REACTIONARIES ARE REAL TIGERS*

(*December 1, 1958*)

Here I want to respond to the question of whether imperialists and all reactionaries are real tigers. My answer is: They are both real and paper tigers, changing from real to paper. Changing means being transformed, real tigers being transformed into paper ones and into their opposite. Everything follows this law, not just social phenomena alone. I answered this question several years ago by saying that strategically we should despise them and tactically we should take them seriously; but why the latter if they are not real tigers? It seems there are still some who have not fully understood this, and we are obliged to make further explanations to them.

Just as everything on earth has duality (i.e., the law of the unity of opposites), the imperialists and all reactionaries also possess duality; namely, they are real tigers and paper tigers as well. In history, the class of slave owners, the class of feudal land owners and the bourgeoisie were full of vitality and revolutionaries, advanced forces and real tigers prior to as well as after taking over ruling power. In the period that ensued they gradually transformed themselves into their opposite, into reactionaries, into backward forces and paper tigers, owing to the steady growth of their opposite, the slave class, the peasant class and the proletariat, and eventually were overthrow or are doomed to be overthrown by the people. Classes that are reactionary, backward and decadent also possess such duality the moment they encounter a life-and-death struggle of the people. On the one hand, real tigers devour people, millions and tens of millions of people. When the people's struggle underwent hard times, twists and turns inevitably emerged. Prior to the victory of 1949, it took the Chinese people 100-odd years and cost them several tens of millions of lives to overthrow the rule of imperialism, feudalism and bureaucrat capitalism in China. Weren't they live tigers, iron tigers, real tigers? Neverthe-

---

* This is an article written by Mao Zedong during the Sixth Plenary Session of the Eighth Central Committee of the Communist Party of China, held in Wuchang.

less, they eventually transformed themselves into paper tigers, dead tigers, beancurd tigers. This is a historical fact. Haven't people seen or heard about this? Truly there are thousands upon thousands of such cases! Therefore, in essence, and in the long run and from a strategic point of view, the imperialists and all reactionaries must be realistically regarded as paper tigers. Upon this ground we should base our strategic thinking. On the other hand, they are live, iron and real tigers, capable of devouring people. Upon this ground we should base our tactical thinking. So it is in combating class enemies, and so it is in combating nature. The 40-Article, 12-Year Program for Agricultural Development[202] and the 12-Year Development Program for Sciences[203] that we issued in 1956 proceed from such a basic viewpoint—the unity of opposites —i.e., Marxism on the duality of the evolution of the universe, the duality in the development of things, and the law that things always take their form of expression as processes and all processes possess duality. On the one hand, we despise it, we take it as insignificant, it doesn't count, we don't care about it, we are able to accomplish it, and we are sure to win victory. On the other hand, we take it seriously, not insignificantly, it does count, we never lower our guard, and we are fully aware that we shall not be able to win victory without arduous and painstaking endeavor. To fear and not to fear is a law of the unity of opposites. There has never been a god of joy who fears nothing and worries about nothing. Everybody is born with miseries. Students fear exams, children fear their parents' favoritism, and there are numerous adversities and calamities, diseases and accidents, 41-degree fevers, as well as what is described as "in nature there are unexpected storms and in life unexpected vicissitudes," all of which we fear. In class struggle and struggle against nature the difficulties we encounter are beyond calculation. However, the majority of human beings, especially proletarians and Communists and excluding cowards and opportunists, always regard to despise all and remain optimistic as of foremost importance. What ensues is to take all seriously, pay attention to each piece of work, stress scientific research, and analyze and study intensively every aspect of contradictions in things, so as to recognize step by step the law of natural progression and the law of social progression. Then it is possible to master these laws and apply them with more ease to solve problems people encounter one by one, handle contradictions and accomplish tasks, and transform difficulties into ease, turn real tigers into paper tigers, the preliminary stage of revolution into the advanced stage, democratic revolution into socialist revolution, socialist collective ownership into socialist state ownership, socialist state ownership into communist state ownership, an annual steel output of several million tons into one of several tens of millions and even hundreds of millions of tons, and a grain output of over 100 *jin* per *mu* into one of several thousands or several tens of thousands of *jin*. Comrades, to bring about these changes is precisely the task we will undertake. Comrades, possibility and reality are two matters of different nature and they form a unity of two opposites. A spurious possibility and a realistic possibility are again two matters of different nature and the two opposites of unity. Our minds must be both cold and hot, this again constitutes the unity of opposites. Boundless enthusiasm is heat. Scientific analysis is cold. At present in our country some people are overheated. They are not willing to cool down their minds or to make analysis, and all they favor is heat. Comrades, such an attitude is not conducive to performing leadership, and those with it may encounter setbacks. It is necessary for such people to alert themselves to it. Some other people prefer cold to heat. They either frown upon or cannot keep pace with some occurrences.[204] Regarding them, we are obliged to make their minds gradually heat up.

(From *Selected Readings from the Works of Mao Zedong*, People's Publishing House, 1986)

A LETTER IN REPLY TO CHAIRMAN FOSTER OF THE U.S. COMMUNIST PARTY

(January 17, 1959)

Dear Comrade Foster:

Many thanks for your letter dated Dec. 19, 1958. I have seen the soul of the great Communist Party of the U.S. as well as the soul of the great U.S. working class and people from your enthusiastic letter.

The Chinese people understand that U.S. imperialism has done a lot of evil deeds to China and to the world. This is the wickedness of the U.S. ruling group, while the American people are good. Although a number of Americans have not yet awakened, bad elements are only a minor part and good people are in the majority. The friendly relations between the Chinese and the American people will break through the obstacle created by Dulles[97] and his ilk after all and extensively develop day by day.

Despite the temporarily unfavorable situation the U.S. Communist Party finds itself in, your struggle is very significant and will surely bear rich fruit in future. There must be an end to darkness. The U.S. reactionary forces are running into snags everywhere, showing they won't last long. Your present situation whereby the enemy is strong and you are weak is but a temporary phenomenon. It will certainly turn to the contrary.

On behalf of the Chinese Communist Party and the Chinese people, please allow me to extend my sincere regards to you, honorable fighter and leader of the U.S. working class, and wish you an early recovery. If it is possible, I warmly welcome you to have medical treatment and recuperation in China.

Please accept my communist greetings.

Mao Zedong
January 17, 1959
(From the manuscript revised by Mao Zedong)

GUARD AGAINST ARROGANCE IN FOREIGN RELATIONS*

(February 13, 1959)

The above examples are incomplete. Maybe some cases of the same kind have not yet been gathered together. Some may not have been clearly verified, and some parts may be exaggerated. Nevertheless, we can learn a lesson from exposure of these mistakes and turn bad deeds to good ones. In short, our achievements in 1958 were great, while shortcomings and mistakes were secondary, like one finger among the ten. We shall commit mistakes if we confuse the primary and the secondary. However, these shortcomings and mistakes are rather serious, because they are related to foreign affairs, so we must correct them, and the sooner, the better. The solution is to educate our working personnel by holding discussion meetings, clearly explaining reasons, guarding against arrogance, exaggeration and impetuosity, resolutely objecting to the extremely erroneous great-nation chauvinism, which is irreconcilable with the Party line, like water and fire, upholding proletarian internationalism and fighting for still greater victories in 1959.

(From the original manuscript)

---

* This paragraph was added by Mao Zedong to the document "Examples of Arrogance, Impetuosity and Under-Estimation of the Enemy in Foreign Relations," prepared by the Foreign Affairs Office of the State Council.

AFRICA'S TASK IS TO STRUGGLE AGAINST IMPERIALISM*

(February 21, 1959)

The task for all of Africa is to struggle against imperialism, against those who follow imperialism, rather than to struggle against capitalism or establish socialism. Anyone proposing to establish socialism in Africa would be making a mistake. The fact is that imperialism, relying on its running dogs, has allied with some Africans to oppress Africa. The nature of the revolution there is a bourgeois democratic revolution, not a proletarian socialist revolution. On the whole, the struggle of all Africa is a protracted one. First, please do not think of immediate victory or an overnight triumph; be prepared for a prolonged struggle. If one is not ideologically prepared for prolonged struggle when imperialism is so powerful, one may be disappointed. Second, please rely mainly on your own efforts, seeking foreign assistance only as a subsidiary. I have these two suggestions for you to consider. I am not familiar with the situation in Africa, nor am I an African. I shall just air my own views for your reference.

The present revolution in Africa is a struggle against imperialism and a national liberation movement. It is a question of national liberation rather than communism; on that we all agree. There are two other points: one is the question of a quick or slow victory. There are only these two possibilities, quick or slow victory. If you are prepared for both, you will not feel disappointed. The other is the question of what force to rely on. Is Africa to be liberated by relying on foreign countries or by relying on the African people themselves? To liberate Africa, it is essential to rely on the African people. African affairs should be run by the Africans themselves by relying on the forces of African people; in the meantime they should make friends throughout the world, including China. China certainly supports you. Whether these two points are right or not is for you to ponder over.

---

* This is the main part of Mao Zedong's talk to representatives of the Union of the Populations of Cameroon and of the youths of Guinea, Kenya and Madagascar.

It seems that present Africa is quite different from past Africa. After the Second World War the anti-imperialist movement in Africa developed greatly in 1958. It is expected that the anti-imperialist movement will develop faster in the future. There is no doubt that various countries will help you. The people of various countries, particularly socialist countries and countries that have won independence, will certainly assist and support you. You need support as much as we and all the socialist countries need it. Who is to support us? The national liberation movement in Asia, Africa and Latin America is the main force supporting us. The working class in western Europe supports us too. Support is therefore a mutual matter. Your anti-imperialist movement is a support to us. It is a support to you when the Soviet Union and China have done well. You may think of China as your friend. We are checking imperialism to divert its forces, so it will not be able to concentrate its forces on oppressing Africa.

(From the verbatim record)

WESTERN PACIFIC AFFAIRS SHOULD BE RUN BY WESTERN PACIFIC COUNTRIES*

(*March 18, 1959*)

I have read both your speech in Beijing and the joint declaration by you and Zhang Xiruo.[205] Far-sighted men will understand that our policy is correct. To our mind, some Americans, especially the United States authorities, have been very shortsighted. For example, they allege that it is up to them to run Western Pacific affairs. I say affairs in the Western Pacific should be managed by Western Pacific countries themselves, and the United States should withdraw its troops from the region, from places such as Japan, the Philippines, Korea and Taiwan. Dulles[97] said we wanted to drive them out of the West Pacific, as if we had done something wrong and the West Pacific belonged to them. I cannot see they will win the argument. Sooner or later, they will leave, because their occupation is temporary. We are not happy about the stand of the present Japanese government in siding with the United States. We think this is only temporary and there will be changes in the future. They may have another view—that China's existence is for a short time only, whereas Chiang Kai-shek will last a long time. According to their view, our joint declaration is out of place, the Socialist Party's view is erroneous and the Chinese view is wrong. We hold different views from theirs. We are confident that time and history will prove our views to be correct.

It is not good that Sino-Japanese relations are severed for the time being, but I think it is only temporary. We have exchanges now, don't we? The Socialist Party has done right to open up the channel of contacts.

There will be trade sooner or later. It is impossible that there will be no business in 10,000 years. We have to leave it as it is with the present practice of the Japanese government. This is the only way open to us. Kishi Nobusuke[206] wants to separate politics from economics and keep contact with Chiang Kai-shek. All right, then, he can go his own way and continue

---

* These are excerpts from Mao Zedong's talk with Asanuma Inejiro, secretary-general of the Japanese Socialist Party.

hobnobbing with Chiang Kai-shek. We can wait as long as necessary. I asked Comrade Liao Chengzhi[207] to list Kishi Nobusuke's hostile speeches about China. We are now using the ways he uses. He, Chiang Kai-shek and the United States stand on one side. Very good. He can do it his way. He still doesn't agree?

If our two countries have good relations, we may do business, which is good for both our countries. So your policy is not wrong. Maybe when you return to Japan, people in the Japanese government will not agree with you. They will say you are mouthing empty words, are siding with the Chinese to drive out the United States, and so on and so forth. We say that you are right that the United States can be and should be driven out. What right does the United States have to occupy our land and your land? It is so fierce just because it has more steel than others. The Americans have two hands, not three hands. They have more steel, but others may accomplish that as well. Others fear the U.S. because they take it as a real tiger. I admit that it is a real tiger, but it may change from a real one into a paper one. Japanese history is a case in point. At the beginning of the Meiji reform[208] in 1868, 90 years ago, you did not have any steel. Isn't that so? You were bullied by foreign countries because you did not have a scientific culture. Over the 90 years you have developed through twists and turns. You are now bullied by the United States, but it is also temporary. The Japanese people are a great nation. How could it be controlled by others? Japan will inevitably become a completely independent and peaceful country.

(From the verbatim record)

SOME PEOPLE IN THE WORLD ARE AFRAID OF GHOSTS AND SOME ARE NOT*

(May 6, 1959)

Some people in the world are afraid of ghosts and some are not. Which is better: to fear ghosts or not to fear ghosts? There are stories of not fearing ghosts in Chinese novels. I think it is the same in yours. I intend to compile a book of stories of not fearing ghosts. Experience proves that we should not fear them. The more you fear them, the more they will appear; if you don't fear them, there will be no ghosts at all. There is a story about an unruly scholar. One night he was sitting in his house when a ghost outside put his head through the window. The ghost, sticking out his tongue, looked very ugly. Its head was so big and its tongue so long. What did that unruly scholar do? He smeared black ink on his face like the ghost and also stuck out his tongue, staring at the ghost for one hour, two hours, three hours, until finally the ghost went away.

There are quite a lot of ghosts in the world today. There is a whole flock of ghosts in the Western world; they are the imperialists. There is also a flock of ghosts in Asia, Africa and Latin-America, who are imperialist running dogs and reactionaries.

Who is Nehru?[209] He is a middle-of-the-roader of the Indian bourgeoisie, different from the Rightists. The overall situation in India is good, I think. There are 400 million people there, and Nehru cannot ignore their will. The Tibet question has become a major issue. There will be a tremendous disturbance which will last for a while, say, half a year, or better, one year. It is a pity that India dare not go on. Our tactic is to let the working people of Asia, Africa and Latin America learn something from this and the Communist parties of these countries learn how not to fear ghosts.

(From a Foreign Ministry document finalized by Mao Zedong)

---

* This is the major part of Mao Zedong's conversation with delegations and envoys of 11 socialist countries, including the Soviet Union.

INDIA IS NOT CHINA'S ENEMY, BUT CHINA'S FRIEND*

(May 13, 1959)

Generally speaking, India is a friendly country toward China and has been so for over 1,000 years. We believe it will still be like this for the next 1,000 or 10,000 years. The enemy of the Chinese people is in the east, where the U.S. imperialists have lots of military bases in Taiwan, South Korea, Japan and the Philippines, all directed against China. China's attention and policy of struggle are focused on the East, on the western Pacific areas, and on the ferocious and aggressive U.S. imperialists, not on India, not on the countries of Southeast Asia or South Asia. Although the Philippines, Thailand, and Pakistan joined the Southeast Asia Treaty Organization,[96] aimed against China, we do not regard these three countries as our principal enemies. Our principal enemy is U.S. imperialism. India did not join the Southeast Asia Treaty Organization. India is not our enemy, but our friend. China will not be so stupid as to make an enemy of the U.S. in the east and an enemy of India in the west. The suppression of the rebellion[210] in Tibet and the democratic reform there will not pose the slightest threat to India. There is a Chinese saying, "As distance tests a horse's strength, so time reveals a person's heart." You will be able to judge whether the relationship between China's Tibet and India is friendly or hostile for the next three, five, ten,[20] and even 100 years. We cannot have two focal points. We cannot take a friend as our enemy. This is our basic policy. The quarrels between our two countries in recent years, especially for the last three months, are merely an episode in the course of the thousands of years of friendship and should not be of concern to the peoples and government authorities of our two countries. The remarks we made in previous paragraphs of this speech[211]—the principled stands and boundary lines between right and wrong—should be discussed. Otherwise, the

---

* This is a paragraph added by Mao Zedong to the reply of the Chinese Foreign Affairs Ministry to Dudd, a foreign affairs secretary of the Indian Foreign Affairs Ministry concerning his April 26, 1959 talk.

present differences between our two countries cannot be solved. But the scope our remarks refer to is only temporary and specific; namely, it is a momentary difference between our two countries, concerning Tibet alone. What do you think, Indian friends? Do you agree with our opinion? Regarding the view that China can focus its attention only to the east and cannot, nor is it necessary to, focus its attention to the southwest, China's leader, Chairman Mao Zedong, on several occasions spoke with India's former ambassador to China, Mr. Nehru, and Ambassador Nehru could well understand and appreciate China's view on this matter. I have no idea if the former Indian ambassador has conveyed these words to the Indian authorities. Friends, China does not assume that you can have two battlefronts either; isn't that so? If so, that is our meeting point. Please think about it. Please allow me to take this opportunity to extend my regards to the Indian leader, Mr. Nehru.[209]

(From the original manuscript)

ON THE QUESTION OF TAIWAN*

(*May and October 1959*)

The United States Must Withdraw Its Troops from Taiwan

(*May 10, 1959*)

The question of Taiwan cannot be solved now because Taiwan is occupied by the United States. The U.S. is not leaving and we do not want to drive it out.

The people in Taiwan greatly dislike the Americans, nor do they like Chiang Kai-shek. Is it good or not to have him there? It is good to have him there now, because while he is pro-American, he wants to rule by himself. There are some others who are pro-American, too, but they want to submit themselves totally to the United States.

A concrete question at present is whether Chiang Kai-shek will be the president next year or not. The United States of America does not want to have him as the president, but we think he should be the president. He wants to have his own army. You know that the people in Taiwan smashed the American embassy on April 24 in 1957.[212] The Americans suspected that it was instigated by Chiang Ching-kuo, son of Chiang Kai-shek; they felt they could not trust him, because he lived in the Soviet Union for about a dozen years and married a Russian woman.

Last year when we shelled Jinmen,[199] there were no American troops except for a working group of a dozen people. Jinmen has no treaty with the United States, while Taiwan has a treaty with it.[117] It was an internal

---

* Excerpts from: 1. Mao Zedong's talk with the People's Chamber delegation of the Democratic Republic of Germany; 2. Mao Zedong's talk with Khrushchev, First Secretary of the Central Committee of the Communist Party of the Soviet Union; 3. Mao Zedong's talk with Communist Party delegations from 17 Latin-American countries.

affair when we bombarded Jinmen. Dulles's policy is for neither we nor Chiang Kai-shek to fight. We say, none of your business, because it is China's territory and whether we fight or not is a matter between us Chinese and you should keep your hands out of it. We have only one connection with the United States, that is, to demand it withdraw its troops from Taiwan. Because of this we are holding negotiations with the United States in Geneva and Warsaw.[201] The United States wants to sign a declaration demanding Chiang Kai-shek not fight us and we not fight Chiang Kai-shek. We say no, because the question of Jinmen, Mazu, Taiwan and Penghu is an internal matter and none of your business. The only question is that you move away.

It appears that we shall continue to negotiate with the United States. They do not agree with us, and we do not agree with them. I do not know how long the negotiations will take. The talks have been going on for three and a half years and I am afraid they may go on for another ten years. They will be the longest negotiations in the world. You should not fear that we might attack Taiwan. When we shell Jinmen and Mazu we are helping Chiang Kai-shek, for the United States wishes to let us have Jinmen and Mazu while it keeps Taiwan. We give both Jinmen and Mazu to Chiang Kai-shek. When Chiang Kai-shek has difficulties, we shall shell Jinmen and Mazu and the United States will let Chiang Kai-shek continue his presidency.

The brink-of-war policy of the United States was mainly wrought out of the Taiwan issue. We adopted a "brink-of-war policy" in return. We shelled Jinmen, Mazu and reinforcement ships of Chiang Kai-shek. Chiang Kai-shek sought help from the United States. The Americans came, but stayed beyond 12 nautical miles. We fired only at Chiang Kai-shek's ships without shelling the American ships, which hoisted American flags to signal us not to aim at them. The United States did not fire a single shot at us, nor did we at them, so we were all at the brink of war.

The American air force abides by the rules to the letter, always keeping its distance from the coast. Once we shot down an American plane because it flew over the border. The United States said nothing and did not ask for compensation. The United States is a big power and has occupied too many places. There were ten fleas under its ten fingers, but it could catch none. Things become difficult when force is divided.

(From the verbatim record)

The Relations Between China's Mainland and Taiwan Are Different from Those Between the Two Germanys, Two Koreas and Two Vietnams

(October 2, 1959)

We have always said that the Taiwan question is an internal affair of China. China must liberate Taiwan. There are two ways of liberation: by peaceful means and by means of war. During the Bandung Conference Premier Zhou Enlai made the statement that we were ready to negotiate with the United States, and negotiations started later. They went on for four years, first in Geneva and then in Warsaw—at first, once a week, later once two weeks and then a month and now once every two months. Neither side wants to suspend the talks. The U.S. stopped for a period. Later we wrote a letter stating that no negotiations were no good and suggesting a date for talking. The U.S. said it could not comply with the date set, but talks could be resumed. Our answer was that the talks could be put off for a year, but negotiations were restored when Jinmen was shelled. The venue for the talks was moved to Warsaw at the suggestion of the U.S. In the negotiations we put forward only one suggestion, that is, that they withdraw their troops from Taiwan. Once the troops were withdrawn, we would have no dispute with them. The rest was between us and Chiang Kai-shek. We could have opened negotiations with Chiang Kai-shek. However, the United States does not agree. It fears having Chiang Kai-shek opened talks with us. Our shelling of Jinmen in fact is not war. We do not want to take over Taiwan all at once. It does not matter if we leave Taiwan in Chiang Kai-shek's hands for ten, 20, or 30 years. We don't have to take Jinmen and Mazu for we do not want to start a war over them.

China's problem is different from that of Germany, not only because of the different population, but also because China was an allied country during the war, a victorious country, while Germany was a defeated country. Germany was divided by international treaty, namely, the Potsdam Treaty.[118] The 38th Parallel[88] in Korea was drawn at the Potsdam Conference. Later, through the Korean War, the line was redrawn through negotiations between Comrade Kim Il Sung and the Chinese Volunteers on one side and the United States on the other. The division between South and North Vietnam was decided at the Geneva Conference.⁹⁵ The split between Taiwan and the mainland has no ruling by any international protocol. That is why the United Kingdom is not happy with the occupation of Taiwan by the United States, and even some Americans resent it.

(From the verbatim record)

The International Issue of the Taiwan Question Should Not Be Confused with the Domestic Issue

(October 5, 1959)

The Taiwan question is very complicated. There is a domestic issue as well as an international issue. As long as the United States is involved, it is an international issue that can be settled only through a peaceful approach, not force. We are still negotiating with the United States, but it has not presented anything new. In the past, the talks were conducted in Geneva; now they are in Warsaw, with the issue unsolved. We demand that the U.S. withdraw its troops, but it does not agree. We can only wait, and we can wait until it withdraws its troops. You comrades may feel at ease that we will not be the first to wage war against the United States. As far as Chiang Kai-shek is concerned, it is a domestic issue. Must it be resolved through force? Not necessarily. We are ready to hold negotiations with Chiang Kai-shek, but he does not want to. We cannot help it and war may break out someday. There are two ways to solve domestic issues, by peaceful means or through force. Some people confuse the international issue with the domestic issue on the question of Taiwan. Taiwan has a population of only several million and it does not matter if we do not recover it (Jinmen included) for some years.

On the question of Taiwan, the United States attempts to create "two Chinas," one big China and one small China. It alleges that Germany has East Germany and West Germany, why can't there be two Chinas? Our answer is that Germany is a defeated country and it was our enemy during World War II. It was divided into two under the Potsdam protocol. China was an allied country during the Second World War. According to the Cairo Conference,²¹³ attended by Churchill, Roosevelt and Chiang Kai-shek,

Taiwan was returned to China by Japan. Taiwan has always been part of China, but it was occupied temporarily by Japan. After being defeated, Japan returned it to China. After his defeat Chiang Kai-shek fled to Taiwan to establish his regime there. Many countries in the world still have diplomatic relations with Taiwan authorities. We oppose "two Chinas" and so does Chiang Kai-shek. We have this point in common.

(From the verbatim record)

IT IS POSSIBLE TO WIN A FAIRLY LONG PERIOD OF PEACE*

(*October 18, 1959*)

The entire international situation is taking a favorable turn. It is barely likely that the West will continue its high-pressure, position-of-strength, cold-war policy. The majority of the Western ruling circles, for instance, the American and the British, are haunted by the fear of a third world war. The reason for a détente, if any, in the cold-war situation is that their previous cold-war policy turned out to be so unfavorable to them that they have changed it a bit and relaxed the situation accordingly. However, things are not that simple, for they have attached equal importance to, one, relaxing the situation a bit and, two, provoking tension again if détente proves unfavorable to them. This is the duality of the bourgeoisie. Their "love of peace" is not in complete conformity with our love of peace. For example, there are differences between the American and the Japanese monopoly capital and between the Japanese monopoly capital and the Japanese people. Differences also exist within the monopoly capital itself, differences between the part of national betrayal and other parts. Even within a clique, such as Eisenhower's,[103] things are not that simple, for there is duality. We have difficulties, but so do they, even more than we. It is possible for us to make use of their difficulties to win a time of peace, not just a short period. It is possible to win a fairly long period of peace. You should make use of their internal contradictions. They indeed encounter difficulties, and it is just because of difficulties that they call for détente; otherwise, why take the trouble for détente? There is no unanimity among Western countries. People in Western countries who love peace always differ from their governments, as do the proletariat from the bourgeoisie. In addition, people in Asia, Africa and Latin America are all against the control of imperialism. Of course, there are stooges of imperialism; however, the broad range of people are opposed to

---

* These are excerpts of Mao Zedong's conversation with representatives of the Japanese Communist Party.

imperialism.

Socialist countries remain united, their camp strengthened. It is no longer easy for imperialists to launch a war. The Soviet Union is fortified, and socialist countries stick together and are consolidated. In such a context the imperialists cannot help having second thoughts about launching a war.

We have all along estimated that the international situation will keep improving, not the other way round. Only one situation needs to be reckoned with; i.e., what if some lunatics want to start a third world war. What's to be done, then? That's why we should take war into account, too. There is a possibility that peace might be undermined, and after détente, tensions will again be created, surprise attacks made, large-scale wars launched, and so on and so forth. Having taken all these situations into account, we say the situation in general has been improving. Judging from the overall conditions, it is possible for us to win ten to 15 years of peace. Supposing this comes true, they will find it more difficult to fight a world war by then. The socialist camp will be much stronger by then than it is now. It will turn out to be rather difficult for Western countries to solve the contradictions among themselves, the Japanese-U.S. contradiction and many other contradictions caused by military bases and agreements.

Supposing you do not succeed in opposing a revision of the Japan-U.S. "Security Pact,"[214] which will subsequently be devised, then this treaty will be presented to the Japanese people again in ten years, serving to educate the Japanese people to strengthen their unity for struggle.

In general, the United States, Britain and France differ from Germany and Japan. That is to say, the United States, Britain and France have quite a few colonies and semicolonies. They have so many places to guard, ranging from Taiwan and South Korea to Turkey, all of which need guarding. In this regard, they are very rich. The United States, though without any colonies, has many semicolonies, such countries and regions as South Korea and Taiwan, to guard and maintain the status quo. West Germany and Japan are different. During World War I Germany was stripped of its colonies, and it did not take any colonies during World War II. Japan expanded its colonies through World War I, but was deprived of all its colonies after World War II. Not resigned to defeat, they intend to resume their occupation of colonies, but are not yet fully prepared, owing to the current control of the United States. They wish to break away from the United States and eventually to engage in expansion. I should like to exchange views with you concerning whether the aforesaid is correct or not.

There should be an estimate of adventurist circles. The most powerful is the U.S. adventurist circles, but it is difficult for it to launch a war of aggression at present, because it is not yet prepared. Nor is it easy for West Germany and Japan, which are under the control of the United States, to launch a war. The reason Kishi Nobusuke[206] has intended to amend Article IX of the Constitution is because this article restrains him from expansion and his wish to revive militarism. There is a slogan of peace and independence in the program of your Party, and this is most applicable to reality.

(From the verbatim record)

DÉTENTE IS BENEFICIAL TO THE PEOPLE OF BOTH THE SOCIALIST COUNTRIES AND THE CAPITALIST COUNTRIES*

(October 26, 1959)

Tensions in the international situation are created by imperialism, but they are turning into their opposite. In large part such tensions have made the imperialists feel things were going against them, against their objectives of preserving capitalism and eliminating socialism. The actions of Dulles[97] have turned out to be counter productive, so the imperialists want to move out of this very narrow path. If tensions were helping them realize their objectives of preserving capitalism and eliminating socialism, it would be unthinkable for them to make any changes. It seems they have come to see the harm and want to make some changes. Moreover, they are afraid of war. Neither of the world wars advanced their interests, as is known to all. A third world war would advance their interests even less. For a country like the United States, the outbreak of war would be most disadvantageous.

Détente is beneficial to the people of both the socialist countries and the capitalist ones and results from the struggles of the socialist countries, the fraternal parties and forces for peace in the world. It would be very good if we could have another decade of peace. It would be fine if China and the Soviet Union could carry out several more five-year plans.

But one should see the other side of the coin, that, in order to maintain its military industries as well as seize interests in other countries, imperialism still needs a degree of tension in the situation. For example, since Khrushchev's visit to America,[215] the United States has set up new rocket-launching bases in some countries and has created an issue out of Tibet in the United Nations. It shows that it still needs to create tension, so we should remain on our guard.

(From the verbatim record)

---

* These are excerpts from Mao Zedong's talk with L.L. Sharkey, General Secretary of the Communist Party of Australia.

THE SINO-NEPALESE BORDER SHOULD BE PEACEFUL AND FRIENDLY FOREVER*

(March 18, 1960)

Chairman Mao Zedong (hereinafter referred to as Mao): We and India have been at odds. Never mind. It will be over soon. We have common interests, because we are both undeveloped countries. It is a false charge that China invaded India. We do not want an inch of others' land. We have a vast land of 9.6 million square kilometers, with a large part uncultivated. It is committing a crime to take others' land and not run one's own country well. Have we invaded Nepal? We do not want a single inch of Nepalese land. Can we sign a border treaty and erect boundary markers?

Prime Minister B. P. Koirala (hereinafter referred to as Koirala): Yes, we can. I have discussed it with Premier Zhou Enlai.

Mao: Do you agree?

Koirala: An official marking of the boundary is needed.

Mao: It is necessary to mark the boundary. Once it is drawn, there can be an unpatrolled zone. The length of the unpatrolled border can be decided through consultation. India and Pakistan have such a treaty and they have a very short border without patrol by either side, just one kilometer. We once suggested to India a 20-kilometer border without patrol by either side. Neither we nor they would go there. They did not agree. If you like, we can have a clause in the treaty stipulating an unpatrolled border area, the length of which can be worked out through consultation. It will be 40 kilometers altogether if each side has 20 kilometers, 20 kilometers if each side has ten kilometers, ten kilometers if each side has five kilometers. It is up to your convenience. How about it?

Koirala: It is worth considering.

Mao: You may think about it. The administration can be local civilians from both sides. Some police and militia may be formed by the local people.

---

* These are excerpts from Mao Zedong's talk with Nepalese Prime Minister B. P. Koirala.

There should be no formal military force. If military troops from both sides keep quite a distance from the area, both sides will be at ease. Boundary drawing and nonpatrol are intended to maintain peace and friendship on the border, so that both sides are at ease and not worried about invasion from the other side. If you are interested, we can sign a friendly treaty of nonaggression as we did with Burma. We shall do wrong if we violate the treaty after we have signed it. We are a big country and we never suspect you will invade us, but you may suspect that we shall invade you. We would commit a blunder if we broke the treaty after it was signed.

Koirala: During our talks Premier Zhou Enlai put forward a draft for a friendly treaty. We shall take it back to the cabinet for decision; there may be some revisions. It may be signed at Kathmandu when Premier Zhou Enlai visits Nepal after his trip to India at the end of April.

Mao: Very good. We have received two of your prime ministers separately and our premier should visit you, making it equal. We thank you very much. It is excellent that we are to set up an embassy in your capital this year. You may set up an embassy here without many people, three or four, maybe seven or eight. It won't be very expensive. It is not difficult to find people out of eight million people.

Koirala: When we are ready to send them, it will not be too many, because we cannot afford it.

Mao: We heard that you are building a highway directly to our country.

Koirala: No. We wanted to build a highway two years ago. It could not go on because of lack of funds. Now technicians from the Soviet Union are helping survey, in preparation for an east-west highway.

Mao: You have to go via another foreign country if you come to our country.

Koirala: No, we can go through a mountain pass between Nepal and Tibet, but it is not a formal road.

Mao: In one year, ten years, or 20 years, sooner or later we shall have a direct road.

Koirala: In our country we are building roads in places that have good prospects for economic development. We are planning to build 900 miles of roads (about 1,300 kilometers) throughout the country.

Mao: Excellent.

Koirala: I invited Jawahalal Nehru[209] and Premier Zhou Enlai to hold talks in our capital, Kathmandu, but they could not.

Mao: It was because Nehru wanted our premier to go to his capital, Delhi. At first we suggested Rangoon, but Nehru did not agree. Now we have agreed to go to Delhi, so he cannot go to Nepal. Thank you for your kindness. You have very good intentions; so did the Burmese prime minister, who wanted the Chinese premier and Indian prime minister to go to Rangoon. When Nehru said that it was not convenient for him, we had to make concessions to him.

Now the Burmese prime minister has invited our premier to Rangoon, and Your Excellency has invited him to go to your country. Premier Zhou Enlai will first go to Burma, then to India to hold talks with the Indian prime minister, and then to your country. The fourth country for him to visit is Cambodia, which has invited us several times and we owe them a debt. There is a fifth country he has to go to, that is, Ho Chi Minh's[216] country. Altogether there are five countries to go to. So, last year's anti-China wave may gradually calm down.

We have had quarrels with India for about a year, but we are still friends. There are often quarrels between friends, between husband and wife, and between brothers. We have had no quarrels with you, Burma, Ceylon[114] and Cambodia. We have serious quarrels with only one country in the world, the United States. It has occupied our Taiwan and has called us "aggressor." We shall call it aggressor, too. We have not occupied a single inch of the land of the United States, even though between China and Honolulu there is Midway Island. Neither have we occupied Japan, while the United States has occupied our Taiwan. I just don't know how we could have become an aggressor.

Now there is one country that wants to have "joint defense" with you against us. I learned that you did not agree. We are pleased. You said that Sino-Indian relations should be solved by themselves and you would not interfere. India alleged that we had invaded you and you made a statement declaring there was no invasion. There is a rumor about our troops intruding into your country. Is there any intrusion, after all?

Koirala: Because there isn't, we made the statement.

Mao: Countries like ours have to take self-reliance as our main principle and seeking external assistance as subsidiary. We are to seek foreign aid, but have to consider which is the main point. You will have the initiative and run things more easily by relying on yourselves.

Your policy is not much different from ours. Our big enterprises were designed and established with the help of the Soviet Union during the ten years from 1950 to 1959. In those ten years we made some progress and now we are relying on ourselves. We had to copy everything from the Soviet Union in the First Five-Year-Plan period because we knew little. For the Second Five-Year-Plan period we gave up copying and worked out a series of our own methods in 1958 and 1959. You may have to go through the same process. It is necessary to copy from a foreign country, then stop copying after a certain period. Students copy teachers when they are educated in schools. They will become teachers upon graduation after several years of education. Certainly you will be teachers in some realms. I mean what I say. It is true that no one will be a student for 100 to 1,000 years. We were students in the past and we are still students. The Soviet Union, the United States and Britain have sophisticated sciences, while we do not. We have to learn from them. Every nation has its forte and foible. It is the same with your country, and Cambodia has many strong points. Every nation, big or small, should learn from other nations' strong points. It is quite good to exchange experience with these countries. We Orientals have a sense of inferiority, feeling inferior to the whites. It is a kind of blind faith that should be breached. It is essential to break the blind faith in them as much as to learn from the West. It is not contradictory to breach the blind faith and learn from them. For instance, we may send students to their countries and import equipment, etc., from them.

I am not against everything from the West; I am only against what the imperialists do to oppress and bully others. We need to learn from their culture and science. Orientals should learn from the West, but thus learning should be carried out without blind faith.

Koirala: On the question of the Nepalese-Chinese border, there are still differences. In our view, there are disputes in four places, based on the historical situation in the past 50 years. Now it is time to settle the disputes.

Mao: Good.

Koirala: In our talks with Premier Zhou we have worked out several principles: first, draw the boundary based on the existing traditionally-accepted boundary line; second, take into consideration the practical situation of jurisdiction by either side at the border; third, try to solve the dispute on the few places; if some cannot be solved, hand them to a joint committee.

Mao: That's good.

Koirala: The principles are good so long as there are disputes between our two sides in specific places, which make us feel uneasy. When I went to Hangzhou, I told Premier Zhou Enlai that I had come to Hangzhou with an uneasy mind. Premier Zhou said I should absolutely feel at ease.

Mao: You should absolutely feel at ease. Burma feared us, but now we have set its mind at rest. The Burmese now know our heart.

Koirala: I met with Prime Minister Ne Win[217] before I came. He asked me to speak frankly with Chairman Mao and Premier Zhou Enlai, so I have spoken about all these things.

Mao: Good. Those disputes are easy to resolve. There are no human beings in the mountain passes. As for disputes over the Himalayas, a joint committee may be established to solve them.

Koirala: To you, the currently disputed places are of no importance, while they matter to us. It is a question of prestige.

Mao: Don't worry; they can be solved.

Koirala: There is another question, a question of sentiment. We call it Sagarmatha, the West calls it Everest and you call it Qomolangma. This place has always been within our boundary, but Premier Zhou Enlai said it was within yours.

Mao: You should not feel uneasy about it.

Koirala: It is a sentimental question.

Mao: It can be solved, half for each side. The southern part is yours and the northern part is ours.

Koirala: How about the mountain top?

Mao: Half for each side as well. Will that be all right?

If it cannot be solved now, we may postpone it as well. The mountain is very high and it can safeguard our security at the border. Neither of us will suffer losses. If all of it is given to you, sentimentally we shall feel sorry. If all of it is given to us, sentimentally you will feel sorry. We can have a boundary marker on top of it.

Shailendra K. Upadhayaya:[218] Who is to do it?

Mao: Difficult to do! We may have a written record of it. We shall inform you when our people are to climb it from your side and you will inform us when your people are to climb it from our side.

Upadhayaya: In the past, mountain climbers had to have a Nepalese visa.

Mao: A mountain climber from a third country intending to climb from your side may obtain a visa from your country.

Pan Zili:[219] In the past, mountain climbers had to have a permit from the local government of Tibet when they wanted to climb it from Tibet.

Luo Guibo:[220] In the past, some foreign mountain climbers obtained visas from our embassy in Switzerland.

Koirala: No.

Mao: The long-time practice is that to climb it from Tibet, one has to get a permit from the local government of Tibet.

Koirala: There are other disputes.

Mao: It is easy to solve them. It is easy to solve them with you, unlike the resolution of disputes with India. Our disputes with India involve scores of thousands of square kilometers.

Koirala: Ours involve only several square kilometers.

Mao: The mountain can be renamed. We shall not call it Everest; that was a name given by Westerners. Neither shall we call it Sagarmatha, nor shall we call it Qomolangma. Let's name it Mount Sino-Nepalese Friendship.

This mountain has the highest summit in the world, with a height of over 8,800 meters. The United States, the Soviet Union, and India have no mountain of this height. Only our two countries have. You may hold an internal meeting to discuss the question and air your suggestions. It may be put off for settlement in the future if no agreement is reached.

Koirala: All right. There are five other places in dispute, three of them major ones.

Upadhayaya: The question is to draw the boundary one mile to the north or one mile to the south.

Mao: That is not hard to solve. With no population, it is easy to solve it.

Koirala: How can we put it to you if it cannot be solved in our talks in Beijing?

Mao: You do not have to talk with me, but continue to talk with Premier Zhou Enlai. You may continue the talks when he visits your country. We shall keep in communication through telegram. The two sides have to reach agreement in the joint committee. If you do not agree, you should insist. If you insist, what can we do? Can we fight a battle? We are optimistic.

Koirala: So are we.

Mao: We want friendship from you, and you from us. This is the crux of the matter. With this central point, everything will fall into place. Isn't that so?

Koirala: *Upadhayaya*: Yes.

Mao: We want to set our minds at ease so that we can make China a country with modernized industry, agriculture, science and national defense. You also need to feel at ease, so as to modernize industry, agriculture, science and national defense. That's good, isn't it?

(From the verbatim record)

WE ARE IN AN ERA WHEN IMPERIALISTS FEAR US*

(*May 3, 1960*)

Welcome, friends. We are all on the same line. Your struggle assists ours. Thank you for your support.

Imperialism is still oppressing us, because our Taiwan is occupied by it. U.S. imperialism does not recognize us, alleging that it sees no People's China. Almost every day it says that we are very bad. This shows that it has seen us; otherwise, how could it say that we are bad? The primary mistake it accuses us of is that we fought a war against Chiang Kai-shek, whom it calls a good guy, while it names us a bad guy, just as it says that, in Cuba, Fulgencio Batista[221] is good, while Fidel Castro[222] is bad. In every country there are people that the United States considers good guys, but the people of the country feel that they are not so good, or even very bad. This is because our views differ.

The United States has money, arms and the atom bomb. It bullies us on grounds that we have no money, few arms and no atom bombs at all. But we and Cuba have militia that are more powerful than the atom bomb. Of course, you in Cuba have a regular army, and so do we. The Soviet Union has a stronger army, and atom bombs as well. Neither the Soviet Union nor we want to fight a war, only to strive for peace. Yet we cannot run the imperialists' affairs, because they have not invited us to be their chief of staff. So it is hard to say how they will manage things.

One thing is certain—we have the support of the people. The great majority of the people in the world are on our side, and on your side as well. That makes 90 percent of the world's population, with at most one tenth supporting imperialism. I do not believe there are more supporters than that. Those who support imperialism are its running dogs, such as Chiang Kai-shek and Batista. Various countries have running dogs, but some are no longer running. Chiang Kai-shek is a case in point. Chiang Kai-shek, staying in

---

* These are excerpts from Mao Zedong's talk with trade union and women's delegations from 14 Latin American and African countries.

Taiwan, is no longer running. He ran away from the mainland to Taiwan, while Batista ran away from Cuba to the United States. There are not many running dogs in the three continents of Asia, Africa and Latin America—out of 100 people, only a few, so together with the imperialists, they account no more than ten out of 100.

American imperialists hope we fear them, and we fear them a little, because they make their running dogs kill people. They have killed a lot, and the people have no alternative but to resist them. The method of struggle is tit for tat, to kill them when they try to kill us. We shall become bold and fearless when we have experience. Imperialism is nothing to fear, for it is one finger out of ten. History has proved that those without guns will defeat those with guns. For instance, the October Revolution in the Soviet Union, led by Lenin, is an example of people without guns defeating those with guns. China is another case in point. We are not gun carriers, but peace lovers, farmers, workers, teachers and businessmen. I was a primary school teacher, unprepared to take up arms. Later, when Chiang Kai-shek did not allow me and the people to live on, we had to take up guns. I learned that at first there were few participants in the July 26 Movement[223] in Cuba; only 82 people sailed back from Mexico. Therefore, those without guns are stronger than those with guns, such as Batista.

Who fears whom after all? Is it that the United States fears you, Cuba, or that Cuba fears the United States?

In my view, the United States fears you. All the imperialists fear the Asian, African and Latin American people. The era when we feared imperialism has gone and now it is time for imperialism to fear us. It has very few people, but it has done very bad things. It protects reactionaries and its running dogs.

We warmly welcome you to visit China. You may think we want to start a war against the United States. We do not want to have war with the United States, nor does Cuba, I believe. But if the United States wants to start a war against Cuba, it is helping and steeling the Cuban people. It fears that the Cuban people are not staunch enough, so it wants to speed up tempering you. The U.S. is steeling and making us stronger when it occupies our Taiwan. Imperialists are tempering and making people stronger by suppressing Africa.

The United States adopts military, economic and political means to suppress and deceive Latin America, but I believe that the people are not afraid. The people are heightening their consciousness. It is so in Africa, Latin America and Asia. In the past, some Chinese, especially rich Chinese, trusted the United States very much, but now they are gradually getting rid of their blind faith. They have upgraded their consciousness.

We have to differentiate between the American people and American imperialists. The American people are good people and the bad guys are imperialists. The same is true of Britain, France, Belgium and Portugal. The people are good, the imperialists bad. The people in West Germany and Japan are good; only the imperialists are bad. We are now learning to tell good people from bad people. Even the imperialists, we do not mean to have no contact with them for 10,000 years. We are now negotiating with the United States in Warsaw.[201] The talks have been going on for several years and will continue to go on. They will continue for ten or 20 years and finally will have a result.

Thank you for informing me of many things and for helping me learn a lot. Ten years ago China was much the same as most of the countries you are representing, and it was like Cuba before January 1 of last year. Our country has been liberated for only ten years. Our people are getting organized for construction, with some achievements, but not great. China is still a very poor country, and we must work hard for at least ten or 20 years before it becomes better. We need your assistance and support; in the meantime, we also support your struggle. It is important to have unity and mutual support. Your struggle is our struggle, and your victory is our victory. Our struggle and victory are also yours. We do not have conflicts of interest with you, but solidarity and friendship. The people in the East are rising up; for example, the South Korean people have been carrying out a great struggle in the past two weeks; in the past week the Turkish people were rising up; there is a big struggle in Japan too. There are American bases in these places, but they are not consolidated and the people, united, will defeat them.

Thank you, friends. Now I should like to propose a toast to celebrate our solidarity and victory, to the present struggle and future victories, and to the victory of all the people in the world in their anti-colonialist and anti-imperialist struggles. At the same time, we support the big-power conference[224] and oppose world war. On the one hand, we oppose world war; on the other, we support the anti-imperialist struggle in various countries. We are using two hands because our enemy is using the two ways to struggle against us.

(From the verbatim record)

IMPERIALISM IS NOTHING TO FEAR*

(*May 7, 1960*)

Welcome, friends. We are friends. We stand on the same front in common struggle against imperialism and colonialism. Most of the imperialist countries do not recognize China. They had virtually ruled China for over 100 years, which turned the country to great poverty, to a state of poverty and blankness. Poverty means deprivation, and blankness means that a lot of people are illiterate. That state of affairs has begun to change. In the past China was an independent country in name only; in reality it was a semicolony of imperialism. Only after decades of struggle did we win liberation. The armed struggle lasted for 22 years. The whole of Chinese mainland was basically liberated in 1949; only Taiwan is still under the occupation of imperialism. At present, U.S. imperialism has established many military bases in the Orient, such as in Japan, Taiwan, South Korea, the Philippines, South Vietnam, Thailand, Pakistan—military bases that pose a great threat to us.

Westerners allege that we Chinese are no good, since we are colored people. They allege that colored people are all no good, that they can accomplish nothing and are neither hygienic nor noble-minded. To them, our race seems no better than you Africans. Westerners also allege that you are no good, but they will not help you develop your industry. The little bit of industry you have managed to develop belongs to the imperialists. So our position is identical to yours.

It is very good for you now to be united. The whole of Africa is united and has become politically awakened, or is in the gradual process of awakening. Your Africa has a population of over 200 million. As you have become united, awakened and organized, imperialism is afraid of you. Imperialism tries to spread feelings of terror. The imperialists kill people or kill people through their running dogs. In China they killed our people through Chiang Kai-shek. Your countries may also have such stooges who do things at the will of

---

* These are excerpts from Mao Zedong's talk with social activists, peace personages and trade union, youth and student delegations from 12 African countries.

imperialism. They are very few in number, at most one out of ten or maybe even fewer. Therefore, the people with whom you can unite are nine out of ten or maybe even more. In fact, imperialism is nothing to fear. Imperialism makes propaganda every day about how powerful it is in order to scare us.

For a period of time in the past we Chinese were afraid of U.S. imperialism and of its running dog Chiang Kai-shek, because they killed people or used other means; for instance, arresting and putting them in jail. In short, they attempted to make us fear them to subdue our fighting spirit. We Chinese were awakened step by step, and gradually we became no longer afraid. We fought face to face against imperialism and its running dogs. To begin with, we were barehanded and did not know how to fight a war. We learned from the imperialists. As you oppress us, should we not oppress you in turn? As one out of ten people oppresses the remaining nine of us, isn't it possible for the nine of us to unite and drive the one away? We concluded we could do so. If one person oppresses the remaining nine of us, it would be unreasonable for the nine of us not to unite and drive him away. Therefore we made revolution for decades. And did we not end in victory?

Our enemy, Chiang Kai-shek, had huge foreign backing, that of none other than U.S. imperialism. He had powerful military forces, munitions, factories and weapons provided by foreigners. He had warships, heavy guns, tanks and airplanes. These we did not have—no heavy guns, no airplanes and no tanks. We had only rifles and light guns. Where did we get them? They were not produced by our munitions factories, but seized, captured in war. It was through Chiang Kai-shek that U.S. imperialism sent us rifles and guns, hence we had rifles and guns. Later we acquired tanks and heavy guns that enabled us to fight major battles. By 1949 we had basically liberated the mainland. Their air force dropped bombs over our heads every day, but this did not frighten us. In the end it turned out that they were afraid of us, not the other way round. Not only was Chiang Kai-shek afraid of us, but the Americans were also afraid of us somehow, because we had united over 90 percent of the people. It is the people who are most important and primary; weapons are secondary and less important. As long as the people are united, arms in hand, imperialists and colonialists will be afraid of us. Of course, fighting a war is not the only means; there are other means, too.

Of the countries that you friends come from, some have not gone through war to seize political power, such as Guinea. In Algeria the war is still going on, which has helped Guinea. Guinean friends also see things this way. Since half a million French troops have been tied up by the Algerians in their country, France does not have many troops left. Imperialism has occupied too many places and made too many things its business. A Chinese saying goes that he who tries to catch ten fleas with ten fingers gets none. Because imperialism has made too many things its business, it cannot get everything under control. Now the United States has occupied too many places in the world. You see, in Asia, Latin America and Africa there are many countries where the United States has military bases. Furthermore, it attempts to dominate Europe. In the past few days some changes have occurred in the international situation. The people of South Korea had no other way out but to rise up against Syngman Rhee,[85] a running dog of the United States. As the people of South Korea rose up, protesting, revolting and demonstrating in the hundreds of thousands, Syngman Rhee collapsed, although he had 75 divisions, while the masses of the South Korean people did not have a single rifle. However, as soon as they rose up, Syngman Rhee collapsed. Of course, the problem is not solved yet. The Americans are still in South Korea and they have chosen a new running dog. The struggle of the South Korean people is likely to go on. The masses in Turkey have also risen up against the running dogs of the United States. So we have been holding mass rallies these days in support of the South Korean people and the Turkish people. The Japanese people are rising up, too. In two days there will be a broad mass campaign. I have learned that hundreds of thousands or even millions of people will rise up against the government of Kishi Nobusuke[206] for entering into a military alliance with the United States.[214] We shall also hold a mass rally to support the masses of the Japanese people.

Some of you may say that South Korea, Japan and Turkey are far from the United States; therefore people are not afraid of the United States and dare to rise up against its running dogs. But please look at Cuba. Where is Cuba? Very close to the United States, only half an hour by flight. In the beginning the Cuban people were barehanded. The Cuban ruler Batista[221] had killed over 20,000 Cubans in just a few years. You may say that China is a big country, with a large population. Cuba is by no means a big country, with only six million people and so close to the United States, and Batista killed as many as 20,000 people. In November 1956 Fidel Castro, a national hero of Cuba, led 82 people in a boat from Mexico to Cuba. They were defeated by the government troops in battle. Of the 82 people, only twelve survived, including Fidel Castro and his younger brother, Raul Castro. They had to move to the mountainous areas and conduct guerrilla warfare. They fought for more than two years, seizing a lot of rifles and guns and even tanks. Batista had to run away. You see, the Cuban people were barehanded at the beginning, whereas the Batista regime was armed to its teeth, with such a big country as the United

States in its support and so close. However, when the people united, they drove Batista away. Has any one of you ever been to Cuba? If not, we suggest that you go to Cuba for a visit. For such a small country to dare to make revolution right beside the United States makes it highly necessary to study the Cuban experience. In that sense, the Cuba revolution has world significance. All the people in Latin-America welcome the people's government of Cuba.

The anti-colonialist and anti-imperialist struggle of Africa has even greater world significance. Instead of one country, many countries are in revolution; instead of millions of people, tens of millions of people and even more are involved in revolutionary struggle for national liberation. We entirely sympathize with you; and we stand foursquare behind you. At the same time, we regard your struggle as support and help for us. We also regard the struggle in Cuba as helping us, as well as the struggle of the whole of Latin America. The struggles of countries such as South Korea, Turkey, South Vietnam and Japan have helped us, too. All the people in Asia have helped us. Of course, first of all the socialist countries have assisted us. The Soviet Union has assisted us. Besides the socialist countries, the broad anti-colonialist and anti-imperialist struggles of the people in Asia, Africa and Latin America have assisted us. By diverting the enemy's strength they reduce the pressure on us. As you have assisted us, we are obligated to assist you. We support and help each other.

At the same time, we support the conference of the big powers.[224] The summit meeting of four countries to be held in France is also a means. To use an expression in Chinese, this is called walking on two legs. To talk with them at the table at the big-power conference is one leg; the anti-colonialist and anti-imperialist struggle of the people in Asia, Africa and Latin America is the other. With two legs one can stand and walk well. With one leg missing one cannot walk. We believe you agree that a world war should not be fought. We are opposed to a world war. However, we are for the people of various countries oppressed by imperialism to have the right to rise up against their oppressors. In order to avert a world war, the people of various countries should rise up against their oppressors. I can mention some examples to be more concrete. Algeria has pinned down half a million French troops. Should a world war break out, France would have fewer forces to participate in the war, since it has only so many troops. The rising of the South Korean people has tied up the U.S. forces stationed in South Korea. The rising of the Turkish people will tie up the U.S. forces stationed in Turkey. If the Japanese people also rise up, they will pin down more U.S. forces. Some people say that if you want world peace, you should not oppose imperialism, lest imperialism be displeased. According to them, no country should wage anti-imperialist struggles. In my view, it is better to walk on two legs. The rising of the people in various countries against their oppressors is one leg, an important one at that, maybe the primary one. To talk with the oppressors at the table at the big-power conference on disarmament, on the solution of the German question and so on is another leg. With these two legs on the move, it would be difficult for a world war to break out. If there were only one leg, it could not be assured that imperialism would not launch a world war. Imperialism is good at deception. Imperialism also has two legs, one being deception, the other, oppression. To the deception of imperialism we are skeptical like you. Then why should we support the big-power conference? To avail ourselves of the opportunity to see things and to expose that leg of theirs is faulty.

I agree with the idea expressed by the Algerian friend just now that countries like or roughly similar to Algeria should be prepared for long-term struggle. It is helpful to be mentally prepared. There are difficulties, sometimes great ones. As I said before, as for the struggle in China, the armed struggle alone took 22 years, whereas your struggle has lasted for only six years. In the 22 years we committed several mistakes, namely, two opportunist mistakes of the Right deviation and three opportunist mistakes of the "left" deviation, costing heavy losses to our strength. Before the Long March our military strength had been 300,000 troops, but fewer than 30,000, less than a tenth, survived, owing to our mistakes. It is important not to waver at a moment like that. Which were stronger, 30,000 or 300,000? Because we had learned our lessons, our fewer than 30,000 troops were even stronger than the 300,000. Later on, our army had the opportunity to grow, and when the Japanese surrendered in 1945, it became one million strong. In 1946 the United States and Chiang Kai-shek attacked us. The United States did not send its own troops, but helped Chiang Kai-shek fight against us. As a result, we lost many places, many cities. Chiang Kai-shek launched an all-out attack on us, and we adopted the tactics of withdrawal in order to wipe out the enemy's effectives. In one year we fought ten campaigns. Although we lost a lot of places, we put out of action more than 100 divisions of enemy forces. Only then did we launch counterattacks. By 1949 we were in the superior position, whereas Chiang Kai-shek's troops were inferior, most having been annihilated by us. We liberated many big cities, such as Shenyang, Beiping, Tianjin, Ji'nan and Zhengzhou. We captured their places and wiped out their main forces. Only then did they ask for peace and send representatives to Beiping. We then adopted the method of walking on two legs. We knew that they asked for peace in order to deceive us. However, if we had not talked peace, the common people would not have believed us; they would have thought Chiang Kai-shek loved peace, whereas we loved war. Well, then, let us talk peace! Send your delegation! It was then that they sent a delegation, which negotiated with us for some three weeks. We told them they should surrender their arms and give their political power to us. Their representatives signed the agreement and sent people back to Nanjing, the seat of the Kuomintang government, asking for approval. They said no. They would not surrender their arms or give up their political power. That tore up their mask of "peace." They refused to sign and we crossed the Yangtze River the next day, stretching out the other leg. The enemy often tries to deceive us; we should be clear about this. Sometimes it is necessary to accept proposals for negotiation and to expose them during negotiation. This is the way two legs walk. It is not surrendering to the enemy; rather it is making the enemy surrender. For instance, the people of the world now demand disarmament, with which we concur, and we should like to see if the United States disarms or not. If they do, so much the better. If they do not, it will prove that they are deceiving. The enemy should be exposed by one method or another. In fact, peaceful negotiation is also a method to expose the enemy. This is our view. We do not believe that Eisenhower[103] loves peace very much. How can an imperialist love peace? What they love is colonialism.

We are pleased to note that so many of our African friends have done away with superstition. Superstition number one is to be afraid of imperialism. You have done away with this and are not afraid of imperialism anymore. However, I believe there are still some people among the 200 million of your African population who are afraid of imperialism, who entertain superstition of imperialism or illusions of it. Therefore you have to work on them. In eight or ten years there will gradually be more and more people, maybe 100 million or more out of 200 million, who will rise up and be entirely free from superstition and not afraid of imperialism. By then victory will be certain. More often than not, people bear much superstition. The superstition of imperialism is but one kind. Another kind is not to believe in one's own strength, to regard it as too small. The Western world is considered good for everything, whereas we yellow people, black people and brown people are considered good for nothing. This is a kind of superstition, too. How could we be good for nothing? I believe whatever the white people can do, we can do, too, and we can do it even better than they, because they are very few in number, only hundreds of millions. Besides, we should differentiate among the white people; not all of them are bad people. Only one tenth are bad people, whereas mine tenths are good ones. They may be taken in for the time being. They are not yet awakened politically, but some day they will be. Here I mainly refer to the proletariat and others who sympathize with them, such as the working people, including the farmers. Among those who are really afraid of nuclear war there are white people, too, including some capitalists. There are contradictions among the imperialist countries, which gives us room to maneuver. They are not that united. The Americans and the British are not that united, nor are the Americans and the West Germans. Adenauer[154] does not see eye to eye with the British. Therefore, for workers the world over and patriotic people oppressed by imperialism there are many allies.

From our own experience, in terms of strategy one must not be afraid of the enemy. Imperialism is weakened, and one, two, even three of its ten fingers have been cut off. In the Soviet Union there are no tsars anymore. The country has become a Leninist Soviet Union. China is also free from the rule of imperialism. Besides these two countries, there are ten more socialist countries. In all the countries the fingers of imperialism have been cut off. Other countries in Asia, Africa and Latin America have won independence. Still others are struggling for it. It can be said that the remaining fingers of imperialism have been injured. For example, Cuba is right beside the United States and it has driven away the running dogs of the United States. In Algeria there is a large chunk of liberated area. Guinea has become independent. In Africa there are more independent countries. It seems a big storm is gathering in Africa. The same kind of storm is also in the making in Latin America. Some people say that in recent years the national liberation movements in Asia have fallen off. Yet on July 14, 1958, a revolution happened in Iraq.[225] In the war over the Suez Canal in 1956,[134] imperialism did not win; Egypt did. Furthermore, the people in South Korea and Turkey have risen in the past few weeks. Seemingly, the Japanese people are very hopeful, too. So now imperialism cannot get to sleep. Friends say that some of our countries have difficulties and worries. We think there is a side of happiness and a side of worry. Looking at imperialism, I can see only the worry side and not the happy one. You think the United States can get to sleep? I don't believe it can. For them, it is just like the Chinese saying: A chain of 15 pails draws well water, seven up and eight down. Therefore, we have full reason to despise them in terms of strategy, to be confident that the imperialist system is doomed and that people the world over will surely stand up. In terms of tactics, we should be cautious. We should carefully study every step to be taken. We should pay attention to them. We should take our work seriously. To combine the two, strategically we should despise the enemy, but tactically we should take them seriously. Only by so doing can one dare to think, dare to speak and dare to act.

You wish to look at the Chinese experience, which we much welcome.

Maybe some of our experience has reference value for you, including the experience of revolution and that of construction. However, I should like to warn you friends that China has its own historical conditions, whereas you have yours. The Chinese experience can be only for your reference.

Our unity is to be celebrated. Because of it, we shall surely win. Our victories are to be celebrated. Let us be united and strive for more victories.

(From the verbatim record)

FIRMLY SUPPORT THE JAPANESE PEOPLE IN THEIR STRUGGLE AGAINST THE JAPANESE-U.S. MILITARY ALLIANCE*

(*May 14, 1960*)

The new Japan-U.S. "Security Pact"[214] is a military alliance that is aggressive in nature and one to oppress the broad masses of the Japanese people and make enemies of China, the Soviet Union and the Asian people. It poses a serious threat to peace in Asia and the world as a whole and, at the same time, is bound to bring serious disaster to the Japanese people. The Chinese and Japanese peoples should oppose the Japan-U.S. military alliance, and so should the Asian people and peace-loving people the world over.

U.S. imperialism is the common enemy of the Chinese and Japanese peoples. It is the common enemy of the people of Asia, Africa and Latin America and of peace-loving people the world over. Imperialism keeps its running dogs in many countries, who are disliked by the people of their own countries. The Kishi Nobusuke[206] government of Japan is such a government. The far-sighted and patriotic personages of the Japanese Liberal Democratic Party have also expressed their unhappiness at the reactionary policy of Kishi Nobusuke. At present, the Japanese people are carrying out large-scale struggle, fighting against the treaty of Japan-US military alliance. In their struggle against the latter, the Japanese people are developing political awareness each day, and more and more people are awakened. The Japanese people are very hopeful. In the past, present and future the Chinese people have supported and will always firmly support the patriotic and just struggle of the Japanese people. The Cuban and other Latin American peoples are supporting the struggle of the Japanese people, and the Japanese people are supporting the struggles of the Cuban and other Latin American peoples.

Not long ago the United States sent a U-2 airplane to invade the Soviet

---

* This is a summary of Mao Zedong's talk with delegations of the Japan-China Friendship Association and the General Council of Trade Unions from Japan and other delegations from Cuba, Brazil and Argentina that were visiting China.

Union and conduct espionage activities. It was shot down by the Soviet Union. The Soviets were very correct in doing so. This event has once more exposed the true face of U.S. imperialism, which is preparing for a war of aggression under the hypocritical disguise of peace, and further attested to the whole world such truth that one can entertain no unrealistic illusions about imperialism. Some people have described Eisenhower[103] as a very peace-loving man. It is my hope that these people will wake up in the face of such facts.

We support the convocation of the summit meeting,[224] no matter whether such a meeting brings results or how big or small such results are. However, the attainment of world peace should mainly rely on the firm struggle of the people of various countries.

What imperialism fears most is the political awakening of the people of Asia, Africa and Latin America, and of the people of countries throughout the world. We should be united to drive U.S. imperialism away from Asia, Africa and and Latin America and send it home.

(From the news release revised by Mao Zedong)

OPPRESSED PEOPLE OUGHT NOT TO YIELD*

(*May 17, 1960*)

A few days ago I met some Cuban friends. Their victory came rather fast, in a matter of only two years or more. At the beginning, merely 82 people took a boat from Mexico to Cuba. They did not know how to fight, but put up an adventurous fight. Of the 82, 70 were killed and 12 survived. Fidel Castro[222] was one of the survivors. What was there for the 12 to do? They moved to the mountains and changed their tactics, which gave rise to development. There were more setbacks later, which educated them. In the end, they attained victory. Cuba's population is smaller than yours, only six million. U.S. imperialism is very close to them, only half an hour by flight. Having fought for over two years, they attained independence on January 1, 1959, and established their own government. I said to them, "You did better than we. We fought for 22 years, whereas you fought for only some two years." They are on an isolated island and have to seek assistance from other countries. The broad masses of Latin American people are giving them assistance. We are giving them some assistance, too. With them the problem of whether the United States will intervene or not is not solved yet. Two possibilities are open: There will be U.S. military intervention, or there will not be. They are redistributing the land, two thirds of which has already changed hands. It will be completed soon.

You should be able to maintain your strength and rely on the masses. You should keep up your efforts, relying mainly on your own efforts while winning over foreign assistance as a subsidiary. In your war efforts be advised not to consume too much of your strength, but rather to keep your main force intact and to consume a bit of enemy strength every day. If your 100,000 troops can be maintained and grow, victory will be yours. Time is not on the side of the French. It is on your side. You have already gone on for six years and you should keep going. In six more years I don't see why you should not gain

---

* These are excerpts from Mao Zedong's talk with the delegation of the Provisional Government of the Republic of Algeria.

victory.

As you have said, the war will last long and you will rely on yourselves and on your own people. We very much agree as we also called for a protracted war. It is also your principle to take first place yourselves. However, other countries have the obligation to give you assistance. You have organized a broad united front that embraces people of all strata. All those opposed to the French are included in the united front. You call it the National Liberation Front, a very good name that can unite many parties. As the war drags on, different views are bound to come up. It will be very good if unity can be maintained. Efforts should be made to unite as many people as possible in order to isolate France and not be isolated.

Imperialists and their running dogs are few in number, accounting for only one tenth of the world's population at most. France has a population of 45 million, but they are not monolithic. Most of them are working people who are being oppressed. You should work among the French people. There are 400,000 Algerians in France, a potential to be tapped to work against French colonialists and help you.

On the surface, U.S. imperialism is powerful, but it has its weaknesses, as it arouses the opposition of many people. The South Korean people, for instance, have risen up against U.S. imperialism and its running dogs. So have the broad masses of the Turkish and Japanese peoples. No one expected the Iraqi revolution to happen on July 14, 1958,[225] a situation that is to your advantage. Nor had anyone expected that the Cuban revolution would be brought to victory on January 1, 1959. Many things are beyond people's expectations. We have not expected them to happen, nor have the imperialists. But they did happen, what can you do? The Cuban revolution is also in your favor. Africa is much different from two years ago. We have met many African and Latin American friends, who are in very high spirits. In Latin America the struggle is spearheaded against the United States, whereas in Africa it is against France, the United Kingdom and Belgium.

We support all anti-imperialist forces; at the same time they give us support. This is the broadest possible united front of the world's anti-imperialist forces. Difficulties are only temporary; the future is always bright. As a friend of yours, I have made the above points for your reference. I believe that you will not accuse me of interfering with your internal affairs. We are Communists. Imperialism says all revolutions are made by Communists, which is pure fabrication. When you were preparing for the revolution, we did not even know about it. Only when your revolution was going on, did we come to hear about it. Nor did we know that you were going to set up a provisional government. After you have established it, we gave our recognition. You have sent several delegations, which we warmly welcome.

We stand by your side, not on the side of De Gaulle.[191] I do not fear to make De Gaulle angry. France does not recognize China, and in Paris there are still representatives of Chiang Kai-shek. So why should China not support you and not have relations with you? The United States has occupied our Taiwan. It recognizes Chiang Kai-shek, not us. They call Chiang Kai-shek "a good guy" and us "bad guys." De Gaulle also calls us "bad guys," and he calls you "bad guys," too. Well then, we are "bad guys" having relations with "bad guys."

Imperialism does not like us, accusing us of committing "aggression." At first, "aggression" against Chiang Kai-shek. Then we fought with the United States in Korea, which brought us the nickname of "aggressor." Imperialism speaks against us. It says that Chiang Kai-shek and Syngman Rhee[85] are very good. The more imperialism speaks against us the happier we are. We would just as soon be cursed for a lifetime. If they were to say we are very good, then would we not be the same as Chiang Kai-shek and Syngman Rhee? Imperialism calls us ugly names and it does the same to you. You have been cursed for five and a half years. You should be prepared to be cursed by imperialism and to be welcomed by the people. Imperialism curses you, but people the world over all welcome you. We are of the same party. Revolutionary people are of the same party and on the same front. Here there are still differences, some believing in communism, some in religion and some in neither of these. There are workers, peasants and revolutionary intellectuals, and also revolutionary national bourgeoisie, but all are united against imperialism. As you know, China carries out a special policy toward the national bourgeoisie. Now they work with us, having the right to vote and participating in the government. We reject only compradore bourgeoisie that sided with Chiang Kai-shek and feudal landlords. Does it mean that compradore bourgeoisie and feudal landlords should be killed? No. They are given a way out. For example, landlords are given a plot of land, which allows them to live on their own labor.

U.S. imperialism has committed aggression against China's Taiwan, yet it says that we have committed aggression and it has not. U.S. imperialism has a "good point"—that it is "peace-loving." It bullies the socialist countries, but the aircraft it sent into the territorial air space of the Soviet Union has been shot down. The United States "loves peace," so it has provided De Gaulle with munitions and airplanes for aggression against Algeria. What it truly loves is something else. It would love to eliminate you, to eliminate us and even to eliminate De Gaulle, so that only it remains. Isn't that so? De Gaulle is collaborating with the United States, but between them there are constradictions. In our struggle we should make use of these contradictions among imperialists.

We have recognized you. The Soviet Union has not done so and there is a reason for it. The Soviet Union does not wish to fall out with France. If it did, the United States and France would act more in concert against you. So the Soviet Union has considered the contradictions among the United States, the United Kingdom and France. To try to win over the United Kingdom and France, it has not recognized you. We cannot play such a role. We cannot give De Gaulle a helping hand, as we have no diplomatic ties with France. Besides, De Gaulle looks down upon us. We have a large population, but only a little amount of steel. France has exploded two atom bombs. We have not a single atom bomb. De Gaulle has reason to look down on us. Those people can see nothing but money, steel and atom bombs. We are obliged that you look up to us. We have no atom bombs. We have only some shabby rifles to give you. In ten years' time we shall have much more steel and also acquire atom bombs. By then your conditions will have changed also. Oppressed people just should not yield. They must have a will. Now it is not long live De Gaulle, long live Macmillan[226] or Eisenhower,[103] but, rather, long live the people of all countries.

(From the verbatim record)

TALK WITH MARSHAL MONTGOMERY ON THE CURRENT INTERNATIONAL SITUATION*

(*May 27, 1960*)

Marshal Montgomery (hereinafter referred to as Montgomery): Would you please tell me your views of the world situation today?
Chairman Mao Zedong (hereinafter referred to as Mao): The international situation is very good, not bad at all, nothing more than the whole world's opposition to the Soviet Union and China.
Montgomery: That is very bad.
Mao: It was created by the United States; not bad.
Montgomery: But it is very bad.
Mao: Not bad, but good. If they do not oppose us, that means we are like Eisenhower[103] and Dulles.[97] Naturally they should oppose us. They are doing it intermittently. Last year it was anti-China and this year anti-Soviet.
Montgomery: That is America's doing, not Britain's.
Mao: Mainly the United States. It also instigated its stooges in various countries to do so.
Montgomery: That's why I say the situation is bad.
Mao: I think the present situation is neither rupture and hot war nor peaceful coexistence, but a third kind, coexistence in a cold war.
Montgomery: That is where the difficulty lies. It is difficult to coexist in a cold war.
Mao: We must solve this problem.
Montgomery: We have to find a solution.
Mao: But we must be prepared for two possibilities—to continue the cold war or to transform the cold war into peaceful coexistence. You are doing transformation work. We welcome it.
Montgomery: Yes, I feel we cannot go on living in this tense situation. Our children have been growing up in the cold war, which is bad for them.

---

* These are excerpts from Mao Zedong's talk with British Field Marshal Montgomery.

Therefore we must change the situation into peaceful coexistence. I do not wish to see my children grow up thinking that there must always be tension in the world.

Mao: This should be analyzed. A cold war has a good point as well as a bad point. The bad point is that it may change into a hot war.

Montgomery: Possibly.

Mao: The good point is that it may turn into peaceful coexistence.

Montgomery: This cannot be called a good point of the cold war.

Mao: We say it is a good point, because the United States has created the tense situation and along with it has created many more opponents, for instance, in South Korea, Japan, Turkey and Latin American countries. Many countries object to American control. The United States has created this for itself.

Montgomery: I am not sure that the United States has created opponents in the Western bloc. There isn't anything like that in the Western bloc, though I hope that is the case.

Mao: I do not mean Europe, which is quite calm. I am referring to South Korea, South Vietnam, Japan, Turkey, Cuba and other Latin American countries, and Africa. In the case of Africa, not only is the United States to be blamed, but the European colonialists should be blamed in the first place. Nevertheless, the United States wants to replace the European colonialists there. That is why I say the good point is that it makes these countries oppose U.S. imperialism, which is shaking the very foundation of the entire capitalist world.

Montgomery: The leader of the Western world is the United States. It is a very strange phenomenon that the Western countries fear their leader will lead them into war, because in the past two world wars the United States joined in when the wars were already fought halfway. Now the Western countries are afraid the United States will take them into war. We must change the situation whereby the leader of the Western pack and the two biggest countries of the Eastern bloc cannot get together for talks. For this reason, the West doubts the leadership of the United States.

Mao: So long as the leadership of the United States is not weakened and this leader strengthened by Britain and France, the situation is not likely to change.

Montgomery: I believe that such a situation will take place inevitably.

Mao: You are British and have been to France. You have been to the Soviet Union twice and now you are visiting China. Is there a possibility that Britain, France, the Soviet Union and China can reach consensus on some major international issues?

Montgomery: Yes, I think it is possible. But because of the leadership of the United States, Britain and France are afraid of doing so.

Mao: Make it a gradual course. We hope that your country will be stronger and France, too. We hope both of you will have a louder voice. In that case, the United States, West Germany and Japan will be contained.

The threat to you and France comes from the United States, West Germany, and Japan in the Far East. These three countries are also a threat to us. We do not feel Britain is a threat to us. Nor do we feel France is a threat to us. The threat to us comes mainly from the United States and Japan.

Montgomery: I feel the most important thing is, which step should we take first in the very complicated situation? I think that the first thing is to withdraw all foreign troops from other countries, and that takes time.

Mao: Mainly the American forces, part of which are in Europe and part in Asia. Britain has only four divisions stationed in West Germany.

Montgomery: Only three.

Mao: While the United States has one and a half million troops stationed overseas in 250 military bases, including those in West Germany, Britain, Turkey and Morocco. In the East, the United States has military bases in Japan, South Korea, Taiwan and the Philippines. It also has military personnel in South Vietnam and air bases in Thailand and Pakistan.

Montgomery: The essential thing is for everybody to return to his home country. We are likely to ease the tense situation if we do the following: first, cease the military occupation of Europe; second, solve the Taiwan question. We can solve the problems only one by one.

Mao: But now the people are doing it. The South Korean people, the Japanese people and the Turkish people are holding demonstrations. A coup just took place in Turkey and one cannot blame it on the Communists.

Montgomery: It is no good to accomplish all at one time. I am a soldier and I understand this. You are also a soldier and you should know it, too.

Mao: You have spent 35 years in the army and I only 25 years.[227] You have spent more years in the army than I.

Montgomery: It's 52 years since I joined the army.

Mao: But I am still chairman of the Communist Party's Military Commission.

Montgomery: That is very good. I have read your military works, which are very well written.

Mao: I do not know what is good in them. I learned from you. You have studied Clausewitz;[228] so have I. He said that war is the continuation of politics in another form.

Montgomery: I have also read Genghis Khan,[147] who emphasized mobility.

Mao: You haven't read *The Art of War*, written by Sun Zi 2,000 years ago, have you? There are lots of good things in it.

Montgomery: Does it have more military principles?

Mao: Some very good principles. It has a total of 13 chapters.

Montgomery: We should come back to the present world from the world 2,000 years ago.

Do you agree with this: When I return to London, I shall mobilize the world's media to put an end to the military occupation in Europe and solve the Taiwan question. Do you agree with starting with these two questions?

Mao: Good. I agree.

Montgomery: I can make the United States feel very embarrassed.

Mao: That also has two points. One is that you do as you said; the other is that the United States is very arrogant and conceited and does not give an inch.

Montgomery: I can make the United States feel very embarrassed.

Mao: It is possible.

Montgomery: I am very familiar with the American situation and I have many American friends who share my views.

Mao: Our policy has also made the United States feel embarrassed.

Montgomery: In the United States many of my friends will agree with me. Many influential persons from the press will agree with me. I have never made the United States feel embarrassed, but now I want to make it feel so.

Mao: The United States now is very passive. Several hundred nooses have tied it up, for it has 250 military bases overseas.

Montgomery: I think I should speak out and say some impolite, candid words, to the Americans.

Mao: The United States has half its troops tied up in its bases. It has three million troops, with one and a half million stationed overseas, including in your Britain and China's Taiwan. We do not have a single military base or a single soldier overseas.

Montgomery: Do you agree with the talk between me and Zhou Enlai on the several principles that the United States should abide by? That is, first, the United States should recognize that Taiwan is part of China; second, the United States should withdraw from Taiwan; third, the Taiwan question should be negotiated between China and Chiang Kai-shek.

Mao: I know and I agree. We do not want to solve problems with the United States by means of war, but it is different with Chiang Kai-shek.

Nevertheless, we shall not use force if he does not use it.

Montgomery: I agree on this.

Mao: The United States made a statement that it is willing to solve international issues through peaceful negotiations without the threat of force or the use of force. We have to wait and see if the statement is reliable or hypothetical. But Chiang Kai-shek has not made such a statement and he objects to negotiations with the Chinese Communist Party, whereas we long ago expressed our desire to solve problems through negotiations with Chiang Kai-shek.

Montgomery: Do you know Chiang Kai-shek?

Mao: He is my old friend. How could I fail to know him? Chiang Kai-shek came into power with help from us. Before he came into power, we had had contacts with Sun Yat-sen.

Montgomery: Chairman Mao and Chiang Kai-shek cooperated during the resistance against Japan, didn't you?

Mao: We cooperated for eight years in fighting the Japanese. Later he cooperated with the United States to fight us.

In the past Britain and Japan were in an alliance to deal with Tsarist Russia. At that time the Far East was yours and China was mainly under your spheres of influence. When did it change? The change started in the First World War. After the Second World War Britain was not able to influence Japan, which went under the influence of the United States. Britain and the United States have a gentleman's agreement to let China be under the sphere of influence of the United States. Mrs. Cripps informed me of this when she visited Yan'an. She said that Britain did not have a say on China issues. From then on, the Chinese people got rid of their hatred of Britain and turned the hatred toward the United States. After Japan's surrender the United States had 90,000 troops in China.

Montgomery: The past hatred was against Britain.

Mao: It was against Britain, and at the same time it was against Japan, too.

Montgomery: We were once the worst foreign devils.

Mao: And the Japanese. Later they are the Japanese and the Americans.

Montgomery: Are you against the United States because it sent General Marshall to China to interfere with China's internal affairs?

Mao: Japan occupied a bigger part of China with help from the United States. Japan lacked iron and crude oil and had very little coal. The United States sent them to Japan on and on. But it fostered a force, causing the Pearl Harbor Incident.[229]

Montgomery: You are not afraid of Japan today, are you?

Mao: Still a little bit, because the United States reinstates Japanese militarism.

Montgomery: Japan is a highly organized industrial country.

Mao: America's major base in the East is in Japan. On the 19th of this month the Japanese Diet forced through a military alliance with the United States.

Montgomery: Does Japan have any ulterior motive against China?

Mao: I think it does.

Montgomery: What kind of motive?

Mao: Of course, it is mainly the United States'. There is one clause in the Japan-U.S. treaty which states that, according to Japanese interpretation, Japan's Far Eastern range includes China's coastal regions.

I have read Eden's[230] memoirs. He talked about the Suez question, the Egyptian question and the question of the Southeast Asia Treaty Organization.[96] He said that when the United States was organizing the Southeast Asia Treaty Organization, Britain wanted India to join, but the United States was firmly against it. The United States said that if Britain had India join, the United States would like Chiang Kai-shek and Japan to join.

Montgomery: India would not take part in it.

Mao: At that time Eden wanted to have India in to deal with the United States. He said, in his reminiscence, he just did not know how Chiang Kai-shek could be compared to Nehru.[209]

Montgomery: I have an interesting question to ask the Chairman: China probably needs 50 years to get everything in shape—the people's living standard greatly improved and housing problems, educational problems and construction problems all solved. What will China's future be by then?

Mao: In your view, we will be aggressive by then, is that right?

Montgomery: No. At least I hope you will not.

Mao: You are afraid that we may be aggressive.

Montgomery: I feel that a country, when it gets strong, should be cautious not to commit aggression. The United States is a case in point.

Mao: Right, absolutely right. Britain was another case in point. Prior to the First World War the most powerful nation in the world was the British Empire. The United States was only a colony of Britain 180 years ago.

Montgomery: The historical lesson is that a country tends to be aggressive when it is very powerful.

Mao: A country is to be driven back when it commits aggression overseas. The North America of George Washington[231] or the British Empire, which is more powerful? Yet, Washington with some shabby rifles drove back the British Empire in eight years.

Montgomery: The American revolution was a good thing. Often revolution is a good thing. Without the American revolution, Canada would not be today's Canada. The Chinese revolution was good, too. So revolution can be good.

Mao: You are very enlightened.

Montgomery: I am a soldier.

Mao: A foreign country is for its people to live in; others should not occupy it, nor do they have the right or reason to squeeze in.

Montgomery: I agree.

Mao: It is a historical lesson that one will be driven out if one gets in.

Montgomery: What will be China's destiny 50 years from now? By then China will be the world's most powerful country.

Mao: Not necessarily. Fifty years from now China's destiny is still 9.6 million square kilometers. China does not have a god, what it has is a Jade Emperor. Fifty years from now the Jade Emperor will still be reigning over 9.6 million square kilometers. We would be aggressors if we occupied an inch of land belonging to others. In fact, we are the "aggressed." The United States has occupied our Taiwan. But the United Nations gave us the title of "aggressor." You are facing an "aggressor." Aren't you afraid?

Montgomery: Before the revolution you suffered aggression by us.

Mao: That was in the past, and now there is no hatred, only a little left over from history. We can establish diplomatic relations and exchange ambassadors with you if your government improves its attitude just a little bit.

Montgomery: I hope so.

Mao: Things will get easier if Britain, France, the Soviet Union and China can get closer.

Montgomery: I hope to see it.

Mao: Why can't you improve your attitude a little? Now the fundamental question is solved; you do not have formal diplomatic relations with Taiwan and have agreed that the Beijing government represents China. You have done the basic things. There are only a few questions—first, you side with the United States when the United Nations discusses the question of the representation of Chiang Kai-shek; second, you have a consulate in Taiwan; third, your government is closer to Taiwan and keeps its distance from China, and many people under Chiang Kai-shek have gone to London from Taiwan and were received by responsible people from your Foreign Office. Also, on the question of Tibet your government stands on the American side. When a

Tibetan rebel went to London, he was received by a responsible member of your Foreign Office.

Montgomery: I don't know about that. Tibet is within China.

Mao: You do not know many of the things done by your Foreign Office. So I think we cannot easily send an official representative to Britain and cannot exchange ambassadors with Britain.

Montgomery: It needs time and patience.

Mao: Our relations will improve with just a little improvement in your attitude.

Montgomery: I feel it is very interesting that you mentioned the question of Britain, France, the Soviet Union and China. I am on very good terms with Macmillan[226] and De Gaulle.[191] De Gaulle has invited me to go to Paris next month to meet him. I shall tell him about this. De Gaulle is a very good man.

Mao: We have two feelings about De Gaulle—that he is not bad and that he has shortcomings.

Montgomery: Everybody has shortcomings.

Mao: We say he is not bad because he has the courage to be independent of the United States. He does not follow the baton of the United States at all. He does not allow the United States to establish air bases in France, and his field army does not obey the orders of the United States.

Montgomery: Nor does his navy.

Mao: The French fleet in the Mediterranean was under the command of the United States, but now he has retrieved his right to command. We appreciate all this very much.

Nevertheless, he has a very big shortcoming. He sent half his army to Algeria to carry out a war, which has tied up his hands and feet.

Montgomery: De Gaulle may say that Algeria is a province of France, and De Gaulle is legally right to say so.

Mao: But the Algerians do not agree and they ask for independence.

Montgomery: That is the trouble, so it must be solved. Legally, Algeria is a province of France. This issue must be settled.

Mao: The Algerian question should be resolved. Algerians told me that France has 900,000 troops in Algeria. I feel it is not that many, probably 500,000 or 600,000. It is very unfavorable for France to have such a large military expenditure in Algeria, every day, every month, every year.

Montgomery: This issue must be solved.

Mao: Yes, it must be. The French army is not good at fighting; in Vietnam they were no match for Ho Chi Minh's[216] troops.

Montgomery: This issue must be settled.

Mao: They have been fighting in Algeria for six years. At first, Algeria had only 3,000 guerrillas, but now it has developed an army of 100,000.

Montgomery: This problem must be solved. De Gaulle's position, to a great extent, relies on a resolution of this issue. If he fails to solve it, he may have to step down.

Mao: It may decide whether he can have equal rights with Britain and the United States in Europe.

Montgomery: He already has them. He insisted on it.

Mao: Not completely. The United States does not buy it. We saw that Macmillan visited France. De Gaulle was solemnly received when he visited London. We were very happy to see it. We hope that your two countries will cooperate.

Montgomery: Macmillan maybe is the best political leader in the West.

Mao: Perhaps. At least he is better than Eisenhower.

Montgomery: Who could be better than he? I mean in the West.

Mao: We hope to see a stronger Britain.

Montgomery: He is the most intelligent and honest in the Western pack.

Mao: People can see that he is quite methodical.

Montgomery: My criterion for a political leader is whether or not he sacrifices his principles for his position. Do you agree with this criterion? If a leader sacrifices his principles for higher position, he is not a good man.

Mao: My opinion is this: A leader should be the spokesman for the great majority of people.

Montgomery: But he cannot sacrifice his principles.

Mao: This is a principle, that he should represent the will of the people.

Montgomery: He must lead the people to do what is best.

Mao: He must be for the people's interests.

Montgomery: But often the people do not know what is best and the leader must lead them to do what is best for them.

Mao: The people know. The people have the final say after all. It was because Cromwell[232] represented the people that the king had to make concessions.

Montgomery: Cromwell represented only a few.

Mao: He was representing the capitalist class against the feudal lords.

Montgomery: But he lost. A few years after Cromwell died and was buried, his corpse was disinterred, beheaded and hanged on the roof of the Parliament building for several years.

Mao: But history has proved Cromwell had high prestige.

Montgomery: Without Cromwell, Britain would not be today's Britain.

Mao: Jesus was nailed to the cross, but he is highly respected.

Montgomery: That was only after he died. When he was alive, he did not have many followers.

Mao: George Washington represented the American people.

Montgomery: But he was assassinated.[233]

Mao: Mohandas K. Gandhi[234] of India was assassinated, but he represented the Indian people.

(From the vertim record)

U.S. IMPERIALISM IS THE COMMON ENEMY OF THE CHINESE AND JAPANESE PEOPLES*235

(June 21, 1960)

You are more than welcome. I am very pleased with the heroic struggle of the Japanese people. Your struggle provides great support to the Chinese people and to the people of the world as a whole. Your struggle is targeted at the largest imperialist country, which once dominated China and helped Chiang Kai-shek with the civil war and which still occupies our territory of Taiwan. It has maintained military bases in Japan, the Philippines, South Korea and Taiwan. Also under its occupation is South Vietnam, not to mention quite a number of other countries west of Pakistan. It is our common enemy. Last year when the leader of the Socialist Party of Japan, Asanuma Inejiro,236 visited China, he made a speech in Beijing, saying that U.S. imperialism is the common enemy of the Chinese and Japanese peoples. At that time, some people considered it too radical. The current struggle of the Japanese people has far exceeded what was meant by the speech last year. The scope and size of the struggle are so large that it goes beyond what one could imagine last year. The struggle started with opposition to the "security pact,"214 opposing U.S. imperialism and its agent, Kishi Nobusuke,206 and demanding national independence and democracy, because the treaty was forced through by Japanese and American reactionaries in the House of Representatives. That is to say that, by nature, the Japanese revolution is a nationalist and democratic one. The workers go on strike not raising economic slogans, but political ones, which is rare in the world. Senior intellectuals have also participated in the struggle. For instance, the day after the "June 15th Massacre"237 Kaya Seiji, president of Tokyo University, called for a protest rally of the whole university, then led the gathering to demonstrate in the streets. The victim was a student of Tokyo University. Her name was Kanba Michiko, now well known to the world. Her father is Kanba Toshio, a professor of law at Central

---

* This is Mao Zedong's talk with a literary delegation from Japan.

University. It seems professors have been organized in their thousands. Women have moved ahead, too. Monks and other religious people have come out. The workers and students are the main force. An even more sizable strike will happen tomorrow.

There are U.S. military bases in Japan. In the past, people could do nothing about them. Although they were annoyed by them, they could not attack them by force. Now you, the Japanese people, have come up with a good method, that is, to carry out a mass struggle involving all the people. Except for U.S. imperialism and its agents in Japan, all forces should unite in the struggle against U.S. imperialism and its agents. In the past, China basically adopted the same method. China also saw armed struggle. However, when the May 4th Movement happened in 1919, there was no armed struggle. It was to oppose the treaty signed at the Paris Peace Conference,[238] which occurred after the First World War. There was no Communist Party of China then. Not until two years later did the Party come into being. In the beginning, there were not many people involved, only scores of them who had been in Marxist groups. In 1926 the Northern Expedition took place, when we cooperated with the Kuomintang. You are all familiar with this period of history. In 1927, when the Northern Expedition reached areas along the Yangtze River, Chiang Kai-shek turned on the Communists, forcing us to fight within the former alliance. Due to Chen Duxiu,[130] Right opportunist in the Party, we were caught unprepared and suffered a surprise attack. China is large in area, and the civil war went on for ten years. Then we fought against the Japanese warlords in cooperation with Chiang Kai-shek. I have talked about events of this period with many Japanese friends. Some say that the Japanese aggression against China was bad. I say, of course aggression was bad, but one should not look only at the bad side of it. On the other side Japan helped China a great deal. Had Japan not captured a good half of China, the Chinese people could not have waked up. From this angle, we should be graceful to the Japanese "Imperial Army." However, you no longer have any burdens, since you do not possess any colonies. On the contrary, you have become a colony or semicolony yourselves. In the sense of the presence of foreign military bases, Japan is a colony, but you have an independent government, though dominated by the United States. In this sense, Japan is a semicolony. Now you no longer owe anyone anything. Instead, a foreign country owes something to you. This foreign country is neither Britain nor France. It is none other than the United States. As a result, the Japanese people have become indignant. I have told many Japanese friends that I do not believe a great nation like Japan will be ruled by others for long. Now who is educating the

Japanese people? U.S. imperialism is serving as your teacher by negative example. At the same time, it is also our teacher by negative example. After 1945 what happened to China had nothing to do with you. It was U.S. imperialism, not Japan, that pushed China around and helped Chiang Kai-shek with the civil war. Therefore, the target of our hatred has transferred from Japan to U.S. imperialism. Our two great nations now have possibilities of cooperation, which is also highly necessary, as both suffer from the oppression of U.S. imperialism. We have a common ground. Now it is the United States that is oppressing the Chinese and Japanese peoples. Does any other country do the same as the United States? How about Britain? Or France? The past spheres of influence of Britain and France in China were gone after the Second World War, and the role of Britain and France was taken over by the United States.

Your history of being oppressed is not so long. Ours is very long, more than one hundred years. However, you are more developed than China in industry, economy and culture. Ours is a backward country. Even today you can see the remains of backwardness. In proportion to population, we have fewer college graduates than you.

All of you present are younger than I am. Most things in the world are the accomplishments of young people—the lesser known, those of relatively low social status and the poor. For instance, James Watt, the British inventor of the steam engine, was a worker by background. You can always find such examples, one way or another. We talked about this in 1958, at the Second Session of the Eighth Congress of our Party. Later, people did some research on the great inventors of the past 300 years. The findings were that 70 percent of them were the lesser known, the young, the relatively low in social status and the relatively poor people. I wonder what the situation is like in your Japan. After all, are all the good things done by the old people, by the big officials? I just don't believe it. It was the young people who put Hagerty[239] under siege and who drove away Eisenhower.[103] The victim of the June 15th Massacre, Kanba Michiko, was young, too. In *China Youth Daily* I read a short essay by a member of your delegation Takeuchi Minoru,[240] which was very well written.

We shall always side with you, with the Japanese people, who call for independence, democracy and freedom, and not with Kishi Nobusuke.

Things are changing in the world and changing very fast. Four or five years ago, when I met many Japanese friends, they would keep silent as we talked about the United States. I think that the Japanese friends were thinking about the issue then and listened to what we were saying. They did not reject it. They were willing to go on listening and did not defend the United States. Now things have changed, as the Japanese people are on the move everywhere in the country. For instance, they put up slogans against the "Security Pact," demanding that the military bases be done away with and the U-2 airplanes be pulled out. They asked the Americans to get out. The people of Okinawa even asked the Americans face-to-face, "How long are you going to keep us under occupation?" The Japanese people of all walks of life have taken action. They are in the millions, which would have been unthinkable four or five years ago. I see that there is great hope for Japan's independence and freedom. It will ensure Japan's independence and peace, and peace in Asia as a whole, to do away with the U.S. military bases and the "Security Pact." Our congratulations on your victory.

Victory is won step by step, so also is the heightening of the awareness of the masses. That includes ourselves; we have raised our political consciousness step by step. I, for one, did not know Marxism-Leninism when attending middle school. My schooling can be divided into two parts. First, I was in an old-style private school learning the stuff of Confucius, that is, feudalism. Then I went to a new-style school, learning the stuff of capitalism. I once believed in the philosophy of Immanuel Kant. Then the objective circumstances forced me and others to organize communist groups and study Marxism. Premier Zhou Enlai did the same. Because at that time I could not afford to go to university, and even if I could have, I could not have gone on studying. I studied at a normal school, training as a teacher. I worked as a teacher and also as a headmaster of a primary school. Then I was determined to be a teacher and never thought of becoming a Communist. Later I opposed the warlords, influenced by *New Youth*. In the beginning *New Youth* was not a Communist magazine. Later I could not teach anymore. Circumstances forced me to work for the students' movement and the workers' movement. Then the Communist Party was in the making. That was in 1919, 1920 and 1921. Premier Zhou, too, could not go on studying. He went to Japan and stayed there for a year and a half, returning to take part in the May 4th Movement. The warlords wanted to put him under arrest, so he went to France on a work-study program. He wrote for a newspaper, *Yishi Bao*, and later they set up a Communist group. In 1927, after the defeat of the Great Revolution, many people went to Moscow to study at Sun Yat-sen University.[241]

The Chinese revolution covered a long journey, going through twists and turns, before it was brought to fruition. In 1840 the Opium War broke out. Between 1851 and 1864 the Taiping Heavenly Kingdom rebelled for 13 years before it ended in failure. The Reform Movement of 1898, with the participation of Kang Youwei and Liang Qichao, also failed. After that many people went to Japan, about 10,000 to 20,000 of them. It was in Japan that China Revolutionary League (Tong Meng Hui) was set up under Sun Yat-sen in 1905. The Revolution of 1911 failed, too, as Yuan Shikai attempted to be emperor. It was followed by the wars among warlords. In 1919 the May 4th Movement occurred. In 1921 the Communist Party of China was founded. In 1923 the General Strike of February 7th happened. In 1925 there was the May 30th Massacre and the struggle against British imperialism. In 1924 the Kuomintang and the Communist Party entered into cooperation and the First National Congress of the Kuomintang was held in Guangzhou. In 1926 the Northern Expedition began. In 1927 Chiang Kai-shek betrayed the revolution, and we went underground and started guerrilla warfare. Between 1927 and 1949 we fought for 22 years, in the War of Agrarian Revolution, the War of Resistance Against Japan and the War of Liberation. During the War of Liberation the target of struggle changed from Japanese imperialism to U.S. imperialism and its running dog, Chiang Kai-shek. It came to a stop in 1949. Last year marked the first decade of New China. In the past over ten years we have carried out socialist revolution and socialist construction; that is what you are seeing now. In the ten years there have been some achievements. However, a decade is not very long after all, and there is not too much success to speak of.

I have told you a lot of history—history I have gone through. It illustrates that it was only step by step that the Chinese people heightened their political consciousness. People of my generation went through the same process. I am convinced that you will develop your political awareness gradually, too. As I said just now, some Japanese did not dare to speak against U.S. imperialism four or five years ago. However, when Asanuma Inejiro visited China last year, he dared to make a public speech in Beijing, saying that U.S. imperialism is the common enemy of the Chinese and Japanese peoples. Barely one year later the Japanese people have launched such a sizable struggle against the "Security Pact." It should be said that the progress is very fast, and that the political awareness has been raised by a large measure. Now people have realized that U.S. imperialism is the common enemy of the Chinese and Japanese peoples. You will move faster than we. It took us more than 100 years to do it, 109 years, to be exact, from 1840 to 1949. To date, you have not done away with the "Security Pact." What you have done away with is the planned visit of Eisenhower to Japan. The "Security Pact" still exists, but it will be done away with some day, which may still take quite some time. It is difficult to predict in which month or which year it will be done away with, but done away with it shall be. Of course, I am not for your fighting a war with the United States.

You can reach your end by means other than war. There is no precedent in other countries yet. Maybe you will make the precedent.

As for achieving independence, there are precedents of reaching the end by means of war and not by means of war. One hundred and eighty years ago America was a British colony. George Washington[231] drove Britain away and it was by means of war that he did so. The independence of India did not arrive by means of war, as the British allowed it to happen. You may find a proper means and it seems you have found some means. It is the method that is being used now—setting up such institutions as the National Conference to Stop the Security Pact, which embraces over 100 organizations, adopting the method of organized struggle under leadership. In the past we did not adopt such methods.

Those of you who have never been to China before may not be in the know about China, but as your visit goes on, you will be. You will see that the Chinese people are friendly to you.

We should assist each other, learn from each other, learn from each other's strong points.

(From the verbatim record)

SO LONG AS THE TWO SIDES KEEP FRIENDLY RELATIONS, THE BOUNDARY ISSUE IS EASY TO SOLVE*

(*September 29, 1960*)

Chairman Mao Zedong (hereinafter referred to as Mao): I remember I suggested that you set up a consulate in Kunming when I first met you. At that time, you thought Kunming was a dark place. Now you have consulate-general there and you can discover it is a very bright city and very friendly to you.

Prime Minister U Nu (hereinafter referred to as Nu): Yes. When friends first meet, they are not familiar with each other. They had no trust in each other before they meet. After they have met each other, naturally the distrust and fear disappear.

Mao: A Burmese detachment crossed the border to our side. You mentioned this to me.

Premier Zhou Enlai (hereinafter referred to as Zhou): They are now in Guizhou engaging in agricultural production. Some of them married Chinese women. They do not want to go back.

Mao: They hoped we would arm them to fight back. We told them that we could accept them, but could not arm them. China and Burma should have friendly relations. There are several dozen of them. They are Kachins,[242] aren't they?

Nu: Yes, they are.

Mao: Now we are about to sign a Sino-Burmese Boundary Treaty. So long as both sides keep friendly relations, it is easy to resolve the boundary issue.

Nu: It is entirely because of the friendly relations of the two countries that the Sino-Burmese Boundary Treaty can be completed so soon; otherwise it would be impossible to complete it. The friendly relations are not of the ordinary kind, which cannot remain friendly for long. The friendly relations

---

* These are excerpts from Mao Zedong's talk with Burmese Prime Minister U Nu.

will last forever if they are established on the basis of the Five Principles.[98]

Mao: Very well said. Mutual non-injury—I don't injure you and you don't injure me. This is the negative side. The positive side is mutual benefit. For a period in the past the Sino-Burmese border was quite tense. Then we sent a general to inspect the border area, and he found it was unnecessary to have it so tense. Afterward, the situation got better. Troops from both sides stationed at the border retreated some distance. There is no reason to keep the situation tense, is there?

Nu: That's right. Chairman, you talked about it when we met last time.

Mao: It is highly unnecessary to make it tense. It is good the armies keep some distance—20-kilometer distance—from each side at the border. We have already reached an agreement with Nepal in this respect.

Zhou: It has already been brought to reality with Nepal.

Mao: There are difficulties to do the same with India. They feel it is not in their favor. Nepal does not fear, so the agreement was reached. There were misunderstandings when we suppressed bandits in Tibet, and we took the responsibility. We have already apologized and made compensation. Business is business. Right is right and wrong is wrong. Were any people killed at our border?

Zhou: There were one or two such incidents at the Sino-Burmese border, but they were resolved as civil disputes between border residents in a friendly way by the local governments from both sides.

Nu: It happened in Wa. Because there was a foundation of friendly relations, it did not develop into a serious incident. China suffered bigger losses, but China did not ask for compensation.

Mao: We have friendly relations. It was a conflict between border residents and not caused by leaders on both sides.

Nu: Border conflicts can be avoided. Chairman, you are right in saying that the armies on both sides should keep some distance; in addition, when education in strengthening friendly relations is carried out among border residents, things go along well. I believe China has done a very good job in this respect.

Mao: I heard that you are giving rice and salt to our one million border residents.

Zhou: They are to give us 2,000 tons of rice and 1,000 tons of salt. They have them ready for distribution to the border residents tomorrow.

Mao: It is a friendly gesture. How and what shall we give in return?

Zhou: We are to give 1.2 million Burmese border residents colorful cloth and porcelain. They will be distributed to the border residents at the time of exchanging of notes when we visit Rangoon on January 4 next year. Prime Minister U Nu has also invited Comrades Chen Yi[243] and Luo Ruiqing[244] and their wives.

Nu: They are welcome to participate in the celebration of the Independence Day on January 4 and I hope they can visit again at the Water Splashing Festival.

Mao: When is the Water Splashing Festival?

Nu: His Excellency Premier Zhou knows very well about the Water Splashing Festival.

Zhou: I joined in the Water Splashing Festival this year. Yesterday we three rode in an open vehicle and "splashed water" as well.

Nu: The chilly wind yesterday made our necks stiff.

Mao: The rainfall will do a lot of good to the planting of wheat.

Nu; I was very happy.

Mao: The past two years have had little rain and some drought, which is more serious this year than last year. I hope we can have a good harvest next year.

Nu: I share your feelings.

(From the verbatim record)

TALK WITH EDGAR SNOW ON TAIWAN AND OTHER QUESTIONS*

(*October 22, 1960*)

Edgar Snow (hereinafter referred to as Snow): On the question of Taiwan, Chairman, I wonder if you have read about a heated debate in the United States between John F. Kennedy[245] and Richard Nixon[246] on the questions of Mazu and Jinmen and American policy on the far east.

Chairman Mao Zedong (hereinafter referred to as Mao): I have read some.

Snow: The debate was so heated that the two names of Mazu and Jinmen often appeared in the newspapers so someone made a joke about it, saying the people had forgotten the two candidates' names, assuming they were called Mazu and Jinmen instead of Kennedy and Nixon.

Mao: It is because the Americans are afraid of war that they use this question for their election campaign. These two islands are very close to the mainland and Kennedy makes use of this point to win votes.

Snow: Nevertheless, it shows there is a great difference of opinion among the American public on this question. Usually people are indifferent about an election campaign, but this question has aroused great interest, for many Americans are against the current U.S. policy. So this is the real issue.

Mao: Nixon has his own idea, saying that these two islands must be protected. He also wants to get more votes. This question has given life to the American election campaign. Nixon has gone too far, as if the U.S. government had an obligation to protect the two islands. The U.S. State Department says that it has no obligation to do so. Whether to protect or not depends on the situation and is to be decided by the president under the circumstances at the time. This is the statement Eisenhower[103] made two years ago.

Snow: Someone asked this question: Under the American Constitution the new president will not take office until the January following his election in early November. If Kennedy is elected and China occupies Jinmen and Mazu

---

* These are excerpts from Mao Zedong's talk with Edgar Snow, an American writer and a friend to China.

on November 6 what's to be done then?

Mao: They asked the question in this way?

Snow: Eisenhower remains president until next January.

Mao: We do not look at the two islands that way. We have made public statements on the question, that is, let Chiang Kai-shek hold the two islands. We will not intercept their supplies. We can even send supplements if they do not have enough provisions. What we want is the whole Taiwan region. Taiwan and the Penghu Islands, including Jinmen and Mazu are all China's territory. As for the two islands, they are now in Chiang Kai-shek's hand; let him hold them. It seems that the American presidential candidates are not clear about this.

Snow: Quite possibly.

Mao: There isn't much to be debated on this question. We want not only the two islands, Jinmen and Mazu, but Taiwan and all the Penghu Islands. This question may annoy us for a long time. It has already been 11 years, and it is quite possible it will drag on for twice that many years or even longer, because the U.S. government is not willing to give up Taiwan. It does not want to give it up, and we do not attack it, so we have had negotiations,[201] first in Geneva, then in Warsaw. We shall not attack Taiwan while the U.S. is there. We want to solve the issue through negotiations rather than force. The U.S. government understands this. Nor shall we attack Jinmen and Mazu; we have stated this openly. Therefore, there is no danger of war and the United States may keep its occupation of Taiwan with its mind at ease. Eleven years have gone. After another 11 years and still another—that will be 33 years—maybe in the 32nd year the United States will give up Taiwan.

Snow: I think the Chairman wants to wait until Chiang Kai-shek's soldiers have become three-legged men.

Mao: It is mainly a question of the U.S. government, not of Chiang Kai-shek or others. If Chiang Kai-shek's men become three-legged, there will still be men with two legs in Taiwan. It is easy to find human beings.

Snow: Is the Chairman serious in thinking it will take 11 years or 22 years for the United States to change its stand? The American situation develops very fast and it will change very fast too. Of course the change has something to do with outside factors. All in all, there will be changes in the situation.

Mao: Maybe. In your article you mentioned one point: that we were more interested in becoming a member of the United Nations than in having the United States recognize China, as if we were more interested in getting into the United Nations. I do not see it that way and it cannot be said so. We instead of Chiang Kai-shek should represent China in the United Nations. It should have been that way long ago, but the U.S. government organized the majority of countries to block our entry. It does not mean there is no good in this. We are not eager to get into the United Nations. Some other countries are eager to have us admitted into the United Nations of course, excluding the United States. Now Britain has no choice but to follow the United States, but its original intention may be the one you talked about, that is, we shall be lawless if we are kept outside the United Nations, it would be better if we were bound by United Nations' rules. Quite a few countries hope China will observe the rules. You know we were guerrillas and accustomed to being unrestrained. It is hard to obey so many rules, isn't it? We shall not suffer any loss if we do not get into the United Nations. What are the good points if we get into the United Nations? Of course, there are some, but not necessarily many. Some countries strive for membership in the United Nations and we don't quite understand their mood. Our country is a united nation. One of our provinces is bigger than some countries.

Snow: I often say so.

Mao: They try to impose an economic blockade against us, just like what the Kuomintang did in the past. We were very grateful to the Kuomintang for setting up an economic blockade against us and making us find a way out by going in for production in our bases. The Kuomintang provided us with pay in 1937, 1938 and 1939, but started blockading us in 1940. We wanted to thank them for forcing us to go in for production and not rely on them. Now the United States has also imposed a blockade on us, which has some good aspects.

Snow: I remember that in 1939 the Chairman told me, "We thank the Kuomintang in eight respects. First, because the Communist Party developed too slowly, so the Kuomintang carried out an economic blockade to help us develop faster." Another respect was since the Communist troops had very few new recruits, Chiang Kai-shek put more people in prison, and so on and so forth. Later these points of the Chairman were proved correct. In fact, the more the people are oppressed, the faster the people's strength develops.

Mao: That is true.

Snow: In one of your articles you said that the law of imperialism is to oppose colonized people's efforts for freedom, to fail, to oppose again, to fail again. The blockade against China was certain to fail, but they have never given up this way of thinking. Now they are brooding over an economic blockade against Cuba. I think it will be a failure, too. It is very hard to comprehend what they want to gain from it. Anyway, it seems that they will impose an embargo against Cuba.

Mao: Now it is a partial embargo. It has no big influence on Cuba. It is possible that they will expand to a total embargo, which will have a bigger impact, but it is impossible for them to block Cuba to death. Cuba will find a way. The situation for Cuba today is after all better than our situation in Yan'an.

Snow: I want to ask another question. In ten to twenty years you will achieve your goal of industrialization. By then the world's economic foundation will have seen tremendous changes, as nuclear power and electronics are applied extensively. Of course by then, maybe earlier, China will have nuclear power. Some Americans think it will be far in the future when China develops nuclear power. However, they fear China will use it irresponsibly once it has the atom bomb.

Mao: No, we won't. How can an atom bomb be used irresponsibly? That won't do. We can't use it irresponsibly if we have it. To use it irresponsibly means committing a crime.

Snow: Even though there is no peace treaty or agreement between China and the U.S., and some Americans think that the United States and China are, in fact, in a semiwar situation, world peace every day relies on China's sense of responsibility, which is first for the Chinese people and then for the whole world, of which China is a part. Do you agree with me on this?

Mao: Right. We hold our responsibility for world peace no matter whether the United States recognizes us or not and no matter whether we are admitted by the United Nations or not. We shall not act in a lawless way like the Monkey King, who created havoc in the heavens, because we are not in the United Nations. We want to maintain world peace with no world war. We hold that problems between countries should not be settled by means of war. Anyway, the maintenance of world peace is not only China's responsibility, but also the United States'. Resolution of the Taiwan question is China's internal affair, which we always stick to. We shall not attack, even though it is so. Will we attack when the Americans are there? No, we won't. Will we attack for certain after the Americans leave? Not necessarily. We want to solve the Taiwan question by peaceful means. Many places in China were resolved by peaceful means. Beijing was liberated peacefully, so were Hunan, Yunnan and Xinjiang. There is hearsay outside China that the Chinese Communist Party, among the communist parties in various countries, is especially naughty, disobedient, unreasonable and reckless. You have been in China for a few months and those words cannot fully be trusted. You said that some outsiders say China is like a big barracks and a big prison. Indeed, it was so in Chiang Kai-shek's China. Then Beijing, Nanjing and Shanghai were indeed barracks.

Since liberation China, through reform and education, has become quite different from what it was.

Snow: I can surely say that my impression is that there are big differences now.

(From the verbatim record)

THE IMPACT OF THE STRUGGLE OF THE JAPANESE PEOPLE IS FAR-REACHING*

(January 24, 1961)

Chairman Mao Zedong (hereinafter referred to as Mao): You are going to stay more days in China, aren't you? I am happy whenever I meet with Japanese friends. We express our condolences over the tragedy of Mr. Asanuma Inejiro.[236]

Kuroda Hisao (hereinafter referred to as Kuroda): As head of the delegation of the Socialist Party, Asanuma Inejiro made a very good speech, declaring that U.S. imperialism was the common enemy of the Chinese and Japanese peoples. We shall carry on and carry forward Asanuma Inejiro's spirit.

Mao: Mr. Asanuma Inejiro grasped the essence of Japanese-U.S. relations as well as the essence of the issue of the various nations in Asia, Africa, Latin America, even in Europe and Canada in North America and that of China. The number of people who agree with this thesis varies from time to time, but with the passage of time, those who agree are bound to become the majority.

The United States does not have a way to establish its rule in various countries, so it must rely on its helpers, who are its allies, that is, the most reactionary handful of people of the country. In China it is those with Chiang Kai-shek as their chieftain. In your country it is Kishi Nobusuke[206] and his gang and the monopoly capitalist clique.

Kuroda: Last year in Japan there was a very big movement against the "Security Pact."[214] The government which represents the monopoly capitalists took the opposite stand. It opposed us and forcibly adopted the "Security Pact". At the same time, China held very big demonstrations in support of us, for which we feel grateful.

Mao: We support each other. In international struggles there is always mutual support. You are in the forefront.

When Asanuma Inejiro visited China in 1959, he mentioned that U.S.

---

* These are excerpts from Mao Zedong's talk with Kuroda Hisao, a Diet member from the Japanese Socialist Party.

imperialism is the common enemy of the Chinese and Japanese peoples. We should have confidence that the majority will agree with this when they understand it, even if not many agree with it for a certain period of time. In 1960, in just one year, Japan saw tremendous changes, and the anti-"Security-Pact" drive reached a momentum and developed into a popular struggle.

Relations between our two countries are abnormal and trade has stopped. When I met the delegation headed by Asanuma Inejiro in East Lake in Wuhan, I said that the severance of relations between China and Japan was temporary and there would be changes with the passage of time. We have already seen changes in trade, but not necessarily politically. Politically there are two sides to it. On the one hand, the Chinese and Japanese peoples have friendly relations as always, friendly relations developed after the Second World War. On the other hand, relations with the Liberal Democratic government and with the monopoly capitalists are not all right. They must wait. It is essential to differentiate between the protagonists of relations with the Japanese people and those with the Japanese government. With regard to relations with the Japanese government, it is necessary to differentiate between the protagonists of the so-called mainstream and those of the so-called anti-mainstream, who are not entirely the same. Matsumura Kenzo,[247] Miki Takeo,[248] Takasaki Tatsunosuke,[249] Kono Ichiro[250] and Ishibashi Tanzan[251] are our indirect allies. The Japanese people are our direct allies; similarly the Chinese people are the direct allies of the Japanese people. There are contradictions within the Liberal Democratic Party; the anti-mainstream is our indirect ally. Do you think there is something in what I said?

Kuroda: The anti-mainstream may be called an indirect alley if it understands China better and becomes a firmer opponent to the "Security Pact."

Mao: The same is true of relations between the United States and European countries. They are not in total consensus with the United States. People all over the world have raised their consciousness, mainly the Asian, African and Latin American peoples. Do you do any work in Africa and Latin America?

Kuroda: We have an Asia Solidarity Committee. With this organization as the center, activities are carried out to struggle against U.S. imperialism and support peace and the national independence movement of the Asian, African and Latin American peoples. We should like to further mobilize and strengthen the activities in the future.

Mao: This is highly necessary.

Kuroda: This year in Asia the main question is the Laos question. The Laotian people are striving for national liberation. The United States makes use of the Japan-U.S. "Security Pact" and Japanese military bases to interfere in Laos' internal affairs. Recently, trade unions, political parties, mass organizations and cultural organizations held a rally against the American use of Japanese military bases in interfering in Laos' internal affairs. They held demonstrations in front of the American Embassy, demanding the United States stop interfering, and they also demonstrated before the Japanese government, demanding it not allow the United States to use Japanese bases.

Mao: This is excellent.

Kuroda: Now the Japanese government is negotiating with the South Korean government to solve the Korean question, with the view of taking the South Korean government as the legitimate government of the whole of Korea. This impedes the peaceful reunification of Korea. The United States takes advantage of the Japan-South Korea talks to strengthen its military forces in South Korea, Taiwan and Japan and to strengthen the military alliance in Northeast Asia. The Japanese people who struggled against the Japan-U.S. "Security Pact" are struggling against the negotiations between Japan and South Korea.

Mao: It is highly necessary to oppose them.

Recently, the Philippines, Taiwan, South Korea and South Vietnam, which have relations with the United States, held "foreign minister talks." The Japanese government, for fear of the Japanese people, did not participate. Therefore, the Japanese people's struggle last year made the Japanese government apprehensive. The Japanese people's struggle has far-reaching influence.

It seems the Japanese people are now between the first and the second high tide against U.S. imperialism. The struggle, at low ebb for the time being, brooding over a second high tide, makes wavelike progress. You know, our Chinese struggle in the past scores of years developed like waves advancing rather than in a straight line every day, every month and every year. So the people's movement you are leading has a bright future. But some people, pessimistic, complain that the movement may get nowhere and some may reproach you Leftists for having led a wrong struggle. At this moment we say the Left should hold out tenaciously. For instance, before the 1911 Revolution the military uprising in April 1911, led by Huang Xing,[252] suffered defeat and all the martyrs were buried in Huanghuagang. After the defeat Huang Xing fled to Hong Kong, feeling he had failed and it would not work; he felt hopeless. Unexpectedly, the 1911 Revolution took place before long and the Qing Dynasty was overthrown. After the defeat of the Russian Revolution in 1905, most of the Social Democratic Labor Party were pessimistic, and the "Creating-God Faction"[253] came into being, Anatoly Lunacharsky for one.

They were all idealists. Lenin wrote *Materialism and Empirio-Criticism*, a philosophical book, to criticize them. Twelve years later the Russian Revolution succeeded, and Lunacharsky became the minister of education in Lenin's government, so he no longer wanted to create God. I think you may find such cases in your history.

Why is it the revolution in your country has not succeeded? It seems that victory may come quite late in countries where capitalism is quite developed. Revolution will first succeed in countries where capitalism is less developed, because the air there is thin and it is easy to break through. Russia and China are cases in point. Africa is another case in point. The monopoly capitalism in Japan is frail compared with that in the seven or eight capitalist powers, such as the United States, Britain, France, Germany and Italy, because, first, Japan was defeated and, second, it is under the control of the United States.

In a sense, these two aspects are advantageous to the Japanese people, I think.

First, the defeat and the loss of all the colonies are in Japan's favor. The Japanese people and revolutionary political parties should understand that the defeat is not a shame. It is a shame for monopoly capitalism, but a victory for the people. You should start a debate on whether being defeated is good or a shame. Some people do not think about it that way, feeling they lost face with the defeat and are guilty of evil doings. This is because they have not differentiated between monopoly capitalism and the people, so they have come to that conclusion. The monopoly capitalist and militarist government instead of the Japanese people should be held accountable for the war in the past. Why should the Japanese people hold the responsibility? If the people are to hold the responsibility, then everybody will oppose the Japanese people. How terrible! In fact, the Japanese militarist government threatened, deceived and forced the Japanese people to become its cannon fodder.

Second, it is necessary to analyze being dominated by the United States. I think the people of a nation will not become conscious without oppression from outside. Now Japan is being oppressed by the monopoly capitalists of Japan as much as by the United States, its ally. This has educated the Japanese people and united them. It has forced the Japanese people to choose between becoming slaves of the U.S. imperialists and monopoly capitalists and rising to strive for independence and freedom. I said long ago that I did not believe a great nation such as Japan would be bullied for long, but it is possible to be suppressed for a short period. Our people were also educated by enemies at home and from abroad, including Japanese militarists. When Minamigo Saburo[254] came from Japan to see me, he first said Japan had invaded China, for which he felt sorry. I told him we did not see it that way. Indeed, Japanese warlords occupied the greater part of China, thus educating the Chinese people; otherwise, the Chinese people could not become conscious or get united. We would still be in the mountains and would not be able to come into Beijing to watch Beijing opera. It was just because the Japanese "imperial army" occupied the greater part of China that the Chinese people were left no way out but to get awakened and armed for struggle and to establish anti-aggressor bases, thus creating conditions for the victory of the Liberation War. So the Japanese warlords and monopoly capitalists did a good thing. I would rather "thank" the Japanese warlords if asked to say "thanks." A great nation like Japan should be independent and have its sovereignty. Japan is more advanced than China in economy and education. Okayama County is said to have seven colleges. Wuxi, in China, has a high education level, but does not have as many as seven colleges. We do not have any county like the Japanese one. It will take quite some time for China to catch up with Japan.

Japan, with a Diet, is a bourgeois democracy. This is your good point and shortcoming as well. China did not have democracy. The Kuomintang arrested and killed people, offering us nothing. It was perhaps a shortcoming or a strong point. Then, what was the way out for us? It lay in learning from Chiang Kai-shek. They could kill, so why couldn't we? After study we learned that the Kuomintang had hands holding guns and swords, while we had hands holding neither guns nor swords. If we could seize weapons from the Kuomintang, we could kill the imperialist running dogs and achieve something, couldn't we?

But you are in a different situation, with a Diet system and some relative democracy. You may make use of it to start a mass movement, since it is not like the Kuomintang, arresting and killing people. I do not know much about your country. Perhaps the Japanese monopoly capitalists are smarter than the Chinese compradors. It seems that you may take advantage of this. They are afraid of the rising up of the common people. For instance, the government could not forbid many Japanese friends from visiting China. Nor could it forbid Chinese people from going to Japan. They could set restrictions, however, because the Japanese government has diplomatic relations with Chiang Kai-shek; in addition, they fear the Communist Party. Takasaki Tatsunosuke has invited Comrade Liao Chengzhi[207] to visit Japan. Comrade Liao Chengzhi, when will you go?

Liao Chengzhi: It's not decided yet.

Mao: Recently, a trade union delegation visited Japan. Nongovernmental exchanges are very good for enhancing mutual understanding and exchanging views and experiences. Contracts of nongovernmental trade have been signed with some big transactions. We have coal, salt, iron ore and soybeans to trade with Japan. China and Japan are close neighbors, so the transportation costs are cheap.

Kuroda: I totally agree. This year will see more and more nongovernmental exchanges.

No matter what the Ikeda[255] administration feels, exchanges between the Chinese and Japanese peoples will increase, the friendly relations will deepen, and a friendship treaty will certainly be signed.

Mao: Very good. There is a bright future.

Kuroda: Our coming to China at the beginning of the year is also for friendship between the two peoples. We have heard a lot of beneficial remarks from our Chinese friends and seen the development of China's socialist construction, which is very helpful to us. We should like to express our thanks and wish the Chairman good health.

Mao: Please give my regards to friends in the Japanese Socialist Party, both those I know and those I do not know.

(From the verbatim record)

AFRICA IS THE FOREFRONT OF STRUGGLE*

(April 27, 1961)

Africa is the forefront of struggle. Some places in Asia, for instance, the Arab countries, are also the forefront of struggle. Take another example, the contradictions between Indonesia and imperialism are not solved yet. A very acute struggle goes on in Laos, which is near Vietnam. So is the struggle in South Vietnam. A mass movement has also been going on in South Korea recently. All these struggles are against imperialism and its running dogs. Furthermore, there was a large-scale mass struggle in Japan last year. Eisenhower[103] had wished to visit Japan, but could not do so, as the Japanese people closed the door to him. At that time we welcomed him by shelling in the Taiwan Straits. The day he arrived in Taiwan, our guns fired the whole day. The reason the Taiwan issue remains unsolved is that the United States has occupied Taiwan. So our country is also in struggle. U.S. imperialism has made trouble everywhere. However, in your Africa it is mainly British, French, Portuguese, Belgian and Dutch imperialism making trouble. As for Latin America, I met a Cuban cultural delegation recently, on the 19th of this month. We did not know then it was the very day Cuba wiped out invaders. Have you heard this news? Cuba has won a battle. Latin America has a population of 200 million. The population of your Africa is also 200 million. The Arab countries have among them a population of 80 million. We should all unite. I have heard that at the current Bandung Conference of the Council for Asian-African Unity[256] the unity of Asia and Africa will be expanded to the unity of Asia, Africa and Latin America.

It is possible for revolution to be successful. Among those countries that did not win victory in the past, has Guinea not won victory already? There are more countries in Africa that have won victory. For instance, the United Arab Republic[196] used to be British territory, and it has won independence, too. In Asia, Indonesia used to be Holland's colony; it has won independence.

---

* This is Mao Zedong's talk with guests from Guinea, Jordan, South Africa, Senegal, Northern Rhodesia (present-day Zambia), Uganda and Kenya.

China used to be a semi-colony of all the imperialist powers. It has become independent, except for Taiwan, which is not liberated yet. The population of Taiwan is only nine million, whereas the entire population of the liberated areas in China is more than 600 million. In another instance Cuba has won independence. It is very worthwhile to study the conditions of Cuba. It is so close to the United States, only 180 kilometers away. It has been independent for over two years, and all the people of the country are truly mobilized to drive away U.S. imperialism and its running dogs. Our country is yet another instance. In the Chinese revolution the armed struggle against imperialism and its running dogs took 22 years.

China underwent all kinds of hardships and difficulties. Only by going through victory, defeat and again victory, through such twists and turns, did we win final victory. Contributing to our defeats were policy mistakes. Our Party once committed Right opportunist mistakes, leading to the defeat of the First Great Revolution, that is the defeat of the Northern Expedition in cooperation with Chiang Kai-shek. After criticizing the Right opportunist mistakes, we carried out armed struggle. However, during the struggle we committed "Left" opportunist mistakes, what we called dogmatic mistakes. Later we criticized such mistakes. Without those mistakes and their correction we could not have found the right path to victory. These lessons do not belong only to us; as international experience they can be studied and taken for reference by all our friends in their struggle against imperialism and its running dogs. It is a bad thing to make mistakes, but it is of benefit, too. It is just like when people become sick, some germs give them immunity, such as in pulmonary tuberculosis. Once one suffers from TB, one will not suffer from it anymore. Typhoid is also like this. Once you get it, you will never have it again. Only because we committed Right and "Left" opportunist mistakes was it possible for our Party and people to find the right line.

Our understanding of conditions in Africa, taking myself as an example, is less than sufficient. We should set up an institute of African studies to conduct research on the history, geography and socio-economic conditions of the continent. As we do not know much about African history, geography and current conditions, it is highly necessary to publish a simple and concise book, which should not be too heavy. One or two hundred pages will do. It is advisable to ask our African friends for help. The book should come out in one year or two. Its content should include how imperialism arrived there, how it oppressed the local people, how it encountered their resistance, how the resistance failed and how the people have risen up again.

Imperialism has created conditions for the struggle of the African people, created conditions for them to bury imperialism. It has created conditions for them to become independent and self-reliant, for it has given rise to the working class and trade union movement among the African people, and it has, out of its own interest, brought education to part of the African people, who have become intellectuals. It seems to me that all of you are such people. Imperialism and its running dogs set up schools for you with the original intention to train intellectuals who would serve their interests. Later some of those people turned to the side of revolution, and a split occurred. In China some of the intellectuals brought up by imperialism and its running dogs followed them, some became advanced elements against imperialism and its running dogs, and still others were middle-of-the-roaders. It was imperialism that forced us onto the road to struggle against it. Imperialism has helped you command the instrument of language. Some of you speak English; others, French, both being main languages. These languages have become common in the colonies. Perhaps you could not have communicated with one another with the different languages native to Africa, but now you can do so by using English and French. Using English and French, people unite against British and French imperialism. This is life: Imperialism has educated its opponents. When we were students, we were not conscious of this. For instance, when China resisted Japanese aggression, many of those who had studied in Japan took part in the War of Resistance Against Japan. Many of the generals had been trained in Japanese military academies. There were others who were not generals, but cultural and political workers. Comrade Liao Chengzhi,[207] for one, speaks Japanese very well. Now the conditions of Japan have changed. As a defeated country, it has been dominated by the United States.

As I said just now, it is possible for the revolution to be brought to fruition. I have raised the examples of Guinea, Cuba, and China to illustrate that the revolution should rely on the masses and win their support. Only by doing so can there be a correct line and can victory be attained. The Democratic Party of Guinea is a party linked to the masses. President Touré is a leader linked to the masses. It will take time for the people to be politically awakened. Their awakening will not occur overnight. It should come through their own experience, from which they draw lessons. That is the way to make progress. As long as there is a core of leadership, like the Democratic Party of Guinea and other revolutionary parties, serving as a core of unity and propagation, the political awareness of the masses of the people will improve step by step.

The political awareness of the people of Asia, Africa and Latin America is on the rise. They have gradually gained a clear understanding of U.S.

imperialism. Just a few years ago their understanding of U.S. imperialism was less than adequate. Now they have gradually gained a good understanding. The United States says that it is not imperialistic on the ground that it possesses no colonies. It somehow seems plausible. True, it has no colony, which can be used to deceive people. However, its virtual colonies go far beyond those of Britain or France. They may as well be termed as semicolonies. For example, it uses the Pan American Union[257] to dominate Latin America and uses military organizations, such as the NATO bloc,[189] the Central Treaty Organization[190] and the Southeast Asia Treaty Organization,[96] to control the broad land masses of Europe and Asia. Now it is using the United Nations to organize aggression against Africa, for example, in the Congo.[258]

Our struggle enjoys your support and your struggle, ours. We support the struggles of all the peoples in the world, including yours, and unite with all friends who are struggling against imperialism and its running dogs, regardless of country or political party.

(From the verbatim record)

CHINA CAN HAVE ONLY ONE REPRESENTATIVE IN THE UNITED NATIONS*

(June 13, 1961)

Chairman Mao Zedong (hereinafter referred to as Mao): When the President came last time, I said that we would not join the United Nations, because Chiang Kai-shek's representative was in it. This has something to do with the Taiwan question. So long as Chiang Kai-shek's representative is in the United Nations, we will not enter it. We have been waiting for 11 years and it does not matter if we wait for another 11 years or longer. We are not eager to enter the United Nations. You do not have a U.N. question, but a West Irian[152] question, which is different from ours.

President Sukarno (hereinafter referred to as Sukarno): At present there are two positions on the question of China's entering the United Nations. One proposes that the Chinese mainland and Taiwan merge and enter the United Nations as one country, and the other proposes that China enter the United Nations first and then struggle with friends in the U.N. to drive out Chiang Kai-shek's representative in the U.N. and make Taiwan return to China. Not long ago, when I talked with Marshal Chen Yi,[243] I told him about the two positions and explained that it was not Indonesia's stand. Anyway, Marshal Chen Yi explicitly expressed that only the former was acceptable; China would like to do it in one step instead of two.

Mao: Only in one step.

Sukarno: I should like to give very good assistance in the struggle to realize your one-step idea.

Mao: If Taiwan is handed back to China, China will join the United Nations. If Taiwan is not considered a country and does not have a central government and is returned to China, the question of its social system may wait for talks in the future. We shall allow Taiwan to keep its social system, which will be decided by the people in Taiwan.

---

* These are excerpts from Mao Zedong's talk with President Sukarno of Indonesia.

Sukarno: Is it like the way the Soviet Union and Ukraine are in the United Nations?

Mao: Not the same.

Sukarno: I did not mean the social system, but whether it could be the same as the Soviet Union and Ukraine having two representatives in the United Nations.

Mao: No. China can have only one representative in the United Nations. Ukraine and Belorussia having representatives in the U.N. has a historical background. After the Second World War Ukraine and Belorussia entered the U.N. and the Soviet Union was also in the U.N. That is how the Soviet Union has three seats in the United Nations. At that time the Soviet Union ran into many difficulties and it had to do so. Nevertheless, there was no question of two Soviet Unions.

(From the verbatim record)

ON THE TWO POSSIBILITIES OF A WORLD WAR*

(August 19, 1961)

On the international situation, our views are identical to those expressed in the Declaration of the Conference of 81 Communist and Workers Parties.[259] It is less than a year since the Moscow meeting, held last November. As to whether a world war will break out or not, the declaration has given an answer, namely, that it is possible for a world war to break out, and it is also possible for it not to break out. There are only these two possibilities. You may say that the question remains unanswered, since it is still uncertain if a war will break out or not. The question rests in: according to the socialist bloc, the Communist Parties and the working people of various countries, war will not break out. The forces of the socialist bloc, the Communist Parties and the working people of various countries are very strong now, and capitalism is also afraid of dying. Therefore it is possible for war not to break out. However, according to imperialism and its running dogs in various countries, war will break out. So we should be on our guard. If we tell people every day war will not break out and everyone falls asleep, what can be done in case war breaks out one morning? We'd rather say that imperialism wants to launch a war and the people should be prepared to deal with it. That is to say, prepare for the worst. If we are prepared, we may avert war. Imperialism opposes us, and it would be very dangerous if we all went to sleep. Cuba is now ever ready. Though the United States has not attacked Cuba directly, it has organized its running dogs to land there. The direct involvement of U.S. imperialism in an attack against Cuba has not happened yet, but over there they are prepared for it.

(From the verbatim record)

---

* These are excerpts from Mao Zedong's talk with a visiting group of cadres from Brazil's Communist Party and a cadre study group.

TALKS WITH MARSHAL MONTGOMERY ON THE THREE PRINCIPLES AND THE QUESTION OF NUCLEAR WEAPONS*

(September 1961)

The Three Principles Are Well Put

(September 23, 1961)

Marshal Montgomery (hereinafter referred to as Montgomery): I should like to talk to the Chairman about the three principles,[260] which I mentioned briefly before. This time I put them forward as a package. For years I can say that I have been in the front row to observe international politics. I worked in the defense institutions of the West. I think that the West has trapped itself in a quagmire, and political leaders in the West seem to find no way to get out of it. My conclusion is that the West totally lacks common knowledge on the questions of Germany and China.

Chairman Mao Zedong (hereinafter referred to as Mao): Not all the West. It is only the United States that lacks common knowledge.

Montgomery: Some others as well.

Mao: They follow the United States.

Montgomery: People in the West cry out more and more for a peaceful world. There will not be a peaceful world unless all the countries withdraw their armed forces and go back to their home countries. Chairman, have you read my speech at the banquet given by Premier Zhou last night?

Mao: Yes, I have.

Montgomery: What do you think of my package of the three principles?

Mao: It is more formidable to put them in one package than to separate

---

* These are excerpts from two talks of Mao Zedong's with British Field Marshal Montgomery.

them; people of various countries can understand them better. Many may oppose them, but more people will welcome them. If they are advanced time and again, once, twice, three times, ten times, 20 times, they will produce effects in the end. You said that you would like to live 100 years, didn't you? You have more than 20 years to live. There is hope to see the problem solved before you go to see God. The three principles are well and correctly put forward.

Montgomery: I want to mobilize world opinion. After my departure from China I am preparing to go to Canada next week and make a television speech in Toronto on October 6.

Mao: That's good.

Montgomery: Afterwards I shall return to London. I shall make another television speech on the evening of October 16.

Mao: Speak up whenever there is the chance.

Montgomery: If the Eastern bloc, at that time, says about my three principles, "Right, we agree; it is a very good suggestion," and if China and Moscow voice the same, it will be a great help. China does not have troops overseas, but the Soviet Union does. If Khrushchev[146] also says, "So long as the United States, Britain and France withdraw their troops from Europe and Germany, I shall bring our troops back to the Soviet Union"—if he says that, it couldn't be better. He has never said this categorically.

Mao: He has said so.

Montgomery: I mean he has never "categorically" said so.

Mao: He agrees with one China, two Germanys and the withdrawal of troops.

Montgomery: I have suggested to Marshal Chen Yi[243] that he talk with Gromyko[261] in the hope that both the Soviet Union and China strongly support my three principles.

Mao: Are you going to the Soviet Union?

Montgomery: I cannot go now.

Mao: If not this year, then next year. If you go there to talk about the three principles, it will give them an opportunity to support you.

Montgomery: I have the idea that when you want to make something happen, you should never make the mistake of offending many people at the same time. I have offended some people by proposing the three principles in China this time. If I go to the Soviet Union, I shall offend more people. That's why I won't go. Chen Yi and Gromyko have been asked to speak about them in the Orient, while I shall dwell on them in Canada and London.

Mao: Have you talked about this with Chen Yi?

Montgomery: Yes, I have.

Mao: Then, it is all right.

Montgomery: I may push it in the West, but I don't want to play a big role in the East. Moscow is in the East, so I do not want to go there. I have a very strong position in my country. If I travel too much in the Communist East, the British people will ask what has come over this chap. It will impair my position. If I want to push this matter, I must keep my position.

Mao: Your position is unshakable. Your basic thought is for peace.

Montgomery: The people will follow me. They will agree with my proposition, though many people in the West disagree with your ideology.

Mao: If they disagree, then, they just don't believe in it.

Montgomery: That's right. I stand for noninterference in each others' internal affairs. Whenever Western countries run into problems, their practice is to divide one country into two. Korea, for example, and Laos and Indochina. They feel that all the problems are solved when a country is divided into two. I do not think that is right and I shall say that every country should withdraw its troops and the Koreans should decide what they want and what they do not want.

Mao: That's right.

Montgomery: This is the only reasonable way.

Nuclear Weapons Are to Scare People, Not to Use

(September 24, 1961)

Montgomery: Now people are discussing the question of nuclear weapons, with many an argument. I have talked with President Liu Shaoqi about China's nuclear policy. Chairman, what's your view on the question?

Mao: I am not interested in nuclear weapons. They are not something to use. The more there are, the harder it will be for nuclear wars to break out. If a war breaks out, it will be a war of conventional weapons. If conventional weapons are used, the arts of war, such as strategies and tactics, can be emphasized, and commanders can change plans to suit the situation. If it is a nuclear war, it will just be a matter of pressing buttons, and the war will be over after a few presses.

Montgomery: President Liu told me that you also want to make some nuclear weapons, because the United States, Britain, France and the Soviet

Union have them.

Mao: Yes, we are preparing to make some, but I do not know when we shall succeed. The United States has so many; it has ten fingers. Even if we succeed in making one, we shall still have just one finger. It is something to scare people, absorbing a lot of money but useless.

Montgomery: I am also thinking that perhaps you put the development of nuclear weapons among the last of your various undertakings.

Mao: That's right. We spend very little money on it. We do not have a solid economic base, with industry just beginning. The United States, Britain, France and the Soviet Union have powerful industrial bases. We are like a poor man or a beggar who walks out in a beautiful suit.

Montgomery: My view is that it is nuclear weapons that prevent the breakout of a third world war.

Mao: I have said that the atom bomb is a paper tiger.

Montgomery: Now many British people are demonstrating to demand the prohibition and destruction of nuclear weapons. I told them, first, withdrawal of troops; second, disarmament; finally, the destruction of nuclear weapons.

Mao: Can an agreement be reached, just as chemical weapons were forbidden during the Second World War, so nobody used chemical weapons? Nobody uses nuclear weapons?

Montgomery: It won't work now. In the first place, the suspicion and distrust between East and West must be got rid of. Hence, it is necessary to return troops to their home countries. That is why I have found no time to visit Japan; I must first work for the realization of my three principles.

Mao: All right. Nuclear weapons are to be prohibited after the realization of the three principles.

Montgomery: I have talked with Marshal Chen Yi and I hope he will talk to the Soviet Union, requesting them to support my three principles.

Mao: He will go to Geneva to participate in the conference on the Laos question.[262] He may meet Gromyko and find a chance to talk about it. I am for it.

(From the verbatim record)

TALK WITH NEPAL'S KING MAHENDRA AND THE QUEEN

(*October 5, 1961*)

Chairman Mao Zedong (hereinafter referred to as Mao): How is everything with Your Excellency? Have all the problems been solved?

Mahendra Bir Bikram Shah Deva (hereinafter referred to as Mahendra): Everything is settled.

Mao: Fair and reasonable?

Mahendra: Yes. We all agree.

Mao: It is good that we agree. There is goodwill on both sides. We hope that you will get along well, and you hope we shall get along well too. We do not want to harm you, nor do you want to harm us.

Mahendra: We fully understand.

Mao: We are equals; we cannot say one country is superior or inferior to the other.

Mahendra: We very much appreciate that way of speaking.

Mao: One ought not to treat other countries unequally. We call it great-nation chauvinism. We educate our Party members and the people not to commit the mistake of great-nation chauvinism. Sometimes there are still problems, such as some cadres treating others with a superior attitude. We have carried out education among them and taken disciplinary measures, so as to help them overcome their shortcomings. Our country is a mixture of all sorts of things: old and new, backward and advanced.

Mahendra: China is a vast country.

Mao: Many traces of backwardness can still be found. Take agriculture, for example. It is a backward sector with very few tractors; mechanization will take quite a few years. The handicraft industry is the main one. We are beginning to have a little modern industry, not much yet. The old society left us too little 12 years ago. In fact, imperialism dominated us for over 100 years and took things away without construction. Take iron and steel, for example. From the Qing Dynasty to the defeat of Chiang Kai-shek the annual output of steel during this period was only 40,000 tons in Chiang Kai-shek's areas. One may say we did not have iron and steel, nor did we have a machine-building industry, nor any geological work. At that time we had just over 200 geological workers, but now we have more than 100,000. It is not easy to discover underground treasures, and at present we do not know what minerals we have. We have to drill wells as deep as one kilometer, two or three kilometers or even deeper, which is beyond any handicraft industry. It needs drilling machines and trained technicians. Oil drilling is just like this; otherwise, we shall have to rely on imported oil. It is the same with things such as coal, iron and nonferrous metals. So we shall develop agriculture and animal husbandry to solve the problem of food and clothing and also go in for heavy industry. Without heavy industry there won't be any steel or machines. It won't do. Your country has a big area.

Mahendra: About 140,000 square kilometers.

Mao: And the population is not small.

Mahendra: About nine million.

Mao: More than that of Australia. I hope you will do a good job in your construction and get richer and stronger every day.

Mahendra: We are making efforts in our development and seeking aid from friendly countries such as China. I hope to talk with Premier Zhou Enlai on our trip.

Mao: Good. Have another talk. With time your country will get along well. Everything in the world develops from nothing to something, from few to many. You are hopeful and your future is bright, but it takes time. You will be more hopeful in a few decades. Our country is still a poor country, but we shall fare better in at least several decades. Marshal Montgomery[263] said that it would take 50 years. I said that it would take 50 to 100 years. A century is not long. It took some ages for Europe and America to develop to today's level. It will be good if it takes China a century to surpass them.

(From the verbatim record)

THE JAPANESE PEOPLE HAVE A BRIGHT FUTURE*

(*October 7, 1961*)

I welcome you very warmly. In Japan, with the exception of the pro-American monopoly capitalists and militarist warlords, all the people are our true friends. You may see for yourselves that the Chinese people are your true friends, for friends may be true or false. However, through practice people can see clearly who are true friends and who are false ones. Some people cannot understand how the Chinese and Japanese can be so close, since they had a war in the past. They do not know that the Japanese people are different from the monopoly capitalists and militarist warlords.

At present, both of us are under oppression. We do not have the right to speak internationally. The government of Japan has joined the United Nations, but we have not. U.S. imperialism has occupied your territory of Okinawa and set up military bases in the country proper. Your country is under semioccupation. Our Taiwan is under the domination of U.S. imperialism. U.S. imperialism has forced the people of our two countries to unite. Both our peoples are under the oppression of U.S. imperialism. We have a common fate and that is why we are united.

It gave me great pleasure to learn that you had arrived in Beijing. Here, on our soil, we greet you with a warm welcome. However, back on your soil, things are different. The responsibility for it does not rest with you, but with the friends of the United States in Japan, namely, the clique of Japanese monopoly capitalists. In China there are also people who are against you, that is, the Chiang Kai-shek clique. An old Chinese proverb goes that things of a kind come together, people of a mind fall into the same group. Kishi Nobusuke[206] and Ikeda Hayato[255] are good friends of U.S. imperialism and the Chiang Kai-shek clique. The Japanese and Chinese peoples are good friends. We should enlarge the scope of such unity and unite with the exception of

---

* This is Mao Zedong's talk with delegations from the Japan-China Friendship Association and Japanese nongovernmental educators.

imperialists and reactionaries in various countries over 90 percent of the people of Asia, Africa, Latin America and the world as a whole. We should actively work on them and on all countries where circumstances permit. We desire that you do the same. If the population of the world is 2.7 billion, then ten percent of it will be 270 million. The remaining 2.43 billion people should be united. All this is known to you, and to say it does not mean that I am brighter than you.

We should work on the people, because not all the 2.4 to 2.5 billion people have political awareness, which rises only step by step. For example, it took time for the people of your country to get awakened politically. Last year the Japanese people set off a major upsurge against U.S. imperialism and the monopoly capitalists. This year the struggle has been on the ebb, which is understandable. One should not be pessimistic about this. High tide, low tide, high tide again and then low tide again, it moves forward like waves. It seems to be low tide, but in fact high tide is in the making. Although there are twists and turns on the road forward, the Japanese people have a bright future. The Chinese revolution went through countless twists and turns. Victory, defeat, victory again and then defeat again; but the final victory belongs to the people. There is hope for the Japanese people.

It is rather strange that in the beginning the people do not have arms. The Chinese people were also unarmed in the past, but they ended up in victory. Originally, I was a school teacher and had no idea that there was a Communist Party in the world, even less thought of joining the Party. Later, oppression left us no alternative but to found the Chinese Communist Party. In 1921 there were only scores of Party members and 12 deputies to the First National Congress of the Communist Party of China.[264] Everybody looked down on us then, saying that the Communist Party was boasting and should never be taken seriously. Among the 12 deputies, some degenerated later. For example, Chen Gongbo[265] and Zhou Fohai[266] turned out to be traitors to China. Zhou Fohai was a returned student from Japan. Another became a Trotskyite. He is now in Beijing, and his name is Liu Renjing.[267] He met Trotsky,[268] who had been driven out of the Soviet Union, in Turkey. Yet another was Zhang Guotao,[269] who turned traitor to the Party. He is now in Hong Kong. Several others laid down their lives. Now the survivors are only Vice-Chairman Dong Biwu, myself, and Li Da.[270] In 1921 there were very few Party members, but the key points were whether we could unite the people and whether we had the correct political line or not.

When you study the experience of the Chinese revolution, I advise you to look at the failures; of course you will look at the successes, too, so that you will be able to compare. Besides studying China's correct political line, principles, policies and military line, you should definitely study the mistakes of "Left" and Right deviation committed in the Chinese revolution.

Among those present here are historians, educators and writers, some scholars specializing in Chinese history. I hope you will study the twists and turns in the course of Chinese history.

You have come to China, for which we thank you, as do all the Chinese people. I have nothing to present to you except a poem by Lu Xun in my own handwriting. In China's dark age Lu Xun was a great revolutionary fighter and a leader on the literary front. This poem is in the old style, which has four lines. The poem goes: "The inky faces of ten thousand people are buried in wormwood,/ And I dare to sing a song of the sorrow that shocks the earth./ My heart reaches far into the universe,/ And I hear surprising thunder where it is quiet." Lu Xun wrote the poem in the darkest years in China before the dawn, indicating he saw light beyond the rule of complete darkness. It is difficult to translate a poem. You may ask Guo Moruo[271] to do it for you. If you concur, we shall conclude our meeting now. I send my regards to the Japanese people.

(From the verbatim record)

THE COUNTRIES IN THE INTERMEDIATE ZONE VARY IN NATURE*

(January 3, 1962)

I thank Japanese friends and all friends who are struggling against the oppression and exploitation of imperialism and its agents, for your struggle is ours, too. We are in the same position. U.S. imperialism pushes the Japanese around and pushes the Chinese around. It can be said that most of the people in the world are oppressed and pushed around by U.S. imperialism. As for our two countries and some neighboring countries, our Taiwan is dominated by the United States, whose Seventh Fleet is stationed there. In your Japan there are many military bases controlled by the United States, which has naval ports, air bases and even bases for the Marine Corps. In addition, South Korea, South Vietnam, Laos and Thailand are all dominated by the United States. Even Britain and France are pushed around by the United States.

The people do not trust the running dogs of the United States. All running dogs of the United States come to no good ends. In Latin America there are quite a few running dogs of the United States, but the people do not trust them. For example, Batista[221] as everyone knows, the people did not trust him and drove him away. The circumstances of South Korea are also worth looking into. The people did not trust Syngman Rhee,[85] and the United States had to remove him. Now they have put up a new replacement in the person of Park Chung Hee.[272] Park Chung Hee and company are dissatisfied with the United States, too. The 700,000 South Korean troops had been under the command of the United States. Now Park Chung Hee and company have managed to get more than 100,000 free from the command of the United States and put them under their own command. The United States was forced to make such a concession. Control by the United States is very tight, and their troops are under the command of the United States as well; and they are not happy about this situation. In Taiwan the United States attempted to nurture an opposition

---

* These are excerpts from Mao Zedong's talk with Yasui Kaoru, chief director of the Japan Council Against A & H Bombs.

to Chiang Kai-shek, headed by Hu Shi,[58] which was suppressed by Chiang Kai-shek. Chiang Kai-shek put his troops under his own command and the U.S. Military Advisory Group are not allowed to go below regiment level. They are allowed to conduct activities only at levels above it. Chiang Kai-shek does not allow the U.S. Army to land in Taiwan and he tells the United States it is sufficient to send the Seventh Fleet and Air Force. "I have my army, so why should you send over your army?" he says. Ngo Dinh Diem[136] is jittery, too. He allows the United States to send over only a military advisory group, not troops. Chiang Kai-shek and Ngo Dinh Diem are constantly in touch. Chiang Kai-shek says to Ngo Dinh Diem, "You should never allow the U.S. Army into your country. If you do, you will be done for." Sarit[273] of Thailand does not allow the United States to station troops in his country, either. Thailand is a member state of the Southeast Asia Treaty Organization.[96] The United States wants to set up military bases there, but Thailand does not allow it to do so. There are contradictions even between them and the United States. Because of their association with the United States, they stink and the people therefore no longer trust them. When the United States sees that the people have no trust in people like Syngman Rhee, it has to replace them. Such are the circumstances.

To a large extent, the position of West Germany is similar to that of Japan. However, the West German people have not come up with a strong trend against the United States and imperialism and for democracy and peace like that of the Japanese people. The monopoly capitalists of West Germany want to collaborate with the United States and resist it at the same time, which is similar to Japan. We call these places the intermediate zone. The socialist bloc can be counted as one side, and the United States, the other. Everything in between can be counted as part of the intermediate zone. However, countries in the intermediate zone are different in nature: countries like Britain, France, Belgium and the Netherlands possess colonies. Other countries have been deprived of colonies, but have strong monopoly capital, such as West Germany and Japan. Some countries have gained genuine independence, such as Guinea, the United Arab Republic,[196] Mali and Ghana. Other countries are independent in name, but dependent in fact. The countries of the intermediate zone are varied in kind and different in nature, but the United States wants to swallow them all up.

U.S. imperialism and its running dogs are the oppressors, exploiters and bullies. The running dogs of the United States in China, Japan and various countries and the United States together form one side of the contradiction, the other side being people the world over, including the working class, peasants, urban petty bourgeoisie, revolutionary national bourgeoisie and revolutionary intellectuals. Britain and France are imperialists, but they are medium-size imperialist countries which the big imperialist power, the United States, wants to eat up; so there are contradictions between them and the United States. They have a hard time too. As such, they may serve as indirect allies of the people. In Japan Matsumura Kenzo,[247] Ishibashi Tanzan[251] and Takasake Tatsunosuke[249] are not too happy with the United States. They are different from Ikeda Hayato[255] and can be taken as indirect allies of the people.

For the Algerian people, French imperialism is not an ally but an opponent, an oppressor that lords it over the Algerian people. It has 600,000 troops at war against the Algerian people. To Africa, Britain, France, Belgium and Portugal are no friends. One advantage is that there are contradictions between them and the United States. In Africa and Asia there are colonies of Britain and France or countries dependent on them, and even in the formally independent countries they retain strong investments. The United States wants to squeeze Britain and France out of those places, to replace old colonialists with new ones. The United States, for example, wants to take over Algeria, for there are very large oil deposits in the Sahara area in southern Algeria. France is developing that area, and there are contradictions between its oil capitalist group and the American oil barons.

You asked about the nature of the Cuban revolution. In my view, the Cuban revolution is a nationalist democratic one, a nationalist one against U.S. imperialism and a struggle against the Batista clique, compradore capital and feudalism. It is yet to be seen which direction it will take in the future. It is definite and firm against imperialism and feudalism. There is no strong national capital there, only small national industry and commerce. It is just like the Japanese monopoly capital in northeast China. Japan did not support Chinese national capital there, but set up small factories with tens or hundreds of workers that did processing for the big Japanese industries. As a result, after the Japanese left, there was no strong national bourgeoisie there as in Shanghai, Tianjin and Beijing. No such class had come into being. France did the same in Vietnam. Japan did the same in Korea, not allowing the Koreans to build their industries, while the Japanese themselves developed some industries. Anshan Steel in northeast China was also built up by the Japanese. I am afraid that the situation in Africa is the same; imperialism will not allow the local people to run big industries. For example, in Guinea there are several big factories, all run by foreigners.

I am very happy to see the Japanese people waging struggles against the oppression of imperialism and monopoly capital. The struggles of the Japanese people against the U.S.-Japan "Security Pact"[214] and against acts of political violence[274] are developing wave upon wave, which is really gratifying. I can sense it directly. Since 1950 I have been meeting Japanese friends almost every year, and it is my feeling that the mental outlook of Japanese friends in recent years has changed a lot from that of 1957 and before. A few years ago I could see in your faces worry and confusion. Your spirit of struggle was suppressed and dared not find expression. Later, especially since 1959 and 1960, things changed. The Japanese people have risen up, no longer afraid of the United States. The United States has lain like a dead weight over your backs. In the past you were prudent and cautious. In recent years you have started to struggle against it. The change that has occurred in the mental outlook of Japanese friends visiting China reflects the growing militant spirit of the Japanese people and the development of their actual struggle.

The Japanese people have become bolder, no longer afraid of devils; that is to say, no longer afraid of the devil of U.S. imperialism, the devil of Kishi Nobusuke,[206] and the devil of Ikeda Hayato. The Japanese people have strengthened their confidence in struggle. We have published a book called *Stories of Not Being Afraid of Devils*. (To Liao Chengzhi[207]) Is there a Japanese version of it? Give them one each.

(From the verbatim record)

OUR RELATIONS WITH ALL AFRICAN PEOPLE ARE GOOD*

(*May 3, 1963*)

You are delegations from a friendly country and friendly government; welcome. All African friends are welcomed by the Chinese people. Our relations with people of all African countries are good, whether they are independent or are fighting for and yet to win independence. There is now a great revolutionary movement for national independence, against imperialism and colonialism, going on in Africa. What's the population in Africa? Two hundred million, I guess. There are another 200 million people in Latin America, a billion and several hundred million in Asia, and other revolutionary people all over the world. We have friends everywhere, so we are not isolated, nor are you. Coming to China you may feel that you are most welcomed by the Chinese people.

Yours is a very good party[275] that maintains close links with the masses, a disciplined party that takes anti-imperialism, anti-colonialism, and the establishment of a national economy as its program, and a party that leads an independent country. We feel very close to you. Our two countries, two parties should help each other, support each other. You won't play tricks on us, neither will we on you. Let us know if we have people doing bad things in your country. For instance, if they look down on you, act self-important, or have a chauvinistic attitude. Do we have such people? If we do, we'll take some actions against them.

Are Chinese experts privileged and better paid than their Guinean colleagues? (To Ye Jizhuang[276]) I'm afraid they are. You should check it up. They should be treated equally, preferably lower. (Ye Jizhuang: Premier Zhou is asking Comrade Fang Yi[277] to check on it.)

Whoever acts like an overlord in your country, not abiding by your laws and engaging in subversive activities, should be driven away. We hope to see

---

* These are excerpts from Mao Zedong's talks with the Guinean government economic delegation and women's delegation.

you stand firm on your feet, not only politically, but also economically, not to be toppled. We are happy to see you stand firm and will be unhappy if you collapse, because your party is a revolutionary party and your government a revolutionary government that has enormous influence in Africa. Work can be done, through you, in many African countries, so as to secure their liberation. You have the responsibility, too. Having won independence yourselves, you should not forget to care for others. This applies to us as well. We should not forget to care for others just because we have won independence. By caring for others I mean giving friendly support and friendly help. You know, we still have difficulties, so the help we have given is not great. In five or ten years' time we may be a bit better off, then we will be in a better position to offer more help. China has a big shortcoming, too many people. These people have to be fed and clothed. So we now have quite a few difficulties, but these difficulties are not insurmountable; they can be overcome. We are now taking measures to overcome them. The Chinese economy and culture are similar to yours in that they have developed from virtually no legacy. You used to be a French colony, whereas we were the semicolony of several countries.

Our circumstances are almost the same as yours, rather close, so we have much in common. We don't feel that we bully you, or you us. We are all colored people; none feels superior to others. Some Western countries are trying to bully us. They think we are born incompetent, have no way out, and are destined to oppression by imperialists for thousands of years. They think that we are unable to administer our country and develop industry, unable to feed and clothe ourselves, and that our science and culture are backward. But why don't they think of who is to blame? It is they who caused the low level of our economic and cultural development. It is they who in the past administered our countries for us. The British said that it was all right for you to administer, but you should learn first—for how many years? Just take your time. But you didn't take your time; you seized political power all at once. We, too, must learn after getting state power. Slowly we shall learn to administer. If we make mistakes, just correct them. Is it only we who make mistakes and not Western countries? They make even greater mistakes. They made the mistake of counterrevolution. We are not fundamentally mistaken. We are waging revolution. Without industry we can gradually develop it; without modern agriculture we can gradually develop modern agriculture. Our science and culture will be upgraded year by year.

(From the verbatim record)

STATEMENT IN SUPPORT OF THE STRUGGLE OF THE AMERICAN BLACK PEOPLE AGAINST RACIAL DISCRIMINATION

(August 8, 1963)

Mr. William Robert, a U.S. black leader who was once chairman of the National Association of Coloured People, North Carolina Branch, and who is now in exile in Cuba, this year has twice asked me to issue a statement to support the struggle of the American black people against racial discrimination. I would like to take this opportunity, on behalf of the Chinese people, to pledge firm support to the struggle of the American black people against racial discrimination and for freedom and equal rights.

There are altogether more than 19 million black people in the United States, occupying almost 11 percent of the whole population. They are in a social position of enslavement, oppression and discrimination. Most of them are deprived of the right to vote. Generally they are obliged to engage in the heaviest and most despised work. Their average wage is only one-third to half of that of the white people. Their rate of unemployment is the highest. In many states, they are not allowed to study in the same school, eat at the same table, or travel in the same bus or train with the white people. The governments at all levels in the United States, the Ku Klux Klan[278] and other racialists constantly arrest, torture and murder black people at will. About 50 percent of the black people dwell in the eleven states of southern U.S., where discrimination and persecution against them are particularly appalling.

The American black people are awakening and their resistance is becoming stronger day by day. In recent years, there is a growing tendency of their mass struggle against racial discrimination and for freedom and equal rights.

In 1957, the black people at Little Rock city in Arkansas waged a fierce struggle against the local public schools which barred black students and pupils. The local authorities used armed force against them, creating the Little Rock Incident which shocked the world.

In 1960, black people in more than 20 states held "sit-in" demonstrations in protest against racial segregation practiced in the local restaurants, stores and other public places.

In 1961, black people held "Freedom Rides" against the racial segregation on buses and trains, which swiftly spread to several states.

In 1962, the blacks of the Mississippi state were suppressed by the local authorities, resulting in blood-shed, when they launched a struggle for equal right to enter university.

This year, the black people's struggle started in the beginning of April from Birmingham, Alabama. The bare-handed blacks were, to our surprise, arrested en masse and suppressed most barbarously just because of holding meetings and demonstrations against racial discrimination. On June 20 the black leader Medgar Evers was murdered in Mississippi. Defying brute force, the enraged masses of black people carried on their struggle even more bravely, and quickly won the support of vast numbers of black and other people of all social strata throughout the country. A nationwide powerful and tumultuous struggle is unfolding at present in almost every state and city in the United States, and it is continuing to upsurge. The American black organizations have decided to stage a "freedom march" on Washington of 250,000 people on August 28.

The rapid development of the struggle by black people is a manifestation of the sharpening of the domestic class and national contradictions in the United States, and it has aroused increasing disquiet among the U.S. ruling circles. The Kennedy administration has adopted an insidious double-dealing approach. On the one hand, it continues to connive at and participate in discriminating against and persecution of black people, even sending troops to suppress them; on the other hand, it has affected a posture of "upholding human rights" and "safeguarding the civil rights of black people," calling on black people "to be patient" and submitting to the Congress a set of so-called "civil rights plans," in an attempt to paralyze black people's will to fight and dupe the general public. However, more and more black people are seeing through these tricks of the Kennedy administration. The fascist atrocities of U.S. imperialism against the black people have disclosed the essence of the so-called U.S. democracy and freedom, as well as revealed the inner link between the U.S. government's reactionary domestic policies and its foreign policy of aggression.

I appeal to the workers, peasants, revolutionary intellectuals, enlightened bourgeois elements and other enlightened personages of the white, black, yellow and brown races all over the world to unite to oppose the racial discrimination of U.S. imperialism and support the American black people's struggle against racial discrimination. National struggle, in the final analysis, is a question of class struggle. It is only the reactionary ruling circles of the white people in the United States that are oppressing the black people. They can in no way represent the overwhelming majority of the white people, the workers, peasants, revolutionary intellectuals and enlightened elements. At present, it is a handful of imperialist powers headed by the United States and the reactionaries who support them who are oppressing, invading and threatening the vast majority of nations and peoples in the world. They are the minority while we are the majority. Among the world's population of three billion they are less than 10 percent at the most. I am convinced that the American black people's just struggle, with the support of more than 90 percent of the people of the world, will surely be victorious. The evil colonialist-imperialist system rose with the enslaving and trafficking of the black people, and it will certainly come to an end with the complete liberation of the black people.

(From *People's Daily*, August 9, 1963)

THE OPPRESSED WILL FINALLY RISE UP*

(*August 9, 1963*)

Chairman Mao Zedong (hereinafter referred to as Mao): I am very glad to see you. I met with a group of African friends yesterday. We and you, feeling equal, are conversing well. We do not impose our view on you, nor do you impose your view on us. We help and support each other and learn from each other's experience in our struggles.

Prime Minister Abdirashid Ali Shermarke (hereinafter referred to as Shermarke): In past days we have had fruitful talks with Premier Zhou Enlai. I feel very satisfied with the result of the talks. I am certain that relations between our two countries are strengthened.

Mao: You talked about politics, economics and other questions?

Shermarke: We talked about the general international situation, especially relations between our two countries. Our two sides have reached agreement on a joint communiqué and an economic and technical cooperation protocol.

Mao: Our economies are not good yet, so we cannot meet your requests now. We are making endeavors and shall make progress in the end, in several years or in decades. By then we shall be able to meet our foreign friends' needs better and to a greater extent. This is our hope that the oppressed nations and peoples in the world make joint efforts in the struggle for political, economic and cultural independence and liberation and strive to be liberated from the oppression of imperialism and colonialism.

You know, our country is not completely liberated yet, because Taiwan is still not liberated. To Western countries, China does not seem to exist, yet, again, it does seem to exist. Dulles[97] said that China seemed to exist as well as not exist. Why is this? During the Korean War Chinese were fighting battles against the United States, so the West felt China's existence. Then why should it not? They assume that China is in bad circumstances and will soon decline, collapse and fall from power; China is hopeless and

---

* This is Mao Zedong's talk with Somali Prime Minister Abdirashid Ali Shermarke.

does not seem to exist. The West holds the same view about the African situation. Westerners think Africa is a place for nonAfricans, but if Africa belongs to the Westerners, does it exist then? Now It seems they are beginning to recognize the existence of Africa. Dozens of African countries have won independence and the people in countries that have not won independence are carrying out struggles. Asian and African countries are a headache to the West; so are Latin American countries. In the past, countries on the three continents served as reserves for Western imperialist countries, and now they feel the three continents are ganging together to cause disturbances and earthquakes.

Shermarke: That's true. They feel that something has gone wrong with these places, running contrary to their will.

Mao: You are disobeying the will of Italy, Britain and France.

Shermarke: Our independence has not been long and we cherish it very much. We ourselves will take responsibility and establish our dignity. For quite a long period in the past we were dominated and now we shall be masters of our own history. In the past the Western colonialists did not treat us as human beings, but only as things.

Mao: They value things only because they are useful. Men are useful when they can create wealth, but useless otherwise. Now we are creating wealth for ourselves instead of for them, so they curse us every day, especially the United States. The main target of your struggle is not the United States, is it? The main target of our struggle is the United States, while Britain, France, Italy and West Germany come behind. The United States has set up many military bases to encircle us; you know this. Do you have diplomatic relations with Japan?

Shermarke: Yes, we do. But Japan does not have an embassy in Somali.

Mao: We do not have diplomatic relations with Japan, because it does not recognize us, but follows the United States.

Shermarke: It is the Japanese government, not the Japanese people.

Mao: The Japanese people are very good and we have very close relations with them. The American people are not against China and we have exchanges with many Americans. The same is true of our relations with Britain, France and other European countries.

Shermarke: To us, the main targets of our struggle are Britain, France and Italy, then the United States. Countries such as Britain, France and Italy take Africa as their sphere of influence. It means when the United States takes an interest in Africa they consider it interference in their internal affairs. The United States finds it hard to accomplish anything without their agreement. They feel that since Africa was their colonies, they have the right to keep their spheres of influence. Now that over 80 percent of African countries have won independence, Africans cherish their dignity and will never allow Africa to be the sphere of influence of others.

Mao: The old practice of taking African countries as one's sphere of influence is no longer feasible. Now over 30 African countries have won independence. Some countries, such as Algeria, have won independence through war, fighting eight years with tens of thousands of soldiers against hundreds of thousands of troops. The fewer defeated the more. Why could tens of thousands defeat hundreds of thousands? Because millions of Algerians backed up and supported the tens of thousands of troops, while the hundreds of thousands of French troops failed to have support from the Algerian people. Most of the one million French among the ten million Algerian population ran away. Another example is the United Arab Republic's fight against Britain and France to maintain sovereignty over the Suez Canal.[134] As a result the British and French fled and now the canal is under the control of the United Arab Republic.

In short, the imperialist front is shrinking, shrinking by a large margin. For instance, their hold in Africa is much smaller and they can no longer control China's mainland. I learned that you do not like the British chargé d'affaires in Beijing.

Shermarke: I do not hold grudges against anybody personally. What we oppose is the British government's past policy. In the past, it made deals seven times with our territory. At that time we were powerless, because we were not independent. But after we won independence, Britain wanted to give our territory to others, so we severed diplomatic relations. That is why Britain now cannot keep its influence in Somali.

Mao: This is very good. When Britain and France used arms to seize the Suez Canal, Egypt broke diplomatic relations with them. They resumed relations only recently. After independence Guinea severed diplomatic relations with France and they were resumed last year.

Shermarke: Yes. These are all lessons and experiences in handling relations with past rulers.

Mao: The United States does not recognize us; Japan does not have diplomatic relations with us; Britain and the Netherlands just have semi-diplomatic relations with us; France, Italy and West Germany do not have diplomatic relations with us as yet, and Turkey, Greece, Portugal, Spain and Belgium, which follow them, do not have diplomatic relations with us.

Now the United States still occupies our Taiwan. If, first, the United States hands back Taiwan to us; second, the United Nations admits us and drives Chiang Kai-shek out; third, the economic blockade is lifted and business is started; fourth, we and the United States recognize each other and establish diplomatic relations—even if all these take place, we shall still be against imperialism and against U.S. imperialists. It is not only a question of China; it is also China's desire to unite with the majority of people all over the world, so as to defeat imperialism. They hate China most for this. We want not only to defeat imperialism domestically, but also to eliminate imperialism worldwide. We do not have many weapons, nor do we have an atom bomb or a developed economy, but we are for the liberation of the people of the whole world from imperialist and colonialist rule. Only then will the people of the world, including us, have tranquillity. Don't you believe it? In the final analysis, imperialism will be defeated.

Shermarke: We believe it. People will work hard for their liberation. If the people who have been under the rule of imperialists and colonialists do not rise up on their own, but rely on the participation of foreign countries, it means interference in their internal affairs.

Mao: The oppressed people will rise up sooner or later.

Shermarke: Freedom is obtained mainly through the local people.

Mao: I totally agree. We feel that backing up means support, offering economic assistance and aid in weapons when necessary. Take Algeria, for example; we offered arms aid.

Shermarke: That's because the Algerian people expressed their desire for independence and appealed for assistance. If the Algerian people had not shown a desire for independence, then what was to be done?

Mao: We could do nothing, absolutely nothing, but wait for the people to awaken and rise to the struggle. China waited for over 100 years before the mainland was liberated, and Taiwan may have to wait several decades. The liberation of the whole world has to wait for quite some time. As for Taiwan, we are not prepared to liberate it by force. One reason is that American troops are stationed in Taiwan and we would be waging war against the United States if our army attacked. Britain does not have a large military force in Hong Kong and we may take over if we want to. But a treaty was signed in the past, under which a small part was ceded and most was leased. The period of the lease is 99 years, with 34 years to go before its expiration. This is a special case and we are not planning to touch it. You may not understand it.

Shermarke: If the Hong Kong people want liberation and to drive Britain away, can you refuse to offer assistance?

Mao: Hong Kong people are Chinese like us. Hong Kong is an important path for trade. If we get control of it right now, it won't benefit world trade, nor will it benefit our trade relations with other countries. It does not mean we shall never touch it. Britain feels at ease now, but may feel uneasy about it in the future.

(From the verbatim record)

STATEMENT AGAINST U.S.-NGO DINH DIEM CLIQUE'S AGGRESSION IN SOUTH VIETNAM AND MASSACRE OF THE SOUTH VIETNAMESE PEOPLE

(August 29, 1963)

Of late, the Ngo Dinh Diem reactionary clique of South Vietnam has stepped up its bloody suppression of Buddhists, college and middle-school students, intellectuals and masses of people in South Vietnam[279]. The Chinese people express the utmost indignation at this and strongly condemn these monstrous criminal acts of the Ngo Dinh Diem clique. Chairman Ho Chi Minh has issued a statement[280] vigorously protesting against the crimes of the U.S-Ngo Dinh Diem clique. We, the Chinese people, warmly support Chairman Ho's statement.

U.S. imperialism and its runningdog Ngo Dinh Diem have adopted the policies of turning South Vietnam into a U.S. colony, launching a counter-revolutionary war and strengthening their fascist dictatorship. These have compelled all sections of the people in South Vietnam to unite extensively to wage a resolute struggle against the U.S.-Ngo Dinh Diem clique.

Hostile to all the people of South Vietnam, the U.S.-Ngo Dinh Diem clique now find themselves encircled by the entire people of South Vietnam. Whatever inhuman weapons U.S. imperialism may use, and whatever atrocious methods of suppression the Ngo Dinh Diem clique may employ, that clique will be unable to escape its final doom of utter isolation and collapse, and U.S. imperialism will have to get out of South Vietnam in the end.

Ngo Dinh Diem is a faithful lackey of U.S. imperialism. But when a lackey has lost his usefulness or even become a liability to U.S. imperialism in pursuing its policy of aggression, then U.S. imperialism will not hesitate to replace him with another lackey. The fate of Syngman Rhee in South Korea is a precedent. An abject lackey who is led by the nose by U.S. imperialism can have no other end than sacrificing his life for U.S. imperialism.

Sabotaging the agreement of the first Geneva Conference, U.S. imperialism obstructed the unification of Vietnam, openly launched armed aggression against South Vietnam, and has waged the so-called "special warfare" there for several years. Again it sabotaged the agreement of the second Geneva Conference and undisguisedly intervened in Laos in an attempt to restart the civil war there. Apart from those who are out to deceive people on purpose or who are extremely naivë, no one will believe that any agreement on a scrap of paper will make U.S. imperialism "drop its cleaver and become a Buddha" or behave itself a little better.

An oppressed people or oppressed nation must not pin its hope for liberation on the "sagacity" of imperialism and its lackeys, but can win victory only by strengthening unity and persisting in struggle. The people of South Vietnam are doing precisely this.

The patriotic and just struggle of the people of South Vietnam against the U.S.-Ngo Dinh Diem clique has won significant victories both politically and militarily. We, the Chinese people, firmly support their just struggle.

I am convinced that the people of South Vietnam will achieve their object of liberating their area through struggle, and contribute to the peaceful unification of their motherland.

I hope that the working class, revolutionary people and progressive personages of the whole world will stand by the people of South Vietnam and, in response to Chairman Ho Chi Minh's call, support and assist the brave people of South Vietnam in their just struggle and oppose the aggression and oppression of the U.S.-Ngo Dinh Diem clique so that the people of South Vietnam may avoid being massacred and achieve thorough liberation.

(From *People's Daily*, August 30, 1963)

THERE ARE TWO INTERMEDIATE ZONES*

(*September 1963; January and July 1964*)

I

All of you are concerned about the situation, particularly the international situation. Some comrades are concerned that the collaboration between the Soviet Union and the United States will bring disadvantages to us. I always believe what Wang Xifeng says in *A Dream of Red Mansions*: "Bigness has the difficulties of being big."[281] Now the U.S. and the Soviet Union both have big difficulties. Rost, chairman of the U.S. Policy Committee, once published an article whose keynote was that both the U.S. and the Soviet Union faced many difficulties and that these difficulties were insurmountable. I don't know this man, but our views happen to coincide at some points. The United States is being rebuffed everywhere, both domestically and internationally; Khrushchev[146] too. Don't forget this point. In the words of Leng Zixing in *A Dream of Red Mansions*, "A centipede does not topple over even when dead."[282] The American magazine *Hammer and Steel* also says that the U.S. is like a hollowed big tree, leafy outside but insect-ridden inside.

In my view there are two intermediate zones: the first, Asia, Africa and Latin America and the second, Europe. Japan and Canada are not happy with the United States. The six-nation Common Market,[283] represented by De Gaulle,[191] is made up of powerful capitalist countries. Japan in the East is a powerful capitalist country. They are unhappy with the U.S. and the Soviet Union. Are the Eastern European countries that satisfied with Khrushchev of the Soviet Union? I don't believe so. Things are evolving and contradictions are revealing themselves. In the past few years the French were trying to assert their independent character, but not to the degree they are today. The contradictions between the Soviet Union and Eastern European countries are

---

* These are excerpts from three talks: (1) at the Working Conference of the Central Committee of the Communist Party of China, (2) with Kikunami Katsumi, Politburo member of the Japanese Communist Party, and (3) Japanese Socialists.

also developing and their relations are very tense. Relaxation in the world situation? Don't be deceived by all that. In my view it is not so easy for the Soviet Union and the U.S. to come to an agreement. Many Atlantic countries will not support the U.S. either. De Gaulle has said everywhere that France will not be a satellite country; their struggle is one of control and countercontrol. Khrushchev claims that we follow the same line as De Gaulle; in fact we have never seen De Gaulle. We mainly rely on the people domestically and internationally, not on the leaders of major countries. People are reliable.

(September 28, 1963)
(From the verbatim record)

II

We have diplomatic relations with the Soviet Union; we are two countries in the socialist camp. But the relations between our two countries are not as good as those between China and the Japanese Liberal Democratic Party or China and the Ikeda[255] faction. This is something we should think about. What's the reason? Because the U.S. and the Soviet Union both have nuclear weapons and want to dominate the world. The Liberal Democratic Party is, however, under American control. So far as its international status is concerned, Japan is secondary to the U.S. and the Soviet Union. Secondary countries also include Britain, France, West Germany, Italy, and so on. Thus we have some work to do. Japanese monopoly capitalists are not that united with the U.S. Though Britain is quite close to the U.S., they are not that united either. France annoys the U.S., and West Germany has become important. It will inevitably confront the U.S.

So when we talk about intermediate zones, we refer to two separate parts. The vast economically backward countries in Asia, Africa and Latin America constitute the first. Imperialist and advanced capitalist countries represented by Europe constitute the second. Both are opposed to American control. Countries in Eastern Europe, on the other hand, are against control by the Soviet Union. This trend is quite obvious.

(January 5, 1964)
(From the verbatim record)

III

The United States reaches out to the entire West Pacific and Southeast Asia. Its reach is too long. The Seventh Fleet, stationed in this area, is the biggest in the U.S.; it has six aircraft carriers, half of America's total number of 12. The Sixth Fleet is stationed in the Mediterranean. When we shelled Jinmen in 1958, the Americans got scared and maneuvered part of the Sixth Fleet eastward. The United States has Europe and Canada under its control; it controls all of Latin America, except for Cuba. It has now reached out to Africa and is waging a war in the Congo.[258]

People all over Asia, Africa and Latin America are opposed to U.S. imperialism. A large number of people in Europe, North America and Oceania are against U.S. imperialism. Some of the imperialists are against U.S. imperialism too. De Gaulle's opposition to the U.S. is evidence. We now put forward the view that there are two intermediate zones: Asia, Africa and Latin America are the first, and Europe, North America and Oceania, the second. Japan belongs to the second intermediate zone too. The monopoly capitalists in Japan are not happy with the U.S.; some openly oppose it. Although there are still others who rely on it, in my view, in the course of time many of these people will finally throw out the Americans sitting on their backs.

(July 10, 1964)
(From the verbatim record)

THE CHINESE PEOPLE RESOLUTELY SUPPORT THE PEOPLE OF PANAMA IN THEIR PATRIOTIC AND JUST STRUGGLE*

(*January 12, 1964*)

Right now the people of Panama are bravely waging a struggle to defend their national sovereignty against U.S. aggression. It is a great patriotic struggle. The Chinese people firmly stand by the Panamanian people and whole-heartedly support their just action of opposing the U.S. aggressors and recovering sovereignty over the Panama Canal zone.

U.S. imperialism is the most vicious enemy of the people of the whole world.

It has not only committed a serious crime of aggression against the people of Panama and doggedly schemed to strangle socialist Cuba, but has all along been plundering and oppressing the peoples of all Latin American countries, and suppressing their national and democratic revolutionary struggles.

In Asia U.S. imperialism forcibly occupies China's Taiwan, and has turned South Korea and South Vietnam into its colonies. It exercises control over Japan with a semimilitary occupation, undermines the peace, neutrality and independence of Laos, plots to subvert the Royal Cambodian Government and carries on intervention and aggression against other Asian countries. Recently it decided to send its fleet to the Indian Ocean, threatening the security of the countries in Southeast Asia.

In Africa U.S. imperialism is stepping up its neo-colonialist policy in an effort to supplant the old colonialists, plunder and enslave the people of the African countries, and sabotage and stamp out their national liberation movements.

U.S. imperialism's policy of aggression and war also seriously threatens the Soviet Union, China and the other socialist countries. It further endeavors

---

* This is the text of an interview given by Mao Zedong to journalists of the *People's Daily*.

to push the policy of "peaceful evolution" in the socialist countries in order to restore capitalism and disintegrate the socialist camp.

Even toward its allies in Western Europe, North America and Oceania, U.S. imperialism likewise pursues a "law of the jungle" policy, trying to trample them under its feet.

U.S. imperialism's plan of aggression for world hegemony has run in a continuous line from Truman, Eisenhower and Kennedy to Johnson.

The people of the countries of the socialist camp should unite, the people of the Asian, African and Latin American countries should unite, the people of all continents of the world should unite, all peace-loving countries should unite, and all countries which are subjected to U.S. aggression, control, intervention and bullying should unite to form a most extensive united front to oppose U.S. imperialism's policy of aggression and war and to safeguard world peace.

Riding roughshod everywhere, U.S. imperialism has put itself in a position of antagonism to the people of the world and landed itself in ever greater isolation. The atomic and hydrogen bombs in the hands of U.S. imperialism cannot overawe people who refuse to be slaves. The raging tide of the people of the world against the U.S. aggressors is irresistible. The struggle of the people of the world against U.S. imperialism and its lackeys will surely win ever greater victories.

(From *People's Daily*, January 13, 1964)

KHRUSHCHEV[146] IS HAVING A HARD TIME*

(January 17, 1964)

We now come across two diplomatic questions, on which we should like to hear your opinions. First, is the United States paying more attention to the Soviet Union or to China? Second, is America actively preparing for a third world war? Some people say yes.

(Adler: On the question of whether the United States is paying more attention to the Soviet Union or to China, the American press says that in the short term the Soviet Union is the principal enemy, whereas from a long-term point of view China is the principal enemy.)

This is what they say, and I have read words to this effect. But imperialists are pragmatists; "long term" is not that important to them, because it is too far away. Now they don't take us seriously, for we have only grenades, no atom bomb. You and other foreign comrades who work with us are not taken seriously either. They think that you are no more than intellectuals working for *Beijing Review* or radio stations and can do nothing but raise a hue and cry. It is a good thing that they don't take us seriously; it is to our advantage.

Nonetheless, they are also paying attention to us.—Rodeuck, a U.S. journalist stationed in Tokyo, is a specialist on China.

In any case the Soviet Union is a big industrialized country, one of the two nuclear powers. Apart from grenades, China has a few more people. In the eyes of Khrushchev a few more people mean only a pile of flesh. He also said, moreover, that in China now five people are sharing one pair of trousers and that people have nothing to eat but wishy-washy gruel. In fact, he said that at just the moment when he had over there too few trousers and too much clear gruel. He doesn't have a much easier life than we do. He said that in his most difficult time just to show his people: Look, how great our country is! We have quite a few trousers and not much clear gruel.

---

* These are excerpts from a talk with Anna Louise Strong, Frank Coe, Sol Adler, Israel Epstein and Sidney Rittenberg.

On the question whether the U.S. is now preparing for a third world war, we expressed our view earlier, and we now still hold that view.

We may look back at history. The United States has always taken part in international wars at the very last. This was the case in the First World War and the Second. Now the U.S. is reaching out too far. As the Sichuanese would say: Catching ten fleas with ten fingers, you end up getting none. If you don't believe it, open your fingers and try to catch one.

Now the United States meets resistance in two Third Worlds. The first Third World refers to Asia, Africa, and Latin America, while the second refers to a number of highly developed capitalist, mostly European, countries, some even imperialist countries. On the one hand, these countries oppress others; on the other hand, they are oppressed by the United States and have contradictions with it. In the first Third World there is a place called South Vietnam. The United States just fails to weigh its people down. Moreover, things of this kind will always crop up in the future.

It is unimaginable for the U.S. to meet resistance in both Third Worlds, only to find that such resistance is absent in the Soviet Union and Eastern Europe.

Khrushchev is having a tough time. According to statistics, since the 20th Congress of the CPSU only a small number of veterans are left in the Presidium of the Soviet Communist Party as a result of leadership changes. That shows it is not stable there, nor is it in Eastern Europe. For instance, there are constant leadership changes in Bulgaria, Hungary, and Czechoslovakia. Some people stepped down after fiercely opposing China, but after they stepped down, they changed their anti-China stance. Take Yugov[285] and Siroky,[286] for example. Why? they opposed China just for the sake of maintaining their power and position; that's why they stopped opposing China after being driven out. This proved two points: First, some people are not truly against China. Second, China now is in a position that evokes opposition from other people and stimulates these people to write articles and deliver speeches to attack it. We have the status that someone has to oppose China to maintain his post.

In fact, Khrushchev has not secured big majority support among the countries in the socialist camp.[287] Romania has differing views; Poland can be counted as only half a supporter. Like the Americans, he wants to control others and tries to make them develop single-product economies, which is not feasible. Romania does not accept it. Cuba is quarreling with him.

After the 20th Congress of the CPSU we began to feel Khrushchev was not following the correct line, but until the first half of 1958 our attitude was one of helping him, for we thought at that time it was not easy for the Soviet people to change leaders.

Later the naval base issue[177] occurred in 1958. Khrushchev visited China that year. Why did he come? Negotiations with the Soviet ambassador to China over the naval base issue broke down. In the end, Khrushchev himself had to come to clear things up. I said to him, "I can give you the whole of China's coastline." He asked, "Then what will you do?" "Go up to the mountains to launch a guerrilla war," I replied. He then said, "It's no use launching a guerrilla war." I said, "You jammed my nose; what else could I do except fight a guerrilla war?"

Then came the Sino-Indian border incident[288] in 1959. Before visiting the United States, Khrushchev issued a statement through Tass indicating that he would remain "neutral" on the Sino-Indian border issue. After visiting the United States, he came to Beijing again. This time he talked about the Taiwan question, asking us to treat Taiwan in the way the Soviet Union treated the Far East Republic[289] in the past. I said to him, "It was you who established the Far East Republic, but we never set up the Chiang Kai-shek clique." He also asked us to release the four or five American convicts then jailed in our prison. Neither of these two questions reached agreement. He said, "Eisenhower told me at Camp David, 'Your trip to Beijing this time will get you nowhere.'"

From the 20th Congress of the CPSU to last July, we found ourselves in a rather passive position. We then turned to a counteroffensive. Like stirring up trouble in the Heavenly Palace, we broke their taboos and commandments. We should never thoroughly yield to their taboos and commandments. They malign us as dogmatists, Trotskyites, empty talkers, sham revolutionaries and nationalists. But they are afraid of our "empty talk." They make verbal allegations that what we say is empty talk, but in fact they take it as pestilence and try very hard to block it. They even jam our broadcasts with the station they use to jam the Voice of America.

They now ask us to stop public debates; they are very nervous. I told the Soviet ambassador last March, "You labeled us as dogmatists, Trotskyites, empty talkers, sham revolutionaries, and nationalists. If that was really what we were, of course you should criticize us; feel free to do so." He said it would be disastrous if things went on that way. I said, "What harm will it do to fight a battle of words? First, heaven won't collapse; second, trees and grass will continue to grow in the mountains; third, women will continue to give birth to children; fourth, fish will swim in the rivers as before. If you don't believe it, go to the riverside and have a look." In a recent letter to us, they quoted these words of mine.

It is not up to one side to stop the debates. A fair agreement accepted by both sides must be concluded, because the two sides represent not just two parties, but parties in scores of countries. Therefore, it is very hard to stop the debates.

(From the verbatim record)

THE CHINESE PEOPLE SUPPORT THE GREAT PATRIOTIC STRUGGLE OF THE JAPANESE PEOPLE*

(*January 27, 1964*)

The anti-U.S. demonstration held by the Japanese people on January 26 was a great patriotic movement. On behalf of the Chinese people, I would like to express to the heroic Japanese people my highest respect.

A large-scale mass movement was launched throughout Japan recently against the introduction and stationing in Japan of the U.S. F-105D nuclear airplanes and nuclear submarines, demanding the closing down of all U.S. military bases, the withdrawal of U.S. armed forces, the return of the Japanese territory of Okinawa, the abolition of the Japan-U.S. "Security Pact," etc. All these things reflect the will and desire of all the Japanese people. The Chinese people wholeheartedly support their just struggle.

Since the Second World War Japan has all along been oppressed by U.S. imperialism politically, economically and militarily. U.S. imperialism has not only oppressed the Japanese workers, peasants, students, intellectuals, urban petty bourgeoisie, religious personages and middle and small businessmen, but also controlled many big entrepreneurs, interfered in Japan's foreign policy and treated Japan as its vassal state. U.S. imperialism is the most vicious enemy of the Japanese nation.

The Japanese nation is a great nation. It absolutely will not allow U.S. imperialism to ride on its back for long. In the past few years the patriotic united front formed by Japanese people of all social strata against the aggression, oppression and control of U.S. imperialism has been expanding. This is the most reliable guarantee of the victory of the Japanese people's

---

* This is the text of a talk given in Beijing by Mao Zedong to Suzuki Hitowo, vice-chairman of the Japan-China Friendship Association and chairman of the Japan-China Trade Promotion Council; Saionji Kooichi, managing director of Japan's Asian-African Solidarity Committee; and Takano Kosa, correspondent of Akahatabo, official newspaper of the Japanese Communist Party.

anti-U.S. patriotic struggle. The Chinese people are convinced that the Japanese people will be able to expel the U.S. imperialists from their territory, and their aspiration for independence, democracy, peace and neutrality will be realized.

The people of China and Japan should unite, the people of the Asian countries should unite, all oppressed peoples and nations in the world should unite, all peace-loving countries should unite, all the countries and peoples who are subjected to U.S. imperialism's aggression, control, intervention and bullying should unite to form an extensive united front against U.S. imperialism, defeat its plans of aggression and war, and safeguard world peace.

U.S. imperialism must get out of Japan, get out of the western Pacific, get out of Asia, get out of Africa and Latin America, get out of Europe and Oceania, and get out of all the countries and places which are subjected to its aggression, control, intervention and bullying!

(From *People's Daily*, January 28, 1964)

CHINA AND FRANCE SHARE COMMON GROUND*

(January 30, 1964)

Welcome. Let's be friends, good friends. You are not Communists. I am not a member of your party. We are against capitalism, and you are probably against communism, but still we can cooperate. There are two common points between us. First, we both are against bullying by big powers. That is to say, never allow any big power in the world to shit over us. I put it in a rather coarse way. Whatever big power attempts to control us, to oppose us, is not permissible, whether it is a capitalist power or a socialist one. You in France have greater means than we. You have made atom bombs and probably have mass-produced them. I'm not against your producing atom bombs, because the bulk of them are in the hands of the United States and the Soviet Union. They always frighten people with them. Second, both want to promote mutual commercial and cultural exchanges. We hope you can knock out the so-called strategic goods embargo against us. Now we are sold only civilian goods, no strategic goods. The Americans don't allow them to be sold. As I say, we are bound to open a breach someday. Petroleum, for example, is a strategic good, so you are not allowed to trade it; we have done some grain business, because grain is not a strategic good. Britain has sold us some aircraft. You can do the same. Why don't you do some business in conventional arms?

The United States is frightening some countries, forbidding them to do business with us. The U.S. is a paper tiger; don't take it seriously; it will break at the slightest touch. The Soviet Union is a paper tiger too; we don't trust it at all. I'm not superstitious. Perhaps you are theists. I'm an atheist and afraid of nothing. It's not acceptable if the big powers try to control us. France is a small country. China too. Only the United States and the Soviet Union are big powers. Do we have to seek their approval on everything and go on pilgrimage to their land? We used to follow the Soviet Union; that was during Stalin's time. I went to Moscow in 1957. At that time, the Soviet Union was not openly against us. Now I won't go there, because it has torn up a large

---

* This is Mao Zedong's talk with a French National Assembly delegation.

number of contracts and doesn't honor its promises. It has collaborated with the U.S. to be openly against us. This is very good; I like it. There must be some reason for big powers like the U.S. and the Soviet Union to be opposed to us. We must have something that deserves their opposition. Now Sihanouk[122] has become unyielding to the United States. Cambodia has only five million people, but it dares to antagonize the U.S.

You can cooperate with us in Asia to resist the U.S. The U.S. is unpopular everywhere. On the 26th this month over a million Japanese demonstrated against the U.S. I once talked to your former Premier, M. Faure,[291] and said I hoped you would do your work well in Europe, to make countries such as Britain, West Germany, Belgium, and Italy distance themselves from the United States and get closer to you. You have said that you would like to establish a Third World, haven't you? It won't do if the Third World has only France. That would be too few and it won't do. You should get the whole of Europe united. I think that with time Britain too will change. The Americans are not so polite to the British either. In the East you may work on Japan. If you can drag Britain to your side, you will extend the Third World from London and Paris in Europe to China and Japan.

Don't follow the British position on the question of Taiwan. Britain has only one difference with us; that is, it does not take a clear-cut attitude toward the status of Taiwan. First, Britain recognizes the People's Republic of China; it doesn't recognize Taiwan. That's good. Second, it votes in our favor in the United Nations; that is good too. The trouble is the third; both Britain and the United States advocate "two Chinas." On this point it shows it acts as America's agent. We have had 15 years of diplomatic ties with Britain. Like you, it asked to mutually accredit ambassadors. We said no. In another 15 years or even several decades we can go without sending an ambassador. It doesn't matter if we cannot get into the United Nations. For 15 years we managed to survive without a U.N. membership. Let Generalissimo Chiang Kai-shek stay in the U.N. for another 15, 30 or even 100 years, we can still survive. It is totally unacceptable for us to recognize "two Chinas," "one and a half Chinas." You may send an ambassador if you want to do so. Don't follow the Bitish—15 years later still a chargé d'affaires. Don't fall into America's trap. If this is not made clear, we won't accept your ambassador and will not send ours either. We must make this clear in advance. When I met Mr. Faure, I made this clear to him. Our Foreign Ministry issued a statement on this; it also notified you in Switzerland, and both came to an agreement. Have you ever sent coded telegrams home? Traveling abroad it would be inconvenient if you didn't have coded communications.

You ought to distinguish yourselves from the British and speak your minds forthrightly. I was a soldier and in war for 22 years. General De Gaulle[191] was a soldier too. Don't talk in a roundabout way; don't play diplomatic ploy.

France is no longer Hitler's[4] France, and China is not under the Japanese. In the past, from Nanjing to Beijing, more than half of China was forcefully occupied by Japan. When the Japanese were driven away, the Americans came in their wake. We managed to drive out both the Americans and Chiang Kai-shek. At that time we had virtually nothing. No aircraft, no tanks, not to mention atom bombs. What we did have were merely some rifles, grenades and light guns. We were grateful to the Americans for having sent us some heavy artillery. It was Chiang Kai-shek who served as our transport brigade commander. We had no munitions factory, no foreign aid whatsoever. You haven't been to our small place, Yan'an, have you? It was very backward there. There was only agriculture and a bit of handicraft industry. Even at that time we were saying that America and Chiang Kai-shek were paper tigers. We also said that Hitler was a paper tiger. Finally he was defeated and dropped dead. Now we say there are two big paper tigers. They are the United States and the Soviet Union. Let's wait and see whether my prediction comes true or not. Please bear in mind that I have told a French parliamentarians' delegation that they are big paper tigers. This does not include the broad masses of the Soviet people, Party members and cadres; they are friendly to us. Some Americans have been deceived. The American people will finally be friendly toward us. By calling them paper tigers, I mean that they have become divorced from the people. Previously Hitler occupied almost the whole of Europe; how mighty of him! You experienced all this.

Thorough and complete disarmament? Do you believe it? There's nothing like that. Now it is thorough and complete armament. It is possible to cut some infantrymen and use the money saved to build atom bombs. France has been able to explode atom bombs. We are a step behind you and have not exploded ours. But we will someday.

There is another common point between us. That is the so-called tripartite agreement. We'll never participate. It is a kind of fraud and blackmail, trying to exert pressure on us. Only they are free to have atom bombs, while we are forbidden to do so. Our two countries did not exchange views in advance. You didn't participate, nor did we.

Some people in Asian countries are against your coming to Asia to support Sihanouk. Only the United States is allowed to occupy South Vietnam; you are not allowed to come to its assistance. U.S. Secretary of State Rusk said in

Tokyo that General De Gaulle wanted to fight in Asia with an olive branch in his hand, but he failed to do so. With an olive branch in one hand and a sword in the other, America has been fighting in southern Vietnam for more than ten years, but the more it fights, the stronger the people's struggle becomes. It has killed two people there with its sword: Ngo Dinh Diem[136] and Ngo Dinh Ru. It did that in a very nasty way. I think you are not happy with it. What's the point of doing this! The so-called new government that had been propped up proved incompetent, too. U.S. policy is too mistaken. We have a saying in Sichuan Province—Catching ten fleas with ten fingers, one ends up getting none.

We both may do some work on Japan. Japan is bound to drive America away someday. I don't mean only the Japanese Communist Party, but also the big capitalists in Japan. Nowadays some big capitalists in Japan are very uncomfortable with America. The problem with Britain is a bit troublesome. It would be good if it ceased to be an American agent one day.

We have no objection if you get along well with the United States. To you it means both unity and struggle. After the Taiwan issue is properly solved, we too shall restore diplomatic ties with the U.S. But even if diplomatic ties are restored, we shall continue to object if America intervenes and controls everywhere as it does today. We demand that American imperialists go away from Asia, Africa, Latin America, and Europe. Europe is the Europeans' Europe; why are Americans there? There is a British House of Lords member, Marshal Montgomery.[263] He was opposed to America's seeking hegemony in the North Atlantic Treaty.[189] He was also against Canada's being too close to America. At that time I told him to go and see General De Gaulle. That was during his second trip to China in 1961, and perhaps he didn't. He is a Conservative. I asked him, "Is it only you who has such views?" "No, there are still others," he replied. He is firmly opposed to America's seeking hegemony in Europe, and he is not a Communist either.

(From the verbatim record)

OPPOSING EXTERNAL INTERVENTION, CARRYING OUT THE EIGHT PRINCIPLES*

(June 14, 1964)

Now the problem facing Africa is to win independence, oppose external intervention, and be independent in military, political, economic and cultural affairs. We all need to oppose external intervention. Construction is now under way in our country. It will take us several decades to catch up with the advanced level of the world. For entire Africa it will also take several decades to catch up with the advanced Western countries. It will be very fast if we can catch up with them in several decades. All the capitalist and imperialist countries in the West have had several hundred years of construction. It took several hundred years for them to develop into what they are now. For us to catch up with them in several decades truly isn't very long, is it? We should be confident. Some say that colored people are inferior to white. In my view, they are not correct in saying this. Colored people, when awakened, may do even better than the West. The most inhabited places in the world are Asia, Africa and Latin America. Many people in Europe and North America are not against us. Among the American people, for instance, many agree with our side. Some American experts work in China as editors and translators and others help us teach in foreign language schools. When we fought against the Japanese, a Canadian doctor[292] worked for us. He died later. We should treat governments, monopoly capitalists and the broad masses of people separately.

Like ours, your country has nothing and everything. First, you have people. Second, yours is a big country in Africa with very good land, where you can develop agriculture and animal husbandry. Third, you may have enormous underground mineral resources. The first of these points is that you have people, very good people.

There is great hope in Africa. People all over the world are watching you rise up. There is no need to go too far back in history. Just ten years ago it

---

* These are excerpts from Mao Zedong's talk with Rashidi Mfaume Kawawa, second vice-president of Tanzania.

was very different from ten years later. Ten years ago, in 1952, the Farouk reign in Egypt was overthrown, but the Suez Canal had not been taken back. Ten years ago the Bandung Conference[111] had not yet convened. The world is changing very fast.

History and the future belong not only to the people in Africa and Asia, but to all the people in various countries in Europe and America. Here I mean the people, not those big capitalists.

We must carry out the eight principles of foreign aid.[293] If we fail to carry out any one of them, it will not do for it will not be to your advantage or to our advantage. What good will it bring us if we go to foreign countries to exploit other people? We ourselves are oppressed; that is to say, Taiwan has not been liberated. Is it reasonable to seek gains from foreigners at their expense when we ourselves are an underdeveloped country? If any Chinese is doing bad things in your country, let us know. We shall call him back, or you can drive him out.

Some people we sent overseas may not be so good. We shall check our work. If anyone is found with a bad attitude toward other countries, he must be ordered to correct this mistake. If he doesn't, we'll call him back. We also have people who defected to capitalist countries. They are not comfortable with socialism. It is all right if some people want to run away. We already have too many people.

We are completely equal. We should speak the truth, rather than say one thing to people's faces and do something else behind their backs.

(From the verbatim record)

WE SUPPORT THE OPPRESSED PEOPLE IN
THEIR WARS AGAINST IMPERIALISM*

(*June 23, 1964*)

War will bring no benefit to us. We must carry out construction, and war will only devastate our ongoing construction. The Kuomintang started the civil war and fought with us for many years. Then we fought against Japan for eight years. We did not go to Japan to fight; Japan invaded China. Going further back, foreign countries committed aggression against China. China has been at war with Britain several times, such as the Opium War,[51] which started in Guangdong in 1840, and the war with the allied forces of the eight powers.[55] The troops of the eight countries, including Britain, occupied Tianjin and attacked Beijing. The Sino-Japanese War from 1894 to 1895[54] was fought in places such as Lüshun and Dalian. Later the Japanese occupied China's northeast. Before that tsarist Russia and Japan fought a war on China's land near Lüshun, Liaoyang and Shenyang.[56] The last was the Second World War, when Japan occupied almost the whole of China. Among all those wars we never fought in other countries; it was always foreign countries which invaded China. There were times Chinese went to fight in foreign countries, but those were in ancient times when Chinese emperors sent expeditionary forces to Vietnam and Korea. Later Japan occupied Korea, and France occupied Vietnam.

In 1911 we overthrew the Qing emperor. Then the war among different factions of warlords took place. At that time there was no Communist Party in China. When the Communist Party came into existence, there were revolutionary wars. But it was not we who wanted to fight; it was the imperialists and the Kuomintang who wanted to fight. In 1921 the Communist Party was founded in China and I became a member. At that time we never prepared for war. I was an intellectual, a primary school teacher. I never learned military affairs, so how could I know how to fight? The white terror

---

* This is the main part of Mao Zedong's talk with a Chilean journalist delegation.

of the Kuomintang wiped out trade unions and peasant associations and killed or arrested large batches of our 50,000 Communist Party members; that made us take up guns and go to the mountains to fight guerrilla wars. Then, after the ten-thousand-*li* Long March, we maneuvered to the north. Previously we had had a 300,000-strong army, but at that time only a little more than 20,000 were left. Just at the time we had fewer men, we corrected our mistakes and took the correct road. Later our forces grew. When Chiang Kai-shek came to attack us after the Japanese had been driven away, our enemies were doomed to lose. We, therefore, won the victory of revolution. So far we have had only 15 years of construction. We cannot change China's backwardness in a short period of time. It will take us at least several decades to accomplish it.

China needs peace. Whoever wants peace will get our support. We don't approve of war, but we shall support wars of the oppressed people against the imperialists. We support the revolutionary wars in Cuba and Algeria. We also support the people in southern Vietnam in their struggle against American imperialists. These revolutions are initiated by the people themselves. In Cuba, for instance, we never asked Castro[222] to wage revolution; he himself rose to revolution, and, believe it or not, it was the United States that brought him to revolution; it was American lackeys who brought him to revolution. Take Algeria, for another example. Did we ask Ben Bella[294] to go to revolution? We never knew this man before, and I've never seen him. They themselves rose to revolution. They set up a provisional government, which we recognize. If they ask for support, we shall give them our support. The imperialists label us "bellicose elements," which is true to some extent, because we support Castro, Ben Bella and people in southern Vietnam in their fight against the United States.

One other time, when the U.S. invaded Korea from 1950 to 1953, we supported the Korean people in their struggle against U.S. imperialists. We openly declared this policy and will never give it up. That is to say, we support the wars against imperialism by people of various countries. If we didn't, we would be committing a mistake and no longer be Communists. Nasser,[139] president of the United Arab Republic, is not a Communist, yet he supported the Algerian revolution. Shouldn't we Communists support Algeria? A hundred eighty years ago, when Washington[231] rose against Britain, France supported Washington; were the French communists then? At that time there was no Communist Party in China or in the world. The Communist Party came into being in the 19th century. Probably our label of "bellicose element" will continue to exist.

One main point is our domestic issue. In China we drove the American stooge Chiang Kai-shek as well as the American forces away, so the Americans are not happy with us. I don't mean the American people; I mean American capitalists. We have some Americans living in Beijing, and they are friendly to us.

The United States would make Latin America its colony economically and, in many cases, politically. The party of the former Brazilian president Goulart, whom I met, was a labor party, not a Communist Party, but the United States couldn't tolerate him, so it overthrew him. Even Ngo Dinh Diem,[136] who was slightly disobedient to the U.S., was killed by it. It is not very peaceful within the United States. Ngo Dinh Diem was killed by the Kennedy[245] government, but only months later Kennedy himself went to see his God.

The United States labeled us "aggressors," but we say they are the aggressors. They allege that we are "bellicose elements," but we say the big capitalists of the American government are bellicose elements. It is up to the world's people to judge who are the real aggressors and bellicose elements. The United States has military bases all around China; it even occupied China's Taiwan. We never occupied a single island of the United States and never invaded any Latin American and African countries. We "invade" only one country in Asia—China. We were at war with the imperialists for several decades and drove them away. This made the U.S. very unhappy; other imperialists were unhappy too, but there is no way they can help. Just as they cannot move Chile away, they cannot remove us from the earth. It's impossible for them to move Cuba away or even very small countries, such as Albania.

The Americans predict our government will collapse either this year or next year. I'm afraid it's not true. In my view we won't collapse this year or next year. What about the year after next? I say we won't collapse. To topple our government would require the U.S. and Chiang Kai-shek combined attacking us. Yet even if they did, they couldn't necessarily achieve what they expected. They once came, but they lost. Southern Vietnam has only a 14 million population, but the U.S. finds itself in a dilemma, difficult to advance or to retreat, and is bogged down in a mire. The U.S. also has a headache in Latin America. We are optimistic on this point. People all over the world are bound to stand up; they want to be masters of themselves, not allow the capitalists to be their masters. Because we believe this, we publicly point it out, so the capitalists are not so fond of us. Then why do so many of them, except the U.S., come to do business with us? Because they don't meddle in our internal affairs. We won't do business with the Americans even if they so wish.

We shall not accept their journalists here. We believe that before the major issues are solved, it's not so urgent to solve these minor and special issues. The Chilean journalist delegation can visit China, but American journalists cannot, although they will someday. The relationship between the two countries will eventually be normalized. In my view it will take another 15 years. Because 15 years have already passed, 15 more years mean 30 years all together. If these are not long enough, just add more years.

(From the verbatim record)

LOOKING AT THE PROSPECT OF THE PEOPLE'S STRUGGLE IN ASIA, AFRICA AND LATIN AMERICA FROM A HISTORICAL PERSPECTIVE*

(*July 9, 1964*)

The prospect of the people's struggle in Asia, Africa and Latin America is a question of common concern. If we are to see its prospect, we must look back at history. By looking at the more than a decade of history since the Second World War in Asia, Africa and Latin America we will be able to see the prospect. Take China, for example. Nineteen years ago Japanese militarists occupied over half our country, and we were at war for eight years. After we won the War of Resistance Against Japan, the Americans came. They supported Chiang Kai-shek to launch the civil war. Before liberation the enemies we had to counter included Japanese militarists, American imperialists, their stooges Wang Jingwei,[295] Emperor Kangde of "Manchoukuo"[296] and Chiang Kai-shek. After we won liberation, a Japanese capitalist named Minamigo Saburo[254] had a talk with me. He said, "I'm very sorry for what we did to you. Japan invaded you." I said, "No, if Japanese imperialism had not committed large-scale aggression and occupied over half of China, it would have been impossible for people all over China to unite against imperialism and for the Communist Party of China to win victory." As a matter of fact, Japanese imperialism acted as our good teacher. First, it weakened Chiang Kai-shek; second, we developed the Communist-led bases and armed forces. Prior to the War of Resistance, our army once numbered 300,000. Because we committed mistakes ourselves, our army was reduced to little more than 20,000. During the eight-year War of Resistance, our army increased to 1.2 million. So you see, Japan helped us a lot, didn't it? This help was not given by the

---

* This is the main part of Mao Zedong's talk with delegates from some countries and regions in Asia, Africa and Oceania who were visiting China after attending the Second Asian Economic Seminar in Pyongyang, Korea.

Japanese Communist Party, but by Japanese militarism, because the Japanese Communist Party never invaded us; it was Japanese monopoly capital and its militarist government that invaded us. Our second teacher, who also helped us, was American imperialism. The third teacher who gave us help was Chiang Kai-shek. At that time Chiang Kai-shek attacked us with a four-million-strong army. After four years of war with him our army grew from the previous 1.2 million to over three million. Over 95 percent of Chiang Kai-shek's army was put out of action, and the fewer than five percent remaining fled to Taiwan.

The lesson China acquired was: Where there is oppression, there is resistance; where there is exploitation, there is resistance. Imperialism, whether Japanese, American or other, can be overthrown. Reactionaries within the country, like Chiang Kai-shek, however strong they seem, can be overthrown too. So much for the Chinese history.

Now the Japanese people are highly conscious. They initiated a mass movement against American imperialism and domestic monopoly capital. What made them rise up? It was the oppression and exploitation by American imperialism and Japanese monopoly capital that taught them; the Chinese Communist Party never taught them to do so. In my view Japanese monopoly capital does not fully approve Japan's being occupied by American imperialism. Some Japanese monopoly capitalists are not happy with the occupation, because under the occupation of American imperialists Japan not only lost its colonies, but is itself subject to American control. Today not only the Japanese people, but some Japanese monopoly capitalists are beginning to oppose American imperialism.

Talking about the history of Asia, Africa and Latin America, great changes have taken place in recent decades. In Africa alone more than 30 countries have won independence. Before 1958 I seldom saw Africans, but in the seven years from 1958 to 1964 I have met with African friends on many occasions. There is a great anti-imperialist and anticolonialist storm in Africa. In Egypt, for instance, the Suez Canal Incident[134] took place in 1956. Who were more powerful, the Anglo-French allies or the Egyptian troops? The British and French were so powerful, but they were sent on the run at the first blow. Now is the Suez Canal in the hands of Egyptians or of the British and French imperialists? Let's take a look at Algeria, where the National Liberation Army fought for eight years. In the later stage of the fighting France dispatched 800,000 troops. The National Liberation Army had only 30,000 to 40,000 men. Who were stronger, the Algerian people or the French imperialists? Let's take another look, at Cuba.

Are American imperialism and its lackey Batista[221] stronger or is Castro[222] stronger? Over 80 of Castro's troops disembarked in Cuba from overseas and after fierce fighting only 12 were left. They hid themselves in the homes of peasants and later rose again in guerrilla warfare. After two years or more they won. We openly supported Vietnam and Algeria in their struggle against French aggression. Did we offend the French government by so doing? No, Ho Chi Minh[216] won; Ben Bella[294] won; France, however, recognized China. So things in the world are changing. Now the French are teaching the Americans that America should draw a lesson from France and stop fighting in southern Vietnam. "We French failed; if you Americans continue to fight, like us you will fail." The United States will probably take the lesson of France. Having fought for three years, but unable to win, it cannot win if it fights on, so it must go. You may see that in three years' time or even longer the U.S. is bound to get out of Vietnam. It will leave places such as Thailand, Laos, the Philippines, South Korea and Japan; it will also leave Taiwan. I cannot figure out an exact time when it will go, but it will certainly go. So long as people unite and strengthen their struggle, all the imperialists and colonialists who oppress Asia, Africa and Latin America will go sooner or later. They may go in a decent way, but what should we do if they refuse to go when we ask them to? Then let's learn from the ways of Castro, Ben Bella, Ho Chi Minh, and even China. When we look back at history, we can know the future.

Talking about people, not reactionaries, no people in any country oppress and exploit people of other countries. Take you, representatives of Asian and African countries, for example; do you oppress the Chinese people? Do you exploit the Chinese people? We don't feel that way. Can the Chinese people oppress you? Can they exploit you? If the Chinese government did so, it would be imperialist, not socialist. If any Chinese show no respect, think themselves superior to you or make trouble in your country, just drive them out. This is the most fundamental principle for the unity of people in Asia, Africa and Latin America against imperialism. Our mutual relations are those of brothers, not father and sons. We should consolidate unity and build a broad united front. Whoever they are, whether black, white or yellow; whatever religion they believe in, whether Catholics, Protestants, Muslims or Buddhists; even some national bourgeois—we should unite with them all, so long as they are against imperialism and its stooges. This does not include stooges who helped imperialism in their countries.

As for the question of how to defeat reactionaries within the country,

I believe we can either adopt peaceful means or resort to force. Some countries called on the broad masses of the people to use force against reactionaries, because those reactionaries had weapons in their hands. This is making use of appropriate opportunities in light of the actual conditions of different countries. If he wants to go to war, I just follow. This method comes from the reactionaries; we learned this from Chiang Kai-shek. If he could strike me, why couldn't I strike back?

Some put weapons first and human beings second. Let's put it the other way round: human beings first and weapons second. Similar to machines, weapons are just extensions of human hands. Are human beings in the hands of weapons or weapons in the hands of human beings? Of course the latter, because weapons have no hands. What weapon has hands? I was at war for 25 years, including the three-year Korean War. Previously I didn't know how to fight; I knew nothing about war. I learned how to fight in the course of the 25-year war. I've never seen any weapons with hands; I see only people have hands and use weapons with their hands. Our "reputation" is very bad. American imperialists labeled us "aggressors." They alleged that we invaded China, which was actually true; we invaded Chiang Kai-shek, but Chiang Kai-shek invaded us first. They said we invaded Korea, but that was because the American imperialists had pushed to the Yalu River and we had to send troops to resist U.S. aggression and assist Korea. They also alleged that we invaded India, but that was because India intruded tens of kilometers into China. After it had been there several years on our territory, we launched a counteroffensive in self-defense, pushing the Indians back to the old border. Along the old border line, which runs for several thousand kilometers, the Indians were all gone; there were no troops left. Then we pulled back to the so-called new border line[297] drawn by imperialism. We don't recognize this line. We withdrew 20 kilometers from there and set up a buffer zone. Imperialists allege that we are "bellicose elements" because we helped Ho Chi Minh in the past and now support southern Vietnam against the Americans. We also supported Ben Bella against the French. We'll give our support wherever it is needed. For this reason our "reputation" is bad and we become "bellicose elements."

The friend from Angola asked what illusions and dangers should be prevented while establishing the national economy. Angola has not been liberated, so armed struggle is still needed. All you can do now is to carry out revolution and develop the economy in the base areas. Portugal will never help you. U.S. help has ulterior motives. To prevent illusions, I think you should guard against illusions about the U.S. As to what dangers might emerge in the course of construction, it is hard to predict as of now. To prevent dangers while establishing the national economy, you need to prevent those coming from imperialism. As to making mistakes in actual work, this is hardly avoidable. All parties make mistakes. The Communist Party of China made many mistakes, some major ones. If mistakes are made, just correct them. Mistakes help people remain sober-minded.

(From the verbatim record)

PEOPLE OF THE WORLD ARE AGAINST KILLING BY ATOMBOMBS*

(*August 22, 1964*)

Welcome to our friends. Thank you very much for coming to visit our country. This is my first meeting with you, but we have common points in our thinking. We are of different nationalities, different countries, and probably different beliefs, but we have a fundamentally common point; that is, to oppose imperialism and colonialism, old and new. Our countries, China included, have no atom and hydrogen bombs. France has atom bombs, but the French friends present here are against nuclear wars, isn't that so? Probably China will produce a small number of nuclear weapons in the future, but we are not prepared to use them. Then why should we produce them if we are not prepared to use them? We shall take them as defensive weapons. Now the nuclear powers, particularly the United States, are frightening other countries with their A-bombs. The United States has big stacks of atom bombs, but used them only twice. That was toward the end of the Second World War when the United States dropped two atom bombs on Nagasake and Hiroshima in Japan, which caused damage to the Japanese people. As a result, however, the name of the United States was muddied among the majority of the world's people. People of the world are against killing by atom bombs, against a third world war, and against meddling in the internal affairs of others by foreign troops in southern Vietnam through "special warfare." The French government acknowledged defeat in Vietnam in the past. At present the U.S. is fighting there. As the French see it, the Americans will be defeated as well. Therefore, France is opposed to solving the Vietnamese and Laotian problems through war; it stands for peaceful negotiations. Here France has acquired a certain right to speak. Japan, too, has a certain right to speak. During the Second World War the Japanese government forced its people into a war of aggression, but things changed afterward. It suffered devastation from Amer-

---

* This is part of Mao Zedong's talk with foreign guests who visited China after attending the Tenth World Conference on the Prohibition of A- and H-Bombs in Japan.

ican atom bombs. So the Japanese people, including some government elements, are against nuclear wars. Like ourselves, most of your countries have no atom bombs. We have diplomatic relations with France, and we have one thing in common—to oppose U.S. aggression. We share the common point not only with our French friends here, but also with De Gaulle.[191] The world has changed; no aggression or intervention in other countries is allowed. Aggression and intervention are doomed to failure. Our friends here represent the majority of the human population; your ideals are bound to come true. Of course, what I said has not become reality; it will depend on our struggle before it can be realized. Imperialism can be defeated, and the people will emerge as victors. I don't believe that people cannot win. In my view you don't believe that you cannot win either. What we want is the liberation of people all over the world.

(From the verbatim record)

WE GREATLY APPRECIATE FRANCE'S INDEPENDENT POLICY*

(September 10, 1964)

President De Gaulle criticized West Germany[298] on July 23. I find this criticism quite pertinent. It forced West Germany to consider whether it was being too obedient to the United States. I think the United Kingdom, too, deserves to be criticized for its overcloseness to the United States.

A few big powers are brandishing nuclear weapons and preaching peace at the same time. You in France also possess nuclear weapons, though not many; you're just beginning. We do not yet have such weapons, but nobody can intimidate us. We have never been cowed by the threat of any strong power, even when we were much weaker.

We greatly appreciate this independent policy of France. One ought not to follow in the wake of a few big powers and echo every word they say. The United Kingdom may be counted as a member of the U.S. side, but there are conservatives who do not agree with the policy of the British government. The world is changing, and it is beyond the domination of one or two big powers. The affairs of each country should be administered by its own people, allowing no foreign intervention whatsoever. You said we too have interfered in Southeast Asia. However, so far we have interfered only by means of "prattle," that is, encouraging and supporting anti-U.S. guerrilla wars. This is not a secret; it is known to the public. We support without the slightest disguise all guerrilla wars against U.S. imperialism and local oppressors anyplace in the world.

(From the verbatim record)

---

* This is part of Mao Zedong's talk with the person in charge of the French Technological Exhibition.

TALK WITH EDGAR SNOW ON INTERNATIONAL ISSUES*

(*January 9, 1965*)

Edgar Snow (hereinafter referred to as Snow): I read the Chairman's military writings before I came to see you. With reference to military experts in southern Vietnam may I say the war in southern Vietnam has entered the stage of mobile warfare, like the third revolutionary civil war in China?

Chairman Mao Zedong (hereinafter referred to as Mao): The third revolutionary civil war which started in 1946 was the war of liberation for the whole country. Chiang Kai-shek then had several million troops, and we, more than one million. Up to this point the war in southern Vietnam has not reached such a scale. You can give the U.S. government some advice. Why should it act like this? Wherever it goes, there is war, and the people there learn how to fight. Still it refuses to leave when it is told to do so. Take Ngo Dinh Diem,[136] for example. Both Ho Chi Minh[216] and I felt that he was not too bad—he ought to have been helped to stay on for a few years. However, some U.S. generals detested, overthrew and killed him. Can there be peace under heaven this way?

Snow: Of course, the Liberation Army of South Vietnam does not have such strength in manpower as the Eighth Route Army or the subsequent Liberation Army, but, likewise, the Saigon regime does not have so many troops as Chiang Kai-shek.

Mao: No, not so many, and they don't know how to fight. They are even inferior to Chiang Kai-shek.

Snow: Can one say that South Vietnam has sufficient strength by itself to withstand external intervention and oppose local reactionaries?

Mao: I think it can. At least it has a more favorable situation than we had during the second revolutionary civil war. We had no direct foreign intervention at that time. Southern Vietnam's advantage is the presence of

---

* This is the main part of Mao Zedong's talk with Edgar Snow, an American writer and a friend to China.

20,000 Americans, who will educate most of the people, including the soldiers and some officers in the army. People opposed to the American troops are not all Liberation Army, just as Ngo Dinh Diem didn't approve of them. Some people in the government army do not either.

Snow: It is very obvious.

Mao: They have bitter quarrels.

Snow: Is it possible to persuade some of the southern Vietnamese troops to join the Vietnamese Communists?

Mao: I think it's possible just like Fu Zuoyi[299] and Tao Zhiyue[300] of Xinjiang, Cheng Qian[301] and Chen Mingren[302] of Hunan.

Snow: Great changes have taken place in the international situation since I last visited China. Africa is awakening. Under such circumstances can I say the current principal contradiction is the contradiction between imperialism and the newly emerging forces in Asia, Africa and Latin America? Is this contradiction more important than that existing among imperialist countries?

Mao: What's your view? I am not very clear about that. Unlike you, I have not visited many places. What do you think? I want you to be my teacher and inform me about the international situation.

Snow: I believe you can answer this question. I'm unable to do so, or I must wait to read your next book. I can see from your writings that you have paid special attention to these events. From these can one conclude that the contradiction between imperialism and the newly emerging forces in Asia, Africa and Latin America is the principal one?

Mao: I think the U.S. President has also said so. The former President on many occasions mentioned that there were relatively few troubles in the United States, Canada and Western Europe, and it was the Southern Hemisphere that was beset with serious troubles. Kennedy[245] talked about this question many times. The special war and the local war he proposed were to deal with this situation. Some sources said he also read my writings on military affairs. It may be true. When the Algerian issue was still without a settlement, some Algerians asked me what to do when not only they were using the theory in my writings but the French were doing the same. It was Ferhat Abbas, the then prime minister, who made these remarks; he had visited China. I replied: "How can you make use of my theory? I wrote on the basis of China's experiences, so my theory is suitable only for a people's war, not a war against the people. Chiang Kai-shek also studied our materials, many of which he acquired in the course of the war, but this by no means retrieved his defeat. Likewise, the French were unable to save themselves from failure just by reading my writings."

Now we are also studying U.S. military writings. Maxwell Davenport Taylor, the U.S. ambassador to southern Vietnam and ex-chairman of the Joint Chiefs of Staff, wrote the book *The Uncertain Trumpet*, from which it seems that he did not quite approve of nuclear weapons. He said nuclear weapons had not been used in the Korean War or in the Chinese War of Liberation. So he doubted whether one could win a war in future by relying on these weapons. He stressed manpower and funds for the army, but also the production of nuclear weapons, letting the two develop in parallel. He said an army was imperative and the U.S. must maintain 800,000 to 900,000 troops. While the army insists on manpower, the air force asks for more aircraft and nuclear weapons, and the navy maintains its own stand. Since Taylor represents the army, he was contending for the army's top priority. Now he has the opportunity to experiment in South Vietnam. He went to South Vietnam last June and it has been less than a year, not as long as his stay in Korea. He will get his experience. I have read the rules and regulations for the U.S. troops to deal with guerrilla warfare in South Vietnam, and they simply enumerate a number of advantages and disadvantages of guerrilla war and conclude that it is possible to wipe out the guerrilla forces in South Vietnam.

Snow: The Americans are politically weak, not militarily.

Mao: That could be. The government of South Vietnam is unpopular. Both the Ngo Dinh Diem regime and the present one are divorced from the masses. It will come to no good end to assist such unpopular governments. The Americans refused to listen to not only my advice, but yours as well.

Snow: They didn't listen to me in the past, that's why they have suffered so many defeats. We can see clearly now that the military and economic gaps between Asia, Africa and Latin America on one side and the developed countries on the other have become increasingly wider, and, meanwhile, what neocolonialism has done makes the gaps even wider. Isn't this the principal contradiction? Is it not only to resist the U.S. but to adapt to this principal contradiction that France changes its policy?

Mao: I have talked with the French. I asked the French National Assembly Delegation if the Third World included France. They said no. Now one side consists of developed countries; the other side, undeveloped countries. The so-called developed countries were not so unanimous; they have never been so. For instance, two world wars took place among the developed United Kingdom, France, Germany, Italy and Japan. Weren't the developed countries fighting one another? Their aim was to contend for the so-called undeveloped countries. Why did they want to fight? Could they not sleep or eat? You haven't taken part in that war; your former President participated in the

Second World War, and so did the incumbent President.

Snow: I was in Russia as a war correspondent then.

Mao: How long did you stay there?

Snow: Two and a half years. I was in the United Kingdom and France after the war. I never killed anybody, but I was almost killed on several occasions.

Mao: How dangerous! But you still went to the front?

Snow: A war correspondent is an accessory of war. I didn't go to the front in Russia, but I went to the front in Germany and France. I visited Stalingrad when it was under German attack.

Mao: Before or after the attack?

Snow: At the time of the surrender of Hitler's[4] troops.

Mao: Hitler was then really terrific, having occupied almost the whole of Europe, excepting east of the Moscow-Leningrad-Stalingrad front. And not counting United Kingdom. He occupied North Africa as well. However, he blundered: If after the Dunkirk evacuation[303] his troops had immediately followed into the United Kingdom, the latter would have been at the end of its tether. A British prime minister told Premier Zhou Enlai in Geneva that the United Kingdom had no more troops at all then, and it was vulnerable everywhere. However, the Germans hesitated to drive forward just because of the English Channel.

Snow: Hitler was impatient to attack Russia at that time. Is there any hope for improvement in Sino-U.S. relations?

Mao: I think there is, but it needs time. Probably it will not be realized during my lifetime, as God will summon me before long. Perhaps you will be able to witness it. According to dialectics, life is limited after all.

Snow: You look very healthy, Chairman.

Mao: I have prepared many times, but always failed to meet death. What could I do? On many occasions death seemed to be at my elbow, including the dangers during war that you have mentioned. Once, a guard, who was at my side, was killed by a bomb, and his blood splashed on me. However, the bomb just didn't hit me.

Snow: This happened when you were in Yan'an?

Mao: A lot of times. Once was on the Long March. After crossing the Dadu River, we were bombed by aircraft and the chief of my guards was killed, but the blood didn't splash on me that time.

You know that I was a teacher in an elementary school before. I never thought of fighting a battle or of organizing the Communist Party. I was then a democrat, almost like you. Later on, I didn't know why, I was engaged in the work of the Communist Party. In short, this was independent of our will. China was oppressed by imperialism, feudalism and bureaucratic capitalism; and there was also the oppression of warlords at one time. This is a fact.

Snow: The objective conditions made revolution inevitable. Such conditions no longer exist. What will the next generation do, since conditions in China have changed?

Mao: I don't know either. That's the business of the next generation. No one knows what they will do. However, there are a couple of possibilities: One is to carry on the revolution; the other is to negate the revolution, do evil deeds, make peace with imperialism, allow Chiang Kai-shek to return to the mainland, and side with a handful of domestic counterrevolutionaries. This is called counterrevolution. You ask my opinion; certainly I don't wish to see the emergence of a counterrevolution. What will happen will be decided by future generations. Taking a long view, future generations will be wiser than we, just as people of the capitalist period are wiser and better than those of the feudal period. Feudalism didn't exist in the United States, but it existed in Europe.

Snow: It can't be said that the U.S. was entirely free of feudalism. One cause of the Civil War[304] was anti-feudalism.

Mao: It was a contention of labor forces; the so-called liberation of Negro slaves in fact meant opening the labor market.

Snow: Although the period of feudal domination in the south was not long, the feudal ideology was quite deep-rooted in the U.S.

Mao: The south is now relatively more backward than the north.

Snow: Do you still think that the atomic bomb is a paper tiger?

Mao: I was just using a figure of speech. It will kill people if it is used. However, it will be eliminated finally, and then it will turn into a paper tiger, because it is no more!

Snow: You must have heard someone say, "Chairman Mao maintains that in case of nuclear war, the people of many countries will be completely wiped out, but China will still have several hundred million people left."

Mao: What do you think?

Snow: In effect you have indirectly replied to the question. It was also mentioned in an article about polemics between China and the Soviet Union.

Mao: I've forgotten the reply.

Snow: I'm afraid I've forgotten too, but in my memory it was referred to in an article as a lie, an assertion planted on you.

Mao: What did it say?

Snow: It said in case of nuclear war, China would still have several hundred million people left. A Yugoslav citizen alleged you told him this when he visited China in the latter half of the fifties.

Mao: I don't remember it, but perhaps I said so. I remember saying only this: We don't want war. We have no atomic bomb. If some other country plans to launch a nuclear war, the whole world may suffer disaster. A disaster will cause casualties. How many casualties? Nobody knows. There must be some. I didn't mean China alone. I didn't believe the atomic bomb could destroy all mankind. If all were destroyed, there would be no government to make peace with. This was mentioned in one of the conversations I had with Nehru[209] in Beijing. He told me that he was the director of the Atomic Energy Commission of India and he knew the destructive power of the atomic bomb. I said it might not be so serious as he asserted, that no government would exist to make peace with after a nuclear war. If one government falls, another government will rise to succeed it. Somebody invariably rises. I didn't say the whole world would perish. I heard that there is a U.S. film called *On the Beach*.

Snow: It is a fictitious novel, describing the destruction of all mankind.

Mao: How awful! Khrushchev[146] has said there is a kind of bomb, something to do with lasers, in his grasp that could destroy all mankind, all animals and plants. Later he repeatedly denied saying this. I never deny what I have said. Please don't deny this alleged rumor on my behalf.

Snow: I also mentioned in my book that you might have said that, aiming to find out the response of the other party.

Mao: This was because a politician of a big power asserted there would be no government then. I was refuting his assertion.

Snow: So it was referred to for the first time under such circumstances?

Mao: Yes, it was in October 1954. The Americans said something about the formidable destructive power of the atomic bomb, and Khrushchev echoed with an arrogant air. They have all surpassed me. I am lagging behind them. Am I right? Rather backward. I read the recent reports on the visit of a number of U.S. experts to Bikini Island.[305] After landing, they found that rats were running here and there as usual, fish were swimming in the lake, the water from the well was still drinkable, plants were flourishing and birds abundant. They had to chop down trees to open a way into the island. This island underwent experiments with nuclear explosions for 12 years, and the experts visited it after six more years. I think creatures had a hard time there within the first one or two years after the explosions, then began to propagate again. Why were the rats not affected at all? Because they hid themselves in holes underground. Why are the plants still so abundant? I judge a lot must have perished, whereas the survivors again started to grow, then flourished after a few years.

Snow: I have seen a film about how all creatures were destroyed not long after the explosion of a hydrogen bomb. Sea turtles came ashore to lay eggs, which failed to breed baby turtles.

Mao: They might be able to breed after some years, but I don't know whether it would be the same for human beings.

Snow: Beetles have the strongest vitality.

Mao: In short, the atomic bomb was only a paper tiger so far as the birds, trees and sea turtles in that place were concerned. Perhaps human beings are a bit weaker than they.

Snow: Human beings are more likely to suffer from toxins made by themselves. The ants consider they rule the world; they are the masters of the world.

Mao: In the eyes of the ants, all men are mere trifles. Ants are relatively big animals. Germs do what men fail to do. The world's total population is only some three billion. A pedologist told me that each *mu* of land contains 400 kilograms of germs. There would be no soil or plant growth without germs. Therefore, don't despise them just because they are so small; they can enter the body of every man, whether he's a president or a journalist. They are very formidable.

Snow: Germs can't be seen at all.

Mao: A man can't live apart from germs. There are innumerable kinds of germs in the human body, and according to medical science, germs such as the colon bacillus and fungi in the mouth cavity are extremely beneficial to human beings. We have identical views on this question. The investigation by U.S. experts on Bikini Island is good data. We have published the data and distributed them to the deputies to the National People's Congress for their reading.

Snow: Is this an open report?

Mao: No, it was written by a Chinese, citing the data of the U.S. experts, and published in *News World* in Hong Kong.

Snow: Nevertheless, you don't think nuclear war to be a good thing?

Mao: Right. Better not launch nuclear war at all. Use conventional weapons if you want to wage war.

Snow: It seems that the Asian, African and Latin American regions have become more and more modernized, and revolutions there are developing more and more vigorously.

Mao: Possibly.

Snow: Can revolutions in Asian, African and Latin American countries achieve complete success without a third world war breaking out?

Mao: It is hard to say. Maybe it requires a relatively long period of time.

Snow: China has given its support to Indonesia's withdrawal from the United Nations. Will this not set a precedent for other countries?

Mao: It is the United States which has set a precedent. In order to prevent China from entering the U.N., it has proposed that China can only enter with a two-thirds majority vote. Isn't China doing quite well without being in the U.N.? Indonesia has withdrawn from the U.N. because it feels that it has not benefited from participation in the organization.

Snow: Can I say China does not want to join the United Nations?

Mao: No. If two thirds of the U.N. members expect us to join that organization, and we refuse to do so, won't they call us nationalistic? However, we demand that the U.N. repeal its slander of China as an aggressor and at the same time designate the U.S. an aggressor. Do you think this argument will work? How could China join the U.N. in the capacity of an aggressor country? The U.S. won't agree either if we call it an aggressor. Hence we don't wish to join the U.N. at present, and likewise the U.S. is not willing we participate, which might prove a hindrance. Both sides agree to a certain extent on this point. Therefore, it is better to let Generalissimo Chiang Kai-shek stay and represent China in the U.N. for the time being! Well, please don't cover this part of our conversation, because we have not yet made it public.

Snow: Would it be possible to have a U.N. without the U.S.?

Mao: The Afro-Asian Conference was held without the participation of the U.S.

Snow: There is also the Games of the Newly Emerging Forces.[306]

Mao: China is a big country and we have a lot of our own affairs to take care of. We are rather busy. China itself is a U.N. Our U.N. has received you; has that U.N. received you yet? When do you plan to leave China?

Snow: After a few days. When I return to the United States this time, perhaps Johnson[284] will let me see him. Have you any message for him?

Mao: No.

Snow: I can take him this word as well.

At present, China stresses maintaining a revolutionary spirit among the young people. The important thing lies in setting an example for similar countries and promoting revolution in other countries, so that the Chinese revolution finds final security, doesn't it?

Mao: On the last point, it is difficult to say. What security do you think there is? Aren't people now talking about disarmament? But in which year will it actually be carried out? Aren't they talking about general and complete disarmament? The Soviet Union talked about it in the past, and now the U.S. is talking about it. We also agree with general disarmament. In fact, the present situation is general and complete expansion of armament instead of disarmament, which is receiving only lip service.

Snow: The North Atlantic Treaty Organization[189] is doing just that. Owing to the proliferation of nuclear weapons, every country is crying for its own atomic bomb.

Mao: Only China is prohibited from having one. We don't wish to possess many atomic bombs. Why do we need many? A few will do, just for scientific experiment.

Snow: You said before that in breaking down the local tyrants and evil gentry in Jiangxi, they called Mr. Soviet a very bad fellow, while throughout the course of the Chinese revolution, the West complained that Mr. Socialism had made a lot of trouble. Now they put the blame on China's atomic bomb.

Mao: This shows that my reputation and that of the Chinese government and the Chinese Communist Party are not good. Why should they oppose China and launch an anti-Chinese tide? When we were still unprepared, suddenly Kennedy was no more. When the Vietnamese people were likewise in bewilderment, Ngo Dinh Diem was no more. Another example is Khrushchev's sudden ouster. God knows! It was done so thoroughly that all his books and pictures were removed overnight.

Snow: Quite a number of European parties have criticized the Soviet party for expelling Khrushchev by such means.

Mao: We don't have many Khrushchev pictures here, but Khrushchev's books are in our bookstores as before. How can the world be without a Khrushchev! His spirit will haunt us, and persons of his ilk will always exist.

Snow: Can we say the proportion of the faults and merits of the new Soviet leadership is 30 percent to 70 percent, i.e., they are 70 percent correct?

Mao: You mean the present Soviet leadership? It's hard to say. Some people say they are engaged in Khrushchevism without Khrushchev.

Snow: Has there been any improvement in Sino-Soviet relations since Khrushchev fell out of power?

Mao: Perhaps a little, but not much. His fall caused us to lose an object of criticism in our articles.

Snow: Some Russians say a personality cult exists in China.

Mao: I am afraid there is a bit. It is alleged that Stalin had a personality cult, Khrushchev not in the least, and the Chinese have one. There is some truth in this. Khrushchev was ousted most probably because he lacked a personality cult.

Snow: I take my acquaintance with you, Chairman, as a great honor, and it also brings me a lot of personal advantages. I hope I can impart your thinking to other people. I sincerely feel that your achievements are great. Of course, I don't mean that everything is ideal, but in brief, you have done many great deeds. It is regrettable that China and the U.S., as well as the Chinese people and the American people, are separated because of historical reasons.

Mao: The two countries will get close to each other through historical reasons as well. We must wait; this will invariably come.

Snow: I don't think a major war will break out between China and the U.S.

Mao: Maybe you are right. U.S. troops may come to China and they may not. They will find things not so easy if they come, and we won't let them reap any benefit. Perhaps they won't come because of this. You can rest assured, as I have said before, that we shall not attack the U.S.

Snow: Some Americans say the war in southern Vietnam will be extended to the north.

Mao: Dean Rusk[307] recently corrected his version, saying he never made such remarks.

Snow: Certainly I don't think the American government will listen to me. A U.S. Congressman called Frank Church suggested that a debate take place on the U.S. policy of interference in the affairs of other countries. He is Johnson's good friend. The rulers of the United States don't understand you, and I'm afraid I myself don't understand you either.

Mao: How so? We shall not make war beyond China, and we shall fight in defense only if the U.S. comes and attacks us. History will be our witness. Why should we go out to attack other people while we are so much occupied with our own affairs? That would be committing a crime. South Vietnam doesn't require our presence there at all. They are able to handle the situation themselves.

Snow: The Americans fighting the war in South Vietnam say China will occupy all of Southeast Asia if they withdraw from South Vietnam.

Mao: How occupy? By our troops or by the local people? The Chinese had better occupy China.

Snow: Are there Chinese troops in South Vietnam?

Mao: No.

Snow: Rusk said the U.S. will withdraw from South Vietnam if China and North Vietnam abandon their aggressive policy.

Mao: We have no aggressive policy to abandon. We haven't committed any aggression. But we do support revolutions; we have to. We shall issue statements and hold meetings to express our support wherever there is revolution. Imperialism dislikes this. We are fond of prattle and empty talk, but send no troops. Can this be called aggression, whereas sending troops is not aggression?

Snow: Formerly people said China was supported by Russia, and now they say South Vietnam is supported by China.

Mao: The victory of the Chinese civil war chiefly relied on U.S. weapons, which proved we had no official support from foreign countries. In fact, South Vietnam obtained their arms from the U.S. In addition, they have often captured soldiers of the South Vietnamese puppet regime to replenish their manpower since last year. It is like us in the past—one source of our manpower was Chiang Kai-shek's troops. They were forced to be soldiers and had undergone some training, so once they were captured, they joined our troops in fighting.

Snow: Why?

Mao: Because they were pressganged by the Kuomintang, and they hated the Kuomintang.

Snow: There is one more point: The Chinese Communist Party and people throughout the country are in accord.

Mao: It was under the pressgang of the Kuomintang that poor peasants became soldiers. Our method was to call meetings for them to pour out their grievances and hold memorial ceremonies for the souls of the dead. If a person was murdered by the Kuomintang, his name would be written on a piece of paper as a memorial to his soul. After settling matters this way, they would join our troops right away and change caps. Why did they wear our caps? Simply because they were afraid of being mistaken for Kuomintang soldiers if they were killed. With this cap on their head, they would be identified as our men.

Snow: To a great extent, South Vietnam is now in such circumstances.

Mao: There must be revolution wherever there is oppression. The course of socialist revolution is just like this. When capitalism developed to a certain stage, the bourgeoisie rose against feudalism. The feudal system didn't exist in the U.S., but there was colonialism—Great Britain. As soon as U.S. capitalism developed to a certain stage, it rose against Britain. For people the world over, who will rise to revolution without being subjected to oppression? The American War of Independence[308] was caused by British oppression. Is it almost 200 years since the American War of Independence?

Snow: The slogan put forward by many revolutionaries during the War of Independence was the same as that raised during the French Revolution[309] later on. The U.S. was the only republic in the world then. The view of the U.S. of the European countries at that time is identical with the U.S. view of China today.

Mao: Washington[231] had a bad reputation, so we can post-humously admit him to the Party.

Snow: The Chinese Communist Party would consider him a reactionary, therefore wouldn't let him join it.

Mao: Being unable to join the Communist Party is a fact, because there wasn't any Communist Party at that time. Still we must acknowledge the revolutionary role played by Washington. He played an advanced role, very progressive, and Abraham Lincoln[310] as well.

Snow: Lincoln was a self-contradictory man and, in the meantime, a great man. He was a humanist. Before I leave China, may I ask you, Chairman, to say a few words to the American people who entertain good feelings toward China?

Mao: I wish them progress. If I wished them liberation, perhaps some people wouldn't agree. I just wish liberation to those who are themselves aware that they have not yet been liberated and have difficulties making a living.

Snow: Your remarks are excellent, Chairman, particularly with reference to what you said before, i.e., China will not go out to attack other people, and China is occupied with its own affairs. I myself have seen this point.

Mao: Whether the Americans need reliberation or not is their own business. They are to be liberated not from British domination, but from the domination of monopoly capital.

Snow: Won't you make some suggestions for the U.S. President?

Mao: It is difficult. The hands of Americans have stretched out to the whole world. We advised them a long time ago to restrain a little. As a rule, they refuse to listen.

Snow: Almost half the U.S. troops are stationed abroad. It seems that a number of U.S. troops in foreign countries have become hostages of the local people.

Mao: This puts the U.S. government into a dilemma: It is embarrassed to quit and likewise embarrassed not to quit. To withdraw is difficult, and refusing to withdraw is also difficult. They will send troops wherever there is any rustle of leaves in the wind, thus they have to be transferred here and there. Sometimes we raised a hue and cry on purpose—for instance, bombarding Jinmen with a few shells. The U.S. felt the Seventh Fleet was not strong enough, just because of these few shells, and hastened to shift part of the Sixth

Fleet, in addition to some naval forces from San Francisco. Then we stopped our shelling, and the American troops had to go back, as they had nothing to do after coming here. Therefore, the American troops are subject to transfer at our mere beckoning, a bit like Chiang Kai-shek's troops.

Snow: They have to have something to do, at any rate.

Mao: They won't remain idle. U.S. monopoly capitalists just want to go somewhere to help the reactionaries. They have to help and they have to quit in the end, like the way they helped Chiang Kai-shek. American troops were stationed in Shanghai, Qingdao, Tianjin, Tangshan and Beijing in the past, but they all left subsequently in a hurry. They lost no time leaving when they were still a great distance from our troops. Britain was rather foolish then; it sent warships to Nanjing to transport its soldiers, which were hit by us. The crux of the matter was that there was in China such a disappointing fellow as Chiang Kai-shek, who always suffered defeat, and in the meantime there was the formidable Liberation Army. If it hadn't been for these conditions, the Americans would have stayed.

Snow: Do you mean that the Americans will withdraw from South Vietnam only under identical circumstances?

Mao: The American troops will not leave South Vietnam now, they may continue to fight for another one or two years. But if they find the war insipid and get tired of it, perhaps they will leave.

Snow: If I didn't misunderstand Premier Zhou Enlai's words, I remember that he told me it would be impossible to settle the issue of South Vietnam through negotiations before the withdrawal of the American troops. Is that right?

Mao: I don't know what Premier Zhou said. I am afraid we have to be prepared for two possibilities. We can negotiate either before or after withdrawal. Or no negotiations at all; let South Vietnam expel the American troops. They may hang on there even after negotiations, as in Korea. We had such experience in Geneva. After the Geneva Conference[95] the U.S. sent troops to replace the French in South Vietnam. To be honest, the presence of U.S. troops in South Vietnam is a good thing; it will temper the people and strengthen the liberation army. To have just a Ngo Dinh Diem won't do, just as to have only a Chiang Kai-shek wouldn't do in China; not until the greater part of China was occupied by Japan and, moreover, the occupation lasted eight years, could the Chinese people be tempered.

(From the verbatim record)

WE HOPE THE ARAB COUNTRIES WILL UNITE*

(*March 23, 1965*)

All revolutionaries and political parties in Asia should unite against imperialism. The strength of one or two countries is insufficient, but they can become a formidable force by uniting together. The entire Arab world is confronting imperialism. We hope the Arab countries will unite.

The hands of the Americans stretch very far, committing aggression everywhere. In 1958 they landed in Lebanon and British troops landed in Jordan, thus creating a tense situation. They were compelled to withdraw only under the pressure of world public opinion. Subsequently, civil war broke out in Lebanon. The U.S. Sixth Fleet is in the Mediterranean Sea and its Seventh Fleet surrounds us. The U.S. has four fleets altogether: The Seventh Fleet is the biggest, then the Sixth Fleet; the Second Fleet is scattered along the U.S. West Coast, and it is the reserve force of the Seventh Fleet; the First Fleet is on the U.S. East Coast, as the reserve force of the Sixth Fleet. Moreover, the U.S. has military bases in Morocco, Libya and other places, while the U.K. also has such bases in Aden and the Persian Gulf.

In resisting Japanese imperialism we stood together with the U.S., U.K. and France. After the surrender of Japan the U.S. helped Chiang Kai-shek launch the civil war to attack us. The U.K. and France were at that time powerless to bother about our affairs. The United States didn't directly participate in the war, only stationed some troops in harbors along the Chinese coast. They withdrew after we had annihilated Chiang Kai-shek's several million troops and when we were about to liberate those harbors. We later encountered them again on the Korean battlefield and fought for three years. The Vietnamese people have also met them now. It seems that the United States is fond of making war. Korea and Vietnam are so distant from the U.S., yet it still sent troops there.

---

* This is the main part of Mao Zedong's talk with a visiting Syrian goodwill delegation.

Both our countries were subjected to colonial oppression. You were under French domination, while we were under the domination of several imperialist powers. They divided China into spheres of influence, one for France, one for Britain and another for Japan. They were all expelled by us afterward. We fought against Japanese imperialism in the northeast for 14 years and in other places for eight years. Japanese imperialism helped us by causing China to unite against it, thus promoting the Chinese revolution. American troops are now occupying our Taiwan, South Korea and many places in Japan, as well as waging war in Vietnam. In fact, such behavior by the U.S. is teaching the Asian people they must unite and carry on a resolute struggle. For example, the Vietnamese people didn't know how to fight a war before, but they are able to do so now. This is the advantage rendered us by imperialism. Imperialism also has its good side, don't you agree?

Sometimes imperialism educates the people through its running dogs, such as China's Chiang Kai-shek, who taught us how to fight by launching the civil war. A person like me was unable to fight, having never even thought of such a thing in the past. However, the running dogs of imperialism forced us to take up arms. There are now wars in Africa: in the Congo,[258] Angola, Portuguese Guinea[311] and elsewhere. Algeria obtained independence after fighting for eight years. War also broke out around the Suez Canal.[134] You won independence when the French were forced to evacuate during the Second World War. Is that right?

We are different in appearance and in religious beliefs. I should say I have no religion, but this by no means hampers our cooperation. I believed in polytheism when I was a child and abandoned it as I grew up. China also has a God, but one different from yours; our god wears Chinese clothes. We help each other, support each other, and do not harm the other party. We won't subvert you, nor you us. We are friendly countries and share a common objective: first, to oppose imperialism and, second, to build up our own country.

We support revolution wherever it takes place. Imperialism hates us very much, calling us bellicose. In fact, the problems of any country can be solved only by the revolution of the local people. External support, though necessary, is only secondary. For example, there are only 14 million people in South Vietnam, yet they are putting up a good fight.

The Arab people are very militant. If you unite, the imperialist conspiracy won't succeed. It should be put this way, that every nation is militant, and victory can be obtained through unity and struggle. It's only a matter of time. The victory of the revolution in China was obtained by undergoing 22 years of fighting: first against the domestic enemy, conducting the Long March, then against Japanese imperialism, and finally against the Chiang Kai-shek reactionaries supported by the U.S. We also committed mistakes during this period, such as Rightist and "Leftist" opportunism. We won after our mistakes were corrected. A man invariably commits mistakes. A political party is like a man. It is impossible not to commit any mistakes at all.

Many examples have proved that imperialism can be defeated, and revolution will be triumphant.

(From the verbatim record)

STATEMENT IN SUPPORT OF THE DOMINICAN PEOPLE'S OPPOSITION TO U.S. ARMED AGGRESSION

(May 12, 1965)

A coup d'état to overthrow the traitorous-dictatorial regime of Cabral[312] took place recently in the Dominican Republic. The Johnson administration of the United States sent more than 30,000 armed troops to carry out bloody suppression. This is a serious provocation by U.S. imperialism against the Dominican people, and also against the people of the Latin American countries and of the world as a whole.

Right now the patriotic Dominican people are putting up a heroic struggle against the U.S. aggressors and their lackeys.

The Chinese people resolutely support the Dominican people in their anti-U.S., patriotic armed struggle. I am convinced that the Dominican anti-U.S. patriotic struggle will win final victory provided there are reliance on the broad masses of the people, unity of all patriotic forces and persistence in protracted struggle, plus the support of the people of the whole world.

U.S. imperialism has never desisted from its actions of control, intervention, subversion and aggression against Latin American countries. This time the U.S. government has thrown to the winds all its deceitful talk of a so-called "good-neighbor policy," "principle of non-interference" and other claptrap, and gone over to naked intervention and aggression against the Dominican Republic, thus revealing all the more the true colors of the U.S. imperialist bandits.

The United States has resorted to armed intervention in Dominica under the pretext of "defending freedom." But what kind of "freedom" is this? It is the freedom to slaughter the people of another country by means of airplanes, warships and guns; the freedom to occupy the territory and trample on the sovereignty of another country at will; the freedom of a robber to kill and plunder; the freedom to tread all countries and peoples underfoot. This is what they do in Dominica, in Vietnam, in the Congo (Leopoldville), and in many other places.

The U.S. armed intervention in Dominica also flaunted the banner of "anti-communism." The "anti-communism" of U.S. imperialism is simply opposition to all people who refuse to be slaves of the United States, opposition to all who would defend the independence, sovereignty and national dignity of their country, and opposition to all who resent U.S. imperialist aggression, control, intervention and bullying. This is what Hitler, Mussolini and Tojo did in the past, and now U.S. imperialism is doing it even more recklessly.

In the eyes of U.S. imperialism, the United Nations, the Organization of American States and all other organs are nothing but tools in its hands. It will use them as long as they serve its purpose, and spurn them when they do not. After being discarded, a tool can be picked up again. Whether it is used or discarded, all depends on whether a tool serves its aggressive purpose or not.

The U.S. aggression against the Dominican Republic has enabled the Dominican people and the people of the other Latin American countries to further realize that they must fight tit-for-tat against the inveterately aggressive U.S. imperialism in order to safeguard their national independence and state sovereignty.

The U.S. armed intervention in Dominica has aroused a new anti-U.S. wave among the people in the Latin American countries and the rest of the world. Heroic Dominican people, your struggle is by no means an isolated one. The people of the Latin American countries are supporting you; the people of the Asian countries are supporting you; the people of the African countries are supporting you; the people of the countries of the socialist camp are supporting you, and people all over the world are supporting you.

Let the people of the countries of the socialist camp unite. Let the people of the Asian, African and Latin American countries unite. Let the people of all continents of the world unite. Let all peace-loving countries unite. Let all countries which are subjected to U.S. aggression, control, intervention and bullying unite. Form a most extensive united front to oppose U.S. imperialism's policy of aggression and war, and to defend world peace.

The struggle of the people of the world against U.S. imperialism is sure to be victorious!

U.S. imperialism, the common enemy of the people of the world, is sure to be defeated!

(From *People's Daily*, May 12, 1965)

FAITH IN VICTORY IS DERIVED FROM STRUGGLE*

(*October 20, 1965*)

You have put up a good fight, both in the south and in the north. People the world over are supporting you, including those who have awakened and some of those who have not yet awakened. The present world is not one of peace and tranquillity, but that is not because you Vietnamese or we Chinese have invaded the U.S.

Not long ago the Japanese newspapers *Asahi Shimbun* and *Yomiuri Shimbun* carried several reports sent back from South Vietnam by Japanese correspondents. American papers called these reports unjust, thus instigating a debate. What I have mentioned is not the *Akahata* of the Japanese Communist Party, but Japan's bourgeois newspapers. It can be seen that public opinion is unfavorable to the U.S. Demonstrations by the American people, mainly the intellectuals at present, against the Vietnamese policy of the U.S. government have been developing.

However, these are external conditions; settlement of the issue still depends on your fighting. Of course, it can also be achieved through negotiations. There were negotiations in Geneva, but the Americans didn't keep their word afterward. We likewise had negotiations with Chiang Kai-shek and the U.S. Rusk[307] once said that the U.S. and China have held the most numerous negotiations. But we stick to one point, that is, the U.S. must withdraw from Taiwan; other questions aren't difficult to solve. The U.S. doesn't agree. The ten years of negotiations between China and the U.S. still harp on the same issue. We will not concede on this. The U.S. suggested exchanging visits of a press delegation with us. It said we could start with minor things, then solve the major questions. We insisted that we ought to begin with the major questions; the minor ones will not be difficult.

Formerly you evacuated your armed forces from the south in accordance with the Geneva agreement.[95] In consequence, the enemy there killed at

---

* This is the major part of Mao Zedong's talk with a Party and government delegation from the Democratic Republic of Vietnam.

random, so you reengaged in armed struggle. At the beginning, you put political struggle before armed struggle. We agreed with you. At the second stage you carried on political struggle in parallel with armed struggle. This we also agreed with. At the third stage you put armed struggle first with political struggle as auxiliary. We further agreed with you. As I see it, as the enemy escalates the war, you escalate your fighting as well. You may have a little difficulty in the next two or three years, but it's hard to say; things may not be this way. At any rate, this factor must be taken into consideration. If you have made all preparations, you won't be too far from the original estimate, even if the most difficult situation occurs. Isn't that fine? Therefore, what is basic is: One, strive for the best and two, prepare for the worst.

You may refer to the experience of Algeria. When the war there was going into its fourth or fifth year, some leaders began to worry about it. Prime Minister Abbas came to me, saying that Algeria had a rather small population, only ten million, among whom one million had already been killed; the enemy maintained an army of 800,000 men, while their regular army was composed of merely 30,000 or 40,000—fewer than 100,000 men even if the guerrilla forces were included. I told them then that the enemy would surely collapse, and the population would grow if they persevered till victory. The French troops withdrew after negotiations, and they have now completed the withdrawal, leaving but a few naval bases. In Algeria it was a national democratic revolution led by the bourgeoisie. Both you and we are Communists, and concerning the questions of mobilizing the masses and carrying out a people's war, Algeria is different from you and us.

Some specific questions in connection with a people's war that I mentioned in my writings are affairs of ten or 20 years ago. You are meeting new situations at present, so a lot of your ways of dealing with them are and ought to be different from ours in the past. We learned how to fight step by step and frequently suffered defeat in the beginning; it was not so smooth as for you.

I haven't yet taken note of what questions you are going to discuss with the U.S. I heed only how to fight the Americans and how to expel them. You may negotiate with them at a certain time, but you ought not to lower your tone; always keep it at a high key. You must be prepared to be deceived by the enemy.

We support you to win final victory. Faith in victory is derived from fighting, from struggle. For instance, the Americans are subject to attack and this experience can be gained only through fighting them. The Americans are subject to attack, I said, and they can be defeated. We must break down that sort of myth, that the Americans cannot be attacked or defeated. We both have had a lot of experience. Both you and we fought the Japanese; you also fought the French, and now you are fighting the Americans.

The Americans have trained and educated the Vietnamese people, and they have likewise educated us and people the world over. In my opinion, it would be no good without the Americans; it is necessary to have this teacher. One must learn from the Americans if one wants to defeat them. The works of Marx didn't teach us how to fight the Americans, nor did Lenin's books. We chiefly learn from the Americans.

The Chinese people and the peoples of the whole world are supporting you. The more friends, the better.

(From the verbatim record)

A CLEAR DISTINCTION MUST BE MADE BETWEEN THE U.S. IMPERIALIST ELEMENTS AND THE AMERICAN PEOPLE*

(*November 25, 1965*)

There is now one thing in the world that deserves our attention. Not only are the broad masses of Japan rising against U.S. imperialism and domestic reaction, but also the broad masses of youth of the United States itself are rising against the U.S. government's policy of aggression in Vietnam. This started in February this year, when the U.S. air force bombed North Vietnam, continued for months, and recently a mass struggle on a fairly large scale has developed in the United States, with some 100,000 young students taking to the streets and holding demonstrations against aggression in Vietnam.

In countries like Japan and the United States, the fact that young students take to the streets to hold demonstrations is an indication that a struggle by broad social strata of people is brewing. Particularly the college students, whose families are not particularly poor—even they are opposed to the reactionaries of their own country. Their struggle will influence the broad masses of people and other social strata, that is, the working class and the peasant class.

The process of the Chinese revolution was also like this, beginning with the May 4th Movement, which was a students' movement. On May 4, 1919 a demonstration was organized and led by the students of Beijing University, and they burned down the residence of a then minister of the government. A revolution does not need very many people to start. The Chinese Communist Party had only a few dozen people in 1921, and almost all were intellectuals. That year the First National Congress of the Chinese Communist Party was held in Shanghai, with the participation of 12 delegates. Before that I wasn't a Communist, and my knowledge was perhaps less than yours is now. I had no idea that there was such a thing as Marxism in the world until the October

---

* This is the principal part of Mao Zedong's talks with the heads of various Japanese delegations and other Japanese friends participating in the Chinese-Japanese Youth Friendship Get-Together.

Revolution, when I came to know about Marxism, about Lenin. In this respect Japan was more advanced. A number of Marxist books had already been translated in Japan before the October Revolution.

There are two movements in the world today: one is that in which you and we are united against our common enemy, and the other the coalition of the imperialist and their pals against us. Here "against us" means not only against the Chinese people but also against the Japanese people as well. The so-called "Three-Prong Plan"[313] has been exposed by some Japanese professors. The secret of the development of bacteriological weapons by the United States at one of its bases in Japan was also exposed by Japanese professors. They might not be Communists but they exposed the dark side of U.S. imperialism as their conscience dictated.

When we oppose U.S. imperialism, our opposition is confined to the imperialist elements only; a clear distinction must be made between the U.S. imperialist elements and the American people. This viewpoint has been confused in China for quite a long time, and was gradually made clear only after decades. Before this, we always thought that the people in a country which committed aggression against China were all bad, thus resulting in an "anti-foreign" policy. It was not until after the May 4th Movement that we came to have a clear conception of this matter. After the founding of the Chinese Communist Party we read a few Marxist books and began to know about the make-up of the world, about political and social structures. Therefore, we rejoice at and welcome the rise of Americans against their own government's policy of aggression. But, unlike you, the Americans have not sent several hundred people over to have a look at China. You managed to do so after a struggle lasting three months, but no such thing has yet happened in the United States. Young American students wish to come to China, but they are prevented from doing so by the U.S. government. They have not yet reached the point of fighting for three months in order to come and see China. We will welcome young American students, but we won't welcome U.S. journalists, or most of them, with the exception of a few individual ones. In this respect Japan's relations with us are different. Japan and China have reciprocally sent journalists and established trade offices. In speaking of how evil your government is, I think it is a little better than the U.S. government, and also a little better than my old friend Chiang Kai-shek. We have neither economic nor personnel exchanges with Chiang Kai-shek; of course, he is not a foreigner.

(From the verbatim record)

STATEMENT IN SUPPORT OF THE AMERICAN BLACK PEOPLE'S STRUGGLE AGAINST VIOLENT REPRESSION

(April 16, 1968)

American black preacher Martin Luther King has been assassinated by the U.S. imperialists. Although King was an apostle of non-violence the U.S. imperialists did not tolerate him but used counterrevolutionary violence to suppress him bloodily. This incident has taught a profound lesson to the broad masses of the American black people, arousing a new blast in their struggle against violent repression, which has swept over 100 U.S. cities. This is unprecedented in American history and shows that very powerful revolutionary power is stored among the 20-million-odd American black people.

The fact that this storm of struggle of black people takes place inside the United States is an outstanding expression of the current overall political and economic crisis of U.S. imperialism. It deals a heavy blow to U.S. imperialism, which is beset with difficulties both at home and abroad.

The American black people's struggle is not only a struggle of exploited and oppressed black people for freedom and liberation, it is a new clarion call for all American people who are exploited and oppressed against the cruel rule of the monopoly capitalists. It is a tremendous support and encouragement for the struggle of the people of the whole world, including the Vietnamese people, against U.S. imperialism. On behalf of the Chinese people, I pledge resolute support for the just struggle of the American black people.

Racial discrimination in the United States is a product of the colonialist-imperialist system. The contradiction between the broad masses of black people and the U.S. ruling clique is a class contradiction. The American black people can achieve complete liberation only by overthrowing the reactionary rule of the U.S. monopoly capitalists and smashing the colonialist-imperialist system. In the United States the broad masses of the black people and those of the white working people share common interests and a common goal of struggle. Therefore, the struggle of the black people is winning more and more sympathy and support from the workers and progressive elements among the white people. The American black people's struggle will inevitably become integrated with the American workers' movement and eventually put an end to the evil rule of the U.S. monopoly capitalists.

In 1963 in my "Statement in Support of the Struggle of the American Black People Against Racial Discrimination" I said, "The evil colonialist-imperialist system rose with the enslaving and trafficking of the black people, and it will certainly come to an end with the complete liberation of the black people." I still uphold that view.

The world revolution has now entered a great new epoch. The struggle of the American black people for liberation is a component part of the general struggle of the people of the whole world against U.S. imperialism, and a component part of the contemporary world revolution. I call on the workers, peasants, revolutionary intellectuals and all who are ready to oppose U.S. imperialism to go into action and give strong support to the American black people's struggle. People of the whole world, unite more closely and launch a protracted and vigorous offensive against our common enemy, U.S. imperialism and its lackeys! It is certain that the day of the total collapse of colonialism, imperialism and all exploiting systems, and the complete emancipation of all the oppressed peoples and nations in the world is not far off.

(From *People's Daily*, April 17, 1968)

WE AGREE WITH VIETNAM'S POLICY TO BOTH FIGHT AND NEGOTIATE*

(*November 17, 1968*)

Since there have been no battles lately, you are inclined to negotiate with the U.S. Negotiation is all right, but it is difficult to negotiate the U.S. away. The U.S. is also ready to negotiate with you because of its awkward situation at present. It has to take care of problems in three regions: America (the U.S.), Europe and Asia. It has lost its balance by stationing a large number of troops in Asia all these years. American capitalists who have investments in Europe are not satisfied. Meanwhile, historically the U.S. was used to letting other countries do the fighting first, then it would join at the halfway mark. Only after the Second World War did it take the lead, in the Korean War and the war in Vietnam. Since the U.S. was in the lead, only a few countries participated. It spared no efforts either in so-called special wars or local wars and is now unable to attend to other countries. For example, its troops in Europe cry out that they haven't enough manpower, veteran fighters and commanders have been transferred, and good equipment has been moved away. No matter whether in Japan, Korea or other places in Asia, its troops are being transferred as well. Does it claim that it has a population of 200 million? However, it cannot withstand attack since its armed forces are limited, and it can only afford to send overseas several hundred thousand troops.

After you have fought for more than ten years, you should not look merely at your own difficulties, but at the enemy's difficulties as well. It has been 23 years since Japan surrendered in 1945, and Vietnam still exists. You have been invaded by three imperialist powers: Japan, France and the U.S. However, your country not only continues to exist, but has developed.

Of course, imperialism is inclined to wage war. Its aim is, first, to put out fire, and you had fire; second, to deal in munitions capital. To put out fire, "fire extinguishers" have to be manufactured; that will make money. The U.S.

---

* This is the major part of Mao Zedong's talk with Premier Pham Van Dong of the Democratic Republic of Vietnam.

has spent over 30 billion dollars every year in your country.

The U.S. is not accustomed to fighting long. Its wars usually last around four years. The fire in your country, instead of being put out, has become increasingly rampant. The U.S. capitalists are divided into different groups. If one group earns more profit than the others, there will be trouble among them owing to the unjust division of the spoils. You can take advantage of these contradictions. The capitalists who are getting less profit will not persist in carrying on the war. This can be perceived from the election campaign speeches of the two parties. Particularly, an American correspondent named Walter Lippmann recently published an article warning the U.S. to be careful of falling into another trap. He said the U.S. had fallen into a trap in Vietnam, and the question now was how to manage to get out of it. He was afraid it might fall into another one. Therefore, your cause is promising.

I had an interview with Chairman Ho Chi Minh[216] in Hangzhou in 1966. At the time the U.S. had again started the war in North Vietnam but had not yet resumed the bombing. In my opinion, the U.S. will probably persist nearly through the year, because this is their year of general election. This problem will always exist no matter who is elected president. Will it continue the war or will it withdraw? I hold that it would incur more difficulties by continuing the war. No European country has participated in this war, and the situation is different from that of the Korean War. Japan is not likely to join, except to render some economic assistance. It has made much money manufacturing arms. I think the U.S. has overestimated its own strength in the past. It is repeating its old practice by excessively dispersing its forces not only in America and Europe, but even in Asia. We are not alone in speaking thus; Nixon[246] said so as well. Originally I didn't believe the U.S. would invade North Vietnam, but it bombed the country afterward, so my words went for nought. Now it has stopped the bombing, so my words have proved effective. Perhaps it will resume bombing, then my words will be ineffective again. However, my words will invariably come true someday when it again stops bombing. Therefore, it is better for you to be prepared against all possibilities.

In brief, the U.S. army hasn't attacked North Vietnam all these years, neither blockading Haiphong nor bombarding the urban district of Hanoi. It has held back a trick or two. Once it spoke of "hot pursuit," but it failed to "hotly pursue" your airplanes, which flew to and fro from China. So this is only empty talk. It has never mentioned anything about your airplanes using our airfields. Take another example. It knew many Chinese were working in your country, yet it didn't say a word, as if this had never happened. As for some of our personnel who are at present not required in your country, they may withdraw to China. Have you discussed this question? We can send them back to you if the Americans return. You can think about who should remain and who should leave. You may keep those who are useful to you and let the rest evacuate. They will go back to Vietnam in future if you need them again. It is the same for your airplanes making use of Chinese airfields. You can use them if you need to and stop using them if there's no need at the time. Things are more or less like this.

I agree with your policy to both fight and negotiate. Some of our comrades are just afraid you might be taken in by the Americans, but I don't think so. Aren't negotiation and fighting alike? In drawing laws from experience in fighting, we may be taken in sometimes. Just as you've remarked that the Americans don't mean what they say. Johnson[284] has openly stated that even treaties sometimes do not count. Yet there is invariably a rule in everything. Like your negotiations, do you wish them to last 100 years? Our Premier said if the negotiations continue another two years without solving any problems, it will be difficult for Nixon to win in the next presidential election.

There's still another point: The South Vietnamese puppet regime is very much afraid of the South Vietnam National Liberation Front. Some people in the U.S. said it is not the Saigon government, but the Liberation Front, that is truly effective and has influence among the South Vietnamese people. This remark was not made in the U.S. Congress but reported by a correspondent, who didn't reveal any names, but merely mentioned that it came from so-called U.S. official sources. This remark poses the question of whose government in South Vietnam truly has prestige: Nguyen Van Thieu[314] or Nguyen Huu Tho[315]? Therefore, outwardly the U.S. boasted how terrific Nguyen Van Thieu was, and declared that he wouldn't go to Paris to attend the negotiations. Actually it was nothing of the sort. The U.S. knows very well that nothing can be settled without the participation of the South Vietnam National Liberation Front.

(From the verbatim record)

THE PEOPLE OF THE WHOLE WORLD UNITE, DEFEAT THE U.S. AGGRESSORS AND ALL THEIR LACKEYS*

(*May 20, 1970*)
This is a statement issued by Mao Zedong in support of the struggle against U.S. aggression and for national salvation waged by the people of the three Indo-Chinese countries.

A new upsurge in the struggle against U.S. imperialism is emerging on a worldwide scale. Since the Second World War U.S. imperialism and its followers have unceasingly launched wars of aggression, while the people of various countries have continuously defeated the aggressors by means of revolutionary wars. The danger of a new world war still exists, and the people of all countries must be prepared for this. However, the main trend of the current world is revolution.

Failing to get their way in Vietnam and Laos, the U.S. aggressors engineered the reactionary coup d'état of the Lon Nol-Srimada clique[316] in Cambodia, flagrantly dispatched troops to Cambodia and resumed the bombing of North Vietnam, thus arousing the indignant resistance of the people of the three Indo-Chinese countries. I warmly support the fighting spirit of Prince Norodom Sihanouk, Head of State of Cambodia, in opposing U.S. imperialism and its lackeys, warmly support the Joint Statement of the Summit Meeting of the Indo-Chinese Peoples,[317] and warmly support the establishment of the Royal National Solidarity Government[318] under the leadership of the National United Front of Cambodia. So long as the people of the three countries of Indo-China strengthen their unity, support one another, and persist in a protracted people's war, they will surely be able to overcome all difficulties and achieve complete victory.

U.S. imperialism not only massacres foreigners, it also massacres white

---

* This is a statement issued by Mao Zedong in support of the struggle against U.S. aggression and for national salvation waged by the people of the three Indo-Chinese countries.

and black people in its own country. Nixon's fascist atrocities have enkindled the raging flames of the revolutionary mass movement in the United States. The Chinese people resolutely support the American people's revolutionary struggle. I am convinced that the bravely fighting American people will win the final victory and that the fascist rule in the United States is doomed to failure.

The Nixon administration is beset with difficulties both at home and abroad. The United States is in the midst of chaos and it is very isolated in the world. Mass movements protesting U.S. aggression against Cambodia have swept across the whole globe. Within ten days of the establishment of the National Solidarity Government of the Kingdom of Cambodia it was recognized by almost 20 countries. The situation of the war of the people of Vietnam, Laos and Cambodia against U.S. aggression and for national salvation is getting better and better. The revolutionary armed struggle of the people in the Southeast Asian countries, the struggle of the people of Korea, Japan and other Asian countries against the revival of Japanese militarism by the U.S.-Japanese reactionaries, the struggle of the Palestinian people and other Arab countries against the U.S.-Israeli aggressors, the struggle of the people of various Asian, African and Latin American countries for national liberation, and the people's revolutionary struggles in North America, Europe and Oceania are all developing vigorously. The Chinese people firmly support the revolutionary struggles of the people of the three Indo-Chinese countries and the people of different countries all over the world against U.S. imperialism and its lackeys.

U.S. imperialism looks like a huge monster, but in fact it is a paper tiger, and it is putting up a last-ditch struggle. Who is afraid of whom in the world today? It is not the people of Vietnam, Laos, Cambodia, Palestine, and the Arab and other countries in the world who are afraid of U.S. imperialism. On the contrary, it is U.S. imperialism that is afraid of the people of those countries. It is panic-stricken at the mere rustle of grass in the wind. Countless facts have proved that a just cause enjoys abundant support, while an unjust cause finds little support. A weak country can defeat a strong one, and a small country can defeat a big one. As long as the people of a small country dare to rise and fight, dare to take up arms and gain control of the fate of their own country, they can surely defeat aggression by a big country. This is a law of history.

The people of the whole world unite, defeat the U.S. aggressors and all their lackeys!

(From *People's Daily*, May 21, 1970)

IMPERIALISM IS AFRAID OF THE THIRD WORLD*

(July 11, 1970)

The British Commonwealth is like a club, to which China also belonged in the past. Britain was doing fairly well at the time of the First World War, but after the Second World War it had too much on its hand and had to concede China to the United States. The U.S. helped Chiang Kai-shek attack us after the surrender of Japan. We were called Communist "bandits"—to differentiate from ordinary bandits. Hence we were not qualified to join the United Nations. How could "bandits" join the U.N.? We have given this question a bit of thought. This country of ours is also a U.N. It's alright if we don't get to that U.N. The imperialists are not fond of people like us, whether it's the presidents of your countries or us Chinese. What can we do? Did you inform the U.K. or U.S. about your coming to Beijing?

Actually, the imperialists aren't having an easy time in this world. They are afraid of not only you but also us. They are afraid of the Third World. We must do away with whatsoever blind faith in imperialism. I don't mean that we should oppose all people of imperialist countries or not learn from their technology. I mean that we must get rid of blind faith in imperialist politics as well as their frauds. However, it is not easy to do so, as this is deeply rooted in the minds of some people. Look, how terrific imperialism is! It has so many atomic and hydrogen bombs, its airplanes fly here and there, its navy intrudes in one place or another, and it occupies other countries everywhere, such as the dispatch of U.S. troops to Cambodia. However, this was the practice of old imperialism—of Britain. Didn't Britain occupy the territories of other people everywhere? It has become a bit wiser now.

(From the verbatim record)

---

* These are excerpts from Mao Zedong's talk with government delegations from Tanzania and Zambia.

INTERNATIONAL ISSUES SHOULD BE SETTLED THROUGH JOINT CONSULTATION*

(*July 13, 1970*)

This world is not very peaceful and tranquil at present. Your ardent love for independence is one thing; frequent interference from others is another. I mentioned last time that a handful of countries in the world are fond of interfering in other countries' independence. You said Hitler[4] was no more, Japanese imperialism has been defeated, France has won independence and China is liberated. However, the present world is still not peaceful. Of course, nobody is invading France now or invading China, except its Taiwan. Nevertheless, I should like to tell you that we are prepared for war, not that we shall invade others, but if other countries invade us, we shall wipe them out. This is not decades ago when anybody could bully China at will.

I advise you to prepare civil air defense besides the Maginot Line[319] and the atomic bomb. Do you have any idea how the world will change? We are not the chief of staff of the big powers. You have been likewise bullied by other countries.

Under the present situation in Europe it seems difficult not only for you but even for the U.K. to launch a war. The so-called allies are hardly reliable. They may be congenial on some questions, while not on others. It will be relatively easy for us to come to agreement, but rather difficult when we negotiate with the United States or the Soviet Union. France hasn't occupied any place in China, nor has China occupied your Corsica.

Consultation is necessary when dealing with international affairs. Domestic questions should be solved by the people of each country themselves, while international issues, instead of being decided by the two big powers, ought to be settled by joint consultation of all countries.

(From the verbatim record)

---

* These are excerpts from Mao Zedong's talk with a government delegation from France.

WE DON'T DEMAND FOREIGNERS RECOGNIZE THE IDEOLOGY OF THE CHINESE PEOPLE*

(*December 6, 1970*)

We don't demand that all foreigners recognize the ideology of the Chinese people, asking them only to acknowledge the integration of the universal truth of Marxism-Leninism with the concrete practice of the revolution of each country. This is a basic principle that I have told you many times. As for other harmful thinking besides Marxism-Leninism, they would come to understand themselves, so there would be no necessity for us to regard conversation with foreigners as a serious problem. You will understand just by reviewing the history of our Party—how it gradually embarked on the correct path after undergoing the lesson of so many erroneous lines; moreover, there is still a problem today, that is, we still have great-nation chauvinism both inwardly and outwardly, which ought to be overcome.

(From the original manuscript)

---

* These are Mao Zedong's comments on a document submitted by the Liaison Department of the Central Committee of the Community Party of China.

IF NIXON IS WILLING TO COME, I AM READY TO HOLD TALKS WITH HIM*

(December 18, 1970)

I welcome Nixon's[246] winning the election. Why? There is a deceptive side of him as well, but there is less of it. Do you believe it? He is accustomed to use hard tactics, but sometimes also soft ones. If he wishes to come to Beijing, please tell him he should do it secretly, not openly—just get on a plane and come. It doesn't matter whether negotiations succeed or fail. Why should we maintain such a deadlock? However, there is no secret in the United States. If the president goes abroad, it is impossible to keep it secret. In coming to China, he is sure to declare his aim is to draw in China in order to make things difficult for the Soviet Union. Hence he does not dare to act this way at present. To punish the Soviet Union is disadvantageous to the U.S., and to punish China is equally disadvantageous.

One of our policies now is refusing to let Americans visit China. Is this policy correct? The Ministry of Foreign Affairs should study it. Leftists, moderates and rightists should all be approved to come to China. Why the rightists? That is to say Nixon, who represents the monopoly capitalists. The reason is that the moderates and leftists are unable to solve any problem, and right now we must straighten things out with Nixon. We have to let him come as a matter of course.

He long ago wrote letters saying he would send a representative to China, which we didn't publish in order to keep them secret. He was not interested in the Warsaw talks[201] and wished to negotiate with us personally. Therefore I say I am ready to hold talks with him if he is willing to come. It doesn't matter if the negotiations succeed or fail, if we quarrel or not, if he comes in the capacity of a tourist or the President. In short, either way will do. I don't think I shall quarrel with him, except to give him some criticism. We shall likewise make self-criticism, i.e. admit our mistakes and faults. For example,

---

* These are excerpts from Mao Zedong's talk with Edgar Snow, an American writer and a friend to China.

our production level is lower than that of the U.S., but nothing else.

It was proposed by Nixon himself that he send a representative to China for negotiations. Documents prove that he would like to negotiate in person either in Beijing or in Washington, without the knowledge of our Ministry of Foreign Affairs or going through the State Department in the U.S. It was extremely mysterious. It was not to be made known. Such information was to be kept top secret.

The U.S. will hold general elections in 1972. I reckon Nixon won't come himself, but may send someone to China during the first half of the year. If he wants to talk with us, that would be the time. He is reluctant to give up Taiwan while Chiang Kai-shek is still alive. What does he have to do with Taiwan? Taiwan's present situation was created by Truman[65] and Acheson[66] and followed by another President; only then did Nixon have any share in the Taiwan question. Then came Kennedy.[245] Nixon visited Taiwan as Vice-President. He said there were more than ten million people in Taiwan, but I say there are over one billion people in Asia and 300 million in Africa, all rising in rebellion.

China and the U.S. will establish diplomatic relations sooner or later. Will China and the U.S. remain for 100 years without establishing relations? After all, we haven't occupied your Long Island!

(From the verbatim record)

THE QUESTION OF WAR BETWEEN CHINA AND THE U.S. DOESN'T EXIST AT PRESENT*

(*February 21, 1972*)

Aggression on the part of the U.S. or aggression on the part of China is a relatively small question, not a big one, because the question of war between our two countries doesn't exist at present. You want to withdraw some of your troops to the U.S., and we won't send any troops abroad. It seems rather strange to both of us that we have always failed to approach each other for the past 22 years. Our present contacts, if counted from the time of playing table tennis[320] together, have lasted fewer than ten months, or if counted from your suggestion put forward in Warsaw, more than two years. We admit to bureaucracy in our work when we flatly refused your proposals to exchange people's visits and do some small business. We, including myself, have insisted for ten years that we not negotiate with you on minor questions pending the settlement of major ones. Later we found that you were correct, so we promised to play table tennis with you.

We became acquainted with each other through the introduction of the ex-president of Pakistan. Our ambassador to Pakistan then was firmly opposed to establishing contact with you, saying we must make a comparison as to who was actually better: ex-President Johnson[284] of the Democratic Party or you, Richard Nixon. Our side didn't much appreciate President Johnson. From Truman[65] to Johnson we weren't happy about them all. In between them a President from the Republican Party was in power for eight years, but at that time you also weren't convinced.

(From the verbatim record)

---

* These are excerpts from Mao Zedong's talk with U.S. President Richard Nixon.

SOVIET POLICY IS A FEINT TO THE EAST AND ATTACK IN THE WEST*

(July 10, 1972)

Is it rather chaotic now in Europe? When I say chaotic, what I mean is there are 60 billion U.S. dollars running rampant in Europe, and, moreover, the U.S. doesn't honor its commitments. My word! It is really a difficult problem. The U.S. is a big despot, separated from Europe only by the Atlantic Ocean. The few big powers are always in discord. We don't wish to see Europe in such chaos. You must watch out for the Soviet Union, whose policy is just a feint to the east and attack in the west. It talks about attacking China, while actually it intends to gobble up Europe. That's dangerous!

(From the verbatim record)

---

* These are excerpts from Mao Zedong's talk with French Foreign Minister Maurice Schumann.

SETTLEMENT OF THE QUESTION OF RESTORATION OF DIPLOMATIC RELATIONS BETWEEN CHINA AND JAPAN STILL DEPENDS ON THE GOVERNMENT OF THE LIBERAL DEMOCRATIC PARTY*

(*September 27, 1972*)

This visit of yours to Beijing makes the whole world tremble with fear, chiefly the two big powers, the Soviet Union and the U.S. They are rather anxious about this: God knows what trick you are playing.

The U.S. is a bit better, but still feels uncomfortable, saying that President Nixon came to China in February without being able to establish diplomatic relations, but now you have gone ahead. So it is just a little uneasy.

An agreement may not be reached after decades, even 100 years, but can also be settled within a few days. Both sides have this necessity at present, this being told me by Nixon[246] himself. He asked me if we had this necessity or not; I answered affirmatively. I said, "I have a bad reputation because I am now collaborating with rightists," and further said, "There are two political parties in your country, the Democratic Party, which is alleged to be relatively enlightened, and the Republican Party, which is rather rightist. But I hold that the Democratic Party isn't up to much; I don't appreciate it and am not interested in it." I told Nixon, "I voted for you when you ran for President. You still don't know."

I also voted for you this time. Just as you said, how could the question of restoration of diplomatic relations between China and Japan be settled if you —the mainstay of the Liberal Democratic Party—didn't come?

That's why some people blame us for collaborating solely with rightists. I maintain that the party not in office is unable to solve any problem. The settlement of the question of restoration of diplomatic relations between China and Japan has to depend on the government of the Liberal Democratic Party.

(From the verbatim record)

---

* These are excerpts from Mao Zedong's talk with Tanaka Kakuei, Prime Minister of Japan.

ON THE QUESTION OF THE DIFFERENTIATION OF THE THREE WORLDS*

(*February 22, 1974*)

Chairman Mao Zedong (hereinafter referred to as Mao): We hope the Third World will unite. The Third World has a large population!

President Kenneth David Kaunda (hereinafter referred to as Kaunda): That's right.

Mao: Who belongs to the First World?

Kaunda: I think it ought to be the world of exploiters and imperialists.

Mao: And the Second World?

Kaunda: Those who have become revisionists.

Mao: I hold that the U.S. and the Soviet Union belong to the First World. The middle elements, such as Japan, Europe, Australia and Canada, belong to the Second World. We are the Third World.

Kaunda: I agree with your analysis, Mr. Chairman.

Mao: The U.S. and the Soviet Union have a lot of atomic bombs, and they are richer. Europe, Japan, Australia and Canada, of the Second World, do not possess so many atomic bombs and are not so rich as the First World, but richer than the Third World. What do you think of this explanation?

Kaunda: Mr. Chairman, your analysis is very pertinent and correct.

Mao: We can discuss it.

Kaunda: I think we can reach agreement without discussion, because I believe this analysis is already very pertinent.

Mao: The Third World is very populous.

Kaunda: Precisely so.

Mao: All Asian countries, except Japan, belong to the Third World. All of Africa and also Latin America belong to the Third World.

(From the verbatim record)

---

* These are excerpts from Mao Zedong's talk with President Kenneth David Kaunda of Zambia.

TALK WITH EDWARD HEATH*

(May 25, 1974)

Edward Heath (hereinafter referred to as Heath): Good morning.
Chairman Mao Zedong (hereinafter referred to as Mao): Good morning.
Heath: I am very glad to meet you. It is my great honor.
Mao: Thank you. You are welcome.
Heath: The welcoming ceremony at the airport was very touching, full of bright colors, active and brisk.
Mao (to Zhou Enlai): Why no guard of honor?
Premier Zhou Enlai (hereinafter referred to as Zhou): Since he is not the incumbent prime minister, we were afraid it might cause misunderstanding and incur unpleasantness with the present prime minister.
Mao: I think it is necessary.
Zhou: We shall arrange a guard of honor at his departure.
Wang Hairong[321]: You aren't afraid of offending Wilson?[322]
Mao: No. (Turning to Heath) I cast my vote for you!
Heath: I think the Soviet Union has a lot of troubles. They are facing domestic economic difficulties and agricultural predicament, and there are also differences within the leadership, over questions of tactics and timing, not over long-term strategy.
Mao: I think the Soviet Union is busy with its own affairs and unable to deal with Europe, the Middle East, South Asia, China and the Pacific. I think it will lose.
Heath: However, its military strength is continually augmented. Although the Soviet Union has encountered troubles at many places in the world, its strength is continuing to grow. Therefore, we deem this to be the principal threat. Does the Chairman think the Soviet Union constitutes a menace to China?
Mao: We are prepared for it to come, but it will collapse if it comes. It

---

* This is the major part of Mao Zedong's talk with British ex-prime minister Edward Heath.

has only a handful of troops, and you Europeans are so frightened of it! Some people in the West are always trying to direct this calamity toward China. Your senior, Chamberlain,[7] and also Daladier[10] of France were the ones who pushed Germany eastward.

Heath: I opposed Mr. Chamberlain then.

Mao: I am chiefly speaking of the public in the U.S. I haven't seen much about the British public talking about the Soviet Union invading China.

Heath: If Europe is weak, it is possible that a Soviet attempt against China would succeed. Therefore a powerful Europe is very important; it will make the Soviet Union worry.

Mao: We shall be glad to have Europe become powerful.

Heath: Does the principal difference between China and the Soviet Union lie in ideology or result from Soviet power politics? How do you, Mr. Chairman, judge Soviet aims and motives with regard to China?

Mao: Differences between China and the Soviet Union began in 1954, because when Adenauer[154] visited Moscow in 1955, Khrushchov[146] told him that China was no end of trouble. It was written thus in Adenauer's memoirs. Have you ever met Adenauer?

Heath: Yes, I have met him lots of times. I talked with him for a whole day once when he went to Italy for a holiday. He always held that the Soviet Union would attempt to take over Europe.

Mao: Not only Europe, but also Asia and Africa. However, its ability is not equal to its ambition.

Heath: It didn't succeed in Africa at all.

Mao: It lost its position in Egypt.

Heath: Its influence is rather weak in the Arab world.

Mao: It is even weaker here in China!

Heath: There isn't the slightest influence here, I think.

Mao: There is some; Lin Biao[323] was their man.

Heath: May I ask you another question, Chairman? How will Sino-U.S. relations develop in future? It seems that relations between China and the U.S. came to a standstill after President Nixon[246] visited China.

Mao: That doesn't matter. Relations are still fairly good. Can you give Nixon some advice and help him tide over the Watergate scandal?[324]

Heath: If he had asked for my opinion at that time, I would have advised him to thoroughly crush that matter 18 months ago. But he didn't ask me at that time.

Mao: So he has faults as well!

Heath: We all have faults.

Mao: My faults are more serious! Eight hundred million people want to eat, and, moreover, China's industry is undeveloped. I can't boast much of China. Your country is a developed country and ours is an undeveloped one. We look forward to the younger generation. I have already received God's invitation, expecting me to call on him.

Heath: I hope the Chairman won't accept this invitation for quite a long time.

Mao: I haven't replied yet.

Heath: I am very interested in what you've just said. China's agricultural production has developed and you are almost self-sufficient in grain; your industry is beginning to develop. Perhaps the U.K. can offer some assistance you need in the way of technology and skills. But how do you, Chairman, inspire over 700 million people to unite and work like this?

Mao: It is a long story. However, we shall be very glad to have your help.

Heath: Good. We are always glad to help you.

Mao: Wonderful. Is your Eden[230] still alive?

Heath: Yes, he is fine. Now he is 76 or 77. He still takes great interest in foreign affairs and international questions.

Mao: He suffered from the Suez Canal issue.[134]

Heath: Yes, he suffered a great deal.

Mao: The Americans let him down. The U.S. has reached out too far. Look, it has reached Japan, South Korea, the Philippines, Taiwan, Southeast Asia, South Asia, Iran, Turkey, the Middle East, the Mediterranean Sea and Europe.

Heath: It was part of U.S. intentions at the time to contain other regions of the world. It has now come to understand that this is impossible.

Mao: Why should it be afraid of communism? We suggest that countries in Europe and Asia, including Japan, should not quarrel with one another. They may quarrel, but not big quarrels.

Heath: I fully agree with you.

Mao: The Americans abused us for more than 20 years.

Heath: Between the Americans and you there exists a sort of love-hate relationship. Their psychological fear of you has now lessened, so they love you all the more.

Mao: Scared like a rabbit! When Kissinger[325] came to Beijing for the first time, he felt as if the Chinese people would eat him. He admitted that he was very nervous the first time, still a bit the second time, but not in the least the third time. However, we feel rather easy toward the Americans.

Heath: We Europeans are glad to hear this. Are you at ease with Japan,

Chairman?

Mao: Yes, we are.

Heath: Do you trust the peaceful intentions of the Japanese?

Mao: We do within a certain period of time. It's hard to say in future. However, we are not afraid of Europe.

Heath: You have no reason to be afraid of Europe.

Mao: But we were in the past.

Heath: That's something that happened long, long ago.

Mao: There's no enmity. It was the allied forces of eight powers[55] in the past, including not only the U.K., but France, Italy, Germany, Austria-Hungary....

Zhou: Also Russia, Japan and the U.S., altogether eight countries that actually represented 12 countries. It happened in 1900.

Mao: All this is now history. Only the question of Hong Kong[326] remains. We won't discuss it at present. We shall consult together at the proper time about what we are going to do. This will be the business of the younger generation.

(From the verbatim record)

NOTES

¹ "Manchukuo" was a puppet regime created by Japanese imperialists after Japan's occupation of northeast China in 1931. It was established in March 1932 in Changchun, with Pu Yi as the president. In March 1934 Manchukuo was renamed Manchu Empire and the president was changed into an emperor. It was abolished following victory in the War of Resistance Against Japan in August 1945.

² Before the outbreak of the Pacific War in 1941 the United States and Britain after several discussions, wanted to sacrifice China in order to reach a compromise with Japanese imperialism. This plot was like the Munich agreement signed between Britain and France and facist Germany and Italy in 1938, which betrayed the interests of Czechoslovakia. That is why it was called Far East Munich or Eastern Munich.

³ Abyssinia refers to Ethiopia.

⁴ Adolf Hitler (1889-1945) was the head of German fascists. He joined the German Workers' Party in 1919 (changed to the National Socialist German Workers' Party, i.e. the Nazi party, the following year). Then he became the party's head. In 1933 he took up the post of chancellor with the support of the German monopoly capitalist class, and the following year he called himself president after the death of President Paul von Hindenburg. He practiced fascist rule and was active in arms expansion and war preparation. In September 1939 he sent German troops to invade Poland and provoked the Second World War. In June 1941 he launched a large-scale attack on the Soviet Union. In April 1945 he committed suicide when troops of the Soviet Union liberated Berlin.

⁵ In August 1935 Georgi M. Dimitrov said in his report to the seventh congress of the Communist International that fascism was unscrupulous chauvinism and aggressive war. In July 1937 he published the thesis "Fascism Means War."

⁶ Franklin D. Roosevelt (1882-1945), a member of the Democratic Party, was president of the United States from 1933 to 1945. On October 5, 1937, he made a speech in Chicago denouncing the aggressive war policies of the fascist countries, which were likened to an incurable pestilence spreading wildly in the world. He called on peace-loving countries to make a concerted effort to win a world where one could breathe freely, have mutual friendship and live without fear and to safeguard laws and principles and oppose activities that violated treaties and infringed human rights. Only in this way, he declared, could peace be guaranteed.

⁷ Neville Chamberlain (1869-1940), leader of the British Conservative Party, was prime minister of Britain from 1937 to 1940. During his tenure of office he carried out an appeasement policy which connived with German, Italian and Japanese fascists in their aggressive wars, hoping that they would be directed at the Soviet Union.

⁸ *New China Daily (Xinhua Ribao)* was the official paper of the Communist Party of China, published openly in Kuomintang-ruled areas. It was first published in Hankou on January 11, 1938, and on October 25 of the same year it was published in Chongqing. In March 1947 it was forced to close down by the Kuomintang government.

⁹ The German-Soviet Treaty of Nonaggression was signed on August 23, 1939, and took effect immediately. The main contents of the treaty were: The two parties would not use military force against each other; one party would not join any group that would oppose the

other party directly or indirectly; if one party was attacked by a third country, the other party would not give any support to the third country; disputes between the two parties would be solved by peaceful means. The treaty would be valid for ten years. On June 22, 1941, fascist Germany tore up the treaty and launched a war of aggression against the Soviet Union.

[10] Edouard Daladier (1884-1970), leader of the French Radical Socialist Party, was premier of France and concurrently foreign minister from 1938 to 1940. He practiced a policy of appeasement and attempted to spearhead the German aggressive war at the Soviet Union.

[11] In October 1935 Italy began to invade Abyssinia (Ethiopia) and occupied it in May 1936. In July 1936 Germany and Italy jointly interfered in the internal affairs of Spain and supported the fascist Franco forces to stage a rebellion against the Popular Front government. After a prolonged war the Popular Front government was defeated in March 1939. German troops occupied Austria in March 1938 and invaded the Sudeten land of Czechoslovakia in October. In March 1939 all of Czechoslovakia came under German occupation. Aided and abetted by the "nonintervention" policy of the British and French governments, fascist Germany and Italy committed a series of acts of aggression and achieved their purpose.

[12] The Anti-Comintern Pact and Additional Protocol to the Anti-Comintern Pact was concluded between Germany and Japan in November 1936. At the same time a secret agreement directly against the Soviet Union was also made. Italy joined the agreement in November 1937.

[13] "Using Chinese to subdue Chinese" was a sinister device of the Japanese imperialists in their aggression against China. To create divisions within the country, they cultivated various Chinese elements to serve as their stooges. After the outbreak of the war they not only employed the openly pro-Japanese clique headed by Wang Jingwei within the Kuomintang, but also made use of Chiang Kai-shek's clique as much as it could to check the Communist Party, which was the most resolute in resisting Japan. Starting from 1939 they ceased large-scale strategic attacks against Chiang Kai-shek forces and gave them political encouragement in their anti-Communist activities.

[14] "Sustaining the war by means of war" refers to the Japanese imperialists' policy of ruthless plunder of the Chinese areas under Japanese occupation to meet the expenses of their aggressive war.

[15] After occupying Wuhan in October 1938, the Japanese imperialists gradually concentrated their main forces to invade the anti-Japanese base areas behind enemy lines led by the Communist Party of China. "Mopping-up campaigns" were the Japanese aggressors' euphemism for their barbarous policy of triple atrocity—"burning all, killing all and looting all."

[16] A reference to the German-Soviet Treaty of Nonaggression signed on August 23, 1939, and the Soviet-Finnish Pact signed in Moscow on March 12, 1940.

[17] Joseph W. Stilwell (1883-1946), a career officer of the United States Army, was once military attaché of the U.S. embassy in China. After the outbreak of the Pacific War he was commander of the U.S. Army in the China-India-Burma (Myanmar) theater and chief of staff of the Chinese theater.

[18] A reference to the Northwest Visiting Group of Domestic and Foreign Correspondents, composed of about 20 foreign and Chinese correspondents from AP, UPI, Reuters, and Tass and from *Da Gong Bao, Central Daily*, and *Saodang Bao*. The group visited Yan'an and northwest Shanxi from June to October of 1944.

[19] Patrick Jay Hurley (1883-1963), a member of the U.S. Republican Party, was appointed U.S. ambassador to China in the latter part of November 1944. He went to Yan'an as the personal representative of Roosevelt. At first he supported abolishing the dictatorship of the Kuomintang and establishing a coalition democratic government, as put forward by the Communist Party of China. Then he turned to support Chiang Kai-shek's policy against the Communist Party and was resolutely opposed by the Chinese people. In November 1945 he

left office.

[20] Here it refers to the Agreement of the Chinese National Government, the Kuomintang and the Communist Party of China (i.e., Draft of the Five-Clause Agreement). This agreement was a revision of the document "For the Basis of an Agreement," drafted by Patrick Jay Hurley and Chiang Kai-shek, in which articles on changing the Kuomintang government into a united national government formed by all the anti-Japanese parties and political personages without party affiliation and reorganizing the military committee into a united military committee formed by all anti-Japanese army representatives were added. The original article that the army of the Communist Party of China should obey and carry out the orders of the Kuomintang government and the military committee and that army officers and soldiers of the Communist Party should be reorganized by the Kuomintang government was revised as follows: All anti-Japanese armies should follow and carry out the orders of the united national government and the military committee and be recognized by the united national government and the military committee. Regulations on guaranteeing people's freedom and rights were added and recognizing the legal status of the Communist Party and all anti-Japanese parties were added. This draft agreement was accepted by Hurley and signed by Mao Zedong and Hurley on November 10, 1944, but it was refused by Chiang Kai-shek.

[21] The Atlantic Charter was issued jointly by the United States and Britain in August 1941 after a series of conferences between President Franklin D. Roosevelt and Prime Minister Winston Churchill aboard the U.S.S. *Augusta* off Newfoundland. It said that the two countries would not pursue territorial or other expansion and would respect various nations' right to choose their own forms of government. They agreed to abolish the Nazi government of Germany and disarm the aggressive countries.

[22] The Moscow conference was held in October 1943 by the foreign ministers of the Soviet Union, the United States and Britain. The Cairo conference was held in November 1943 in Cairo, the capital of Egypt, by the heads of state of China, the United States and Britain. The Teheran conference of the Soviet Union, the United States and Britain was held in the capital of Iran from November to December 1943. The Crimea conference of the Soviet Union, the United States and Britain took place in February 1945 at Yalta. At all these international conferences the signatories recorded their resolve to defeat fascist Germany and Japan through common endeavor and, after the war, to prevent the revival of the forces of aggression and the remnants of fascism, maintain world peace and help the peoples of all countries realize their aspirations for independence and democracy.

[23] From August to October 1944 representatives of the Soviet Union, the United States, Britain and China met at Dumbarton Oaks, a mansion in Georgetown, Washington D.C., in accordance with the decisions of the Moscow and Teheran conferences. They formulated proposals for a world organization that became the basis for the United Nations. As the representative of China's Liberated Areas and a member of the Chinese Delegation, Dong Biwu attended the United Nations Conference on International Organization, which was held in San Francisco from April to June 1945, with the participation of representatives from 50 countries.

[24] See J. V. Stalin, the first part of "The Historical Roots of Leninism" from *The Foundations of Leninism*, Foreign Languages Publishing House, Moscow, 1947, p. 13.

[25] The Xi'an Incident is also known as the Double-Twelve Incident. In the desperate situation of the stepped-up aggression of the Japanese imperialists, who wanted to turn China into their colony, General Zhang Xueliang of the Northeast Army and General Yang Hucheng of the 17th Route Army, influenced by the anti-Japanese national united front policy of the Communist Party and the anti-Japanese movement of the Chinese people, demanded that Chiang Kai-shek stop the civil war and fight against the Japanese aggressors. Chiang Kai-shek refused their demand and went to Xi'an to deploy troops against the Communist Party. On December 12, 1936, Zhang Xueliang and Yang Hucheng jointly detained Chiang Kai-shek in

Lintong near Xi'an. This is the famous Xi'an Incident. After the incident the pro-Japan section in the Kuomintang, headed by He Yingqin, wanted to take advantage of this opportunity to launch a large-scale civil war. The Communist Party persisted in the principle of a peaceful solution of the Xi'an Incident. Thanks to the arduous efforts of its representatives Zhou Enlai, Bo Gu (Qin Bangxian) and Ye Jianying, who worked together with Zhang Xueliang and Yang Hucheng, the Xi'an Incident was peacefully resolved. This promoted the formation of an anti-Japanese national united front.

[26] Here, "an American" refers to Colonel David D. Barrett, head of the U.S. Observation Group in Yan'an. The Observation Group was dispatched to Yan'an in 1944 by the U.S. armed forces which participated in the war against Japan, after approval by the Communist Party of China.

[27] The Council of Foreign Ministers was established in accordance with the Potsdam Accords, representing the United States, the Soviet Union, China, Britain and France. From September 11 to October 2, 1945 the foreign ministers of the Soviet Union, China, the United States, Britain and France held their first meeting in London to discuss peace treaties with Italy, Romania, Bulgaria, Hungary and Finland, countries that had joined Nazi Germany in its war of aggression, and the issue of dealing with the Italian colonies. In the discussion of the draft peace treaties with Romania, Bulgaria and Hungary, the United States and Britain made the unjustifiable demand that the democratic governments of the three countries should resign or be reorganized; the United States and Britain's proposal to give France the power to discuss these peace treaties, which was a violation of the Potsdam Accords, was rejected by the Soviet Union; and the Soviet Union's proposal to discuss the establishment of a committee of surveillance over Japan was rejected by the United States. Therefore, no agreement was reached at this meeting.

[28] See "Some Points in Appraisal of the Present International Situation" of this book, pp. 43-44.

[29] A reference to the Seventh National Congress of the CPC held in Yan'an from April 23 to June 11, 1945.

[30] Anna Louise Strong (1885-1970), progressive American writer and correspondent, visited China many times from 1925 on. She visited China for the fifth time in June 1946. In August of the same year Mao Zedong met her in Yangjialing, Yan'an, and had this talk. She settled in China in 1958. In 1962 she began to compile *Letters from China* regularly to introduce to foreign readers the new China's achievements in construction. Her works during this period include *China's Millions, One-Fifth of Mankind, The Chinese Conquer China*, etc.

[31] To help Chiang Kai-shek start civil war against the people, U.S. imperialists gave his government a very great amount of aid. By the end of June 1946 the United States had equipped 45 Kuomintang divisions. It had trained 150,000 Kuomintang military personnel—army, naval and air forces, secret agents, communications police, staff officers, medical officers, supply personnel, etc. U.S. warships and aircraft transported to the front against the Liberated Areas 14 Kuomintang corps (41 divisions) and 8 regiments of the communications police corps, or over 540,000 men in all. The U.S. government landed 90,000 of its marines in China and stationed them at such important cities as Shanghai, Qingdao, Tianjin, Beiping and Qinhuangdao. They guarded the lines of communication for the Kuomintang in northern China. According to data disclosed in *United States Relations with China* (The White Paper), released by the State Department on August 5, 1949, the total value of various kinds of U.S. aid given to the Chiang Kai-shek government from the beginning of the War of Resistance Against Japan in 1937 to 1948 was more than 4,500 million dollars (the overwhelming bulk of U.S. aid given during the War of Resistance had been hoarded by the Kuomintang for the ensuing civil war against the people). But the actual amount of U.S. aid to Chiang Kai-shek far exceeded this total. The U.S. White Paper admitted that U.S. aid was equivalent to "more than 50 percent

of the monetary expenditures" of the Chiang Kai-shek government and was of "proportionately greater magnitude in relation to the budget of that Government than the United States has provided to any nation of Western Europe since the end of the war."

[32] February Revolution refers to the Russian bourgeois democratic revolution in March (February in the Russian calendar) 1917. At that time workers and soldiers (basically consisting of peasants) staged an armed uprising and overthrew the tsarist autocratic rule. After the victory of the revolution workers and peasants in various places organized the Soviets of Workers, Peasants and Soldiers, while the bourgeoisie organized a provisional government, creating a situation wherein two governments existed simultaneously. In the October Revolution of the same year, under the leadership of the Bolsheviks and Lenin, the proletariat overthrew the bourgeois regime and established a socialist state under proletarian dictatorship.

[33] Benito Mussolini (1883-1945), fascist dictator of Italy, joined the Socialist Party in his early years and later was expelled. In 1921 he organized a fascist party and in 1922 established a fascist dictatorship, seizing power through violence. In 1939 he formed a political and military alliance with Germany and started World War II, following Germany, the next year. In July 1943, owing to military failure and the rise of an anti-fascist movement in Italy, his autocratic power collapsed. On April 28, 1945, he was executed by Italian guerrilla forces.

[34] The Information Bureau of the Communist and Workers' Parties was founded at a meeting held in Warsaw, Poland, in September 1947 by representatives of the Communist and Workers' Parties of Bulgaria, Romania, Hungary, Poland, the Soviet Union, France, Czechoslovakia, Italy and Yugoslavia. It ceased operation in April 1956. The Information Bureau's call to people of the world to rise up against the imperialist plan of enslavement, mentioned here by Mao Zedong, was the Declaration on the International Situation adopted at the September 1947 meeting of the Information Bureau.

[35] The December Meeting refers to the meeting of the Central Committee of the Communist Party of China held December 25-28, 1947, at Yangjiagou, Mizhi County, northern Shaanxi. The meeting discussed and adopted Mao Zedong's report the Present Situation and Our Tasks and the document Some Points in Appraisal of the Present International Situation.

[36] Vyacheslav M. Molotov (1890-1986) was deputy chairman of the Council of Ministers of the Soviet Union from 1946 to 1953.

[37] Andrey A. Zhdanov (1896-1948) was secretary of the Central Committee of the Communist Party of the Soviet Union (Bolsheviks) starting from 1944 and responsible for ideological work.

[38] J.V. See Stalin, "The October Revolution and the National Question," *Selected Works*, People's Publishing House, 1979, Vol. I, Chinese edition, p. 126.

[39] Referring to Deng Xiaoping, Rao Shushi, Chen Yi and Liu Bocheng.

[40] On April 20-21, 1949, while the People's Liberation Army was fighting its way across the Yangtze, the *Amethyst* and three other British warships intruded into the river, an inland waterway of China, and fired on the army, trying to obstruct the crossing. In the ensuing military conflict, British firing caused 252 casualties. The People's Liberation Army returned the fire; the *Amethyst* was disabled and forced to anchor near Zhenjiang; the three other British warships escaped. The British authorities requested the *Amethyst* be allowed to leave, and its captain, acting on the orders of Brind, commander-in-chief of the British Far Eastern Fleet, conducted negotiations with the army's representative. While negotiations were continuing, on the night of July 30 the *Amethyst* forced her way alongside a passenger ship, the *Liberated Jiangling*, which was going downstream off Zhenjiang, and escaped by using that ship as a shield. When the army signaled a warning to the *Amethyst* to stop, she opened fire, collided with and sank a number of junks and escaped from the Yangtze River.

⁴¹ On April 26, 1949, speaking in the British House of Commons, Winsten Churchill, chief of the British Conservative Party, slandered as an "atrocious outrage" the action taken by the Chinese People's Liberation Army in counterattacking the British warships that had fired on the army and demanded that the British government "get in Chinese waters one aircraft carrier, if not two, capable of ... effective power of retaliation."

⁴² On April 26, 1949, British Prime Minister Clement R. Attlee declared in the House of Commons that British naval vessels had been within their rights in going up the Yangtze on their "peaceful missions," because they had the permission of the Kuomintang government of China. At the same time, speaking about the negotiations the British representative was holding with the representative of the Chinese People's Liberation Army, Attlee lied, saying that the Chinese People's Liberation Army "would be prepared to allow the ship [the *Amethyst*] to proceed to Nanjing but only on condition that she should assist the People's Liberation Army to cross the Yangtze."

⁴³ The British government, on May 19, 1948, gave the Kuomintang government the heavy cruiser *Chongqing*, the largest cruiser in the Kuomintang navy. On February 25, 1949, the officers and men of the cruiser revolted in Wusongkou, Shanghai, renounced their allegiance to the Kuomintang government and joined the Chinese People's Navy. On March 19 of the same year the U.S. imperialists and the Kuomintang authorities sent heavy bombers and sank the *Chongqing* off Huludao in Liaodong Gulf in northeast China.

⁴⁴ Huang Hua, born in 1913, Cixian County, Hebei, was then a member of the CPC Nanjing Committee and director of foreign affairs of the city's Military Control Committee.

⁴⁵ Leighton Stuart (1876-1962), an American born in Hangzhou, China, started missionary work in China in 1905 and in 1919 became president of Yanjing University, which was established by the United States in China. In July 1946 he was appointed U.S. ambassador to China. When Nanjing was liberated in April 1949, he stayed on in Nanjing to wait and see. In August of the same year he left China.

⁴⁶ On April 30, 1949, Li Tao, director of the Operation Department of the Central Military Commission, entrusted by Mao Zedong, made a statement as spokesman of the People's Liberation Army of China that sternly denounced the outrages of the British warship *Amethyst* and other warships by intruding into the Yangtze River and bombarding the People's Liberation Army. See "On the Outrages by British Warships—Statement by the Spokesman of the General Headquarters of the Chinese People's Liberation Army" in this book.

⁴⁷ Fu Jingbo was then private secretary to Leighton Stuart, U.S. ambassador to China.

⁴⁸ During the early years of the War of Liberation some democratic personnel tried to find a third road—outside the Kuomintang landlord and capitalist dictatorship and the people's democratic dictatorship led by the Communist Party of China. This road, in fact, was the road of British and American capitalist dictatorship.

⁴⁹ Wu Song is a hero in the famous novel *Outlaws of the Marsh* who killed a tiger with his bare hands on Jingyang Ridge. The story is very popular among the people.

⁵⁰ The U.S. White Paper, *United States Relations with China*, was published by the U.S. State Department on August 5, 1949. Dean Acheson's Letter of Transmittal to President Truman was dated July 30, 1949, after the White Paper had been compiled. The main body of the White Paper, divided into eight chapters, deals with Sino-U.S. relations from 1844, when the United States forced China to sign the Treaty of Wangxia, to 1949, when victory was basically won throughout the country in the Chinese people's revolution. The White Paper goes into particular detail about how, in the five years from the last part of the War of Resistance Against Japan to 1949, the United States pursued a policy of support for Chiang Kai-shek and of anti-communism, opposed the Chinese people by every possible means and finally met defeat.

[51] Forced by opposition from the Chinese people to her traffic in opium, Britain sent forces in 1840-42 to invade China under the pretext of protecting trade. Chinese troops, led by Lin Zexu, fought a war of resistance. People from Guangzhou spontaneously organized armed resistance to fight the British aggressors, who suffered serious blows. People from Fujian, Zhejiang, Jiangsu and other places rose spontaneously in struggles against Britain. In 1842 British troops invaded the Yangtze valley and forced the decadent Qing government to sign the first unequal treaty in modern Chinese history —the Treaty of Nanjing. The main contents of the treaty included cession of Hong Kong Island, large reparations for Britain, opening Shanghai, Fuzhou, Xiamen, Ningbo and Guangzhou as trading ports and reducing the import customs on British goods, with rates agreed to by both China and Britian.

[52] The war unleashed jointly by Britian and France in 1857, also known as the Second Opium War. In 1856 British invaders carried out provocations against China in Guangzhou. In 1857 Britain and France jointly unleashed a war of aggression against China, with the United States and tsarist Russia supporting them from the sidelines. The Qing government which was then devoting all its energy to suppressing the peasant revolution of the Taiping Heavenly Kingdom, adopted a policy of passive resistance toward the foreign aggressors. From 1857 to 1860 the Anglo-French allied forces occupied such major cities as Guangzhou, Tianjin and Beijing, plundered and burned down Yuanmingyuan Garden in Beijing and forced the Qing government to conclude the Treaty of Tianjin and the Treaty of Beijing. The main provisions of these treaties included opening Tianjin, Niuzhuang (later changed to Yingkou), Dengzhou (later changed to Yantai), Taiwan (Tainan), Danshui, Chaozhou (later changed to Shantou), Qiongzhou, Nanjing, Zhenjiang, Jiujiang and Hankou as treaty ports and granting foreigners special privileges for travel, trade and missionary activities in China's interior and giving special inland navigation rights to foreign ships. From then on, foreign aggression forces extended over all China's coastal provinces and penetrated deep into the hinterland.

[53] From 1882 to 1883 French aggressors invaded the northern part of Vietnam. From 1884 to 1885 the aggressors extended their aggression to China's of Guangxi, Taiwan, Fujian and Zhejiang. Chinese troops, led by Feng Zicai, resisted staunchly and won a series of victories. Notwithstanding the victories, the corrupt Qing government signed the humiliating Treaty of Tianjin, which permitted the French to trade in the Sino-Vietnamese border areas in Yunnan and Guangxi provinces, granted them privileges and permitted their aggression forces to penetrate southwestern China.

[54] The Sino-Japanese War of 1894, which was deliberately provoked by Japanese militarists. The war broke out as a result of Japan's aggression against Korea and her provocations against Chinese land and naval forces. Then Japan mounted a large-scale offensive over northeast China. In this war the Chinese forces put up a heroic fight, but China suffered defeat, owing to the corruption of the Qing government and its lack of preparation for resistance. As a result, the Qing government concluded in 1895 the shameful Treaty of Shimonoseki with Japan, under which it ceded Taiwan and its islets, the Penghu Islands and Liaodong Peninsula (later, pressured by Russia, Germany and France, Japan agreed to return it to China, with the Qing government paying 30 million taels of silver as redemption money), paid war reparations of 200 million taels of silver, permitted the Japanese to set up factories in China's port cities, and opened Shashi, Chongqing, Suzhou and Hangzhou as treaty ports.

[55] In 1900 eight imperialist powers—Britain, France, Japan, tsarist Russia, Germany, the United States, Italy and Austria—sent a joint force to attack China in an attempt to suppress the Yi He Tuan uprising which opposed foreign aggression. The Chinese people resisted heroically. The allied forces of the eight powers captured Dagu, Tianjin and Beijing. At the same time tsarist Russia sent its own troops to intrude into China's northeast. On September 7, 1901, the Qing government concluded a treaty with the eight imperialist countries; its main provisions were that China pay the enormous sum of 450 million taels of silver as war reparations and grant the countries the special privilege of stationing troops in Beijing and in

the environs of Beijing, Tianjin and Shanhaiguan.

⁵⁶ This was the imperialist war fought between Japan and tsarist Russia in 1904-05 to grab China's northeast and Korea. As the war was fought mainly in the area of Fengtian (now Shenyang) and Liaoyang and around the port of Lüshun in China's northeast, it caused enormous losses to the Chinese people. Tsarist Russia was defeated and Japanese imperialism took the dominant role in China's northeast. Mediated by the United States, Russia concluded the Treaty of Portsmouth with Japan. At the end of the war tsarist Russia also recognized Japan's exclusive control over Korea.

⁵⁷ On September 18, 1931, Japanese troops stationed in China's northeast launched an attack on Shenyang. This aggression was called the September 18 Incident by the Chinese people. After the incident Chinese troops stationed in Shenyang and other places carried out the order of nonresistance by Chiang Kai-shek, so Japanese troops rapidly occupied China's Liaoning, Jilin and Heilongjiang provinces.

⁵⁸ Hu Shi (1891-1962), native of Jixi, Anhui, studied in the United States in his early years and returned to China in 1917. He served as professor and dean of the Faculty of Arts of Beijing University, chief editor of the weekly *Independent Review*, ambassador of the Kuomintang government to the United States, and President of Beijing University. He went to the United States in 1949 and returned to Taiwan in 1958, serving as president of Academia Sinica.

⁵⁹ Fu Sinian (1896-1950), native of Liaocheng, Shandong, studied in Britain and Germany when he was young and returned to China in 1926. He served as professor, dean of the Faculty of Arts, and head of the history and Chinese departments of Zhongshan University. Beginning in 1928, he served as director of the Institute of History and Languages for a long time and, for a while, concurrently as acting president of Academia Sinica. He also was a councilor of the National Political Council, professor of Southwest Associated University, and acting president of Beijing University. In 1948 he was elected a member of the Legislative Yuan. He went to Taiwan in January 1949 and concurrently served as president of Taiwan University.

⁶⁰ Qian Mu (1895-1990), native of Wuxi, Jiangsu, once served as professor of Yanjing University, Beijing University, Qinghua University, Beiping Normal University, Southwest Associated University and Sichuan University; chief editor of *Qilu Journal* (*Shandong Journal*); director of Wuhua Institute of Culture and History of Kunming; and dean of the Faculty of Arts and concurrently head of the Department of History of Jiangnan University, Wuxi. He went to Hong Kong in 1949, then to Taiwan in 1967 and served as an academician of Academia Sinica and a special research fellow of the Palace Museum in Taipei.

⁶¹ See Mao Zedong's "On the People's Democratic Dictatorship," *Selected Works*, Vol. IV, Foreign Languages Press, Beijing, 1967, English edition, p. 418.

⁶² George C. Marshall (1880-1959), U.S. Democrat, was former U.S. Secretary of State and Secretary of Defense. He was the special envoy to China sent by President Truman in December 1945. He participated in the negotiations between the Communist Party and the Kuomintang in the name of "mediation" and supported the Kuomintang government in launching a civil war. In August 1946 he admitted failure in his "mediation" and soon returned to the United States.

⁶³ Following the Japanese surrender in 1945 the armed forces of the United States landed in China and were stationed in Beiping, Shanghai, Nanjing, Tianjin, Tangshan, Kaiping, Qinhuangdao, Jinghai, Qingdao and other places, in violation of China's territorial sovereignty and interfering in her domestic affairs. In addition, they repeatedly invaded the Liberated Areas. On July 29, 1946, U.S. troops in Tianjin, in cooperation with Kuomintang troops, assaulted the town of Anping, Xianghe County, Hebei Province. This is the Anping Incident referred to in the text. On March 1, 1947, U.S. troops made a military reconnaissance of the position of the People's Liberation Army at Heqibao, situated between Changchun and Jiutai in northeast-

ern China. On June 16, 1946, U.S. troops in Tangshan, Hebei Province, raided Songjiaying and other places; in July the same year they raided Sanhe Village, Luanxian County, and Xihenan Village, Changli County, both near Tangshan. Of the numerous attacks on Eastern Shandong Peninsula, the most widely known were one by U.S. aircraft and warships on Langnuankou and Xiaoli Island, Mouping County, on August 28, 1947, and one by U.S. forces on Wangtuanyuan Village, north of Jimo County, on December 25, 1947, in coordination with Kuomintang troops. In all cases in which U.S. forces committed acts of aggression by invading the Liberated Areas the Chinese People's Liberation Army or the local people's armed forces took just action in self-defense.

[64] Claire Lee Chennault (1890-1958) was at one time U.S. air adviser to the Kuomintang government during the War of Resistance Against Japan and organized the American Voluntary Group (also known as the Flying Tigers and later renamed the 14th Air Force) to support China's anti-Japanese war. After the Japanese surrender he organized a group of U.S. 14th Air Force personnel into Civil Air Transport to help the Kuomintang fight the civil war.

[65] Harry S. Truman (1884-1972), member of the U.S. Democratic Party, was U.S. president from 1945 to 1953.

[66] Dean Acheson (1893-1971), member of the U.S. Democratic Party, served as Secretary of State of the United States from 1949 to 1953.

[67] After the end of World War II, owing to the war and natural disasters, Western Europe was in a state of political turbulence and economic recession. In order to control Western Europe and widen its foreign market, U.S. Secretary of State George C. Marshall made a speech on June 5, 1947, putting forward a plan of so-called U.S. aid to rehabilitate Europe. In July 1947 16 countries, including Britain, France and Italy, held a meeting in Paris and decided to accept Marshall's proposal and establish the Committee for European Economic Cooperation (later changed to the Organization for European Economic Cooperation. The European Recovery Program, subsequently drawn up on the basis of the speech, was known as the Marshall Plan. The signing of the Economic Cooperation Act in April 1948 by President Truman started the official carrying out of the Marshall Plan.

[68] Jiang Taigong lived in the Zhou Dynasty. According to legend, he once fished in the Weishui River, holding a rod without hook or bait three feet above the water and saying, "The fish that is destined to be caught will come up." (From *Stories About King Wu's Expedition Against the Yin Dynasty*.) "Food handed out in contempt" refers to alms handed out as an insult. It is an allusion to a story in the *Book of Rites* that tells of a hungry man in the state of Qi who would rather starve to death than accept food given him insultingly.

[69] Wen Yiduo (1899-1946), native of Xishui, Hubei, was a famous poet, scholar and professor. In 1943 he began to take an active part in the struggle for democracy out of bitter hatred for the reactionary and corrupt Kuomintang government. After the War of Resistance Against Japan he vigorously opposed the Kuomintang's conspiracy with U.S. imperialism to start a civil war against the people. On July 15, 1946, he was assassinated in Kunming by Kuomintang agents.

[70] Zhu Ziqing (1898-1948), native of Shaoxing, Zhejiang, Chinese man of letters and professor, was born in Donghai, Jiangsu. After the War of Resistance Against Japan he actively supported the student movement against the Chiang Kai-shek regime. In June 1948 he signed a declaration protesting the revival of Japanese militarism, which was being fostered by the United States, and rejecting "U.S. relief" flour. He died in Beiping on August 12, 1948, from poverty and illness.

[71] Han Yu (768-824) was a famous writer of the Tang Dynasty. "Eulogy of Bo Yi" was an essay he wrote. Bo Yi, who lived toward the end of the Yin Dynasty, opposed the expedition of King Wu of Zhou against the House of Yin. After the downfall of the House of Yin he fled to Shouyang Mountain and starved to death rather than eat grain produced under the Zhou

regime.

⁷² See *Lao Zi*, Chapter 74.

⁷³ See Li Mi's *Chen Qing Biao* (*Memorial to the Emperor*).

⁷⁴ The Common Program refers here to the Common Program adopted at the First Plenary Session of the Chinese People's Political Consultative Conference held on September 29, 1949. The Common Program laid down China's basic policies on politics, military affairs, economy, culture and education, ethnic groups, and foreign affairs at that time. It was a program for building the country enacted by various democratic parties, people's organizations, ethnic groups and people from all walks of life under the leadership of the Communist Party of China. It was the common goal and political basis for united action of the Chinese people for a certain period of time. It functioned as the provisional constitution before the adoption of the Constitution of the People's Republic of China in 1954.

⁷⁵ A reference to the Sino-Soviet Treaty of Friendship and Alliance signed in Moscow on August 14, 1945, by the Chinese Kuomintang government and the Soviet government. The main contents include: The two countries give each other all necessary military and other assistance and support in the war against Japan, and the two countries adopt measures in concert after the war to prevent fresh Japanese aggression. The agreements on China's Changchun Railway, on Dalian and on Lüshunkou were also signed the same day, and the two governments exchanged notes on the problem of Outer Mongolia. China stated that if a plebiscite in Outer Mongolia after the defeat of Japan confirmed the wish for independence, the Chinese Kuomintang government would recognize the independence of Outer Mongolia. The agreements stipulated that Changchun Railway would be managed jointly by China and the Soviet Union for 30 years; Lüshun would be a common naval base for the two countries for 30 years; and Dalian would be a free port. As a result the Soviet Union gained some special rights and interests from China. The treaty would be valid for 30 years. After the founding of the People's Republic of China the treaty was invalidated, following the regulation in notes exchanged on the signing of the Sino-Soviet Treaty of Friendship, Alliance and Mutual Assistance in 1950.

⁷⁶ On February 14, 1950, the People's Republic of China and the Union of the Soviet Socialist Republics signed the Sino-Soviet Treaty of Friendship, Alliance and Mutual Assistance in Moscow. Its main contents include: Both sides would adopt all necessary measures to stop aggressive action by Japan and its allied nations, and both sides would act according to the principles of equality and mutual benefit and mutual respect of sovereignty and territorial integrity to develop economic and cultural aid and cooperation. The treaty went into effect on April 11, 1950, and would be valid for 30 years. In view of the great changes in the international situation, the Seventh Meeting of the Standing Committee of the Fifth National People's Congress, held on April 3, 1979, decided that the treaty would not be extended after it expired.

⁷⁷ Anastas Mikoyan (1895-1978) was vice-chairman of the Soviet Council of Ministers in 1950.

⁷⁸ Dong Biwu (1886-1975), native of Huang'an (present-day Hongan), Hubei Province, served as vice-premier of the Government Administration Council and concurrently director of the Politics and Law Committee of the Central People's Government in 1950.

⁷⁹ Li Fuchun (1900-1975), native of Changsha, Hunan Province, served as vice-chairman of the People's Government of Northeast China and deputy director of the Committee of Finance and Economics of Northeast China in 1950. On January 10, 1950, he joined a Chinese government delegation to Moscow for economic talks with the Soviet Union.

⁸⁰ The Lüshun-Dalian question refers to the joint use of Lüshunkou naval base by China and the Soviet Union. On February 14, 1950, the governments of China and the Soviet Union signed a Sino-Soviet Treaty of Friendship, Alliance and Mutual Assistance and agreements on China's Changchun Railway, Lüshunkou and Dalian. The agreement stipulated that Soviet troops would withdraw from Lüshunkou after the signing of a peace treaty with Japan, but no

later than the end of 1952. On September 15, 1952, Zhou Enlai and Andrey Y. Vishinsky, foreign minister of the Soviet Union, signed an exchange of notes extending the joint use of China's Lüshunkou naval base, because Japan had not concluded a peace treaty with the People's Republic of China and the Soviet Union. After the end of the Korean War the governments of China and the Soviet Union issued a joint communiqué on October 12, 1954, to announce the withdrawal of Soviet troops from China's Lüshunkou.

[81] Andrey Y. Vishinsky (1883-1954) served as foreign minister of the Soviet Union in 1950.

[82] The Economic Cooperation Administration was a foreign aid organ established by the American government in April 1948. Here the materiel left in Shanghai refers to the goods left behind in Shanghai by the China branch of the American Economic Cooperation Administration for Chiang Kai-shek in fighting the civil war.

[83] In July 1949 the Department of Finance and Economics of the Central Committee of the Communist Party of China and north China's financial and economic committee were merged into a Central Financial and Economic Committee directly under the Chinese People's Revolutionary Military Commission. On this basis the Financial and Economic Committee of the Government Administration Council under the Central People's Government was officially set up on October 21, 1949, unifying national financial and economic work. It was rescinded in September 1954.

[84] On June 27, 1950, U.S. President Harry Truman proclaimed that America had decided to prevent the Chinese government from liberating Taiwan by armed force. Shortly afterward, the U.S. Seventh Fleet was ordered to set out for the Taiwan Straits.

[85] Syngman Rhee (1875-1965) served as president of South Korea (R.O.K.) from 1948 to 1960.

[86] Southern Manchuria referred to Zhuanghe, Andong (now Dandong), Tonghua, Linjiang and Qingyuan east of the Shenyang-Dalian Railway and the Liaozhong area southwest of Shenyang.

[87] It was changed to October 19 later.

[88] When Japan surrendered in August 1945, the United States and the Soviet Union agreed that the 38th parallel of north latitude on Korean territory would be the temporary line of demarcation, when they accepted the surrender of Japanese troops. Soviet troops would accept the surrender north of the line and American troops south of the line, hence the "38th Parallel." When the Korean War broke out in June 1950, the Democratic People's Republic of Korea had already been established north of the parallel, while the area south of the line was under the rule of the Syngman Rhee group supported by American imperialism. The United States then sent troops, in the name of the United Nations, to intervene and landed on Inchon, on the west coast of Korea. Then the troops crossed the "38th Parallel" and mounted a large-scale offensive toward the Chinese-Korean border, which seriously threatened the safety of China. In order to resist U.S. aggression, aid korea and safeguard home and country. the Chinese People's Volunteers fought side by side with the Korean People's Army and gave the U.S. aggressors a heavy blow. The U.S. was forced to sign an armistice agreement in July 1953.

[89] Peng refers to Peng Dehuai, Gao to Gao Gang, He to He Jinnian (deputy commander and concurrently chief of staff of the Northeast Military Area at that time), Deng to Deng Hua (commander of the 13th Army of the People's Liberation Army at that time), Hong to Hong Xuezhi (deputy commander of the 13th Army of the PLA), Xie to Xie Fang (chief of staff of the 13th Army of the PLA).

[90] Reference is to South Korean troops.

[91] Reference is to Zhou Enlai.

[92] On October 26, 1950, Indian Deputy Foreign Secretary Krishna Menon talked with

Shen Jian, political counselor of the Chinese embassy in India, about Chinese troops entering Tibet. He said the Indian government regretted it, if the news were true, and delivered a copy of the Indian government's note to the Chinese government on the Tibetan question. Shen Jian pointed out that the often-used expression of China "invading" Tibet, which also appeared in the note, was not correct. It was not invasion when Chinese troops entered Tibet, which was Chinese territory. It was just like Indian troops entering India's Uffar Pradesh or Bombay, which people could not say it was an invasion. Menon said that India hoped China could solve the Tibetan question by peaceful means. Shen Jian said that the Chinese government had always wished to solve the Tibetan question by peaceful means, but that did not mean Chinese troops could not enter Tibet.

[93] A reference to the Security Treaty of the United States, Australia and New Zealand signed on September 1, 1951 in San Francisco. It took effect on April 29, 1952, and was valid for an unspecified time. The treaty, consisting of 11 articles, mainly stated that the signatories would independently and jointly adopt self and mutual assistance to keep and develop independent and collective military capability; if any signatory state was threatened, consultation should be conducted among them, and if subjected to armed attack, concerted action should be taken.

[94] Aneurin Bevan (1897-1960) was a leader of the British Labour Party, and member of a delegation of the British Labour Party to China.

[95] This refers to the international conference held in Geneva, Switzerland, from April 26 to July 21, 1954, discussing the peaceful solution of the Korean problem and the restoration of peace in Indochina. China, the Soviet Union, the United States, Britain and France participated in the discussion of both subjects. North and South Korea, and 12 countries other than the United States, Britain and France, which took part in the invasion of Korea, also participated in the discussion of the Korean problem. The Democratic Republic of Vietnam, Laos, Cambodia and the puppet regime of South Vietnam also participated in the discussion of the Indochina problem. No agreement was reached on the Korean problem. An agreement to stop hostilities in the three countries of Indochina and the Final Declaration of the Geneva Conference (together known as the Geneva Accords) were concluded, thus realizing the cessation of the Indochina war.

[96] Instigated by the United States, the Southeast Asia Collective Defense Treaty, also known as the Manila Treaty, was signed in Manila, capital of the Philippines, on September 8, 1954, by the United States, Britain, France, Australia, New Zealand, the Philippines, Thailand and Pakistan. It was a military alliance which stated that self-assistance and mutual assistance would be used to resist armed attacks. An "understanding" raised by the United States was attached to the treaty. Here "invasion and armed attack" was explained as only "suitable for Communist invasion." In a related protocol, Cambodia, Laos and Vietnam were designated as the "protection area." The Southeast Asia Treaty Organization was set up when the treaty went into effect on February 19, 1955. The Statement on the Neutrality of Laos, adopted at the Geneva Conference in July 1962, did not recognize its so-called protection of Laos. In 1967 France refused to send an official delegation to take part in the ministerial level council of the organization. On November 8, 1972, Pakistan announced its withdrawal from the organization. In June 1977 the organization was disbanded.

[97] John F. Dulles (1888-1959), member of the U.S. Republican Party, represented the American government at international conferences many times after World War II. He served as adviser to the Truman Administration in 1950 and Secretary of State of the United States from 1953 to 1959. In international affairs he advocated a "cold war," practiced a "brink-of-war" policy, threatened to carry out "large-scale nuclear retaliation" and practiced "peaceful evolution" tactics toward socialist countries. In 1950 he took part in plotting an American invasion and occupation of the Chinese territory of Taiwan by taking advantage of the Korean

War. In 1954 he was instrumental in the signing of a mutual defense treaty of the United States and Taiwan by American and Taiwan authorities, attempting to legalize the U.S. occupation of Taiwan and make Taiwan a long-term U.S. military base.

[98] The Five Principles of Peaceful Coexistence refers to the principles of mutual respect for territorial integrity and sovereignty, mutual nonaggression, noninterference in each other's internal affairs, equality and mutual benefit, and peaceful coexistence. From December 1953 to April 1954 Chinese and Indian government delegations held talks in Beijing on the two countries' relations vis-a-vis China's Tibet. The five principles were put forward by Premier Zhou Enlai at the beginning of the negotiations in his talks with the Indian delegation; later they were officially put into the preface of the Agreement on Trade and Transportation Between China's Tibet and India. The formulation of the five principles was used in the joint statement by Premier Zhou Enlai and Prime Minister Jawaharlal Nehru of India and in many other international documents. The five principles, as the norm of relations between countries, have been widely recognized and used.

[99] N. Raghavan (b. 1900) served as Indian ambassador to China from September 1952 to October 1955.

[100] The Locarno Pact was adopted at the Locarno Conference in Switzerland on October 16, 1925, by Britain, France, Germany, Italy, Belgium, Poland, and Czechoslovakia and officially signed in London, England, on December 1, 1925. The treaty consisted of a protocol and seven agreements. The most important one was the treaty of mutual guarantee between Germany, Belgium, France, Britain and Italy, which stipulated that the signatory states would guarantee nonaggression of the German-French border and German-Belgian border, comply with the agreement to demilitarize the Rhine land of Germany as stipulated by the Treaty of Versailles, and settle all disputes through diplomatic channels. In March 1936 the German fascist government scrapped the agreement and sent troops to the Rhine land, and in April 1939 the Locarno Pact was announced as ended. In the early 1950s Authony Eden, foreign secretary of Britain, advocated a collective security system like the Locarno Pact in Southeast Asia, which was not realized because of the opposition of the United States.

[101] See *Mencius*, "Teng Wen Gong."

[102] Here it refers to the war of resistance waged by the Vietnamese people against French aggression. After World War II Vietnam proclaimed its independence and established the Democratic Republic of Vietnam. In order to re-establish colonial rule over Indochina, France invaded Vietnam in September 1945. To defend their national independence, the Vietnamese people waged a courageous struggle against the French aggressors. In May 1954 the Vietnamese people won decisive victory after the Dienbienphu campaign. According to the Geneva Agreements, the 17th parallel of north latitude was used as the temporary line of demarcation for cease-fire by the Vietnamese People's Army and French troops. France recognized the independence of Vietnam and withdrew its troops from Indochina, so the Vietnamese people's war of resistance against France ended in victory.

[103] Dwight D. Eisenhower (1890-1969), member of the U.S. Republican Party, served as U.S. president from 1953 to 1961.

[104] See Qu Yuan, "Shaosiming," *Nine Odes*.

[105] Yuan Zhongxian (1904-1957), native of Changsha, Hunan, served as ambassador of the People's Republic of China to India from September 1950 to February 1956.

[106] On April 29, 1954, the governments of China and India signed an Agreement on Trade and Transportation Between China's Tibet and India. It stipulated that the five principles of peaceful coexistence were the norm for relations between the two countries and determined the various methods for trade and pilgrimage of people from China's Tibet and India. The main contents concerned the following: the setting up of a trade representative's office in each other's country; businessmen and pilgrims of both countries to trade or make regular pilgrimages in

designated places and pass through designated mountain passes and roads; regulations on diplomatic personnel, government functionaries and nationals of the two countries passing through each other's territory. The agreement went into effect on June 3, 1954, with a period of validity of eight years. In June 1962 the agreement expired.

[107] Kublai Khan (1215-1294) was the founder and first emperor of the Yuan Dynasty. He reigned from 1260 to 1294. During his reign he made many incursions into the neighboring countries of Japan, Korea and Vietnam in order to expand his sphere of influence. From 1283 to 1288 he sent troops to invade Burma twice, which were met with fierce resistance from the Burmese people.

[108] A reference to remnants of Kuomintang troops who fled into Burma (Myanmar) from 1949 to 1950.

[109] From April 28 to May 2, 1954, the premiers of Burma, Ceylon, India, Indonesia and Pakistan held a meeting in Colombo, capital of Ceylon, at which they proposed holding an Asian-African Conference. The second meeting of the five countries, held in Bogor, Indonesia, on December 28-29, 1954, decided on jointly sponsoring an Asian-African Conference in 1955. The communiqué of the meeting declared that the purpose of the Asian-African Conference was to promote close cooperation and good-neighbor relations among these countries; discuss the social, economic and cultural problems and relations of the participating countries; discuss problems of common interest to the people of Asian and African countries, such as national sovereignty and racial and colonial problems, and the international status of the Asian and African countries and their people and how they could contribute to world peace and cooperation. The five countries participating in the meeting were also called the Colombo countries.

[110] A reference to the Joint Communiqué of the premiers of China and Burma, issued in Rangoon, Burma, on June 29, 1954, by Premier Zhou Enlai of China and Prime Minister U Nu of Burma. It confirmed that the Five Principles of Peaceful Coexistence were the norm guiding relations between China and Burma and reiterated that the people of various countries had the right to choose their own state systems and way of life and other countries should not interfere; revolution could not be exported and the people's common will of a country brooks no outside interference; the people of China and Burma should keep close ties in order to continue to strengthen their friendly cooperation.

[111] Also known as the Bandung Conference, the Asian-African Conference was held from April 18 to 24, 1955, in Bandung, Indonesia, and participated in by 29 Asian and African countries, including the five initiators, Burma, Ceylon, India, Indonesia and Pakistan, and Afghanistan, Cambodia, the People's Republic of China and Egypt. Problems of national sovereignty, struggle against colonialism, world peace and economic and cultural cooperation of the participating countries were discussed widely at this meeting and a Final Communiqué of the Asian-African Conference was issued, which put forward ten principles on world peace and cooperation.

[112] Yao Zhongming, born in 1914 and native of Dong'e, Shandong, served as ambassador of the People's Republic of China to Burma from August 1950 to January 1958.

[113] A reference to the Communiqué on the Talks of the Premiers of China and Burma published in Beijing on December 12, 1954. Its main contents were as follows: a reiteration that the Five Principles of Peaceful Coexistence remained the guiding principle of the relations between the two countries; establishment of consulates-general in appropriate cities between the two countries; the opening of airlines, the resumption of highway communications and the signing of a postal agreement to promote economic and cultural exchanges between the two countries; protecting the legal rights and interests of the nationals of both sides and urging them to abide by the laws and social customs of the residing country; and solution of boundary issues through normal diplomatic channels.

[114] Ceylon is the present Democratic Socialist Republic of Sri Lanka.

[115] In 1953 China established the Xishuangbanna Dai Autonomous Region and Dehong Dai and Jingpo Autonomous Region in Yunnan Province. In 1955 and 1956 they were changed into autonomous prefectures.

[116] Clement Attlee (1883-1967), former prime minister of Britain, was leader of the Labor Party of Britain in 1954.

[117] After the Korean War broke out in June 1950, U.S. President Harry Truman ordered the U.S. Seventh Fleet to intrude into the Taiwan Straits, while he announced armed interference in the Korean civil war. In order to legalize its invasion of China's territory, the United States signed a mutual defense treaty with Taiwan authorities on December 2, 1954. The treaty stipulated that the United States would help Taiwan maintain and develop armed forces; if Taiwan suffered an "armed attack," the United States would take action to deal with the "common danger"; and the United States had the right to deploy its ground, naval and air forces in Taiwan, the Penghu Islands, nearby places and other territories decided on by both sides through consultation. The treaty went into effect on March 3, 1955. On the establishment of diplomatic relations between the United States and the People's Republic of China, the U.S. government announced on December 15, 1978 that the mutual defense treaty signed by the United States and Taiwan would be terminated. On January 1, 1980, the treaty was formally abrogated.

[118] The Potsdam Conference, also known as the Berlin Conference, was held in Potsdam, southwest of Berlin, Germany, from July 17 to August 2, 1945, by top leaders and foreign ministers of the Soviet Union, the United States and Britain. The conference agreed to establish a council of foreign ministers of China, the Soviet Union, the United States, Britain and France to prepare for the signing of treaties after World War II and to discuss other problems among the member states. The conference discussed the principles for handling German politics and economy during occupation by the Soviet Union, the United States, Britain and France, including the disarmament of Germany, eradicating or controlling German military industry, destroying all organizations and systems of the Nazi party, arresting and sentencing Nazi war criminals, and Germany's compensation and policies in dealing with Italy, Bulgaria, Finland, Hungary and Romania. On August 2, 1945, the participating states signed the Berlin (Potsdam) Conference Protocol and Berlin (Potsdam) Conference Communiqué, generally known as the Potsdam Agreement.

[119] A series of documents signed in Paris in October 1954 by the United States, Britain, France and other member states of the North Atlantic Treaty Organization with the Federal Republic of Germany was generally called the Paris Protocol. It included documents on terminating the occupation of Federal Germany, a Western European alliance, the North Atlantic Council, and a bilateral agreement between France and Federal Germany. The Protocol reiterated the "right" to station troops in Federal Germany and West Berlin by the United States, Britain, and France and other "rights" as stated in the Bonn Treaty. It also allowed Federal Germany to join the Treaty of Brussels and the North Atlantic Treaty as a sovereign state, and to rebuild its army. Wording forbidding aggression by Federal Germany in the Treaty of Brussels was dropped, and the treaty was renamed the "Western European Alliance," to which Federal Germany and Italy were invited to be member states. In addition, the Saar was to be governed by a special commissioner elected by popular vote but appointed by the Western European Alliance organization. The Paris Protocol became effective May 5 and 6, 1955.

[120] Hideki Tojo (1884-1948), war criminal, participated in plotting the September 18th Incident for invasion of China in 1931. Afterward, he was appointed commander of military police and chief of staff of the Japanese Kwantung Army. From 1940 to 1941 he was minister of war, actively advocating expanding the aggressive war in China and preparing for a war with the United States and Britain. When he was prime minister, from 1941 to 1944, he launched

the Pacific War and expanded the aggressive war from China to the Pacific and Southeast Asia. After Japan's surrender he was arrested and sentenced to death by hanging by the International Military Tribunal for the Far East in 1948.

[121] Tito (1892-1980), former Yugoslav leader and famous activist of international communist movement, was one of the founders of the nonalignment movement. In World War II he led the people of various ethnic groups of Yugoslavia to wage a war against fascism and for national liberation. In 1945 he founded the Federal People's Republic of Yugoslavia (changed to the Socialist Federal Republic of Yugoslavia in 1963). In 1955 he served as general secretary of the League of Communists of Yugoslavia, president of the Republic and chairman of the Federal Executive Council.

[122] Norodom Sihanouk (b. 1922) served as prime minister and concurrently foreign minister of Cambodia from 1955. He was elected head of state in 1960. When Lon Nol staged a coup d'état in 1970, Sihanouk organized a National United Front and a government in exile in Beijing and served as chairman of the United Front and head of state.

[123] Prince Wan Waithayakon, or Krommun Naradhip Bongsprabandh (1891-1976), served as minister of foreign affairs of Thailand in 1956.

[124] Carlos P. Romulo (1899-1985), former foreign minister of the Philippines, was a special envoy of the president of the Philippines to the United States in 1956 and the representative of the Philippines at the Asian-African Conference.

[125] Malaya is now part of Malaysia.

[126] "On the Historical Experience of the Dictatorship of the Proletariat" was an article published by the Editorial Department of *People's Daily* on April 5, 1956. It was written according to the opinions discussed by the Enlarged Meeting of the Political Bureau of the Central Committee of the Communist Party of China.

[127] Wang Ming and others gained the leading positions of the Party Central Committee at the Fourth Plenum of the Sixth Central Committee of the CPC through the support of the Communist International and its representative in China, Pavel A. Mif, in January 1931. They confused democratic revolution with socialist revolution, and equated the struggle against the bourgeoisie, to the struggle against imperialism and feudalism; they denied the obvious changes in domestic class relations after the September 18th Incident of 1931 and looked upon the intermediate forces as the most "dangerous enemy"; they continued to carry out the "theory of cities being the center" and advocated that the Red Army seize key cities first, to achieve victory in one province or many provinces to bring about victory throughout the country. In military affairs they first carried out adventurism, then turned to conservatism and "flightism." Organizationally, they became sectarians practicing ruthless struggle against and merciless blows to people who did not agree with their wrong ideas. Wang Ming's "Left" adventurism dominated the Party for about four years, bringing great losses to the revolutionary cause. In January 1935 the Political Bureau of the Central Committee of the CPC held a meeting in Zunyi that established the correct leadership of the new Central Committee, headed by Mao Zedong, thus ending the domination of Wang Ming's "Left" adventurism in the Party Central Committee.

[128] In December 1937, when Wang Ming of Resistance had just come back from the Soviet Union, he made a speech on "How to Continue the War of Resistance Against Japan in the Whole Country and Win Victory" at a meeting of the Political Bureau of the Party Central Committee and put forward many Right capitulationist ideas. Later, when he was secretary of the Changjiang Bureau of the Party Central Committee, he issued some declarations and wrote decisions and articles containing wrong ideas. He believed in the Kuomintang more than in the Communist Party, did not dare to launch mass struggles, develop a people's army and expand the liberated areas in Japanese-occupied areas, and advocated that "everything goes through the united front," giving the leadership of the anti-Japanese war to the Kuomintang.

Owing to the domination of the correct line in the Party, represented by Mao Zedong, Wang Ming's mistakes had influence only in some regions. Wang Ming's right capitulationism was criticized in the enlarged meeting of the Sixth Plenum of the Sixth Central Committee of the CPC held from September to November 1938 and the policy and principles of the Party independently leading the armed struggle against the Japanese aggressors were reaffirmed.

[129] In the Beijing opera *The Famen Temple* Jia Gui is a trusted lackey of Liu Jin, a Ming Dynasty eunuch. When Zhao Lian, head of Meiwu County, goes to see Liu Jin, Liu asks him to take a seat and Zhao Lian also invites Jia Gui to sit down. Jia Gui refuses to do so, giving the excuse that he is used to standing in attendance.

[130] Chen Duxiu's Right opportunism refers to the right capitulationist mistake represented by Chen Duxiu in the first half of 1927. At that time Chen Duxiu gave up the Party's leadership of the peasant masses, urban petty bourgeoisie and middle bourgeoisie and, in particular, gave up the Party's leadership of the armed forces. He advocated "alliance above all" and denied struggle by adopting a policy of compromise with and capitulation to the anti-Communist and anti-people plots of the Rightists in the Kuomintang. As a result, when Chiang Kai-shek and Wang Jingwei, representatives of the big landlords and big bourgeoisie, successively betrayed the revolution and launched surprise attacks on the people, the Communist Party of China and the people could not organize effective resistance, thus causing the defeat of the First Revolutionary Civil War. In August 7, 1927, an emergency meeting was held by the Central Committee of the Communist Party of China in Hankou, which summed up the experiences and lessons of the failure of the revolution and ended the rule of Chen Duxiu's Right capitulationism in the Party Central Committee.

[131] Li Lisan's "Left" opportunism refers to the "Left" adventurism represented by Li Lisan during the Second Revolutionary Civil War. The resolution on "New Revolutionary High Tide and the Victory of One Province or Several Provinces First," adopted on June 11, 1930, by the Political Bureau of the Party Central Committee, led by Li Lisan, advocated that various places in the country take immediate measures to prepare for uprisings. Before long, an adventurist plan to organize armed uprisings in the key cities of the country and concentrate the Red Army of the whole country to attack the key cities was adopted. Then the Party, Youth League and trade union leading organs at various levels were changed into Action Committees at various levels to prepare for an armed uprising, thus ceasing all their normal work. The Third Plenum of the Sixth Central Committee of the Communist Party of China, held in September 1930, corrected the mistake of Li Lisan's "Left" adventurism.

[132] In June 1935 the First Front Army of the Red Army on the Long March joined forces with the Fourth Front Army in Maogong, Sichuan. At that time the Party Central Committee had decided on the strategic principle of going to north China to establish a Shaanxi-Gansu base. Zhang Guotao, who had led the Fourth Front Army for a long time, did not foresee the possibility of establishing bases in north China and refused to carry out the decision of the Party Central Committee to go north. He ordered the Fourth Front Army and part of the Central Red Army to go south, retreating to the border areas of Sichuan and Xikang. He maneuvered to split the Party and the Red Army and openly established another central committee. Owing to the hard work and resolute fight of Zhu De, Liu Bocheng and the commanders and soldiers of the Fourth Front Army, Zhang Guotao was forced to rescind the second central committee and go north with the Second and Fourth front armies in June 1936. They arrived in northern Shaanxi in December the same year.

[133] Gao Gang was once a member of the Political Bureau of the Party Central Committee, vice-chairman of the Central People's Government, secretary of the Northeast China Bureau of the Party Central Committee and chairman of the State Planning Commission. In 1953 he and Rao Shushi, head of the Organization Department of the Party Central Committee, plotted to split the Party and seize the supreme power of the Party and state. They were exposed and

criticized in the Fourth Plenum of the Seventh Central Committee of the Communist Party of China, held in February 1954. The National Conference of the Communist Party of China held in March 1955 summed up this important struggle and adopted a resolution to expel them from the Party.

134 The Egyptian incident refers to the Suez Canal crisis. The Suez Canal, in northeastern Egypt, is an international waterway connecting the Mediterranean and Red seas. Located at the juncture of Europe, Asia and Africa, it is very important strategically. It was opened to navigation in 1869, and Britain and France monopolized the stock of the Suez Canal Company, earning huge profits. Britain built a military base in the area of the canal, the biggest base in a foreign country. After World War II the Egyptian people struggled unremittingly to regain sovereignty of the Suez Canal. On July 26, 1956, the government of Egypt announced it would take back the Suez Canal Company. The Chinese government and governments and leaders of many other countries in the world made statements supporting the just action of Egypt. In October 1956 Britain, France and Israel launched a war to invade Egypt and seize back the canal, but they failed.

135 London Conference, held in London from August 16 to 23, 1956, refers to the international conference suggested by the United States, Britain and France to discuss the problem of the Suez Canal. It was participated in by Britain, France, Italy, the Netherlands, the Soviet Union, Japan, Ceylon, India, Ethiopia, the United States, New Zealand, and others, totaling 22 countries. Egypt did not participate in the conference. The United States, Britain and France wanted to adopt a plan to practice "international control" over the Suez Canal, which was opposed by some countries, such as the Soviet Union, India and Ceylon, so the plan did not get through.

136 Ngo Dinh Diem (1901-1963) was president, prime minister and defense minister of the former South Vietnamese puppet regime, the "Republic of Vietnam." He and his younger brother were killed in a military coup d'état on November 1, 1963, plotted by the United States.

137 In July 1956 the Egyptian government announced it would take back the Suez Canal Company. In order to control the Suez Canal again, Britain, the United States and France held a meeting of 22 countries (but not Egypt) in London in August of the same year to discuss the Suez Canal problem. At the meeting John F. Dulles, U.S. Secretary of State, put forward a plan of international administration of the Suez Canal. This plan stressed that the Suez Canal was of international character, so that the canal company was an international organ that could not be nationalized. It suggested establishing an International Suez Canal Administrative Bureau, enjoying extraterritoriality, to practice international condominium over the Suez Canal. This plan, depriving Egypt of sovereignty over the Suez Canal, was not adopted at the meeting and later was refused by the Egyptian government.

138 This refers to King Faruk (1920-1965), the last king of Egypt. He was overthrown by the Free Officers Group, led by Gamal Abdel Nasser, in 1952.

139 Gamal Abdel Nasser (1918-1970) was then president of the Republic of Egypt. He had led the Egyptian people in their struggle to take back the Suez Canal and resist the aggression of Britain, France and Israel.

140 A reference to the Five Nations Suez Canal Committee organized by Australia, Ethiopia, the United States, Sweden and Iran in August 1956, plotted by Britain, the United States and France. It forced the Egyptian government, threatened by armed force, to accept a plan of "international control" over the Suez Canal through negotiations. Nasser, president of Egypt, accepted the invitation for negotiations, but he firmly opposed the stand of the "committee" in the negotiations, so the activities of the "committee" ended without result.

141 The Third International means the Communist International, which was established in March 1919 under the leadership of Lenin. The Communist Party of China joined the Communist International in 1922 and became a branch. The presidium of the Executive

Committee of the Communist International adopted a decision in May 1943 to disband the Communist International. In June 1943 the Communist International was formally disbanded.

[142] Georgi M. Dimitrov (1882-1949), a Bulgarian, was a famous activist in the international communist movement. He served as general secretary of the Executive Committee of the Communist International from 1935 to 1943.

[143] After the War of Resistance Against Japan broke out, an enlarged meeting of the Political Bureau of the Central Committee of the Communist Party of China was held in August 1937 at Luochuan, northern Shaanxi. The Ten Point Program of Resistance Against Japan and for National Salvation of the Communist Party was approved in this meeting. Integrating resistance against Japan with striving for democracy and improving people's lives, the program proposed mobilizing all forces to defeat the Japanese imperialists and fight a full-scale war against Japan. Wang Ming returned to China from the Soviet Union in November 1937. He opposed the correct line of resistance against Japan formulated by the Central Committed of the Communist Party of China under the banner of the Communist International. In December 1937 Wang Ming, as a member of the delegation of the Communist Party of China, arrived in Wuhan and issued a Statement of the Central Committee of the Communist Party of China on the Present Situation without authorization. He put forward six tasks to be realized in the anti-Japanese war and canceled the proposals for political and economic reform in the Ten Point Program and for abolishing the dictatorship of the Kuomintang. He also advanced the idea that the people's anti-Japanese armed forces, led by the Communist Party, should accept the unified command of the Kuomintang government. That meant the Communist Party of China would abandon its independent position in the War of Resistance Against Japan and leadership over the united front, which were contrary to the Ten Point Program.

[144] Winston Churchill (1874-1965), politician of the Conservative Party of Britain, served as prime minister of Britain during wartime from 1940 to 1945 and led the British people to fight against the German fascists. From 1951 to 1955 he was again prime minister of the British government.

[145] The Yalta Conference, also known as the Crimea Conference, was held by the heads of the Soviet Union, the United States and Britain in Yalta, Crimea, from February 4 to 11, 1945. The military plan for the final defeat of Germany was coordinated and the problems of postwar arrangement of Europe and struggle against Japan were discussed; the Communiqué of the Crimea Conference of the Soviet Union, the United States ad Britain was signed, and agreements on the problem of occupying and administering Germany by different districts and on the Polish problem were reached. An agreement of the Soviet Union, the United States and Britain on Japan was secretly signed (Yalta Agreement for short). It stipulated that the Soviet Union would join the war against Japan within two or three months after the end of the European war; the United States and Britain promised to maintain the status quo of Outer Mongolia; Russia's lost territory after the Japanese-Russian War of 1905 and various rights over China's northeast would be restored and the Kurile Islands would be returned to the Soviet Union. The Soviet Union agreed to sign a pact of alliance and friendship with China's Kuomintang government.

[146] Nikita Khrushchev (1894-1971) became first secretary of the Central Committee of the Communist Party of the Soviet Union in September 1953 and chairman of the Council of Ministers in March 1958. He was dismissed from these posts in October 1964.

[147] Genghis Khan (1162-1227), original name Temujin, was Emperor Taizu of the Yuan Dynasty. In 1206 he consolidated all the Mongol tribes to form the Mongol Khanate. He became the Great Khan, the reign title of Genghis Khan. He led expeditionary armies to invade Central Asia, West Asia and Eastern Europe many times and caused great havoc to those areas.

[148] O. V. Yudin (1899-1968), Soviet philosopher and academician, served as a member of the Central Committee of the Communist Party of the Soviet Union from 1952 to 1961.

He was ambassador of the Soviet Union to China from 1953 to 1959.

[149] A reference to the article "Trotskyism or Leninism?" by Stalin (see J. V. Stalin, *Works*, People's Publishing House, 1956, Vol. VI, Chinese edition, p. 281-309).

[150] The three articles refer to "Stalin, Friend of the Chinese People," published by *Xinzhonghua Bao* (*New China's News*) on December 20, 1939, "Congratulatory Speech for the Celebration of Stalin's 70th Birthday" in Moscow on December 21, 1949, and "The Greatest Friendship," published in *People's Daily* on March 9, 1953, in memory of Stalin.

[151] A reference to the five permanent members of the United Nations Security Council: the Soviet Union, China, the United States, Britain and France. China's seat as a permanent member of the United Nations Security Council was still illegally occupied by Taiwan's Kuomintang authorities in 1956.

[152] West Irian refers to the western part of New Guinea and its offshore islands in Indonesia (today's Irian Jaya). When Indonesia won its independence in 1949, the Dutch government, supported by the United States, continued to occupy this area. The Indonesian government tried many times to solve the problem of West Irian through negotiations, but it was obstructed repeatedly. In order to safeguard the nation's independence and sovereignty, the Indonesian people launched a mammoth movement of recovering West Irian and an armed struggle against colonialism, which forced the Dutch government to agree to negotiate. On May 1, 1963, the Netherlands returned West Irian to Indonesia.

[153] Huang Zhen (1909-1990), native of Tongcheng, Anhui, served as ambassador of China to Indonesia from November 1954 to June 1961.

[154] Konrad Adenauer (1876-1967) was chancellor of the Federal Republic of Germany from 1949 to 1963. He became chairman of the Christian Democratic Union in 1956.

[155] Round Table Conference Agreement is the general term for the series of agreements signed in November and December of 1949 by the governments of the Kingdom of the Netherlands and the Republic of Indonesia on the problem of turning over sovereignty. The agreement stipulated that the government of the Netherlands should turn over sovereignty to Indonesia and establish a Dutch-Indonesian union, but the Netherlands would still keep its control over West Irian. According to the agreement, Indonesia won only nominal independence and, in fact, did not get rid of the colonial control of the Netherlands. To safeguard true national independence and sovereignty, the Indonesian government waged a struggle and abrogated the Round Table Conference Agreement in April 1956.

[156] A reference to the friendship visits of a Chinese government delegation, headed by Premier Zhou Enlai, from January 7 to 11 and January 17 to 19, 1957.

[157] After the German troops failed in their all-round offensive on the Soviet Union in the summer of 1942, they turned their attack to the south flank of the Soviet-German battlefield. On July 17, 1942, German troops started a fierce attack on Stalingrad in an attempt to occupy this city, cut off transportation on the Volga, seize the Caucasus oilfields in the south and attack Moscow in the north. The five front armies of the Soviet troops fought bravely, along with the people, and eliminated a great number of the enemy in the defensive warfare. On November 19, 1942, Soviet troops switched to counterattack and encircled 330,000 German troops on November 23, which were wholly annihilated on February 2, 1943. In this campaign the German army lost 1.5 million troops and the Soviet army seized strategic initiative, marking a turning point in the war between the Soviet Union and Germany and in World War II.

[158] Reference is to the anti-government political event in Hungary in October-November 1956.

[159] Howard Fast (b. 1914), American writer. He joined the Communist Party of the United States of America in 1942. His works exposed the darkness of capitalist society and reflecting revolutionary movements in American history. Once a member of the World Peace

Council, he announced his withdrawal from the Communist Party of the USA after the 20th Congress of the Communist Party of the Soviet Union and the Hungarian incident.

[160] Here it refers to the northeastern area of China.

[161] During the Korean War the United States intervened militarily in Korea by organizing the "U.N. forces" composed of armies of 16 countries: Britain, France, the Netherlands, Belgium, Luxembourg, Australia, New Zealand, Canada, South Africa, Ethiopia, Turkey, Greece, the Philippines, Thailand, Colombia and the United States.

[162] The Vanguard Program was drawn up by the United States to launch man-made earth satellites, through which the United States hoped to put America at the very front of space technology.

[163] Harry Pollitt (1890-1960) was then chairman of the Central Executive Committee of the Communist Party of Great Britain. John Gollan (1911-1977) was then the general secretary of the Central Committee of the Communist Party of Great Britain.

[164] One acre is about six *mu*.

[165] According to the Korean armistice agreement, a neutral nations supervisory commission, made up of four senior officers from countries that did not send armies to take part in the Korean hostilities, should be founded. The four officers were from Switzerland, Sweden, Poland and Czechoslovakia.

[166] This refers to the meeting held in Nanning, Guangxi from January 11 to 23, 1958 by the Party Central Committee. Some of the leading comrades of central and local authorities attended the meeting to discuss the 1958 national economic plan and state budget, and how to improve methods of work.

[167] Chen Yun (1905-1995), born in Qingpu, Jiangsu Province (now part of Shanghai), was then a member of the Standing Committee of the Central Political Bureau of the CPC, vice-chairman of the Central Committee of the CPC and vice-premier of the State Council.

[168] A representative meeting of the Communist and workers' parties of socialist countries was held in Moscow during November 14-16, 1957. Twelve delegations from ruling Communist or Workers' Parties attended the meeting. They were from Albania, Bulgaria, Hungary, Poland, the German Democratic Republic, Romania, Czechoslovakia, the Soviet Union, Vietnam, Mongolia, Korea and China. The meeting adopted the Declaration of Communist Parties and Workers' Parties of Socialist Countries (also called the Moscow Declaration), which summed up the experience of the international Communist movement, presented the communist Parties' tasks of fighting for peace and struggling for socialism, formulated the norm of relationship between socialist countries and parties and called on the Communist Parties to apply Marxism-Leninism with creativity. This meeting, to some extent, played a positive role in strengthening the international Communist movement and socialist cause.

[169] A reference to the May 14, 1958 report by the leading Party group of the Second Ministry of Machine Building to Chairman Mao and the Central Committee of the CPC. The report mainly introduced how the Soviet experts in the Third Beijing Industrial and Architectural Design Institute were helped to familiarize themselves with China's national conditions and policies of construction, so that they could proceed from actual conditions and work in cooperation with their Chinese colleagues.

[170] Xiaoping, i.e., Deng Xiaoping, born in 1904 in Guang'an, Sichuan Province, was then the general secretary of the Central Committee of the CPC and vice-premier of the State Council.

[171] In 1955 the Central Committee of the CPC and Mao Zedong began to discuss the idea of achieving greater, faster, better and more economical results in building socialism and took it as the guiding principle of socialist construction. In March 1958 Mao Zedong summarized this guideline at the Chengdu meeting held by the Central Committee of the CPC

as the general line of "Go all out, aim high and achieve greater, faster, better and more economical results in building socialism." In May of the same year the Second Session of the Eighth National Congress of the CPC formally adopted the general line and its main points, which were set forth comprehensively in the work report given by Liu Shaoqi representing the Central Committee. This general line affirmed the main task of the Party at the time was to carry out socialist economic construction, which reflected the wish of the broad masses to end the backwardness of the country's economy and culture. Its shortcoming lay in ignoring objective economic law.

172 On April 18, 1958, Soviet Defense Minister Rodion Y. Malinovsky wrote to the Minister of National Defense of China, Peng Dehuai, asking to set up a joint special long-wave radio station in China. On June 12 the Chinese government replied that China would not agree to the establishment of the station unless it was funded and wholly owned by China. The Soviet Union could help China with technology and equipment and the two countries could use the station together. Because the Chinese government insisted on the conditions, the Soviet Union was forced to agree to help with setting up the station by providing a loan. On August 3 the two countries signed the agreement and concluded contracts concerning equipment and the engagement of experts. Later, because the Soviet Union recalled its experts and tore up the contracts, China completed the long-wave radio station on its own.

173 Liu refers to Liu Shaoqi. Lin Biao was then vice-chairman of the Central Committee of the CPC and vice-premier of the State Council. Xiaoping, i.e., Deng Xiaoping, was then the secretary general of the Central Committee of the CPC and vice-premier of the State Council. Zhou refers to Zhou Enlai. Zhu refers to Zhu De and Chen to Chen Yun, who was vice-chairman of the Central Committee of the CPC and vice-premier of the State Council. Peng Zhen was then a member of the Secretariat of the Central Committee of the CPC and vice-chairman of the Standing Committee of the NPC. Chen Yi was then a member of the Political Bureau of the Central Committee of the CPC, vice-premier of the State Council and minister of foreign affairs.

174 On June 5, 1958, Peng Dehuai, member of the Political Bureau of the Central Committee of the CPC, vice-premier of the State Council and Minister of National Defense, said in his report to Mao Zedong and the Central Committee of the CPC that since the Soviet Union still insisted on setting up a special long-wave radio station jointly with China and suggested that it send experts to China in early June for site selection, prospecting, design, and drafting the agreement, it looked as if the Soviet Union would not soon accept China's proposal. In order not to delay the prospecting and design, China could allow the Soviet experts to come for some technical work, leaving problems of investment and operation to later discussions.

175 A reference to Mao's revision of part of the record of the conversation between Peng Dehuai and Dorovanov, general military advisor of the Soviet Union, on June 4, 1958.

176 See "Li Lou Shang," *Mencius*.

177 On June 28, 1958, China, at the suggestion of Soviet military experts, asked the Soviet Union for technical assistance to develop nuclear submarines for the Chinese navy. That year on July 21 Ambassador Yudin of the Soviet Union conveyed to Mao Zedong Khrushchev's idea that since the Soviet Union did not have an ideal coast for the development of nuclear submarines, the Soviet Union proposed establishment of a joint nuclear submarine fleet with China that would take advantage of the favorable conditions of China's coastal areas. Because the proposal impaired China's sovereignty, China withdrew the request for technical assistance from the Soviet Union for development of nuclear submarines.

178 In March 1950 and July 1951 the governments of China and the Soviet Union concluded four agreements with regard to the establishment of four Sino-Soviet joint-stock companies in China: the Sino-Soviet Civil Aviation Company, the Sino-Soviet Oil Company, the Sino-Soviet Nonferrous and Rare Metal Company and the Sino-Soviet Shipbuilding

Company. Although these enterprises under joint operation played a positive role in China's economic construction at the time, the Soviet Union's attempt to change them into economic entities independent of China's sovereignty impaired China's interests in some ways. For that reason the Chinese and Soviet governments signed on October 12, 1954 a joint communiqué in which the Soviet side promised to sell China its shares in the four Sino-Soviet joint-stock companies before January 1, 1955. After the turnover of the stocks the Sino-Soviet Civil Aviation Company was taken over by the Chinese Civil Aviation Bureau, and the other three companies were renamed respectively Xinjiang Oil Company, Xinjiang Nonferrous Metal Company and Dalian Shipyard.

[179] Grigory Zinovyev (1883-1936), a member of the Central Political Bureau of the Russian Social Democratic Workers' Party (Bolsheviks) on the eve of the October Revolution, was seriously criticized by Lenin for being against the armed uprising and revealing its plan. Later he became chairman of the Petrograd Soviet and chairman of the Executive Committee of the Communist International. He was removed from the Party in 1927, and put to death in 1936.

[180] Nikolay Bulganin (1895-1975) was chairman of the Council of Ministers of the Soviet Union at that time.

[181] O. V. Kuusinen (1881-1964) was a member of the Central Presidium of the Communist Party of the Soviet Union and of the Central Secretariat.

[182] Mikhail Suslov (1902-1982) was then secretary of the Central Committee of the Communist Party of the Soviet Union.

[183] A reference to China's 156 large and medium-sized industrial projects to be built with assistance from the Soviet Union during the First Five-Year Plan period. These projects were established in turn during the years 1950-1954 through repeated consultation between the two countries' governments, and the number was reduced to 154 later. In 1960, because the Soviet Union unilaterally tore up the agreement, only 150 projects were carried out.

[184] Lavrenty Beria (1899-1953), vice-chairman of the Council of Ministers of the Soviet Union in 1949.

[185] Andrei Kovalyov was the top leader in charge of the Soviet experts in China in 1958. He accompanied Mao Zedong to the Soviet Union in December 1949.

[186] Nikolai Fedorenko, Soviet Sinologist. He was the Chinese interpreter in the Soviet diplomatic service for a long time and Cultural Attaché of the embassy of the Soviet Union in China.

[187] Kemal Atatürk (1881-1938), who represented the national merchant capitalists of Turkey, led its national liberation movement and the bourgeois-democratic revolution after World War I. He founded a bourgeois republic in Turkey in 1923 and was elected its first president.

[188] On April 27, 1958, Vice-President Nixon of the United States attended the inaugural ceremony of the new president of Argentina and afterward paid visits to seven Latin American countries: Uruguay, Paraguay, Bolivia, Peru, Ecuador, Colombia and Venezuela. During the visits protests against the Latin American policy of the United States took place in the seven countries. While in Venezuela Nixon was forced to abort his visit and return to the United States.

[189] A military setup consisting of major Western countries, founded in April 1949 when the United States, Britain, France, the Netherlands, Belgium, Luxembourg, Norway, Portugal, Italy, Denmark, Iceland and Canada signed a military alliance treaty in Washington. Greece and Turkey acceded to the treaty in 1952, and the Federal Republic of Germany and Spain were admitted in 1955 and 1982 respectively.

[190] A military alliance organized by Britain and the United States to control the Middle

East and contain the Soviet Union. It was founded according to the Baghdad Pact in November 1955 and was renamed the Central Treaty Organization in August 1959. Turkey, Iraq, the United Kingdom, Iran and Pakistan were members and the United States joined the organization as an observer. In July 1958 Iraq's monarchy was overthrown and the new government formally withdrew from the pact in March 1959. It was dissolved on September 28, 1979, after Iran, Pakistan and Turkey withdrew the same year because of increasing differences toward international affairs among its members.

[191] Charles De Gaulle (1890-1970), French general and politician who led france's resistance movement against the armed occupation of fascist Germany during the Second World War. In 1944 he became head of the provisional government and in June 1958 he became premier of France. In December, when the Fifth Republic was founded, he was elected President.

[192] He Yingqin (1890-1987) was born in Xingyi, Guizhou. He was chief of the general staff of the Military Committee in the Kuomintang government and Minister of War during the War of Resistance Against Japan.

[193] Here the 19 countries refers to the countries that had established diplomatic relations with China at that time: Afghanistan, Pakistan, Cambodia, Burma, Nepal, Ceylon (Sri Lanka), Yemen, Iraq, India, Indonesia, the United Arab Republic (formed after merger of Egypt and Syria in February 1958), Denmark, Finland, the Netherlands, Norway, Sweden, Switzerland, Liechtenstein and the United Kingdom. The 11 socialist countries refers to Korea, Mongolia, Vietnam, Albania, Bulgaria, Poland, the German Democratic Republic, Czechoslovakia, Romania, the Soviet Union and Hungary.

[194] On September 9, 1958, *People's Daily* published a news report about the speech. It was revised by Mao Zedong. Here is an abstract of the part on the international situation:

Chairman Mao said the current situation was favorable to people all over the world striving for peace. The general trend was for the east wind to prevail over the west wind. He said that the American imperialists had occupied China's territory of Taiwan for nine years and had recently sent their armed forces to invade and occupy Lebanon. The United States had established several hundred military bases all over the world. Taiwan, Lebanon and these bases were nooses around the necks of the American imperialists. Not others, but American imperialism produced the noose and put it on its neck. Besides, it handed the other end of the noose to the Chinese people, people in Arabic countries and all the people who loved peace and opposed aggression. The longer the American invader stayed in those areas, the tighter the noose would be around his neck.

Chairman Mao also said that the American imperialists produced tense situations throughout the world, so that they could invade other countries and keep the people in bondage. The American imperialists thought the tense situations were always favorable to them. On the contrary, they aroused the world's people's opposition to the American invader. Chairman Mao said, if the American monopoly capital group insisted on its policy of aggression and war, it would be hanged for sure by people throughout the world, and so would its accomplices.

Chairman Mao placed hope on the coming negotiations at the ambassadorial level between China and the United States in Warsaw. He said, "If the two countries really want to solve problems, there can be some achievements. Now the world is paying close attention to the negotiations."

[195] Smout was commander of the American troops stationed in Taiwan in 1958.

[196] The United Arab Republic was formed by Egypt and Syria in 1958. Syria withdrew in 1961 and founded the Syrian Arab Republic. In 1971 the United Arab Republic was renamed the Arab Republic of Egypt.

[197] A reference to a letter from Zhou Enlai to Mao Zedong in which Zhou asked for Mao's

instructions on the tactics to be adopted in the talks between China and the United States and the military struggle along the coast.

[198] Wang Bingnan (1908-1988), born in Fengtian (now Qianxian), Shaanxi Province, was Chinese ambassador to Poland and the chief representative in talks at the ambassadorial level between China and the United States in 1958. Ye Fei, born in 1914 in Nan'an, Fujian, was the provincial Party committee secretary, governor of Fujian Province and the political commissar of the Fujian Military Area in 1958.

[199] In July 1958, with U.S. support, the Taiwan Kuomintang government declared it would "counterattack the mainland" and bombarded coastal villages and towns of Fujian Province. In order to give a heavy blow to the Kuomintang army and oppose United States interference in China's sovereign rights, the Fujian front army of the People's Liberation Army was ordered beginning on August 23 to bombard military installations and artillery positions of the Jinmen garrison and blockade Jinmen Island to disrupt the supply of goods for the Kuomintang army. At the beginning of September the United States dispatched large contingents of reinforcement to the Taiwan Straits area and assigned naval vessels and airplanes to escort the transport vessels of the Kuomintang army, openly intruding in Chinese territorial waters. Chinese front troops made another all-out bombardment against the Kuomintang army on Jinmen and its warships on September 8. By January 7, 1959, the PLA had made altogether seven large-scale bombardments with 13 air battles and three naval battles, in which 36 Kuomintang aircraft were shot down or damaged, 17 warships sunk or damaged and over 7,000 Kuomintang soldiers killed. The Jinmen artillery fire continued until China established diplomatic relations with the United States on January 1, 1979.

[200] A reference to the United States' armed intervention in Lebanon in 1958. In May 1958 uprisings occurred in parts of Lebanon opposing the government's implementation of policies contrary to its national interest. On July 15 the United States violated the U.N. Charter, sent troops to Lebanon, and intervened in Lebanese internal affairs on the pretext of "protecting American citizens" and "protecting Lebanese sovereignty." Strongly condemned by Lebanese people, people in the Middle East and people all over the world the American aggressive troops were forced to withdraw from Lebanon on October 25.

[201] A reference to ambassadorial talks between China and the United States. On April 23, 1955, Premier Zhou Enlai stated at a meeting of heads of delegations from eight Asian and African countries that the Chinese government was willing to talk with the U.S. government about alleviating the situation in the Far East, especially tension in the Taiwan area. On July 25 the same year China and the United States reached agreement on ambassadorial talks and the first talks were held in Geneva on August 1. Thereafter the talks were discontinued because of the United States' lack of sincerity. When the Jinmen bombardment began in August 1958, the U.S. government publicly expressed willingness to resume the talks, and the two parties resumed talks in Warsaw on September 15. Up to February 20, 1970, a total of 136 sessions of Sino-American ambassadorial talks were held, but no progress was made on the alleviation and eradication of tension in the Taiwan situation owing to the United States' insisting on interfering in Chinese affairs.

[202] A reference to the National Program for Agricultural Development, 1956-1967 (draft), submitted by the Central Committee of the Communist Party of China and issued in January 1956. A revised draft was issued in October 1957 and formally approved by the Second Session of the Second National People's Congress in April 1960. The program's 40 articles formulated development plans for agriculture, animal husbandry, forestry, fishery, subsidiary production, rural commerce, credit, transportation, post and telecommunications, broadcasting, science, culture, education and public health.

[203] A reference to the Long-Term Program for the Development of Science and Technology, 1956-1967 (draft). Following the CPC Central Committee's instruction on quickly

changing the backward situation in the economy, science and culture, the State Council, starting from April 1956, organized over 600 Chinese scientists and specialists as well as over 20 Russian specialists to work out the draft after half a year's research and discussion. The program set forth 57 important scientific and technological tasks that were urgently needed by the state's construction and 616 key questions and pointed out the development direction of various sciences. Implementation of the program promoted the speedy development of Chinese science and technology.

[204] Originally "the ones who are taking a wait-and-see attitude or ready to settle political accounts belong to this group" followed this sentence. On September 16, 1961, Mao Zedong deleted the above sentence when he went over a collection of study materials for cadres that contained this passage.

[205] A reference to the joint declaration by Zhang Xiruo, president of the Chinese People's Institute of Foreign Affairs, and Asanuma Inejiro, head of a visiting delegation from the Japanese Socialist Party, on March 17, 1959, in Beijing.

[206] Kishi Nobusuke (1896-1987), former president of the Japanese Liberal Democratic Party; prime minister of Japan from February 1957 to June 1960. He pursued a hostile policy to China during his term of office.

[207] Liao Chengzhi (1908-1983), native of Huiyang, Guangdong Province. He was vice-director of the International Liaison Department of the CPC Central Committee, vice-director and director of the Commission of Overseas Chinese Affairs from 1949 to 1959.

[208] Meiji was the reign name of the Japanese emperor Mutsuhito. Meiji reform was a bourgeois movement during the Meiji period beginning in 1868. The reform abolished the shogunate system of feudal separatist rule and established a unified centralized state. Through a series of reforms Japan took the capitalist road and gradually realized capitalist modernization.

[209] Jawaharlal Nehru, prime minister of India from 1947 to 1964.

[210] On March 10, 1959, with the support of foreign powers, Tibet's local reactionary ruling clique publicly announced the "independence of Tibet," intentionally breaking the Agreement on the Peaceful Liberation of Tibet. On March 19 armed rebels launched an all-out attack on the People's Liberation Army stationed in Tibet and representative organs of the central government. On March 20 the PLA in Tibet counterattacked the rebels in Lhasa and later rooted out armed rebellions in other areas. This action protected the unification of the country and the solidarity of the nation and opened the way for Tibet's democratic reform.

[211] The main content of these paragraphs was: China completely disagreed with Mr. Dudd's statement that China was responsible for the abnormal relations between India and China; Tibet was an inalienable part of Chinese territory, rooting out the rebellion and promoting democratic reform were China's internal affairs, and no other country had a right to interfere by any means and on any justification; prior to and after the rebellion in Tibet there were many speeches and activities in India that libeled China and interfered in China's internal affairs; the fact of serious interference in China's internal affairs and the harm caused to Sino-Indian friendship could not be changed by explanations of "freedom of speech" or any other "freedoms"; the words and deeds of the leaders of the Indian government in publicly showing contempt of the documents China formally released, criticizing the Chinese government, and warmly welcoming the Dalai Lama, whatever the subjective intentions were—undoubtedly had the effect of encouraging Tibetan rebels.

[212] On March 20, 1957, Sergeant Reynolds, an American soldier stationed in Taiwan, shot to death Liu Ziran, a Chinese who happened to pass by American soldiers' residence. On May 23 the military court of the American military advisors' group acquitted Renault of the crime. On May 24 tens of thousands of people held anti-U.S. demonstrations in Taipei and other cities. The demonstrators stormed and destroyed the American embassy in Taiwan and its information office and surrounded the headquarters of the American military advisors' group

as well as the Taipei city police station. The Kuomintang government mustered its armed forces to suppress the demonstration while Chiang Kai-shek apologized to the American ambassador and offered to compensate for the loss of the embassy.

[213] The Cairo Conference was a meeting of the heads of three countries of China, the United States and Britain, Chiang Kai-shek, Franklin D. Roosevelt, and Winston Churchill in Cairo, Egypt, November 22-26, 1943. The meeting discussed joint operations against Japan and how to handle Japan after victory. The Cairo Declaration was issued on December 1, pledging that Japan would be deprived of all Pacific islands occupied since World War I, that all territories seized from China, including the northeast, Taiwan and the Penghu Islands, would be restored to China, that Japan would be driven out of territories seized in its desire for expansion, that Korea would be granted independence and that an unconditional surrender would be demanded from Japan.

[214] The Japan-U.S. "Security Pact" was a military alliance treaty signed in San Francisco on September 8, 1951, simultaneously with the conclusion of a peace treaty between the two countries. It went into effect on April 28, 1952. The pact stipulated that the United States had the right to station troops and set up military bases in Japan to protect Japan's "security." In January, 1960, the pact was revised and resigned as the Japan-U.S. Treaty of Mutual Security and Cooperation. Its main contents were as follows: developing Japan's ability to resist armed aggression; Japan's responsibility to protect the American army stationed in Japan to cope with common threat; the United States continually practicing its right to station troops in Japan and use military bases; encouraging economic cooperation between the two countries, etc. The new treaty was forcefully adopted by the House of Representatives of the Diet on May 19 and came into effect on June 23. The Japanese people strongly opposed both the old and new pacts.

[215] September 15-27, 1959, Nikita Khrushchev visited the United States and held talks with President Eisenhower at Camp David on the issues of Germany, Berlin, arms reduction, nuclear testing and bilateral relations.

[216] Ho Chi Minh (1890-1969), founder of the Vietnamese Communist Party, was elected president and concurrently premier of the Democratic Republic of Vietnam. After 1951 he was chairman of the Central Committee of the Vietnam Workers' Party. He led the Vietnamese people in wars of resistance against France and the United States.

[217] Ne Win refers to U Ne Win (b. 1911). At that time he was Prime Minister and Minister of Defense of Burma.

[218] Shailendra K. Upadhayaya was Minister of Internal Affairs and Justice of the Kingdom of Nepal at the time.

[219] Pan Zili (1904-1972), native of Huaxian, Shaanxi Province, served as Chinese ambassador to India and Nepal at the time.

[220] Luo Guibo (b. 1908), native of Nankang, Jiangxi Province, served as Vice-Minister of Foreign Affairs at the time.

[221] Fulgencio Batista (1901-1973), former president of Cuba. He ruled dictatorially while in office, arousing an uprising of the Cuban people. In 1959 his dictatorship was overthrown by the people.

[222] Fidel Castro (b. 1926). In 1953 he led the people to rise up against Fulgencio Batista's dictatorship; the dictatorial government was overthrown and a revolutionary government established in January 1959. Later he served as first secretary of the Central Committee of the Cuban Communist Party, chairman of the Council of Ministers, and president of the Council of State.

[223] The July 26 Movement was a revolutionary organization set up by Fidel Castro of Cuba. On July 26, 1953, Castro led over 100 young revolutionaries in an attack on the Moncada military barracks in Santiago, which was the first armed uprising against Batista's dictatorship.

The July 26 Movement was set up after the failure of the uprising, and Castro went to Mexico to prepare for further armed uprising. In November 1956, with 82 revolutionaries belonging to the July 26 Movement, Castro returned to Cuba and set up a revolutionary base in the Sierra Maestra to continue the struggle. On January 1, 1959, the Batista dictatorship was overthrown, bringing the Cuban revolution to fruition. The July 26 Movement was merged with the United Revolutionary Party of Cuba in 1961 and in 1965 was renamed the Cuban Communist Party.

[224] The heads of the governments of the Soviet Union, the United States, Britain and France met in Paris on May 16, 1960. The conference discussed the further easing of relations between the Soviet Union and the United States in Europe and the means to solve significant international problems. During the conference Nikita Khrushchev demanded that Dwight D. Eisenhower apologize for the accident on May 1, 1960, when an American U-2 high-altitude spy plane invaded the territorial airspace of the Soviet Union. When Eisenhower refused, Khrushchev quit the conference, thus the conference miscarried.

[225] After World War II the Faisal Dynasty of Iraq adopted a policy subservient to the capitalist countries and took strong steps to suppress the opposition movement of the people. On July 14, 1958, a military coup was launched by the patriotic armed forces, with General Kassem as the leader and the support of the Iraqi people; the rule of the Faisal Dynasty was overthrown and the Iraqi Republic founded.

[226] Hardd Macmillan (1894-1986), member of the British Conservative Party and British prime minister from 1957 to 1963.

[227] A reference to the 22-year revolutionary war from 1927 to 1949 and the three-year war to resist U.S. aggression and aid Korea.

[228] Kerlvon Clausewitz (1780-1831), Prussian general and famous bourgeois military strategy theoretician. He wrote *On War*. To Clausewitz war was not an end in itself, but "a continuation of political intercourse with the admixture of different means."

[229] On December 8, 1941, Japan made a surprise attack on Pearl Habor, the largest U.S. naval and air base in the Pacific area, without a declaration of war. Nineteen U.S. naval vessels were sunk or severely damaged and over 200 planes destroyed or damaged. The U.S. Pacific Fleet suffered a serious loss. The United States declared war on Japan that day; thus the Pacific War broke out.

[230] Anthony Eden (1897-1977), former British prime minister and famous diplomat, published his memoirs in three volumes.

[231] George Washington (1732-1799), first president of the United States. As commander-in-chief of the American Army during the American War of Independence, he turned the loosely organized and poorly armed local army into a regular army capable of confronting British troops and finally won victory in the war. He was elected president in 1789.

[232] Oliver Cromwell (1599-1658), major military and political leader during the period of British bourgeois revolution in the 17th century, leader of the Independents, representative of the bourgeois new aristocracy. He defeated the king's troops and established a republic in 1649. In 1653 he took the position of lord protector and ruled the land on a military dictatorship basis.

[233] Montgomery made a mistake here. George Washington died of illness at home on December 14, 1799.

[234] Mohandas K. Gandhi (1869-1948), leader of the Indian independence movement, had been president of the Indian National Congress and for a long time led India's struggle for independence from British colonial domination. He was assassinated on January 30, 1948.

[235] The talk was published in *People's Daily*, June 25, 1960. The following are extracts:

Chairman Mao Zedong pointed out that the victorious struggle of the Japanese people against U.S. imperialism and its agents in Japan and for national independence, democracy and freedom constituted a very great support to the Chinese people and people all over the world in their struggle to oppose U.S. imperialist aggression and to safeguard world peace.

Chairman Mao said that compared with a few years ago there had been a greater awakening of the Japanese people. Broad sections of the Japanese people had come to recognize that U.S. imperialism was the common enemy of the Chinese and Japanese peoples and of peace-loving and just-minded people throughout the world. This struggle would have been inconceivable in the past, judging by its large scale, broad character and long duration. It seemed that the Japanese people had found an excellent method under present circumstances to oppose the new "Japan-U.S. Security Treaty," oppose the U.S. military bases and drive out the U.S. imperialist aggressive forces. This is the method of uniting the broadest possible forces, excluding U.S. imperialism and its agents, and carrying out nation-wide mass struggle against them.

Chairman Mao said that he did not believe that a great nation like Japan would be subject to foreign rule for long. He said that there were very hopeful prospects for Japan's independence and freedom. The independence and peace of Japan would be ensured after the abolition of the "Japan-U.S. Security Treaty" and U.S. military bases.

Chairman Mao pointed out that victory is won step by step and the consciousness of the masses is also raised step by step. Chairman Mao wished the Japanese people still greater success in their patriotic, just struggle against U.S. imperialism. He expressed respect for the heroic sacrifice of Kanba Michiko. He said that Kanba Michiko had become a world-famous Japanese national heroine.

[236] Asanuma Inejiro (1898-1960), former chairman of the Japanese Socialist Party and social activist. He led a delegation from the Japanese Socialist Party to China twice. In March 1959 he declared in a speech in China that "U.S. imperialism is the common enemy of the Chinese and Japanese peoples" and made contributions to the promotion of friendship between China and Japan as well as the normalization of Sino-Japanese relations. He was assassinated by a Rightist in Tokyo on October 12, 1960.

[237] The massacre took place when the Kishi Nobusuke government of Japan suppressed the demonstrators. On June 15, 1960, a demonstration was held by 100,000 people from all walks of life in Tokyo to oppose the Diet's approval of the Japan-U.S. Treaty of Mutual Security and Cooperation and American President Eisenhower's visit to Japan. The demonstrators were suppressed by armed police and attacked by right-wing Japanese groups. Two students from Tokyo University were killed, including Kanba Michiko; nearly 300 persons were injured.

[238] From January 18 to June 28, 1919, a peace conference was held in Paris by 27 countries, including both victorious and defeated ones of World War I. The aim of the conference was said to draft peace treaties with Germany and "establish world peace after the war," but in fact it was a conference for the victorious capitalist countries to share the war loot and redivide the world. The Treaty of Versailles was signed and the Convenant of the League of Nations was approved. The peace conference ignored China's sovereignty and position as a victorious country and illegally decided that Japan would inherit the privileges of Germany in Shandong before the war, which touched off the May 4th patriotic movement by the Chinese people. The Chinese delegation refused to sign the treaty.

[239] James Hagerty served as press secretary for the U.S. president in 1960. On his arrival at Tokyo Airport as a vanguard of Eisenhower's Japan tour, Hagerty was under siege by 25,000 anti-American Japanese for over an hour.

[240] A reference to the essay "May the Friendship Between Young People in China and Japan Develop forever," published in *China Youth Daily* June 17, 1960, and written by Japanese writer Takeuchi Minoru.

[241] Sun Yat-sen University, or Sun Yat-sen Chinese Laborers University, founded in Moscow in 1925, was renamed as Chinese laborers Communism University in 1929 and closed

in the autumn of 1930.

²⁴² The Kachins, one of the ethnic groups in Burma, most of whom resided in Kachin state in north Burma, were of the same origin as the Jingpo people of China.

²⁴³ Chen Yi (1901-1972), native of Lezhi, Sichuan Province, served as vice-premier of the State Council and Minister of Foreign Affairs at that time.

²⁴⁴ Luo Ruiqing (1906-1978), native of Nanchong, Sichuan Province, served as vice-premier of the State Council, chief of the general staff of the People's Liberation Army and vice-minister of national defense.

²⁴⁵ John F. Kennedy (1917-1963), American Democrat. He was a senator and the Democratic Party's candidate for the presidency in 1960, and in November the same year he was elected U.S. president. He was assassinated in 1963.

²⁴⁶ Richard Nixon (1913-1994), American Republican. He was U.S. vice-president, Republican candidate for the presidency in 1960 and elected president in 1968. During his term he sent Henry Kissinger, national security adviser, on a secret mission to China in July 1971 to break the diplomatic deadlock that had existed for a long time between the two countries. In February 1972 Nixon visited China for the first time and issued the Sino-U.S. Joint Communiqué with China in Shanghai. Relations between China and the U.S. thus began to normalize.

²⁴⁷ Matsumura Kenzô (1883-1971), former adviser of the Japanese Liberal Democratic Party and member of the House of Representatives. He visited China five times after 1959. Before China and Japan resumed diplomatic relations, he was the chief person on the Japanese side to conduct contact on trade between China and Japan. During his visit to China in September 1962 he signed a Japan-China General Agreement on Trade with China. In 1964 he took over from Takasaki Tatsunosuke and was in charge of matters a Japan-China memorandum on trade.

²⁴⁸ Miki Takeo (1907-1988), former president of the Japanese Liberal Democratic Party and prime minister. In the early part of the 1960s he served as director-general of Economic Planning Agency and concurrently director-general of Science and Technology Agency of the Japanese Cabinet, holding the view that Japan should actively develop political, economic and cultural relations with China.

²⁴⁹ Takasaki Tatsunosuke (1885-1964), member of the Japanese Liberal Democratic Party and former member of the House of Representatives. In the beginning of the 1960s he served as minister of international trade and industry in the Japanese Cabinet and head of the examination committee of comprehensive trade relations between China and Japan and was active in promoting trade between China and Japan. In 1962 he led a delegation to China and signed a Japan-China nongovernmental trade memorandum with Liao Chengzhi.

²⁵⁰ Kono Ichiro (1898-1965) served as Minister of Agriculture and Forestry and of Construction in the Japanese Cabinet in the early 1960s.

²⁵¹ Ishibashi Tanzan (1884-1973), former president of the Japanese Liberal Democratic Party and prime minister, served many times as chairman of the Japan-China Economic and Trade Exhibition Committee in the beginning of the 1960s. He was elected adviser to the Alliance of Diet Members for Promoting the Resumption of Japan-China Diplomatic Relations in December 1972. He visited China in 1959 and 1963.

²⁵² Huang Xing (1874-1916), native of Shanhua (now Changsha), Hunan Province. In 1904 he founded Hua Xing Hui, an anti-Qing revolutionary society in Changsha. In 1905 he helped Sun Yat-sen prepare for the establishment of Tong Meng Hui and was in charge of general affairs in its Executive Department. He led many armed uprisings organized by Tong Meng Hui. After the Wuchang Uprising in 1911 he served as wartime commander-in-chief of the military government and Minister of War in the Nanjing Provisional Government. In 1913

he served as commander-in-chief of the anti-Yuan Shikai army in Jiangsu.

[253] The Creating-God Faction was a religious philosophy trend that appeared from 1905 to 1907 after the failure of the Russian bourgeois democratic revolution. A. Bogdanov and Anatoly Lunacharsky were its representatives. Having lost faith in the future of revolution, they advocated to "perfect" Marxism, agitated to create a "socialist" religion without God and announced that religion was the only organizing force of socialism, attempting to combine Marxism with religion. After 1912 the Creating-God Faction was quickly shattered by the upsurge of the Russian revolutionary movement.

[254] Minamigo Saburo served as president of the Japan-China Import and Export Workers' Union in 1955. He visited China twice in 1956. In 1958 he came to China with a Japanese commercial delegation to sign the Fourth China-Japan Trade Agreement.

[255] Ikeda Hayato (1899-1965) served as president of Japan's Liberal Democratic Party and prime minister of Japan from 1960 to 1964.

[256] This refers to the fourth session of the Council for Asian-African Unity, which was held in Bandung, Indonesia, from April 10 to 13, 1961. More than 40 countries from Asia and Africa were represented. The conference passed a general declaration and 24 resolutions opposing new and old colonialism, particularly the new colonialism of the United States. It also passed a resolution opposing the establishment of military bases in Asia, Africa and Latin America. The conference called on the people of Asia and Africa to strengthen unity and support all countries in their just struggle against imperialism and colonialism.

[257] Pan American Union, an international organization comprising the United States and Latin American countries. Founded in April 1890 as the International Conference of American States, it changed its name to Pan American Union in 1910 and again to Organization of American States in April 1948. It now has 30 member states. Its aims are peaceful resolution of conflicts among member countries and guaranteed collective security for all member states; the solving of political, legal and economic problems among members; cooperation to guarantee sovereignty, and territorial integrity and independence; acceleration of the integration of Latin American countries. However, from its founding, the organization was under the control and manipulation of the United States and became its tool to expand to Latin America. After the 1970s an increasing number of Latin American countries condemned the United States for its economic exploitation and discriminating trade policy, and the United States' role as leader of the organization began to decline.

[258] Now the Democratic Republic of the Congo.

[259] This refers to the Declaration of the Conference of the Communist and Workers' Parties of Various Countries passed at the Conference of the Communist and Workers' Parties of Various Countries held in Moscow in November 1960. The declaration took up such burning topics as the world situation, the fight for peace, national independence, democracy and socialism. It pointed out that American imperialism was the common enemy of people all over the world, and the national liberation movement was an important force in the prevention of world war. It reaffirmed the correctness of the Moscow Declaration of 1957.

[260] This refers to the three principles put forward by British Marshal Montgomery in a bid to ease the tension in international situations: all countries would acknowledge that there was only one China (the People's Republic of China), that there were two Germanys and that all armed forces should withdraw to their own territory.

[261] Andrei Gromyko (1909-1989) served as Soviet foreign minister from 1957.

[262] This refers to the conference held in Geneva from May 16, 1961, to July 23, 1962. Also called the Second Geneva conference, it discussed ways to peacefully solve the Laotian issue. The 1954 Geneva Accord stipulated the neutral status of Laos and the principle of respect for Laos' sovereignty, independence, unity and territorial integrity and of its internal affairs

being immune from outside interference. However, the United States interfered and carried out aggression in Laos in breach of the accord and instigated in 1960 the civil war in Laos. In his effort to resolve the Laotian issue by peaceful means, Sihanouk, head of state of Cambodia, proposed to convene the conference. The conference included many of the 1954 Geneva conference participants, such as Cambodia, Laos, Vietnam Democratic Republic, South Vietnam, China, the Soviet Union, the United States, the United Kingdom and France, and some other countries, including India, Canada, Poland, Thailand and Burma. Two documents—The Declaration of Laos' Neutrality and Protocol on the Declaration of Laos' Neutrality—were signed at the conference.

[263] Bernard L. Montgomery (1887-1976), British marshal and viscount, was one of the commanders of the allied troops in World War II. He later served as chief of the general staff of the British armed forces and deputy commander-in-chief of the NATO armed forces. He visited China in 1960 and 1961.

[264] The First Congress of the Communist Party of China was held in Shanghai on July 23, 1921. Twelve representatives of the communist groups throughout China and Japan attended the conference: Mao Zedong, He Shuheng, Dong Biwu, Chen Tanqiu, Wang Jinmei, Deng Enming, Li Da, Li Hanjun, Zhang Guotao, Liu Renjing, Chen Gongbo and Zhou Fohai. Also present were Bao Huizeng who was designated by Chen Duxiu to represent him at the congress and G. Maring, representing the Communist International. The congress discussed and passed the Party's first program and a resolution on the Party's tasks. The central leading organ was elected. This congress marked the founding of the Communist Party of China.

[265] Chen gongbo (1892-1946) was from Ruyuan, Guangdong Province. He attended the First National Congress of the Chinese Communist Party in July 1921 as the representative of the Guangdong communist group. He broke away from the Communist Party in 1925 to join the Kuomintang. After the outbreak of the War of Resistance Against Japan he followed Wang Jingwei and surrendered to the Japanese invaders. He served as head of the legislative Yuan, head of the Executive Yuan and acting chairman of the puppet government headed by Wang Jingwei.

[266] Zhou Fohai (1897-1948) was from Yuanling, Hunan Province. He studied in Japan in 1917 and attended the First National Congress of the Chinese Communist Party in July 1921 as a representative residing in Japan. He broke away from the Communist Party to join the Kuomintang in 1924. After the outbreak of the War of Resistance Against Japan, he followed the steps of Wang Jingwei, surrendered to the Japanese invaders and became deputy head of the Executive Yuan of the puppet government headed by Wang Jingwei.

[267] Liu Renjing (1902-1987) was from Yingcheng, Hubei Province. He attended the First Natinal Congress of the Chinese Communist Party in 1921 as the representative of the Beijing communist group. He studied at the International College of Leninism in Moscow in 1926 and later became a member of the Trotskyite faction. He was expelled from the Party in 1929. He served as counsellor in the Counsellors' Office under the State Council after the establishment of the People's Republic of China.

[268] Leon Trotsky (1879-1940) served as a Politburo member in the Central Committee of the Russian Social Democratic Workers' Party (Bolsheviks) and chairman of the Petrograd Soviet during the October Revolution. After the victory of the revolution, he served as chairman of the Revolutionary Military Commission and member of the executive committee of the Comintern. After Lenin died, he opposed Lenin's theory and line on socialist construction in the Soviet Union. He was expelled from the Party in November 1927 and from the Soviet Union in January 1929. He was assassinated in Mexico in August 1940.

[269] Zhang Guotao (1897-1979) was from Pingxiang, Jiangxi. He attended the First National Congress of the Chinese Communist Party in 1921 as the representativec of the Beijing Communist group and served consecutively as member of the Party Central Committee,

Politburo member, member of the standing committee of the Politburo, secretary of the Hubei-Henan-Anhui Sub-bureau of the Party Central Committee and concurrently chairman of its military committee, and deputy chairman of the Provisional Central Government of the Chinese Soviet Republic. During the Long March in 1935 he opposed the Party Central Committee's decision to move the Red Army to north China and engaged in activities to split the Party and the Red Army. He established his own central committee, which he relinquished under pressure in June 1936. Upon arrival in northern the Shaanxi, he was elected deputy chairman and then acting chairman of the Shaanxi-Gansu-Ningxia Border Area government. He fled from there to join the Kuomintang special agents in April 1938 and became a traitor to the Chinese revolution. He was soon expelled from the Communist Party. He went to Taiwan in November 1948 and moved to Hong Kong the next year. He migrated to Canada in 1968 and lived there until he died of illness in 1979.

[270] Li Da (1890-1966), was from Lingling in Hunan Province and a philosopher. As a representative to the First National Congress of the Chinese Communist Party, he was elected head of propaganda in the Central Bureau. He served as president of Wuhan University after the founding of the People's Republic of China.

[271] Guo Moruo (1892-1978) was from Leshan, Sichuan Province. At the time he was deputy chairman of the Standing Committee of the National People's Congress, deputy chairman of the National Committee of the Chinese People's Political Consultative Conference and president of the Chinese Academy of Sciences.

[272] Park Chung Hee (1917-1979) served as South Korea's chairman of the Supreme Committee for National Rejuvenation in July 1961 and acting president and president of South Korea from March 1962.

[273] Sarit Thanarat (1908-1963), former supreme commander of Thai armed forces. He seized power after a coup d'etat in 1958 and imposed authoritarian military rule over the country. In February 1959 he named himself premier. He was also chairman of the Anti-infiltration Special Committee and the Central Committee for National Security and Suppression of Communists.

[274] This refers to the Act on the Prevention of Violent Political Actions. It was put forward by Japan's Ikeda Hayato government in June 1961 to enforce the Japan-U.S. Treaty of Mutual Security and Cooperation (commonly called "New Japan-U.S. Security Treaty"). The act prohibited Japanese people from gathering and demonstrating near the Diet, prime minister's residence and the court. All groups were required to report to the Public Security Investigation Agency their name, aim, address of office, names of their officers, income and activity plans. The government's intention was that once the act was passed in the Diet, it would have the legal right to suppress the Japanese people's anti-imperialist patriotic movement. The act was forcibly passed in the Legal Affairs Committee in the House of Representatives on June 2. On June 3 and 6 four million people throughout Japan demonstrated against the act. Under such massive pressure the Ikeda Hayato government gave up the effort to have the act passed in the Diet.

[275] This refers to the Parti Democratique de Guinée. Founded in May 1947 the PDG became the governing party of Guinea after it declared independence in 1958. The PDG changed its name to the National Party in November 1978. After the military took the highest power in Guinea in 1984, they disbanded the party.

[276] Ye Jizhuang (1893-1967) was from Xinxing, Guangdong Province. At that time he served as vice-minister of the Finance and Trade Office of the State Council and minister of foreign trade.

[277] Fang Yi (b. 1916) was from Xiamen, Fujian Province. At that time he served as vice-minister of the State Planning Commission and director of the Foreign Economic Liaison General Administration.

²⁷⁸ The Ku Klux Klan is a racist terrorist organization in the United States. It was formed by slave owners in the South in May 1866 to suppress blacks and defend the slave system. Its major activities include spreading racist ideas and using lynching, kidnaping and mass murder to intimidate blacks and progressive people. It was a tool in the hands of the reactionary power in the United States in promoting racism and implementing fascist rule.

²⁷⁹ On May 8, 1963, around 20,000 Buddhists took to the streets in Hue in South Vietnam to demonstrate against the Ngo Dinh Diem regime's decision to ban Buddhist sacrifice-offering services. The authorities violently suppressed the demonstration, killing 12 people and injuring 17. On June 11 Quang Duc, an eminent Buddhist monk in his seventies from Saigon, burned himself to death to demonstrate against the authorities' violence toward Buddhists. On June 16, despite harsh suppression, 700,000 residents in Cho Lon of Saigon attended the funeral ceremony for Quang Duc. Soon after that four Buddhist monks committed self-immolation by setting fire to themselves. The struggle started by Buddhists quickly expanded to become a mass struggle involving students, intellectuals and common residents. The authorities used harsher methods, burning temples and closing schools. Gas shells were used to disperse demonstrators. On August 20 the South Vietnam authorities imposed martial law throughout the country and arrested Buddhists and people who had taken part in the demonstration. This provoked more demonstrations, involving people from all walks of life on a bigger scale.

²⁸⁰ On August 28, 1963, Ho Chi Minh, president of the Democratic Republic of Vietnam, issued a statement on the situation in Vietnam. In the statement Ho pointed out that the crimes committed by the Ngo Dinh Diem clique—the burning of temples, persecution of nuns and monks, closing of schools, detaintion of teachers and students—were intolerable. He called on his compatriots in South Vietnam, no matter whether intellectuals, peasants, workers or merchants and regardless of political inclination and religious belief, to unite to fight for democracy and freedom (including religious belief). The statement asked the U.S. imperialists to withdraw from South Vietnam, indicating that the issue of South Vietnam could be resolved only by the South Vietnamese themselves. It appealed to people who loved peace throughout the world to give stronger support to the just struggle waged by the South Vietnamese people.

²⁸¹ See Chapter Six of *A Dream of Red Mansions*.

²⁸² See Chapter Two of *A Dream of Red Mansions*.

²⁸³ The six-nation Common Market refers to the European Common Market, established by France, the Federal Republic of Germany, Italy, the Netherlands, Belgium and Luxembourg in January 1958.

²⁸⁴ Lyndon Johnson (1908-1973), member of the Democratic Party and president of the United States (1963-1969).

²⁸⁵ Anton Yugov (b. 1904) served as prime minister of Bulgaria from April 1956 to November 1962.

²⁸⁶ Viliam Siroky (1902-1971) was prime minister of Czechoslovakia from March 1953 to September 1963.

²⁸⁷ This refers to Albania, Bulgaria, Hungary, Vietnam, the Democratic German Republic, China, Korea, Mongolia, Poland, Romania, the Soviet Union, Czechoslovakia and Cuba.

²⁸⁸ In August 1959 Indian troops invaded Lungjug in China's Tibet, the first armed confrontation on the Sino-Indian border since new China was founded. Soon after that the Indian army crossed the line of actual control by both sides in the western and eastern sectors of the border area and stirred up constant trouble. It even established military strongholds inside Chinese territory. The Chinese government lodged strong protests to the Indian government and suggested that the border issue be settled through negotiations. This was rejected by the Indian government. In October 1962 Indian troops launched a large-scale offensive against

Chinese border troops, who were forced to counterattack and drive back the Indian troops. In its effort to solve the border issue peacefully the Chinese government issued a statement on November 21 announcing that Chinese troops would start a ceasefire along the Sino-Indian border the next day. From December 1 on, Chinese troops withdrew 20 kilometers from the line of actual control by both sides on November 7, 1959. China, on its own initiative, freed and repatriated all Indian POWs and returned all weapons captured in the war. Chinese border troops finished withdrawal by February 1963.

[289] The Far East Republic, also called Chita Republic, was a democratic parliamentary republic formed in April 1920 in the region to the east of Lake Baikal in the former Soviet Union. It was integrated into the Soviet Union in November 1922.

[290] Okinawa, main island of the Ryukyu Islands of Japan, was occupied by the United States in June 1945 during World War II. In 1951 the Japanese authorities agreed to American trusteeship of the island according to a U.S.-Japanese "peace treaty" signed in San Francisco. The Japanese people struggled for the return of Okinawa for a long time. On May 15, 1972, jurisdiction was restored to Japan according to an agreement of the two governments.

[291] Edgar Faure (b. 1908), member of the French Radical Socialist Party, served as French premier twice, in 1952 and 1955 to 1956. He visited China three times after 1957.

[292] Reference is to Norman Bethune (1890-1939). After the outbreak of the Chinese War of Resistance Against Japan in 1937 he came to China at the beginning of 1938 as head of a Canadian-American medical team and arrived at Yan'an at the end of March. Before long he went to the Shanxi-Qahar-Hebei border area and worked there for over a year. He died on November 12, 1939, at Tangxian, Hebei Province, due to an infection during emergency surgery.

[293] Reference is to the Chinese Government's eight principles of foreign aid: First, the Chinese Government always bases itself on the principle of equality and mutual benefit in providing aid to other countries. It never regards such aid as a kind of unilateral alms but as something mutual. Second, in providing aid to other countries, the Chinese Government strictly respects the sovereignty of the recipient countries, and never attaches any conditions or asks for any privileges. Third, China provides economic aid in the form of interest-free or low-interest loans and extends the time limit for the repayment when necessary so as to lighten the burden of the recipient countries as far as possible. Fourth, in providing aid to other countries, the purpose of the Chinese Government is not to make the recipient countries dependent on China but to help them embark step by step on the road of self-reliance and independent economic development. Fifth, the Chinese Government tries its best to help the recipient countries build projects which require less investment while yielding quicker results, so that the recipient governments may increase their income and accumulate capital. Sixth, the Chinese Government provides the best-quality equipment and material of its own manufacture at international market prices. If the equipment and material provided by the Chinese Government are not up to the agreed specifications and quality, the Chinese Government undertakes to replace them. Seventh, in giving any particular technical assistance, the Chinese Government will see to it that the personnel of the recipient country fully master such technique. Eighth, the experts dispatched by China to help in construction in the recipient countries will have the same standard of living as the experts of the recipient country. The Chinese experts are not allowed to make any special demands or enjoy any special amenities.

[294] Ahmed Ben Bella (b. 1918) was one of the leaders of the Front de Libération Nationale of Algeria. In 1956 he was arrested by the French colonialist authorities for actively taking part in organizing a nationwide armed uprising against France. In 1958 he was elected in absentia first deputy prime minister when the Algerian provisional government was founded. He was set free and returned to Algeria in 1962. In September 1962 the Democratic People's Republic of Algeria was established and he was elected premier. In September 1963 he was

elected the first president and assumed the title of supreme commander of the armed forces, and in April 1964 he served as general secretary of the Front de Libération Nationale.

²⁹⁵ Wang Jingwei (1883-1944), native of Shanyin (today's Shaoxing), Zhejiang, and born in Sanshui, Guangdong. After the September 18 Incident in 1931 he became head of a pro-Japan group in the Kuomintang and advocated compromise with Japan. In March 1938 he served as Kuomintang's vice-president and in December of the same year he publicly surrendered to the Japanese aggressors. After 1940 he served as chairman of the bogus national government and head of its Executive Yuan.

²⁹⁶ Reference is to Aisin-Gioro Pu Yi (1906-1967), the last emperor of the Qing Dynasty. He was forced to abdicate after the founding of the Republic of China in 1912. In March 1932 he became "chief executive" of the bogus Manchoukuo, organized by Japanese imperialists, and in March 1934 his title changed to Emperor of Manchoukuo, with Kangde as its reign name. He was captured by the Soviet army after Japan's surrender in 1945 and handed over to the government of the People's Republic of China in August 1950. He received a special pardon in December 1959 and then served as a member of the National Committee of the Chinese People's Political Consultative Conference in 1964.

²⁹⁷ Reference is to the McMahon Line, which was an illegal border line created by British colonialists and Tibetan local authorities by secret protocol without acknowledgment by representatives of the Chinese central government. The line put 90,000 square kilometers of Chinese territory in the eastern sector of the China-India border into India which was then under the administration of British colonialists. The Chinese government never ratified or acknowledged this line. In 1953 India occupied roughly all the Chinese territory south of the line.

²⁹⁸ On July 23, 1964, French President De Gaulle accused in a news conference the U.S. of breaking the Geneva Agreement and interfering in Indochina's affairs. He also criticized the foreign policy of the Federal Republic of Germany as not "European and independent."

²⁹⁹ Fu Zuoyi (1895-1974), native of Ronghe (today's Linyi), Shanxi, once served as chief commander of the North China "Bandit Suppression" Headquarters and chairman of the Qahar provincial government. He led his army to accept peaceful redesignation by the People's Liberation Army in January 1949, which contributed greatly to the peaceful liberation of Beiping and Suiyuan. After the founding of the People's Republic of China he served as a member of the Central People's Government Council, vice-chairman of the Council of National Defense, vice-chairman of the National Committee of the Chinese People's Political Consultative Conference, and minister of water conservancy and electric power.

³⁰⁰ Tao Zhiyue (1892-1988), native of Ningxiang, Hunan, once served as commander of the Xinjiang Garrison Headquarters of the Kuomintang government. In September 1949, he led his army to cross over to the side of the PLA. After the founding of the People's Republic of China he served as deputy commander of the Xinjiang Military Area of the PLA, commander of the Xinjiang Production and Construction Corps, member of the Council of National Defense, member of the Standing Committee of the National People's Congress, and vice-chairman of the National Committee of the Chinese People's Political Consultative Conference.

³⁰¹ Cheng Qian (1882-1968), native of Liling, Hunan, once served as director of the Kuomintang Changsha Pacification Office and chairman of the Hunan provincial government. He and Chen Mingren launched an insurrection with his army, so that Hunan Province was liberated peacefully. After the founding of the PRC he served as a member of the Central People's Government Council, vice-chairman of the Standing Committee of the National People's Congress, vice-chairman of the Council of National Defense, an executive member of the National Committee of the Chinese People's Political Consultative Conference and governor of Hunan Province.

³⁰² Chen Mingren (1903-1974), native of Liling, Hunan, once served as deputy director

of the Central China Military and Political Govenor's Office and commander of the First Army of the Kuomintang government. He and Cheng Qian launched an insurrection with his army, so that Hunan Province was liberated peacefully. After the founding of the PRC he served as deputy commander of the Hunan Provincial Military Command of the PLA, army commander, and corps commander, a member of the Council of National Defense, and an executive member of the National Committee of the Chinese People's Political Consultative Conference.

[303] Dunkirk is a port city in northern France. Here reference is to the retreat of British and French troops from Dunkirk at the beginning of World War II. In May 1940 German forces attacked Belgium, the Netherlands, and Luxembourg and invaded France; British and French troops were defeated. A total of 220,000 British expeditionary troops and 200,000 French troops had to retreat to Belgian and French coastal areas, facing the danger of annihilation. From May 27 to June 4 over 300,000 British troops and most French troops were evacuated from Dunkirk to England across the English Channel. Though many weapons and equipment were lost, the armed effectives were saved.

[304] Reference is to the American Civil War of 1861-1865, which was caused by the contradiction between the slave system of the southern plantation owners and the wage labor system of the northern bourgeoisie. During the war President Lincoln of the Union government, who represented the interests of the northern bourgeoisie, promulgated the Homestead Act and the Emancipation Proclamation and took other democratic measures to arouse the spirit of workers, peasants and blacks, so the Union forces won the war in the end. American capitalism was further developed through the war.

[305] Bikini Island is an atoll in the Marshall Islands. The island came under U.S. administration in 1947 and was an American nuclear test base.

[306] The Games of the Newly Emerging Forces was held in Djakarta, capital of Indonesia, from November 10 to 22, 1963. The sports meet was first advocated by Indonesian president Sukarno and then decided on at a meeting held in Djakarta by representatives from ten countries (Cambodia, China, Guinea, Indonesia, Iraq, Mali, Pakistan, the Democratic Republic of Vietnam, the United Arab Republic and the Soviet Union) and observers from Ceylon (today's Sri Lanka) and Yugoslavia. A total of 2,000 athletes from over 40 countries and regions of Asia, Africa, Latin America and Europe attended the sports meet.

[307] Dean Rusk (b. 1909), member of the U.S. Democratic Party, served as Secretary of State from 1961 to 1969.

[308] American War of Independence, also called North American War of Independence. In 1775 the people from 13 North American colonies began a bourgeois revolutionary struggle for independence from British colonial administration. On July 4, 1776, the Declaration of Independence was published, formally announcing separation from Britain. Defeated, Britain signed the Paris Peace Treaty granting independence to the United States.

[309] French Revolution refers to the French bourgeois revolution from 1789 to 1794, which broke out under circumstances of an extremely decayed feudal system and ever sharper contradictions among the first (monks), second (aristocracy) and estates (masses, peasants, urban populace and the bourgeoisie). The revolution overthrew the French feudal dictatorial system and promoted the development of capitalism as well as bourgeois revolutionary movements in other European countries.

[310] Abraham Lincoln (1809-1865), member of the American Republican Party, United States president from 1861 to 1865. He led the war against the southern slave system and promulgated the famous Homestead Act and Emancipation Proclamation.

[311] Portuguese Guinea is today's Republic of Guinea-Bissau.

[312] On April 24, 1965, young military officers of the Dominican Republic launched a coup d'état with the support of the people, overthrew the pro-American Cabral dictatorial

government and established a constitutional government. After the coup over 30,000 United States troops invaded the Dominican Republic. They were met with heroic resistance from the Dominican people.

313 "Three-Prong Plan" was a secret military plan exposed by Okada Haruo, a Diet member of the Japanese Socialist Party, on February 10, 1965. The plan was made after intensive scheming by Japan's "Defense Agency" in 1963, according to which the United States, Japan and South Korea would fight China and the Democratic People's Republic of Korea if a "Second Korean War" broke out. In Japan, a national general mobilization would be declared and "wartime legislation" would be enacted to suppress patriotic democratic forces.

314 Nguyen Van Thieu (b. 1923) served as president of the "Republic of Vietnam," i.e., the South Vietnam puppet government at that time.

315 Nguyen Huu Tho (b. 1910) served as chairman of the presidium of the Central Committee of the South Vietnam National Liberation Front at the time.

316 On March 18, 1970, Lon Nol, former Cambodian prime minister, minister of national defense and commander-in-chief of the Cambodian royal armed forces, and Srimada, vice-prime minister, launched a coup at the instigation and with the support of the United States while the Cambodian head of state Prince Sihanouk was abroad. Prince Sihanouk was replaced by Cheng Heng as the new head of state. Thus state power fell into the hands of a pro-American clique of Lon Nol-Srimada-Cheng Heng.

317 On April 24 and 25, 1970, the Summit Meeting of the Indo-Chinese Peoples was held, attended by the National United Front of Cambodia, Laotian Patriotic Front, South Vietnam National Liberation Front and a people's delegation from the Democratic Republic of Vietnam. The meeting discussed the situation in Indo-China and the common task of Cambodia, Laos and Vietnam. The Joint Statement of the Summit Meeting of the Indo-Chinese Peoples was published on April 25. It strongly condemned the crime committed by the American imperialists' invasion of Indo-China and called on the peoples of Indo-China to strengthen their unity and struggle bravely against their common enemy—American imperialism and its running dogs —until they won complete victory.

318 After the coup launched by the Lon Nol-Srimada clique on March 18, 1970, Cambodian patriotic people from all walks of life held a congress in Beijing on May 3 and 4 and established the Royal National Solidarity Government under the leadership of the National United Front of Cambodia with Samdech Penn Nouth as prime minister. After the government's establishment the National United Front together with the Cambodian people and revolutionary troops, fought a people's war against the United States and the Lon Nol-Srimada clique until victory in 1975.

319 Maginot Line was a positional defense work built in the 1930s by France on its northeast border in preparation for Germany's attack. It was named after André Maginot, major designer and war minister at that time. In May 1940 German troops got round the line through Belgium to invade France and made it useless.

320 In April 1971 China invited the United States Table Tennis Team, which had been to Nagoya for the 31st World Table Tennis Championships, to visit China. This played an important role in resuming friendly communication between the peoples of the two countries.

321 Wang Hairong (b. 1942) served as deputy director of the Protocol Department of the Ministry of Foreign Affairs at the time.

322 Reference is to James Harold Wilson (b. 1916), leader of the British Labor Party and Britain's prime minister from 1964 to 1976.

323 Lin Biao (1907-1971), native of Huanggang, Hubei, joined the Communist Party in 1925. In May 1958 he was elected vice-chairman of the CPC Central Committee and member of the Standing Committee of the Political Bureau at the Fifth Plenum of the Eighth Central

Committee of the CPC. In 1959 he was appointed vice-chairman of the Military Commission of the CPC Central Committee and Minister of National Defense. During the "cultural revolution" he organized an counterevolutionary clique and schemed to launch a coup to usurp the highest power of the Party and the state. When the intrigue was exposed, he betrayed the country and fled China by plane in the early morning of September 13, 1971, and was killed in a plane crash in Mongolia. The CPC Central Committee decided to expel him from the Party in August 1973.

[324] On June 17, 1972, some Republican Party members working for Nixon's reelection broke into the headquarters of the Democratic Party in the Watergate Building to install an electric bug. Shortly after Nixon's reelection the break-in was exposed. In July 1974 the Judiciary Committee of the House of Representatives approved articles of impeachment, based on evidence gathered. In August 1974 Nixon had to resign.

[325] Henry Kissinger (b. 1923) served as Secretary of State of the United States from 1973 to 1977. In July 1971 he came to Beijing as National Security Adviser to President Nixon to hold talks with Premier Zhou Enlai on the normalization of relations between the two countries. He visited China many times after that.

[326] The Hong Kong question refers to questions left over from history. Hong Kong (including Hong Kong Island, Kowloon and the New Territories) was China's territory since ancient times. In 1840 Britain launched the Opium War and forced the Qing government to sign the Treaty of Nanking, ceding Hong Kong Island to Britain. In 1856 British and French troops instigated a second Opium War and the Convention of Beijing of 1860 ceded the tip of Kowloon Peninsula. Again, in 1898, the British forced the Qing government to sign the Convention Respecting the Extension of Hong Kong Territory, leasing a large part of Kowloon Peninsula and over 200 nearby islands (later collectively called the New Territories) from China for 99 years until June 30, 1997. The Chinese people have consistently opposed the above three unequal treaties.

POSTSCRIPT

Mao Zedong on Diplomacy was jointly compiled by the Ministry of Foreign Affairs of the People's Republic of China and the Party Literature Research Center Under the Central Committee of the Communist Party of China.

The title of the Chinese edition of the book is in the calligraphy of Jiang Zemin, General Secretary of the CPC Central Committee.

Thanks are due to Qian Qichen, Li Qi, Jiang Xianzhi and Tian Zengpei for their advice concerning the editorial work of this book.

The entire manuscript of the book was read and approved by Comrades Jin Chong and Pei Jianzhang. The staff of the Ministry of Foreign Affairs who took part in the editorial work are Shi Rui (head of the editorial group), Xu Mingyuan and Wang Zhuxiang, with the assistance of Yu Wuzhen, Li Xiling, Gu Jiaji, Xing Geng, Luo Yisu, Zhang Chengxun, Zhang Huiqing, Wu Deji, Fang Baohua and Tian Wenjin.

The staff of the Central Party Literature Research Center who took part in the editorial work are Wu Zhengyu, Lu Zhenxiang and Cao Zhiwei, together with Shen Xueming, Zheng Zhaohong, Han Honghong, Deng Pei, Zheng Jianying, Zhang Hongzhi, Li Qingtian and Tan Youping, who supplied the notes.

The editors received much help from the archive departments of the Ministry of Foreign Affairs, the Central Party Literature Research Center and other relevant units.

图书在版编目(CIP)数据

毛泽东外交文选:英文/中华人民共和国外交部,中共中央文献研究室编.
—北京:外文出版社,1998
ISBN 7-119-01141-3

Ⅰ.毛… Ⅱ.①中…②中… Ⅲ.①毛泽东著作-对外关系-专题汇编-英文
②对外关系-毛泽东著作-专题汇编-英文
Ⅳ.A46

中国版本图书馆 CIP 数据核字 (95) 第 01849 号

责任编辑　吴灿飞
封面设计　蔡　荣

毛泽东外交文选

中华人民共和国外交部
中共中央文献研究室　编

*

ⓒ外文出版社
外文出版社出版
(中国北京百万庄大街 24 号)
邮政编码 100037
北京外文印刷厂印刷
中国国际图书贸易总公司发行
(中国北京车公庄西路 35 号)
北京邮政信箱第 399 号　邮政编码 100044
1998 年(小 16 开)第 1 版
(英)
ISBN 7-119-01141-3/A·8(外)
06860
1-E-2989P